The Official Book
of the FAI Cup

First published in 2011 by
Liberties Press
Guinness Enterprise Centre | Taylor's Lane | Dublin 8
Tel: +353 (1) 415 1224
www.libertiespress.com | info@libertiespress.com

Trade enquiries to Gill & Macmillan Distribution
Hume Avenue | Park West | Dublin 12
T: +353 (1) 500 9534 | F: +353 (1) 500 9595 | E: sales@gillmacmillan.ie

Distributed in the UK by
Turnaround Publisher Services
Unit 3 | Olympia Trading Estate | Coburg Road | London N22 6TZ
T: +44 (0) 20 8829 3000 | E: orders@turnaround-uk.com

Distributed in the United States by
Dufour Editions | PO Box 7 | Chester Springs | Pennsylvania 19425

Copyright © Seán Ryan, 2011
The author has asserted his moral rights.

ISBN: 978-1-907593-33-8
2 4 6 8 10 9 7 5 3 1
A CIP record for this title is available from the British Library.

Cover design by Graham Thew
Internal design by Liberties Press
Printed by ScandBook

The Official Book of the FAI Cup

Seán Ryan

Acknowledgements

No man is an island, and no writer works in isolation, so there are plenty of people to thank for bringing *The Official Book of the FAI Cup* to publication, and I only hope that I don't forget anyone. I am especially grateful for the interest shown by FAI CEO John Delaney, who pushed this project along, and his colleague, Gerry McDermott, who was there when I needed him. Thanks also to Eddie Murphy, CEO of Ford Motors, for giving the project the financial push required. Regarding the research, I had many allies up and down the country, all of whom helped get me over the line in time to meet my deadline. So thanks to Gerry Desmond (Cork), Ray Scott (Waterford), Brian O'Brien (Limerick), John McIntyre (Galway), John Hudson (Dublin), Jim Murphy (Dundalk), Richie Kelly and Arthur Duffy (Derry), Bartley Ramsay (Donegal), and Joe McGrath of the Irish Referees' Society. A big thank you also to the many players and managers who made themselves available for interviews and who shared the stories that made this project worthwhile. Thanks too to the staff of the National Library, Kildare Street, and that Dublin gem, the Gilbert Library in Pearse Street, where I spent many happy hours. I am grateful also to Terry O'Rourke for his work on an earlier project, which was useful on this occasion, and to Ray McManus of Sportsfile for his help in sourcing so many historic photos. It was a pleasure to be taken on by a publisher, Seán O'Keeffe of Liberties Press, who was so encouraging, and his wonderful staff, Daniel Bolger, Clara Phelan, Caroline Lambe and Alice Dawson, who have kept me on the rails through the months spent working on this book. Finally, I am extremely grateful to Irish soccer legend Kevin Moran for writing the foreword. He adds a touch of class just where it's needed.

Contents

Foreword
by Kevin Moran

Little did I know when I lined out for the UCD graduates team Pegasus in the FAI Cup against Dundalk on 13 February 1977, that it would lead to a whole new world of professional football being opened up to me. The legendary Manchester United scout, Billy Behan, had been tipped off about me by our manager Ronnie Nolan, another Irish soccer legend.

My job that day was to mark Dundalk's danger man, right-winger Jimmy Dainty. By all accounts I did OK, because Billy said afterwards that I had done enough to convince him that I could make it to the top. My subsequent career with Manchester United, Sporting Gijon, Blackburn Rovers and the Republic of Ireland, which featured FA Cup Finals, European Championship Finals and World Cup Finals, gave some credence to Billy's remark.

For me, the FAI Cup was a stepping stone to greater things, as it has been since for players like two of my former schoolboy colleagues at Rangers in Templeogue, Pat Byrne and Gerry Ryan, as well as Ashley Grimes, Ronnie Whelan, Paul McGrath, Roy Keane, Kevin Doyle, Seamus Coleman, Stephen Ward and others too many to mention.

It is a competition that brings out the best in players because of its winner-take-all formula. In that respect it's similar to the GAA's Championship, in which I enjoyed great years with the Dublin team. In fact, if it weren't for Billy Behan's intervention at that FAI Cup game in 1977, I would probably have been content to pursue my sporting ambitions in Gaelic football rather than soccer.

Last year was the ninetieth FAI Cup Final, so Seán Ryan has done us all a favour by researching and writing up the history of those ninety years. My story is in here, in the 1977 chapter, and in these pages you can learn all about the great characters – players and managers – who have participated in this competition since its inception in 1922.

Apart from the football history, there is a lot of social history in these pages too. For example, how the Civil War impacted on the career of the great Jimmy Dunne, or why the Troubles in the North in the 1920s didn't allow Alton United take the Cup back to Belfast, or how the Brideville players used their wartime clothing coupons to purchase jerseys for their Cup run in the 1940s.

It all makes for an enthralling read, while the results section for each year can be dipped in to time and again to check out the fortunes of your favourite teams and players.

With the backing of the FAI and Cup-sponsors Ford, I feel sure that Seán is on a winner with *The Official Book of the FAI Cup*.

Enjoy this nostalgic trip through some of the great days of Irish soccer!

1922

Revolver Halts the 'Terrors'

Shamrock Rovers have covered themselves in glory down the years in the FAI Cup, but such was not the case in 1922 when, as a Leinster League side, they contested the very first competition for the then Free State Challenge Cup. The competition was run off in the interim period between the ending of the Black-and-Tan War and the start of the Civil War, and the background of those turbulent times had a part to play.

Rovers became known as 'the terrors of football' as they fought their way to the Leinster League title and then to the final of the Free State Cup. Their robust style, epitomised in players like William 'Sacky' Glen, Dinny 'Nettler' Doyle and the legendary Bob Fullam, plus their vociferous support drawn from the Ringsend area, intimidated most opponents – but their Cup final opposition, St James's Gate, were a worthy exception.

Most of the Gate's players had proved their mettle in Cup competition when winning the All-Ireland Intermediate Cup in 1920 and they had just finished convincing winners of the inaugural Free State League Championship. In addition, their half-back line of Ernie McKay, Frank Heaney and Bob Carter was reckoned to be so tall that 'you'd need a ladder to get over them', as 'Sacky' Glen later put it.

Rovers accounted for League clubs Olympia, Dublin United and Bohemians on their way to the final; while the Gate, who were naturally installed as favourites, had beaten Jacobs and Shelbourne after a replay.

The final ended in a 1–1 draw, but it was the aftermath of the replay which showed those early Rovers in a bad light. The Gate prevailed by 1–0 and, when the final whistle went, some Rovers supporters climbed over the palings and attacked the winning team. Rovers players joined in the fray, and when the Gate eventually made their way to their dressing room they were followed by at least three of the Rovers team.

Rovers' captain, Bob Fullam, had a score to settle with Charlie Dowdall. Apparently they had tussled during the game and, when Fullam protested, Dowdall put his finger to his nose, a gesture which didn't go down well with the Ringsender.

Fullam was one of the Rovers players who invaded the Gate's dressing room but, as he advanced on Dowdall, the latter's brother Jack, who had just recently seen active service with the IRA, produced his revolver – and that was the end of that. At least, it put a sudden end to Rovers' invasion, but the matter was thrashed out again when an FAI Committee investigated the after-match incidents. As a result of their findings, Bob Fullam received one month's suspension, John Joe Flood three months, and Dinny Doyle six months. In addition, Rovers' Committee were reminded that the club is responsible for the conduct of its players.

It was a sorry start to a great club's involvement with the Blue Riband of Irish soccer, but it is to their credit that they learned their lesson and proceeded to play a brand of football that won for them the admiration of the Dublin public. Even though hit by the suspensions of three key players, they ran away with the Free State League title at their first attempt the following season and established themselves as the glamour club of Free State football, a title they have only relinquished on rare occasions since.

First Round

14 January	Dublin United	8	Frankfort	1
	Capstick 3, Millings 3,		Gillespie	
	B. Byrne, Harling			
	Olympia	1	Shamrock Rovers	3
	C. Pemberton		Flood, Cowzer 2	
	St James's Gate	3	Jacobs	1
	O'Shea, Kelly 2		Smith	
	West Ham	0	Shelbourne	0
	(Belfast)			
	YMCA	3	Athlone Town	4
	Lee 2, Wilson		James Sweeney 2, Ghent,	
			John Sweeney pen.	

Bye: Bohemians

First Round Replay

21 January	Shelbourne	2	West Ham	1
	Cannon 2		Kerr	
	(Belfast)			

Second Round

28 January	Bohemians	7	Athlone Town	1
	Kirwan 3, Robinson 2,		James Sweeney	
	McIlroy, Willits			
	Shamrock Rovers	5	Dublin United	1
	Fullam 2, Cowzer 2,		Ardiff	
	Flood			

Byes: Shelbourne and St James's Gate

Semi-Finals – Dalymount Park

18 February	St James's Gate	0	Shelbourne	0
25 February	Shamrock Rovers	1	Bohemians	0
	Flood			

Semi-Final Replay – Dalymount Park

4 March	St James's Gate	2	Shelbourne	1
	Duncan, Dowdall		Hamilton	

Final – Dalymount Park

17 March	St James's Gate	1	Shamrock Rovers	1
	Kelly		Campbell	

St James's Gate: Paddy 'Bucky' Coleman, Tom 'Spud' Murphy, J 'Fatty' Kavanagh, Ernie McKay, Frank Heaney, Bob Carter, Johnny Carey, Jack Kelly, Paddy 'Dirty' Duncan, Charlie Dowdall, Johnny Gargan

Shamrock Rovers: Billy Nagle, John J.J. Kelly, Peter 'Weaser' Warren, William 'Sacky' Glen, Joe 'Buller' Byrne, Harry Birthistle, Charlie Campbell, Bob Cowzer, John Joe Flood, Bob Fullam, Dinny 'Nettler' Doyle

Referee: M. Broderick (Athlone)　　　　　　　　　　Attendance: 15,000

Final Replay – Dalymount Park

8 April	St James's Gate	1	Shamrock Rovers	0
	Kelly (43m)			

St James's Gate: Bill O'Shea for Carter
Shamrock Rovers: Unchanged

Referee: M. Broderick (Athlone)　　　　　　　　　　Attendance: 10,000

1923

The Men From The Falls

Comparisons between the standards of soccer, North and South, were inevitable in the years immediately after the split of 1921 and, in that respect, Free State morale suffered a bad blow when the Cup was won in 1923 by a junior team from The Falls Road, Belfast.

At the time, Belfast Celtic were out of Irish League football – they returned in 1924 – and many of the players, who would normally aspire to playing with Celtic, paraded their talents in The Falls League, whose clubs affiliated to the Free State FA.

Alton United, who won the Belfast & District competition to qualify for the Cup proper, had a good pedigree as they had won the All-Ireland Junior Cup in 1920, under the title United, only acquiring the Alton pre-fix when they moved into Clubrooms above the Alton Bar. Their captain and centre-half, Michael Brennan, was a member of both Cup-winning teams and later played for Tranmere Rovers and Belfast Celtic. He was also chosen as a reserve for the IFA's international team. In later years he was a well-known boxing referee.

Most of the Alton players were labourers working on the Belfast docks. As amateurs, their progress to the Cup final, which was played on St Patrick's Day in Dalymount Park, was a costly business and they needed financial assistance from The Falls League to subsidise their trip to Dublin.

En route to the final they disposed of Midland Athletic, Shelbourne United and Fordsons, but they were regarded as rank outsiders in the final against a star-studded Shelbourne side that had beaten Bray Unknowns, Cup-holders St James's Gate, and Jacobs. Shelbourne's half-back line included the legendary Val Harris and Mick 'Boxer' Foley, both international players with years of English soccer under their belts.

Harris, Foley and goalkeeper Paddy Walsh were all seeking to become the first players to win IFA and Free State Cup medals. Harris had won IFA Cup medals with Shelbourne in 1906 and 1920; while Foley and Walsh were teammates in the 1920 success. Harris had also won an All-Ireland medal in Gaelic football with Dublin in 1901.

The fact that the country was still in an unsettled state was underlined by Alton United's dramatic arrival in Dublin on Cup final day, when they were escorted from Amiens Street station to Dalymount by an armed guard provided by the IRA. Whether this had an intimidating effect on their opponents is impossible to ascertain, but Shelbourne certainly played well below their usual form and went under 1–0. Centre-forward Jimmy Harvey also had the unwelcome distinction of becoming the first player to miss a penalty in a Cup final, shooting straight at goalkeeper Maginnis when the score was 0–0. Shelbourne supporters firmly believe this defeat set in train a Cup hoodoo which wasn't dispelled until they won the Cup for the first time in 1939.

Although Alton's players received their medals, they were not able to take the Cup back to Belfast because of the troubles in the North at the time. In fact, they didn't have a very long reign as Cup-holders for, apart from not taking the Cup home, shortly afterwards they decided to affiliate to the IFA for the 1923-24 season.

First Round

6 January	**Alton United**	4	**Midland Athletic**	0
	McSherry, Ward 3			
	(Abandoned 2nd half: bad light)			
	Athlone Town	1	**Shamrock Rovers**	2
	McNulty		Fagan 2	
	Bohemians	1	**Shelbourne United**	2
	Robinson		McLean, Redmond	
	Fordsons	W/O	**Rathmines United**	SCR
	Jacobs	4	**Pioneers**	0
	Smith 3, Byrne			
	Olympia	0	**St James's Gate**	1
	(At St James's Park)		Duncan	
	Shelbourne	9	**Bray Unknowns** 0	
	Doyle 5, Williams 2, Wilson, Delaney			
	Dublin United	3	**Sligo Celtic**	3
	P. Carroll, Rushe, Murtagh		Tiernan 2, Dykes	

First Round Re-Fixture

13 January	**Alton United**	5	**Midland Athletic**	0
	Ward 3, Duffy, Brennan pen.			

First Round Replay

14 January	**Sligo Celtic**	0	**Dublin United**	0

First Round Second Replay

28 January	**Dublin United**	3	**Sligo Celtic**	1
	Rushe 2, McGuinness		Lynch o.g.	

Second Round

20 January	**Shelbourne United**	1	**Alton United**	1
	McLean		Duffy	
	St James's Gate	1	**Shelbourne**	2
	Kelly		Wilson 2	
21 January	**Shamrock Rovers**	1	**Jacobs**	2
	Fullam pen.		Houston, Smith	

4 February	Dublin United	2	Fordsons	3
	Campbell, Rushe		O'Sullivan 3	

Second Round Replay

27 January	Alton United	2	Shelbourne United	0
	Ward, McSherry			

Semi-Finals – Dalymount Park

17 February	Alton United	4	Fordsons	2
	Ward 3, Brennan pen.		Buckle 2	
3 March	Shelbourne	2	Jacobs	0
	Harvey, Williams			

Final – Dalymount Park

17 March	Alton United	1	Shelbourne	0
	McSherry			

Alton United: James Maginnis, Edward McNeill, Hugh Bell, Paddy Devlin, Michael Brennan, Bobby Loughran, Andy McSherry, Billy Duffy, Sammy Ward, Jack Russell, Hugh McCann

Shelbourne: Paddy Walsh, Paddy 'Yoddy' Kavanagh, James 'Sally' Connolly, Dan Delaney, Val Harris, Mick 'Boxer' Foley, Eddie Brierley, Stephen Doyle, Jimmy Harvey, Ralph Ardiff, Sammy Wilson

Referee: M. Broderick (Athlone)　　　　　　　　　　Attendance: 14,000

1924

Hannon Shows How

Soccer in Ireland, in the early years of the twentieth century, was known as a 'garrison game', due to the fact that it flourished in those towns and cities which housed a garrison of the British occupying forces. So it was no surprise when the first all-provincial final in the Free State Cup featured teams from Cork and Athlone, towns which had housed substantial British garrisons only three years previously.

The strength of the game in these towns is best underlined by the fact that Athlone Town, the winners of the 1924 final, fielded no less than seven local players. Two of the others were from the same county, with goalkeeper Paddy O'Reilly (from Dublin) and centre-half John Joe Dykes (Sligo), the only outsiders.

Athlone, who disposed of Midland Athletic, Shelbourne and Bohemians on the way to the St Patrick's Day final against Fordsons, didn't concede a goal in their victorious campaign and this feat wasn't equalled until 1958. Ironically, Fordsons, who were a non-League team at the time, only conceded one goal in their Cup run – and that was the lone goal of the final.

Fittingly, the goal was scored by inside-right Dinny Hannon, probably the most famous Athlone player of all time. By 1924 he was in the twilight of his career, the majority of which had been spent with Bohemians. As a student first and later as a solicitor, he had been a loyal member of the Dublin club and helped them to their historic win in the IFA Cup in 1908.

19

Although he was an amateur, he was capped six times by the IFA between 1908 and 1913, and he also won five amateur caps between 1908 and 1920. While with Athlone, he won two amateur caps with the Free State team in the 1924 Olympic Games in Paris. Athlone's Cup success enabled him to become the first holder of both IFA and Free State FA Cup medals.

Hannon was probably a surprise scorer in the final for, while he was the most experienced Athlone player, he only rarely figured on the scoresheet. Centre-forward James Sweeney was the Town's most prolific marksman at the time but, strangely, he didn't manage a Cup goal this season. Another player who caught the eye in this team was wing-half Tommy Muldoon, who was snapped up by Aston Villa shortly after. Not so fortunate was right-back Joe Monahan who, some years later, lost his Cup medal, which he had attached to his watch-chain, while gaffing a pike on Lough Rea. Despite the best efforts of divers from as far afield as Limerick, it was never recovered.

Fordsons were a works team, just two years in existence, based in the Ford factory in Cork. They had the advantage, like St James's Gate, the Guinness brewery team in Dublin, of attracting good players who were anxious to secure employment. Two of their players, goalkeeper Billy O'Hagan and inside-left Harry Buckle, were Irish internationals and, with League status granted for the following season, more notable signings were planned. Success wouldn't be long denied the Cork club.

First Round

5 January	Athlone Town	2	Midland Athletic	0
	Collins, Lyster			
	Bohemians	1	Shamrock Rovers	0
	Roberts			
	Brooklyn	1	Bray Unknowns	2
	Houston		O'Brien o.g., Carroll	
	St James's Gate	3	Pioneers	2
	Duncan, Dowdall, Kelly		Murphy, Fisher	
3 February	Clifton	0	Shelbourne United	2
	(Cork)		Keegan, Quigley	

Byes: Fordsons, Jacobs, and Shelbourne

Second Round

19 January	Bohemians	1	Bray Unknowns	0
	Robinson			
	Shelbourne	0	Athlone Town	2
			Ghent, Collins	
27 January	Jacobs	0	Fordsons	2
			D. Collins 2	
17 February	St James's Gate	2	Shelbourne United	1
	Kelly, Keogh		Doyle	

Semi-Final – Shelbourne Park

16 February	Bohemians	0	Athlone Town	0

Semi-Final – The Mardyke, Cork

2 March	Fordsons	4	St James's Gate	0
	D. Collins 3, Pinkney			

Semi-Final Replay – Shelbourne Park

1 March	Athlone Town	2	Bohemians	0
	Ghent, Lyster			

Final – Dalymount Park

17 March   **Athlone Town**   1   **Fordsons**   0
              Hannon (20m)

Athlone Town: Paddy O'Reilly, Joe Monahan, Jimmy Hope, Terry Judge, John Joe Dykes, Tommy Muldoon, Norman Lyster, Dinny Hannon, James Sweeney, Eddie Collins, Frank Ghent

Fordsons: Bill O'Hagan, Jeremiah O'Mahony, D. Millar, Leo Maher, Jack O'Sullivan, Paddy Barry, Frank Hunter, Laurence Pinkney, Jock Malpas, Harry Buckle, Dinny Collins

Referee: J. J. Kelly (Dublin)   Attendance: 21,000

It's a Record!

- Derry City and Alton United (1923) are the only Northern Ireland-based winners of the FAI Cup. Alton were unable to take the Cup to Belfast, however, because of civil unrest, so Derry were the first club to bring the cup north of the border.

- Shelbourne, Bohemians and Derry City are the only clubs to win both the FAI and the IFA Cups. The Dublin clubs were successful in the IFA Cup before the 1921 split, from which the FAI was formed, while Derry remained in the IFA until 1973, only entering the FAI's jurisdiction for the 1985-86 season.

1925

The Four Fs

Shamrock Rovers, who had burst on the scene in 1922 by reaching the Cup final as a non-League side and then ran away with the League in their first season in 1922-23, lost their way somewhat when forwards Bob Fullam and John Joe Flood departed for Leeds United. However, their return for the 1924-25 season launched Rovers into one of the most glorious chapters in the club's illustrious history.

Rovers completed the Grand Slam of League, Shield and FAI Cup and they did it without losing a match. In twenty-seven League and Shield games, they won twenty and drew seven, with a goal difference of ninety-four for and twenty against. A lot of their success was due to their famous Four Fs – Fullam, Flood, Billy 'Juicy' Farrell and John 'Kruger' Fagan – whose understanding up front yielded a sack-full of goals.

Fullam was also an outstanding captain – because he hated losing and because he was the original players' player, always pleading their cause for an extra bonus or, where necessary, a better basic. His fellow players respected him and accepted his bluntly spoken diatribes if their performance wasn't up to scratch. Many a game was won by Fullam's earthy half-time summary of his teammates' shortcomings.

The slogan 'Give it to Bob' was a popular one and referred to Fullam's lethal left foot, which was regarded as virtually unstoppable. Apart from shooting talent, Fullam was also an able midfield general and was credited with bringing the best out of his wing partner, Fagan.

Flood, who later had a spell with Crystal Palace, operated at inside-right but could also perform on the right wing, while centre-forward Farrell was a former Bray Unknowns player who was noted for his pace, his dribbling skills and his opportunism. 'Sacky' Glen said of Farrell: 'He had more ways of scoring than any player I have ever seen.'

Farrell, who had joined the Milltown club the previous season, really blossomed with the return of Fullam and Flood, and was the club's top scorer in a record-breaking year. So good was he, in fact, that Jimmy Dunne, later to become one of the English League's most prolific scorers, was forced to accept reserve team football at Rovers and was eventually transferred to New Brighton. Sadly, Farrell's great career was brought to a tragic halt when he was badly injured in a motorbike accident on his way home from training in 1926. Although he made a courageous attempt at a comeback, it was not a success.

Fullam and right-full Alec Kirkland had won IFA Cup medals with Shelbourne in 1920, while goalkeeper Paddy O'Reilly was winning his second Free State Cup medal in successive seasons, having been successful with Athlone in 1924.

The final was a Ringsend 'derby', with Shelbourne providing the opposition, and Dalymount Park was packed to capacity with a record crowd of 23,000 watching the proceedings. The gates had to be closed fifteen minutes before the kick-off. For the first time an English referee was in charge of the final and the honour fell to Mr J. T. Howcroft (Bolton), who had refereed the 1920 English FA Cup Final.

Later in the season, Rovers travelled to Belfast to take on Irish League champions Glentoran, and they gave the game in the South a most welcome boost when they scored a memorable 2–0 win in what was billed as an All-Ireland Championship decider.

First Round

3 January	Bohemians	0	Shamrock Rovers	2
			Farrell 2	
	Jacobs	2	Brooklyn	6
	Hickey 2		M. McCabe 5, Hinch	
	Shelbourne	3	Fordsons	3
	Lea, Doran 2		Hannon 2, Kelly	
10 January	Athlone Town	5	Cork Bohemians	3
	John Sweeney, James		O'Driscoll, O'Leary 2	
	Sweeney 3, Ghent			

First Round Replay

| 11 January | Fordsons | 0 | Shelbourne | 1 |
| | | | · Cowzer | |

Byes: Pioneers, Drumcondra, Bray Unknowns, St James's Gate

Second Round

17 January	Bray Unknowns	4	Pioneers	0
	Byrne 2, McLean,			
	Cunningham pen.			
	Brooklyn	0	Shelbourne	4
			Doran 3 (1 pen.), Cowzer	
	Drumcondra	0	Athlone Town	2
			James Sweeney 2	
	St James's Gate	0	Shamrock Rovers	1
			Jordan	

Semi-Final – Dalymount Park

| 14 February | Shelbourne | 4 | Athlone Town | 0 |
| | Doran 2, Maguire, Cowzer | | | |

Semi-Final – Shelbourne Park

| 28 February | Shamrock Rovers | 2 | Bray Unknowns | 1 |
| | Flood, Kirkland | | Newman pen. | |

Final – Dalymount Park

17 March	Shamrock Rovers	2	Shelbourne	1
	Fullam (23m), Flood (61m)		Glen o.g. (65m)	

Shamrock Rovers: Paddy O'Reilly, Alec Kirkland, Patrick 'Doc' Malone, William 'Sacky' Glen, Dinny 'Nettler' Doyle, Ned Marlowe, Charlie 'Spid' Jordan, Bob Fullam, Billy 'Juicy' Farrell, John Joe Flood, John 'Kruger' Fagan

Shelbourne: Paddy Walsh, Frank Daly, Paddy 'Yoddy' Kavanagh, – Kelly, Val Harris, Mick 'Boxer' Foley, – Laxton, Bob Cowzer, John Doran, Terry Mulvanny, Sammy Wilson

Referee: J. T. Howcroft (Bolton)   Attendance: 23,000

It's a Record!

- Thirteen of the thirty-two counties have produced FAI Cup-winning clubs – Dublin, Cork, Limerick, Waterford, Louth, Wicklow, Westmeath, Longford, Galway, Sligo, Derry, Donegal and Antrim.

1926

O'Hagan Thwarts Fullam

The turning-point in the 1926 final occurred when Fordsons' goalkeeper, Billy O'Hagan, saved a penalty struck by Shamrock Rovers' captain, Bob Fullam, with the scores level at 2–2. It was rare for Fullam to miss from the spot but the sequel to his miss on this occasion gave him a lot of satisfaction in years to come.

When the ball broke loose, after O'Hagan's initial save, it was 50/50 between the goalkeeper and the penalty-taker, but Fullam decided not to contest the issue. 'That decision was the best of my life,' he told his brother, Monsignor Thomas Fullam. 'When the ball came out, I could have hit it but I would have killed O'Hagan so I held back.'

O'Hagan's bravery inspired his teammates, who notched the vital third goal to win before yet another record crowd (25,000). In fact, O'Hagan proved an inspiration right through the Cup campaign as he saved a penalty in the first round tie against Shelbourne and then twice saved a penalty in the last fifteen minutes of the second round tie in Athlone.

O'Hagan was from the North, as were five other members of the Fordsons team – Jimmy Carabine, Barney Collins, Malachy McKinney, Paddy Kelly and Harry Buckle – and, if Buckle's case is anything to go by, Orange bigotry probably did the Cork club a few unwitting favours!

Buckle was an Irish international who played with Sunderland, Bristol Rovers and Coventry before returning to his native Belfast to work at ship-building with

Harland & Wolff and continue his football career on a part-time basis with Belfast Celtic.

Discrimination was rife in the shipyards and Catholics were very much in the minority. It was probably through his football connections that Buckle managed to find work there at all. Even that didn't save him, however, when the Troubles started and the Orangemen came searching for scapegoats on which to vent their anger. Along with seventeen or so other Catholics, Buckle was thrown into Belfast Lough – and the message was clear.

A foreman, who was friendly with him because of his football prowess, took him aside and advised him to get out while the going was good. Buckle took the hint and moved to Wales before getting into his ship-building trade again in Cork. From there he was snapped up by Fords and became a key member of the team.

Buckle, at forty-four, was the oldest player ever to win an FAI Cup medal, and was renowned for the fact that he never headed the ball. He always took the ball down to his feet and made full use of his arms and elbows to keep would-be tacklers at bay. In the final he made one magical run from practically the halfway line, beating the entire Rovers defence only to slip the ball wide. A veteran he may have been, but the skill was still there.

Fordsons right-full Jack Baylor achieved another distinction in 1937 when he became the first Cup medal winner to referee a Cup final. English referees were the custom in the early days of the Cup and, on 9 January 1926, a Mr Baker and his son made history when they refereed Cup ties in Dublin. Baker Snr. was in charge of Bohemians v. Shamrock Rovers, while Baker Jnr. deputised for a Mr Winnell and took charge of Shelbourne v. Fordsons.

First Round

9 January	**Athlone Town**	4	**Brideville**	0
	Brooks, Ghent, James			
	Sweeney, Henry pen.			
	Bohemians	0	**Shamrock Rovers**	0
	Bray Unknowns	5	**St James's Gate**	2
	Byrne 2, McFarlane,		Donnelly, Dowdall	
	Carroll, T. Cunningham			
	Fordsons	2	**Shelbourne**	2
	Roberts, D. Collins		Watters, Simpson	
	Lindon	4	**Pioneers**	2
	Hoey 3, Flanagan		Chervi, M. Murphy	
10 January	**Jacobs**	5	**Barrackton Utd**	1
	Smith 4, Byrne		McVeigh pen.	

First Round Replays

16 January	**Shamrock Rovers**	2	**Bohemians**	2
	Fagan, Farrell		Stynes 2	
	Shelbourne	1	**Fordsons**	2
	Robinson		Kelly, Roberts	

First Round Second Replay

20 January	**Shamrock Rovers**	2	**Bohemians**	0
	Farrell pen., Marlowe			

Second Round

23 January	**Lindon**	1	**Jacobs**	1
	Carey		Moore	
	Athlone Town	2	**Fordsons**	3
	James Sweeney 2		Hannon, Roberts,	
	(1 pen.)		Barry	

Byes: Bray Unknowns and Shamrock Rovers

Second Round Replay

31 January	**Jacobs**	4	**Lindon**	2
	Smith 2, Moore 2		Hoey pen., Flanagan	

Semi-Final – Shelbourne Park

| 6 February | Shamrock Rovers | 0 | Jacobs | 0 |

Semi-Final – Victoria Cross, Cork

| 21 February | Fordsons | 4 | Bray Unknowns | 1 |
| | Buckle, Kelly, Sullivan 2 | | McFarlane | |

Semi-Final Replay – Dalymount Park

| 20 February | Shamrock Rovers | 3 | Jacobs | 0 |
| | Jordan, Fullam, Flood | | | |

Final – Dalymount Park

17 March	Fordsons	3	Shamrock Rovers	2
	Roberts (3m),		Farrell (1m), Fagan (28m)	
	Barry 2 (60m, 85m)			

Fordsons: Bill O'Hagan, Jack Baylor, Jimmy Carabine, James 'Sally' Connolly, Jack O'Sullivan, Barney Collins, Malachy McKinney, Paddy Kelly, Dave Roberts, Harry Buckle, Paddy Barry

Shamrock Rovers: Paddy O'Reilly, Patrick 'Doc' Malone, Alec Kirkland, William 'Sacky' Glen, Dinny 'Nettler' Doyle, Ned Marlowe, Charlie 'Spid' Jordan, John Joe Flood, Billy 'Juicy' Farrell, Bob Fullam, John 'Kruger' Fagan

Referee: A. E. Fogg (Bolton)   Attendance: 25,000

1927

Non-League Surprise

Down the years there have been many good performances in the FAI Cup by the winners of the Intermediate Cup but, strange to relate, none have managed to repeat the performance of the first winners, Drumcondra, who went all the way in 1927 to complete a unique double.

In its first year, the Intermediate Cup was known as the Qualifying Cup, and Drumcondra had to travel to Cobh to beat the local Ramblers in the final. Both teams qualified for the FAI Cup but, whereas Cobh lost to Brideville in the first round, Drumcondra beat Jacobs and Bohemians on their way to a final meeting with Brideville, whom they beat 1–0 after a replay.

Drumcondra were then a Leinster Senior League team aspiring to League of Ireland status, but their Cup success didn't earn them that distinction as there were no vacancies and League officials obviously felt the time was not right to extend the League. However, Drumcondra proved their form was no flash in the pan by reaching the Cup final again in 1928 and, although they were beaten 2–1 by Bohemians, they secured the sought-after place in the League for 1928-29 when Athlone Town resigned.

Tom Moore, left-back on that Drumcondra team, recalled that it was their great team spirit which carried them through so many tough Cup ties. 'The players played whether they were injured or not,' he remarked.

Captain of Drumcondra was centre-half Joe Grace, who had played for Belfast Celtic in a distinguished career and was a father figure to the Drums team. In 1926 he earned the distinction of being capped for Ireland against Italy while playing in the Leinster Senior League, a feat that has never been repeated.

Drumcondra figured in another piece of history in their 1928 Cup run when their 3–0 semi-final win over Fordsons in Cork was the first soccer match to be broadcast on Irish radio. The commentary was by John Murphy (Pioneers) and Jim Brennan, who was Chairman of the Free State League.

Shelbourne Park was used as a venue for a Cup final for the first time in 1927 when the replay was held there and, as the score was 0–0 after ninety minutes, extra time was used for the first time to decide the issue.

Brideville, Drumcondra's victims in the final, were a team based in Dublin's Liberties and were only in their second season of League football. They won the FAI Junior Cup in 1924 and the Leinster Senior Cup the following year, but the FAI Cup always eluded them. Had they been successful against Drumcondra, theirs would have also been a unique feat, for they finished bottom of the League that season.

The passion of Mary Jane Cunningham, the wife of Shamrock Rovers' Chairman Joe, for the Hoops was very much in evidence after their shock first round defeat to Bray Unknowns. The winners' full-back, Joe Williams, renowned for his robust style, had to run the gauntlet of Mary Jane's umbrella as he left the pitch, so upset was she at some of his fearsome tackling. Nine years later, Williams, who worked for Cunningham's bookmaking firm, was in the Hoops' team Cup-winning team.

First Round

8 January	Athlone Town	1	Shelbourne	4
	James Sweeney		McMillan, Meek 2, Robinson	
	Bohemians	6	Dundalk	1
	Matthews 2, O'Flaherty, Dennis, Bermingham, Bowden o.g.		Bushe	
	Bray Unknowns	3	Shamrock Rovers	0
	Rogers 2, Byrne (At Shelbourne Park)			
9 January	Brideville	2	Cobh Ramblers	1
	Maguire, Killeen		Kelleher	
	Jacobs	0	Drumcondra	3
			McCarney 2, Murray	
	Fordsons	2	St James's Gate	1
	Heaney o.g., Fleming		Booth	

Second Round

22 January	Shelbourne	5	Bray Unknowns	1
	Doran 3, McMillan 2		Rogers	
	Fordsons	2	Bohemians	3
	Keenan 2		White 2, Matthews	

Byes: Brideville and Drumcondra

Semi-Final – Dalymount Park

5 February	Brideville	2	Shelbourne	0
	Murtagh 2			

Semi-Final – Shelbourne Park

19 February	Drumcondra	3	Bohemians	1
	Swan, Coyle, Murray		Matthews	

Final – Dalymount Park

17 March **Drumcondra** 1 **Brideville** 1
McCarney (24m) McCarthy (79m)

Drumcondra: Jim Cleary, John 'Myler' Keogh, Tom Moore, Con Coyle, Joe Grace, P. Maxwell, Donie Fleming, George Swan, Owen McCarney, Eddie Cullen, Johnny Murray

Brideville: Celestine Gamblin, George Lennox, John Siney, Gerry Donovan, Harry Armstrong, Johnny Fox, Phil Murtagh, Mick Maguire, Fran Watters, Paul O'Brien, Percy McCarthy

Referee: J. T. Howcroft (Bolton) Attendance: 25,000

Final Replay – Shelbourne Park

9 April **Drumcondra** 1 **Brideville** 0
Murray

(After extra time.)

Both teams unchanged

Referee: J. T. Howcroft (Bolton) Attendance: 10,000

It's a Record!

• The original FAI Cup was purchased for £68/10/-, and was retired after the 2006 Cup final.

1928

Bohemians' Grand Slam

The Bohemian team that won the Free State Cup in 1928 is reckoned to have been the best that ever represented the famous Dublin club. In addition to the Cup, they also won the League, the Shield, and the Leinster Cup – the latter a trophy which had eluded the great Shamrock Rovers team of 1924-25.

There wasn't a weak link in the team – and the mentors knew it. And rather than weaken the team, they went to great lengths to keep it together, as the story of Jeremiah 'Sam' Robinson, the right-back, indicates.

As a result of some horseplay in the dressing room after training one night at Dalymount, a bucket of hot water was accidentally tipped over Robinson's leg, causing the skin to peel away and leaving the scalded leg in an exceedingly raw and tender state. It seemed a foregone conclusion that he would miss Bohemians' forthcoming game, but Bohemians' doctor and mentor, Dr Hooper, had other ideas. 'He bandaged me up like a turkey cock and I played,' was how Robinson described it. 'They didn't want to disturb the team,' he added. 'With that team it wasn't a case of were we going to win, it was how much we were going to win by.'

A vital cog in the team was inside-right Billy Dennis, who scored the winning goal in the final against Drumcondra. An Englishman, he wouldn't have joined the Bohemian ranks but for the course of true love.

Originally a miner, he joined the British Army, North Staffordshire Regiment, in 1918, and was stationed on the Curragh in 1919. He became friendly with an Irish girl, Mary O'Leary, and after a tour of duty in India he asked her to marry him. She agreed – on condition that she didn't have to leave Dublin. So Billy returned to Dublin to get married and later joined Bohemians, having played a couple of games for Port Vale as an amateur before he left England.

Another 'outsider' who had a big influence on that Bohemian team was the club's first full-time coach, Bobby Parker, a former Hearts player. Although a man of few words, he had the respect of all the players.

He was also instrumental in spotting the potential of left-winger Peter Kavanagh, who turned up to watch a game and was drafted in when one of the selected eleven failed to arrive. Parker pestered Kavanagh to sign after that and finally succeeded. At eighteen, Kavanagh was the youngest member of the Grand Slam team and was naturally a target for the cross-Channel scouts, with Glasgow Celtic eventually winning the race. Sadly, a knee injury finished his career while he was still in his early twenties.

Another key man was centre-half Johnny McMahon, who came from Derry. A member of the Garda Band, he had a fearsome shot that earned him many goals and, apart from amateur internationals, he was also honoured at full international level by the IFA. He is the only League of Ireland player to be accorded that honour.

Bohemians' win meant that four of the first seven winners of the Cup – St James's Gate, Alton United, Drumcondra and Bohemians – were amateurs but this trend was not maintained in the succeeding years, with only Bohemians (1935) and Home Farm (1975) breaking the professional clubs' stranglehold on the Cup.

First Round

7 January	**Athlone Town** Henry 2, James Sweeney	3	**Drumcondra** McCarney 4, Swan 3, Keogh, Doyle	9
	Bohemians White 3, Dennis 2, Thomas, Robinson	7	**Cobh Ramblers**	0
	Jacobs Herron, Boyne	2	**Strandville** McGrane	1
	Shelbourne McCleery, Robinson	2	**Brideville**	0
8 January	**Bray Unknowns** Sloan 4, Rogers 2	6	**Bendigo** Cummins	1
	Cork Bohemians Noonan, Buckley	2	**Fordsons** Heinemann, Dowdall, O'Sullivan, Hannon	4
	St James's Gate Farrell 2, Ennis, Booth	4	**Cork City**	0
	Shamrock Rovers Campbell, Luke, Fagan	3	**Dundalk** Kane, Barrett 2	3

First Round Replay

12 January	**Dundalk** Withers, Carroll 2, Mathieson	4	**Shamrock Rovers** O'Brien	1

Second Round

21 January	**Bohemians** McMahon 2 (1 pen.) White 2, Bermingham	5	**St James's Gate**	0
	Shelbourne McIlvenny, MacMillan, McCleery	3	**Dundalk** Barrett	1
22 January	**Fordsons** Connolly 2, Heinemann 2	4	**Jacobs**	0
25 January	**Bray Unknowns** Carroll 2	2	**Drumcondra** Murray 2	2

Second Round Replay

29 January	Drumcondra	4	Bray Unknowns	1
	McCarney 3, Doyle		Newman	

Semi-Final – Dalymount Park

4 February	Bohemians	1	Shelbourne	1
	McMahon pen.		McCarthy o.g.	

Semi-Final Replay – Dalymount Park

19 February	Bohemians	0	Shelbourne	0

Semi-Final – The Mardyke, Cork

19 February	Fordsons	0	Drumcondra	3
			McCarney, Doyle 2	

Semi-Final Second Replay – Dalymount Park

22 February	Bohemians	4	Shelbourne	1
	Dennis, Daly o.g.,		Kinsella	
	White, C. Robinson			

Final – Dalymount Park

17 March	Bohemians	2	Drumcondra	1
	White (35m), Dennis (75m)		Keogh (25m)	

Bohemians: Harry Cannon, Jeremiah 'Sam' Robinson, Jack McCarthy, Johnny McIlroy, Johnny McMahon, Bob Thomas, Jimmy Bermingham, Billy Dennis, Jimmy White, Christy 'Boy' Robinson, Peter Kavanagh

Drumcondra: Charlie O'Callaghan, Jimmy Kelly, Tom Moore, Con Coyle, Joe Grace, P. Maxwell, Stephen Doyle, George Swan, Owen McCarney, John 'Myler' Keogh, Johnny Murray

Referee: J. Langenus (Belgium)   Attendance: 25,000

1929

Start of an Affair

Shamrock Rovers' great love-affair with the FAI Cup started in earnest on 5 January 1929, with a first round defeat of great rivals, Shelbourne. That marked the start of an unbeaten five-year Cup run which didn't end until 24 January 1934, when Rovers were surprisingly beaten at home in a first round replay by St James's Gate.

Three players – John Burke, William 'Sacky' Glen and John Joe Flood – shared in each of that five-in-a-row, establishing a record of consecutive Cup medals that wasn't broken until 1969, when Pat Courtney, also of Shamrock Rovers, won his sixth successive medal. While Glen and Flood were from Ringsend, Rovers' traditional home, Burke was from Cahir, County Tipperary, and had been spotted playing for junior club Cahir Park. He scored on his debut as an inside-forward in the 1927-28 season, but coach Johnny Dundon solved one of Rovers' problems when he switched Burke to left-back, a position in which he won international honours.

Burke was a much-travelled footballer, having played while serving with the British Army in England, France, Germany and India. He fought in both World Wars and was among those evacuated from Dunkirk in 1940.

The Tipperary man married into the same family as Rovers boss Joe Cunningham, and his son, Mickey, followed in his footsteps, winning two Cup medals in 1955 and 1956 with Rovers, from the right-back position. Although he never emulated his father at international level, Mickey was honoured on many occasions at inter-League level. Family rivalry was keen in the 1950s when John was trainer-coach for a spell to Sligo Rovers' Dublin players.

Another member of Rovers' 1929 team has links with later Cup glory for the Milltown men: centre-half Tom Caulfield's grandson, Liam O'Brien, was a member of the Rovers' team which won the Cup 1985.

Rovers' victory over Bohemians in a replay also saw the start of a tradition which lasted until 1984, when it was ended by UCD. In the intervening years, Rovers built up a seeming invincibility in Cup final replays. Rovers' 1929 victory also marked the first occasion any club won the Cup twice.

When the Harcourt Street railway line was in operation, it passed through Milltown on its way to Bray and, as a result, Rovers picked up some useful talent from the seaside town. Billy 'Juicy' Farrell, centre-forward on the great 1924-25 team, was probably the best known, but by 1929 his place had been taken by another Bray man, Jack Sloan.

First Round

5 January	**Bohemians**	**2**	St James's Gate	0
	McMahon, Bermingham			
	Richmond Rovers	0	**Dundalk**	**2**
	(At Dundalk)		Stewart, Fitzhenry o.g.	
	Shamrock Rovers	**3**	Shelbourne	2
	Sloan 2, Flood		Maguire, R. Thomas	
6 January	**Bray Unknowns**	**2**	Brideville	1
	Rogers 2		S. Robinson	
	Drumcondra	**3**	Fordsons	1
	Watters, McCarney, McDonald		Heinemann	
	Fermoy	0	**Richmond United**	**1**
			Fagan	
	Jacobs	1	Dolphin	1
	Carlisle		Kenny	
	Waterford Celtic	1	Cork Bohemians	1
	Haygood		Lynch pen.	

First Round Replays

9 January	**Cork Bohemians**	**4**	Waterford Celtic	1
	Buckley, O'Sullivan 2, Geaney		Arrigan	
	Dolphin	2	**Jacobs**	**3**
	Burch, Hand pen.		Owens, Carlisle, Ronan	

Second Round

19 January	Bohemians	2	Jacobs	2
	O'Kane, Deegan o.g.		Carlisle, Hickey	
	Dundalk	**6**	Bray Unknowns	2
	Carroll 4, Mathieson, Egan		Payne, Rogers	
	Shamrock Rovers	**4**	Richmond United	0
	Golding, Sherwin 2, Flood			
20 January	**Drumcondra**	**3**	Cork Bohemians	1
	McCarney 2, McDonald		Kane	

Second Round Replay

23 January	**Jacobs**	**2**	**Bohemians**	**4**
	Kelly pen., Carlisle		Horlacher, Bermingham, McMahon pen., White	

Semi-Final – Tolka Park

2 February	**Shamrock Rovers**	**3**	**Dundalk**	**0**
	Sloan 3			

Semi-Final – Shelbourne Park

16 February	**Bohemians**	**2**	**Drumcondra**	**0**
	McMahon pen., Andrews			

Final – Dalymount Park

18 March	**Shamrock Rovers**	**0**	**Bohemians**	**0**

Shamrock Rovers: Paddy O'Reilly, Jim Maguire, John Burke, William 'Sacky' Glen, Tom Caulfield, Ned Marlowe, Joe 'Lye' Golding, John Joe Flood, Jack Sloan, Bob Fullam, Alfred Sherwin

Bohemians: Harry Cannon, Mick O'Kane, Jack McCarthy, Paddy O'Kane, Johnny McMahon, Alec Morton, Jimmy Bermingham, Billy Dennis, Jimmy White, Fred Horlacher, Peter Kavanagh

Referee: A. H. Hull (Burnley)   Attendance: 22,000

Final Replay – Shelbourne Park

6 April	**Shamrock Rovers**	**3**	**Bohemians**	**0**
	Flood 2 (5m, 65m), Fullam (50m)			

Shamrock Rovers: Charlie Campbell for Sherwin
Bohemians: Unchanged

Referee: A. H. Hull (Burnley)   Attendance: 15,000 (approx.)

1930

'Babby' Denies Brideville

A number of Cup finals have been decided by 'handball' goals which went undetected, but the first such verifiable goal occurred in the 1930 final, when Shamrock Rovers recorded a second successive win, beating Brideville 1–0.

David Byrne, who was known as 'Babby' because he was the youngest of a Ringsend family of eleven, admitted that the winning goal in the last minute of the game, which was credited to him, was illegal. He remembered the circumstances well: 'A very high ball was floated across and I got in between Charlie Reid, who had dropped back to defend, and the goalie Charlie O'Callaghan. I jumped up, my hand hit the ball first and it went in. I got into more trouble over scoring that goal because a draw seemed on the cards and that would have meant more money.'

Byrne also recalled a curious incident from the semi-final against Fordsons, which was played in the Mardyke in Cork: 'I scored with two minutes to go but the referee, who was from Sheffield, disallowed it. Coming off the pitch I said to him: "You made a mistake there, ref", and he replied, "Well, you won't lose anything by it".' How right he was, with Rovers romping to a 3–0 replay win in the Iveagh Grounds in Dublin.

Although he stood barely 5'5", centre-forward Byrne was known as the 'scourge of goalkeepers', for he never let them alone, snapping terrier-like at them to force them into errors, which was then permissible under the rules. Very fast off the mark, many a goalkeeper discovered he had hopped the ball once too often in his area and 'Babby' had pounced to dispatch it to the net.

Byrne won a League medal with Rovers in 1926-27 and then transferred to Bradford City, where he played a handful of games and did reasonably well before returning to Shelbourne, with whom he won a second League medal in 1928-29. It was back to Rovers then and four successive Cup medals in the famous five-in-a-row team. 'Babby' weighed in with goals in the 1930 and 1933 finals.

Following the latter final, he was transferred to Manchester United but got little chance to prove his worth there, despite scoring three goals in four appearances, and moved on to Coleraine. From there he went to Larne and it was his goals which earned the County Antrim club a place in the 1935 IFA Cup final, which they lost 1–0 to Glentoran after two 0–0 draws.

His Cup luck was out again when he returned to the Free State League, as he missed out on the 1936 final while with Shamrock Rovers and the 1939 final while with Shelbourne. Capped three times – he scored on his debut against Belgium in 1929 – 'Babby' Byrne was one of the early characters of Free State football and was the first player to register one hundred goals in the League of Ireland.

While Byrne scored the goal that mattered in the Cup in 1930, Bohemians' centre-forward Bill Cleary also wrote his name into the record books with a six-goal haul in a first round re-fixture away to Bray Unknowns, which Bohs won 7–3. Cleary's feat has never been equalled.

First Round

4 January	Bray Unknowns	0	Bohemians	1
	(Abandoned: bad weather)		Daly o.g.	
	Shamrock Rovers	1	Shelbourne	1
	Golding		Davis	
5 January	Brideville	1	Waterford Celtic	0
	Blair			
	Cork Bohemians	1	Dundalk	2
	Delea		Aitken 2	
	Dolphin	5	Mullingar Celtic	1
	Hand 2 (1 pen.), Swan 3		Henry	
	Drumcondra	3	Fordsons	3
	Murray, Rowles o.g., Fleming		Blair, Lindsay 2	
	Glasnvin	2	Cahir Park	1
	Drumgoole 2		Ryan	
	Jacobs	3	St James's Gate	4
	Corcoran 2, Temple		Westby 4 (1 pen.)	

First Round Re-Fixture

8 January	Bray Unknowns	3	Bohemians	7
	Gorman, Hogan 2		Cleary, McMahon	

First Round Replays

8 January	Fordsons	3	Drumcondra	1
	Lindsay, T. Dickson, Owens		Murray	
	Shelbourne	0	Shamrock Rovers	0

First Round Second Replay

15 January	Shamrock Rovers	3	Shelbourne	1
	'Babby' Byrne 2, Flood		Luke	

Second Round

18 January	Shamrock Rovers	4	St James's Gate	2
	Golding, Byrne 2, Flood		Westby, Wilson	
19 January	Brideville	1	Dolphin	1
	Bermingham pen.		Hand	

Dundalk	5	**Glasnevin**	0
Aitken, Patton 2, Beadles,			
Kelly o.g.			
Fordsons	1	**Bohemians**	0
T. Dickson			

Second Round Replay

22 January	**Dolphin**	2	**Brideville**	2
	Hand 2		C. Reid, Charles	

Second Round Second Replay

29 January	**Brideville**	5	**Dolphin**	1
	Gaskins 2, Blair, Reid,		Swan	
	O'Brien			

Semi-Final – Shelbourne Park

1 February	**Brideville**	2	**Dundalk**	1
	Gaskins, Patton o.g.		Patton	

Semi-Final – The Mardyke, Cork

16 February	**Fordsons**	2	**Shamrock Rovers**	2
	T. Dickson 2		Byrne, Fullam	

Semi-Final Replay – Iveagh Gardens, Crumlin

2 March	**Shamrock Rovers**	3	**Fordsons**	0
	Flood, Golding, Sloan			

Final – Dalymount Park

17 March	**Shamrock Rovers**	1	**Brideville**	0
	Byrne (90m)			

Shamrock Rovers: Paddy O'Reilly, Peppino 'Pudge' Cervi, John Burke, William 'Sacky' Glen, Tom Caulfield, Ned Marlowe, John Joe Flood, Jack Sloan, David 'Babby' Byrne, Joe 'Lye' Golding, Bob Fullam

Brideville: Charlie O'Callaghan, Paddy Kenny, Paddy Bermingham, Joe O'Reilly, Bill Charles, Johnny Fox, Jack Smith, Peadar Gaskins, Davy Blair, Charlie Reid, Paul O'Brien

Referee: Capt A. Prince-Cox (London)   Attendance: 17,000

1931

Heartbreak for Dundalk

From the very start of their League career, Dundalk made great efforts to win the Cup, starting with a sensational first round replay victory over Shamrock Rovers in their first campaign in 1928. In each of the following two seasons they advanced to the semi-final, but lost to Rovers and Brideville, respectively.

The advent of Joey Donnelly and Gerry McCourt in 1931 heralded the next stage of the club's development, with wins over Jacobs, Cork Bohemians and Dolphin, securing a place in the final against Shamrock Rovers. The goals of Donnelly and McCourt, who were to remain loyal servants of the club for many years, were largely responsible for the achievement of this milestone in the club's history.

When McCourt scored again in the first half of the final, it looked as though history was to be made, for Rovers were playing well below form in the controversial absence of captain Bob Fullam. However, a change of policy on Dundalk's part in the second half, when they opted to hold on to what they had rather than increase their lead, handed the initiative to Rovers.

Time was running out – and the Dundalk colours were already attached to the Cup – when Rovers attacked and, in controversial circumstances, equalised. When the ball was played into the Dundalk goalmouth 'Sacky' Glen, who was up helping his attack, handled the ball. The Dundalk defence hesitated, expecting the whistle, but it never came. The ball was played through to Paddy Moore and he touched it into the net for a goal that still rankles with Dundalk fans. In fairness, it should be stated that reporters at the game felt the referee had consistently allowed play to go on when the ball was unintentionally handled and Glen's offence probably came into that category.

Rovers duly won the replay – as they were to win every Cup final replay they contested until 1984, when Moore scored the only goal of the game. Again it was controversial, as Moore told Donnelly afterwards that he had punched the ball in! The return of Bob Fullam for the replay – where he won his fourth and last Cup medal – was a crucial factor.

That Dundalk team was not only one of the unluckiest, but also one of the best, as they proved when they beat Scottish Cup-winners Glasgow Celtic, 2–1. It may have been an end-of-season friendly, but there was a free-for-all in the dressing room afterwards. 'They didn't like being beaten,' recalled Joey Donnelly!

Apart from Dundalk, there was one other loser that year – Rovers' reserve goalkeeper, Billy Behan, later to win fame as a referee and as Manchester United's scout in Dublin. Behan had filled in for the injured Paddy O'Reilly in the Cup semi-final and final, but was replaced for the replay. Despite his contribution, he was overlooked when the medals were being distributed. However, after spells with Shelbourne and Manchester United, he returned to Rovers and captured that elusive medal in 1936.

First Round

28 December	**Cork Bohemians**	3	**Drumcondra**	2
	Delea, Hayes 2		Feeney, Griffiths	
10 January	**Shamrock Rovers**	2	**Shelbourne**	1
	Flood, Byrne		Connolly	
11 January	**Cork**	0	**Bohemians**	0
	Dolphin	3	**Brideville**	2
	Somers 2, Lennox pen.		Reid, Bermingham pen.	
	Dundalk	4	**Jacobs**	2
	McCourt, Donnelly, Stewart, Firth		Forrest, Owens	
	St James's Gate	2	**Bray Unknowns**	2
	Gleeson, Swan		McNally 2	
	St Vincent's	1	**Edenville**	3
	(Cork) Herrick		Bell 2, Lewis	
	Waterford	5	**Rossville**	3
	Arrigan, Crawford, Mitchell, Graham 2		Byrne, W. McCormack 2	

First Round Replays

15 January	**Bohemians**	1	**Cork**	0
	Cleary			
	Bray Unknowns	4	**St James's Gate**	3
	McNally 3, Buchanan		Wilson 2, Swan	

Second Round

7 February	**Bohemians**	5	**Edenville**	1
	Ellis, O'Sullivan, Cleary 3		Bell	
8 February	**Dundalk**	3	**Cork Bohemians**	1
	McCourt 2, Donnelly		Delea	
	Shamrock Rovers	5	**Bray Unknowns**	1
	Byrne, Flood 2, Golding 2		McNally	
	Waterford	2	**Dolphin**	3
	Scurry, Common		Patterson, Somers, Carroll	

Semi-Final – Iveagh Grounds, Crumlin

8 March	Dundalk	1	Dolphin	1
	Slowey pen.		Carroll	

Semi-Final Replay – Dalymount Park

11 March	Dundalk	3	Dolphin	1
	Donnelly, McCourt, Hirst		Somers	

Semi-Final – Shelbourne Park

28 March	Shamrock Rovers	3	Bohemians	0
	Moore 3			

Final – Dalymount Park

18 April	Shamrock Rovers	1	Dundalk	1
	Moore (84m)		McCourt (33m)	

Shamrock Rovers: Billy Behan, Peppino 'Pudge' Cervi, John Burke, William 'Sacky' Glen, Tom Caulfield, Owen Kinsella, Luke 'Diller' Delaney, Paddy Moore, David 'Babby' Byrne, John Joe Flood, Joe 'Lye' Golding

Dundalk: Sam McMullen, Johnny McKeown, Gordon Clancy McDiarmuid, Jack Slowey, Ted Reed, Dicky Johnston, Gerry McCourt, Owen McCahill, Billy 'Ledger' Firth, Henry Hirst, Joey Donnelly

Referee: H. N. Mee (Nottingham)   Attendance: 20,000

Final Replay – Dalymount Park

9 May	Shamrock Rovers	1	Dundalk	0
	Moore (37m)			

Shamrock Rovers: Paddy O'Reilly for Behan, Bob Fullam for Delaney
Dundalk: Unchanged

Referee: H. N. Mee (Nottingham)   Attendance: 10,000

1932

Moore Exits on a High Note

Paddy Moore is reckoned by many to have been the best centre-forward ever produced by Ireland and his name is indelibly linked with the FAI Cup, having scored the winning goal in each of the three finals he contested with Shamrock Rovers in 1931, 1932 and 1936.

A native of Ballybough on Dublin's north side, he made his way to Rovers via Clonliffe Celtic, Bendigo and Richmond Rovers. As a schoolboy his skill became so widely admired that crowds flocked to watch him in action in the Phoenix Park. He made his FAI Cup debut with the Richmond Rovers team, beaten 2–0 by Dundalk in the first round in 1929, and then moved to Shamrock Rovers where he made a sensational start to his career with a steady stream of goals in the Shield campaign.

Moore spent the 1929-30 season with Cardiff City but only got one league game with them and returned to Rovers for the 1930-31 season, when his goals were the ones that mattered in the Cup semi-final (a hat-trick against Bohemians) and final.

A switch to centre-forward – he had been operating at inside-right – for the 1931-32 season started the goals flowing and he led Rovers to magnificent victories in the Cup, League and Shield. Only the Leinster Cup eluded them, and it was significant that Moore was injured and missed the game in which Dolphin dismissed the men from Milltown.

Dolphin, formed by the Butchers' Social Union, were worthy opponents for

Rovers in the latter's Cup final bid for the four-in-a-row. According to 'Sam' Robinson, who played on Bohemians' Grand Slam team of 1927-28 before joining Dolphin, 'Dolphin were the greatest football team ever in the Free State. You could play three matches for Dolphin and not be tired, whereas you could play one match for Bohs and you'd be tired out of your standing.'

Unfortunately, like a lot of good footballing sides, Dolphin never really got the reward for their talents. In the short seven years of their existence as a League club, they won the League and Leinster Cup once, but failed to capture the Cup, twice losing to Shamrock Rovers in finals. In 1932, they established a Cup record for an away win when they beat St James's Gate 10–0. Included among the scorers was eighteen-year-old Alec Stevenson, later to win fame with Glasgow Rangers and Everton.

In the 1932 final, Dolphin were unlucky to come up against Paddy Moore at the height of his powers; his lone goal was sufficient to take the Cup to Milltown for the fifth time. The glamour pairing attracted a record crowd of over 32,000, almost three times bigger than at the first final ten years previously. Without doubt, the FAI Cup had arrived.

Two of the Rovers' players, Moore and right-full Jimmy Daly, along with Brideville wing-half Joe O'Reilly, were transferred the following month to Aberdeen, where Moore proved a big hit until the effects of his latent alcoholism took over. Sadly, alcoholism wasn't recognised for what it was in those days and, with no treatment available, Moore's great career was cut tragically short – although there were many great moments still to come before he bowed out in 1938.

The 1932 final was the first to be played on a Sunday, a decision reached despite many objections. The record crowd produced receipts of £1,710, almost double those for the IFA Cup in Belfast.

First Round

27 December	Drumcondra	3	Cork Bohemians	1
	Brown, Sherwin, Crofts		Foley pen.	
9 January	Bohemians	8	Cobh Ramblers	0
	White 2, Dennis 2,			
	Horlacher 4			
	Bray Unknowns	1	Cork	2
	Quinlan		Cunningham, Ferguson	
	Edenville	2	Jacobs	1
	Mundow pen., D. Kane		Ward	
	Shamrock Rovers	9	Ormeau	3
	Moore 4, Smith, Fullam 2,		Morton, Snowe, Hughes	
	Matthews 2			
10 January	Brideville	1	Waterford	4
	Reid		Forster 4	
	Dundalk	1	Shelbourne	2
	Kelly		T. Carroll, Walsh	
	St James's Gate	0	Dolphin	10
			Shiels 5, McKay o.g.,	
			Patterson 2, Stevenson 2	

Second Round

6 February	Bohemians	2	Drumcondra	0
	Dennis, White			
	Shamrock Rovers	4	Edenville	2
	Kinsella, Moore 2, Byrne		Mundow pen., Kane	
7 February	Dolphin	3	Cork	2
	Smith, Shiels 2		Ferguson, Paton	
	Shelbourne	4	Waterford	2
	Walsh, Carroll 2, Jones		O'Brien, Sampy pen.	

Semi-Final – Iveagh Grounds, Crumlin

5 March	Shamrock Rovers	3	Bohemians	2
	Moore 2, Smith		Horlacher, Foy	

Semi-Final – Milltown

27 March **Dolphin** **3** **Shelbourne** **1**

Somers, Smith, Paterson Jones

Final – Dalymount Park

17 April **Shamrock Rovers** **1** **Dolphin** **0**

Moore (75m)

Shamrock Rovers: Mick McCarthy, Jimmy Daly, John Burke, William 'Sacky' Glen, Vincent Matthews, Owen Kinsella, David 'Babby' Byrne, John Joe Flood, Paddy Moore, Jock McMillan, Jimmy Smith

Dolphin: Jimmy Power, Bobby Nisbet, Larry Doyle, Jeremiah 'Sam' Robinson, Gerry Kelly, Jimmy Watt, Albert Smith, Alec Stevenson, Jimmy Shiels, Johnny Somers, Danny Paterson

Referee: I. Caswell (Blackburn) Attendance: 32,000

It's a Record!

- Cork Hibernians' Miah Dennehy (1972) and Bray Wanderers' John Ryan (1990) are the only players to score hat-tricks in FAI Cup Finals.

- William 'Sacky' Glen and Johnny Fullam won eight Cup medals: Glen with Shamrock Rovers and Shelbourne; Fullam with Shamrock Rovers and Bohemians.

1933

'Nettler' Gets the Sack

Tommy 'Nettler' Doyle took over the centre-forward role for Shamrock Rovers when the great Paddy Moore was transferred to Aberdeen in 1932. He made a success of it too, finishing in the League with seventeen goals and winning a Cup medal but, as he said himself, 'I wouldn't even be fit to lace Paddy Moore's boots.' However, Tommy, whose brother Dinny won a Cup medal with Rovers in 1925, got a shock when he was left out of the team to play Dolphin in the 1933 Cup final. He scored three goals in the four Cup games, so it was a bit of a bombshell but, as he recalled later, 'I just took it – that's what you did at that time.' No explanations were given, but Jimmy Daly, who had been transferred as a full-back with Moore to Aberdeen, was brought in at outside-right and David 'Babby' Byrne moved in from the wing to take Doyle's place.

The re-arranged team nearly came unstuck, for Dolphin were 3–0 up at one stage before Rovers rallied to force a 3–3 draw with goals from Byrne, Jimmy Buchanan and Vincent Matthews. The latter two were part of the cross-Channel colony which had built up in Milltown in the early 1930s as the club gradually lost its Ringsend look. Matthews was a former England centre-half from Sheffield United, probably recommended by Jimmy Dunne, while Buchanan and outside-left Jimmy Smith were from Scotland.

While prepared to pay for cross-Channel talent, Rovers apparently didn't appreciate the local players, and Doyle said, 'I had a terrible job getting a few bob out of them, so the following season I signed for Southport and later went to

Wigan Athletic.' He later found his way back to League of Ireland football with Reds United.

The replay was in complete contrast to the first game. 'I think I scored the quickest-ever goal in a final,' recalled 'Babby' Byrne. 'It was the first kick of the ball I got. A throw-in came from John Joe Flood who passed to me and that was it. We were 2–0 up after twenty minutes and it was all over.' Controversial choice Daly got the other two goals that gave Rovers a 3–0 win and the FAI Cup for the fifth successive season. Tommy Doyle had to be content with his medal as twelfth man.

The 1933 Cup campaign saw the final chapter in the playing career of Billy Lacey, probably the most versatile player ever produced by Ireland. Lacey, who started his senior career with Shelbourne, made his name in England with Everton and Liverpool, with whom he won League medals, before he returned to League of Ireland football with Shelbourne in 1926. He also had a spell with Linfield, winning an IFA Cup medal in 1919, and was a regular on the international team for many years. He was a member of the British Championship-winning team of 1914, when he scored two goals in a famous 3-0 victory over England in Middlesboro. Towards the end of his career, he was capped on three occasions by the FAI, each time in a different position – outside-right, inside-right and right-full! By 1933 he had retired but he answered a cry for help from Cork Bohemians and helped them win their first round tie against Bray Unknowns.

First Round

26 December	Tramore Rookies	0	Drumcondra	8
			Murray 3, Merry 2,	
			Baggot 2, Bracegirdle	
31 December	Shelbourne	5	Jacobs	0
	Griffiths, McConnell 2,			
	McDaid, Diamond			
1 January	Bray Unknowns	0	Cork Bohemians	0
	Rossville (Dublin)	1	Cork	6
	Quirke		J. Rorrison 3, Kirkwood,	
	(At Mardyke)		Clarke, Cameron	
	Dundalk	1	Dolphin	1
	Carroll		Clarke o.g.	
	Shamrock Rovers	3	St James's Gate	1
	Buchanan, Doyle, Flood		Ebbs	
	Sligo Rovers	3	Brideville	1
	Westby, T. Callaghan, Fallon		Thomas pen.	
	Waterford	0	Bohemians	4
			Dennis, Cleary	

First Round Replays

4 January	Cork Bohemians	0	Bray Unknowns	0
	(Abandoned 38m)			
	Dolphin	2	Dundalk	1
	McCarney 2		Carroll	

First Round Replay Re-Fixture

11 January	Cork Bohemians	2	Bray Unknowns	2
	Doherty, Delea		Hannon, Hogan	
	(After extra time.)			

First Round Second Replay

| 18 January | Bray Unknowns | 1 | Cork Bohemians | 2 |
| | A. Rigby | | Hayes, Crawford | |

Second Round

21 January	**Bohemians**	7	**Cork Bohemians**	1
	Ellis, McMahon, O'Dempsey 2,		Delea	
	Cleary 2, Horlacher			
22 January	**Cork**	1	**Shamrock Rovers**	1
	O'Keeffe		Buchanan	
	Dolphin	2	**Drumcondra**	1
	Kendrick, Reid		Baggot	
	Shelbourne	5	**Sligo Rovers**	2
	Diamond 4, Holmes pen.		P. Monaghan, Donnelly	

Second Round Replay

| 25 January | **Shamrock Rovers** | 3 | **Cork** | 0 |
| | Doyle 2, Flood | | | |

Semi-Final – Shelbourne Park

| 11 February | **Shamrock Rovers** | 3 | **Bohemians** | 1 |
| | Byrne, Buchanan, Smith | | Ellis | |

Semi-Final – Dalymount Park

| 26 February | **Dolphin** | 1 | **Shelbourne** | 0 |
| | McCarney | | | |

Final – Dalymount Park

17 March	**Shamrock Rovers**	3	**Dolphin**	3
	Byrne (13m), Buchanan (51m),		Lennox (11m, pen., 17m, pen.),	
	Matthews (70m, pen.)		Fallon (52m)	

Shamrock Rovers: Mick McCarthy, Peadar Gaskins, John Burke, William 'Sacky' Glen, Vincent Matthews, Owen Kinsella, Jimmy Daly, John Joe Flood, David 'Babby' Byrne, Jimmy 'Scot' Buchanan, Jimmy Smith

Dolphin: Leonard Slater, George Lennox, Larry Doyle, Jimmy Watt, Gerry Kelly, Joe Kendrick, Jimmy Bermingham, Tony Weldon, Owen McCarney, Johnny Somers, Willie Fallon

Referee: W. F. Bunnell (Preston)   Attendance: 30,000

Final Replay – Dalymount Park

26 March   **Shamrock Rovers**   **3**   **Dolphin**   **0**
Byrne (1m), Daly 2 (38m, 66m)

Shamrock Rovers: Unchanged
Dolphin: Charlie Reid for Bermingham

Referee: W. F. Bunnell (Preston)   Attendance: 25,000

It's a Record!

- Drumcondra and Alton United are the only non-League of Ireland teams to win the Cup. Alton (1923) played in the Falls League in Belfast, while Drumcondra were a Leinster League team when they won the Cup in 1927.

- Shamrock Rovers are the only club to win the Cup five times and six times, each in succession. Apart from Rovers, Cork Hibernians, Shelbourne and Longford Town are the only clubs that managed to retain the Cup.

1934

Buckle Emulates his Father

History was made in the 1934 final when Cork's outside-right, Bobby Buckle, emulated his father Harry's achievement of 1926 by winning a Cup medal. A versatile player, Buckle junior usually played full-back but was played on the wing in the final to add more aggression to the attack.

In fact, it was their versatility which won Cork the Cup, as the winning goal in the final against St James's Gate was scored by John Kelso, who had been moved from defence to centre-forward and responded with vital goals in the two semi-final games as well as in the final. After an earlier spell in the attack had been ended by an ankle injury, he recovered just in time for the semi-final tie with Dundalk.

Cork almost completed the double, being denied the League title by a point and claiming, with some justification, that a goal scored by Buckle in a crucial game should not have been ruled out for offside. However, they had their own share of luck, too, as a Hugh Connolly handball in the semi-final replay went unpunished when it looked a definite penalty.

The 1934 team has never been rated among the great Cork teams, but it had the necessary balance, as Buckle recalled: 'We had a star goalie in Jimmy 'Fox' Foley; Harry Chatton had command as a centre-half; Johnny Paton was the general, controlling matters – he might only do four things in a match but something would come out of those four – and he got everybody working, and Timothy Jim O'Keeffe was the finisher.'

Foley was in great form during that Cup run, as Eddie Bellew of Bray Unknowns recalled: 'We were losing 1–0 in the Mardyke when Paddy Jordan floated the ball across and, as I couldn't get to it, I put my hand up and tapped it in. Foley went mad when the referee allowed the goal but he had his revenge when we played them in Bray. No matter what we did he saved – he was tremendous – and Cork got through 2–0.' Foley, who was capped seven times, was snapped up by Glasgow Celtic after the Cup final and later played for Plymouth Argyle before returning to finish out his career with the great Cork United team of the 1940s. Jordan, who was credited with that goal in Cork, and who also scored twice in the first round in Waterford, was the father of Formula One supremo Eddie Jordan.

Chatton, a former Shelbourne and Dumbarton player, was an Irish international, while Paton had made his name with Glasgow Celtic and had won a French Cup medal the previous season. However, O'Keeffe was the real star of the team – a winger with an eye for goal whose tally of three caps was poor reward for his talent. He won a second Cup medal with Waterford in 1937 and was transferred afterwards to Hibernian for a record League of Ireland fee of £400.

Beaten finalists St James's Gate also had a talented left-winger in Mattie Geoghegan, who was transferred to Belfast Celtic but returned to win a Cup medal with the Gate in 1938. Player-coach Charlie Dowdall, back after a number of years in Cork, was the sole link with the Gate team that won the Cup in 1922.

First Round

13 January	**Drumcondra**	1	**Shelbourne**	1
	Hunt		Leonard	
	Jacobs	0	**Dolphin**	5
			O'Donnell 2, Tucker,	
			Kendrick, Bermingham	
14 January	**Bohemians**	9	**Tramore Rookies**	0
	Rogers 5, Dennis, Ellis,			
	O'Dempsey, Jordan			
	Cork Bohemians	1	**Cork**	1
	Hogg o.g.		O'Keeffe	
	Dundalk	4	**Sligo Rovers**	0
	Burke 2, Delea, G. Godwin			
	St James's Gate	1	**Shamrock Rovers**	1
	Geoghegan		Daly	
	Waterford	0	**Bray Unknowns**	3
			Jordan 2, Hunt	
21 January	**Queen's Park**	2	**Brideville**	2
	Walsh, F. Bermingham		Quinlan, Cooke o.g.	

First Round Replays

17 January	**Cork**	3	**Cork Bohemians**	1
	O'Keeffe 2 (1 pen.), Paton		Doherty	
	Shelbourne	2	**Drumcondra**	5
	Brady 2		Meehan 2, McCosh 2, Merry	
24 January	**Brideville**	0	**Queen's Park**	2
			MacDonnell, E. Bermingham	
	Shamrock Rovers	1	**St James's Gate**	2
	Smith		Dowdall, Rigby	

Second Round

27 January	**Dundalk**	1	**Bohemians**	0
	G. Godwin			
	Queen's Park	1	**Dolphin**	1
	MacDonnell		Fallon	
28 January	**Cork**	1	**Bray Unknowns**	1
	Haddow		Jordan	

Drumcondra	0	St James's Gate	2
		Kennedy, Geoghegan	

Second Round Replays

31 January	Bray Unknowns	0	Cork	2
			Haddow, O'Keeffe	
	Dolphin	1	Queen's Park	0
	Dalton o.g.			

Semi-Final – Shelbourne Park

10 February	St James's Gate	1	Dolphin	0
	Kennedy			

Semi-Final – Dalymount Park

11 February	Cork	2	Dundalk	2
	Haddow, O'Keeffe		Atkins, Delea	

Semi-Final Replay – Dalymount Park

4 March	Cork	1	Dundalk	1
	Kelso		McCourt	

Semi-Final Second Replay – Milltown

7 March	Cork	2	Dundalk	1
	Paton pen., Kelso		Carroll	

Final – Dalymount Park

17 March	Cork	2	St James's Gate	1
	O'Keeffe (28m), Kelso (49m)		Comerford (19m)	

Cork: Jimmy 'Fox' Foley, Bobby Hogg, Tom Burke, Paddy Lennon, Harry Chatton, Hughie Connolly, Bobby Buckle, Andy Haddow, John Kelso, Johnny Paton, Tim O'Keeffe

St James's Gate: Ned Pidgeon, Jack Hoey, Joe Moylan, Harry Simpson, Charlie Lennon, Dickie Murray, Billy Kennedy, Brendan Comerford, Alf Rigby, Charlie Dowdall, Mattie Geoghegan

Referee: I. Caswell (Blackburn)   Attendance: 21,000

1935

Illegal Players Lose Out

The 1935 final is renowned, with that of 2006, as the highest-scoring Cup final, with Bohemians edging out Dundalk 4–3, but it also has another claim to fame – it featured the highest number of illegal players (two), and both lined out for Dundalk. The proximity of Dundalk to the border with Northern Ireland obviously proved too much of a temptation in those days when the Cup came round and the players listed as Mills and Gaughran in the final lineout were, in fact, prominent Irish League players.

Jimmy 'Ginger' Mailey, who later had a legitimate spell with Dundalk and also played for Plymouth Argyle, was right-winger Mills's correct identity; while the outside-left, who assumed the name Gaughran, was a player called Craig from Glenavon. 'They played on Saturday in the Irish League and then on Sunday with Dundalk,' recalled Joey Donnelly, inside-right on that Dundalk team.

In the first round tie away to Shamrock Rovers, which Dundalk won 1–0, the border club fielded Black of Portadown, one of the best players in the North, under the name Gernon. Rovers obviously smelled a rat and subsequently objected to two of the Dundalk players, but they lost the objection as they couldn't prove their point.

More to Dundalk's credit that year was the chance they took with full-back Billy O'Neill by moving him to centre-forward. O'Neill, capped eleven times for Ireland at right-back, more than justified the switch with a vital goal in each round of the Cup.

That Cup campaign also proved a turning-point in the life of Bohemian inside-right Paddy Farrell, an Athlone man who had joined Bohs from Home Farm. Earlier in the season he had been in the reserve team, but coach Billy Lacey, the former Liverpool star, spotted a fault in his running action and corrected it in sessions on the cinder track which then lay behind the Tramway goal in Dalymount. It made a different player of Farrell.

Promoted to the first team, he scored in the 5–2 second round defeat of Waterford and then scored the winner in the semi-final replay against League champions Dolphin. That brought him to the attention of Scottish club Hibernian, who wanted to sign him straight away. His mother, a widow, was against it but withdrew her opposition when he promised to attend Edinburgh University and prepare for a career after football.

There followed a hectic two months of study for Farrell as he swotted for his matriculation examination, but this was all placed in jeopardy when, in the Cup final, he suffered a bad injury. However, Hibernian remained interested and Farrell sailed through his matriculation.

His contract with Hibernian was unique for, apart from a signing-on fee of £800, Hibs also undertook to pay his university fees as he studied dentistry and they arranged his training so that it didn't interfere with his lectures. He spent five years with Hibs, was capped three times and qualified as a dentist. After serving in the RAF during the war, he set up in private practice in Hull.

First Round

13 January	Distillery	1	Butchers (Cork)	1
	Recusin		Staunton	
19 January	Reds United	3	Bohemians	3
	Doyle, Lappin 2		Ellis 2, French	
20 January	Cork	0	B + I	0
	Dolphin	1	Bray Unknowns	0
	Rogers			
	Drumcondra	3	Tramore Rookies	0
	Kavanagh, Meehan, McCosh			
	Shamrock Rovers	0	Dundalk	1
			O'Neill	
	St James's Gate	1	Sligo Rovers	1
	McCann o.g.		J. McDaid	
	Waterford	4	UCD	2
	Ryan 2, Irvine, Walsh		Hooper, Doherty	

First Round Replays

16 January	Butchers (Cork)	0	Distillery	0
23 January	Bohemians	4	Reds United	3
	Nolan 2, Dwyer, Menton		Lappin, D. Flood, Finnegan	
	Cork	3	B + I	0
	Neville, O'Keeffe, Madden			
	Sligo Rovers	3	St James's Gate	1
	J. McDaid 2, Smith		Martini	

First Round Second Replay

23 January	Distillery	3	Butchers (Cork)	0
	Dorney, Redmond, Molloy			

Second Round

9 February	Bohemians	3	Waterford	2
	Ellis 2, Horlacher 2, Farrell		Ryan, Irvine	
	Distillery	1	Dundalk	2
	Ward		O'Neill, 'Mills' pen.	
10 February	Drumcondra	0	Dolphin	2
			Paterson	

Sligo Rovers	5	Cork	1
Monaghan 2, J. McDaid,		O'Neill	
G. McDaid, Bradley			

Semi-Final – Dalymount Park

2 March	Dolphin	1	Bohemians	1
	Paterson pen.		Ellis	

Semi-Final Replay – Dalymount Park

6 March	Bohemians	2	Dolphin	1
	Ellis, Farrell		Watt	

Semi-Final – Dalymount Park

24 March	Dundalk	2	Sligo Rovers	0
	'Gaughran', O'Neill			

Final – Dalymount Park

14 April	Bohemians	4	Dundalk	3
	Menton (1m),		O'Neill (15m),	
	Jordan (26m, 27m),		McCourt (31m),	
	Horlacher (35m)		T. Godwin (71m)	

Bohemians: Harry Cannon, Aloysius Morris, Bill McGuire, Paddy O'Kane, Paddy Andrews, Andy Maguire, Jimmy Menton, Paddy Farrell, Pleb Ellis, Fred Horlacher, Billy Jordan

Dundalk: Peter McMahon, Billy Powell, Len Richards, Gerry Godwin, Tommy Godwin, Henry Hurst, 'Mills', Joey Donnelly, Billy O'Neill, Gerry McCourt, 'Gaughran'

Referee: Mr Booth (Preston)   Attendance: 21,799

1936

Scully and Madden Make News

Nineteen thirty-six was the year of Paul Scully and Owen Madden, with Jimmy Turnbull and Paddy Moore relegated to supporting roles even though they scored the bulk of their clubs' goals in a campaign which saw Shamrock Rovers capture the Cup for the seventh time at the expense of red-hot favourites Cork.

Scully was a teenage left-winger with a cannonball shot, who benefited enormously from playing alongside the great Paddy Moore. Top scorer for Rovers in the League, Scully also produced the goods in the Cup, scoring in each round en route to the final. His tears were understandable then, when, the Thursday before the final, the teamsheet was posted up after training and his name was missing, with reserve wing-half Denis 'Dinger' Dunne taking his place.

Dunne was probably the luckiest player ever to win a Cup medal, for he made no impression at Milltown before or after his surprise selection for the Cup final. The Cunningham family had just taken over Rovers and Dunne's selection was merely the forerunner to some other strange Cup final selections they indulged in over the years.

On this occasion, they almost had a players' strike on their hands for, with minutes to go before the kick-off, not a single Rovers player had stripped, in protest at Scully's omission. The matter was only resolved at the last minute by the direct intervention of Scully, himself who pleaded with his teammates not to risk suspension on his account.

The Cunninghams also flexed their muscles by objecting to the referee appointed for the final, and the fact that both linesmen were from Munster. They eventually withdrew their objection to the referee, but linesman Jack Baylor (Cork) was replaced by J. Ralph (Dundalk).

Meanwhile Cork had their own problems, although they didn't surface until after the final. Owen Madden, their teenage inside-left and reckoned to be the best player Cork ever produced, had signed for Norwich City after the semi-final win over Drumcondra. In a direct reversal of the 'open door' policy which League of Ireland clubs used to sign disenchanted English League players, he had accepted a signing-on fee from the East Anglian club, making him a Norwich player when he played for Cork in the final.

He later went on tour with the international team and scored on his debut in Hungary in a 3–3 draw. However, he also picked up an injury in that game and had to return to Norwich for treatment. The Cork club officials, annoyed that they were getting no fee from Madden's move, reported him to the FAI Council which promptly suspended him. In the true hypocritical manner that surrounded all the official action of this case, Madden was reinstated in 1939 and called up for the international match to be played in Cork against Hungary. He accepted the lifting of the suspension but declined the invitation to play.

Jimmy Turnbull was probably the most talked-about player in Irish football that season, hitting a phenomenal thirty-seven goals in twenty-two League games and then getting a record eleven goals during the FAI Cup campaign. A champion sprinter, it was his goalscoring as much as anything that made Cork such hot favourites in the final. He duly obliged with a goal against Rovers, but Paddy Moore had the last word and it was his performance and winning goal which saw Cork return to the Lee empty-handed. There was consolation for Turnbull the following year when he scored all the goals in Belfast Celtic's 3–0 win over Linfield in the IFA Cup Final.

First Round

1 January	GSR	1	Reds United	4
	R. Buckle		J. J. Flood, Sinnott 2, Wright	
11 January	Bohemians	7	Waterford	0
	Jordan 2, Gaughran 3, Horlacher, O'Kane			
12 January	Cork	2	Bray Unknowns	2
	Turnbull 2		Reynolds, Bellew	
	Dolphin	1	Drumcondra	0
	Leonard pen.			

(Abandoned: encroachment of spectators)

	Dundalk	7	B + I	1
	Sayers 3, Donnelly 2, Morgan, McCourt		M. Kavanagh	
	Hospitals Trust	2	Sligo Rovers	5
	P. Molloy 2 (1 pen.)		Monaghan, Mulreany 2, G. McDaid 2	
	Shamrock Rovers	1	St James's Gate	1
	M. Byrne		Comerford	
	Tramor Rookies	1	Brideville	5
	Flaherty		McGonagle 4, Murphy	

First Round Re-Fixture: Tolka Park

16 January	Dolphin	3	Drumcondra	6
	Rogers 2, Bermingham		Kerr 3, Donnelly 2, Bermingham o.g.	

First Round Replays

15 January	Bray Unknowns	1	Cork	6
	Reynolds		Connelly, Turnbull 2, Little, Foy, McKane	

(After extra time.)

	St James's Gate	1	Shamrock Rovers	2
	Hoey pen.		'Babby' Byrne, Scully	

Second Round

8 February	Bohemians	1	Cork	1
	Horlacher pen.		Turnbull	
	Dundalk	**2**	**Reds United**	**1**
	Sayers, Mailey		Doyle	
9 February	**Drumcondra**	**1**	**Sligo Rovers**	**1**
	Donnelly		McCann	
	Shamrock Rovers	**5**	**Brideville**	**1**
	Reid, Moore 2, Daly o.g., Scully		O'Reilly pen.	

Second Round Replays

12 February	Sligo Rovers	1	Drumcondra	1
	O'Neill		Donnelly	

(After extra time.)

19 February	Cork	3	Bohemians	2
	Turnbull 2, Connolly		Horlacher 2	

Second Round Second Replay

19 February	Drumcondra	3	Sligo Rovers	2
	Donnelly, Meehan, Keohane		Monaghan 2	

Semi-Final – Dalymount Park

1 March	Shamrock Rovers	2	Dundalk	2
	Moore, Glen pen.		Morgan, McCourt	

Semi-Final Replay – Iveagh Grounds

4 March	Shamrock Rovers	2	Dundalk	1
	Ward, Scully		O'Neill pen.	

Semi-Final – The Mardyke, Cork

22 March	Cork	5	Drumcondra	2
	Turnbull 3, King, O'Reilly		Meehan, Donnelly	

Final – Dalymount Park

19 April	Shamrock Rovers	2	Cork	1
	Moore (46m), Reid (53m)		Turnbull (80m)	

Shamrock Rovers: Billy Behan, Joe Williams, Peadar Gaskins, William 'Sacky' Glen, Jim Blake, Owen Kinsella, Mick Byrne, Paddy Moore, Charlie Reid, Joe Ward, Denis 'Dinger' Dunne

Cork: Bill Harrington, Hugh Foy, Charlie Wade, Bill Williams, Billy Little, Hugh Connolly, Jack O'Reilly, Bertie King, Jimmy Turnbull, Owen Madden, Andy Percy

Referee: I. Caswell (Blackburn)   Attendance: 30,946

It's a Record!

* Three generations of the Whelan family have won FAI Cup medals. Grandfather Ronnie won with St Patrick's Athletic (1959 and 1961), son Paul captained Bohemians to victory in 1992, and grandson Gavin scored one of the goals that helped Drogheda United win the Cup for the first time in 2005.

1937

Noonan Misses the Bus

When 1937 Cup finalists Waterford and St James's Gate met a few weeks before their big date in a League game at Kilcohan Park, the Gate held all the aces and won comfortably 4–2. It was obvious to all concerned with Waterford that changes would have to be made if the Cup was to be won. However, the selectors dropped a bombshell when they decided to drop centre-forward Johnny Walsh and replace him with right-back Eugene Noonan, who had been given a roasting by Mattie Geoghegan in the League game. Noonan had never played centre-forward before, while Walsh had scored in practically every round of the Cup. Scotsman Hugh Foy, who had been understudy to right-half Waltie Walsh all season, came in at right-full, the same position he filled in the 1936 Cup final for Cork.

'I was on the train to Dublin when the club chairman Gerry Whelan came to me and said that they had decided to play me at centre-forward,' recalled Noonan. 'I protested, asserting I had never played in the position in my life, but the chairman said I must obey orders. That was shock number one, but the second was even worse for, coming out of the hotel after lunch, I found that the Waterford bus had gone! I looked at the crowds clinging to the trams and wondered would I ever see Dalymount Park, but finally I got a foot on board and clung on until we reached Phibsboro.'

Noonan always admitted that the Cup final was not one of his better games, but he did prove effective. 'I hardly knew where I was for the first twenty minutes,' he said, 'but when Johnny McGourty side-footed the ball across, its swerve beat Charlie Lennon, the Gate centre-half, and dropped at my feet to be tapped with the left and pushed into the net with my right.' Noonan was a Corkman, as was Waterford's other goalscorer that day, left-winger Tim O'Keeffe.

The tears flowed freely as captain Tom Arrigan lifted the Cup in what was only the Suirside club's fifth season of League football. The Shield had been captured earlier and, with the League going to Sligo Rovers, all the major trophies had a provincial destination for the first time.

Arrigan, who formed with local Waltie Walsh and North of Ireland man Terry Fullerton one of the strongest half-back lines in the country, had returned to his native Waterford after three successful seasons with Glentoran, during which he won Cup medals in 1933 and 1935 and captained the Glens to their 1935 IFA Cup triumph. John 'Fatty' Phelan, the third local player on the team, was captain when Waterford reached the 1941 final and by then he had made an unusual switch – from outside-right to centre-half – and was picked for Inter-League honours in the latter role.

The Waterford team, who earned a £5 bonus for winning the Cup, were all full-timers with the exception of Phelan. Wages were £3.50 for everybody except the star left-wing pair of former Everton star McGourty and O'Keeffe, who each received £4. Waltie Walsh had been a part-timer like Phelan on £1.50 but turned full-time midway through the season.

Davie Christopher from nearby Butlerstown was the team's trainer. He had served in that capacity with Scottish club Hibernian and completed an FAI Cup double when he trained the Shelbourne team that won the Cup in 1939. He was a former professional sprinter.

First Round

9 January	Fearons Athletic	4	Bray Unknowns	1
	Leonard, Byrne 2, Reid		Kelly	
	Shelbourne	1	St James's Gate	1
	Slater		Geoghegan	
10 January	Cork	3	Queen's Park	2
	Whitenell, King, Symonds pen.		D. Ryan, J. Bermingham	
	Drumcondra	1	Brideville	1
	Donnelly		Gill	
	Longford Town	2	Evergreen	1
	McManus, P. Clarke		Fitzgerald	
	Shamrock Rovers	1	Dolphin	0
	Boyle			
	Sligo Rovers	6	Bohemians	1
	Monaghan, Litherland 2, Duncan, Hughes 2		O'Kane	
	Waterford	3	Dundalk	3
	O'Keeffe pen., Phelan, McGourty		Smith pen., Donnelly, Halpin	

First Round Replays

13 January	Drumcondra	3	Brideville	2
	Meehan, Donnelly 2		Johnston 2	
	St James's Gate	4	Shelbourne	2
	Geoghegan, Kennedy, Rigby 2		Slater pen., Doyle	
14 January	Dundalk	1	Waterford	1
	Mailey		O'Keeffe	

First Round Second Replay

21 January	Waterford	3	Dundalk	1
	J. Walsh 2, Gill		Donnelly	

Second Round

7 February	Cork	0	Fearons Athletic	0
	(Abandoned 55m: bad weather)			
	Longford Town	2	Drumcondra	1
	W. Clarke, P. Clarke		Meehan	

St James's Gate	6	Sligo Rovers	2
Rigby 4, Merry 2		Monaghan, Gourley	
Waterford	2	Shamrock Rovers	0
O'Keeffe 2			

Second Round Re-Fixture

| 10 February | Cork | 0 | Fearons Athletic | 1 |
| | | | Hogan | |

Semi-Finals – Dalymount Park

10 March	Waterford	4	Longford Town	1
	O'Keeffe, Arrigan, J. Walsh, Phelan		P. Clarke	
21 March	St James's Gate	4	Fearons Athletic	0
	W. Byrne 3, Comerford			

Final – Dalymount Park

| 18 April | Waterford | 2 | St James's Gate | 1 |
| | Noonan (35m), O'Keeffe (75m) | | Merry (80m) | |

Waterford: Alf Robinson, Hugh Foy, Jock McDonnell, Waltie Walsh, Terry Fullerton, Tom Arrigan, John 'Fatty' Phelan, George Gill, Eugene Noonan, Johnny McGourty, Tim O'Keeffe

St James's Gate: John Webster, Alec Stewart, Jimmy Daly, Joe O'Reilly, Charlie Lennon, Maurice Cummins, Billy Kennedy, Billy Merry, Alf Rigby, Dickie Comerford, Mattie Geoghegan

Referee: J. Baylor (Cork)   Attendance: 24,000

1938

The Honourable 'Wagger' Byrne

When Willie 'Wagger' Byrne scored a hat-trick in the 1937 Cup semi-final, he could be forgiven if he thought he had secured his place on the Cup final team. However, the selectors thought differently and it was a tearful Byrne who watched from the Dalymount Park stand as his St James's Gate teammates lost to Waterford. The words of the selectors – 'you're young and your chance will come' – had a hollow ring about them as far as the twenty-three year old Byrne was concerned.

Still, he did his utmost to fulfill their prophecy the following season, scoring vital goals in the first and second rounds of the Cup as the Gate advanced to the semi-finals at the expense of Cork and Limerick. The semi-final proved a difficult task, the opposition being provided by Leinster League side Distillery, reckoned by many the best non-League team ever, who were just about to embark on a four-in-a-row in the Intermediate Cup. It took a piece of typical Byrne skill to win the penalty which decided the issue in the replay.

It had been a great season for Byrne, his link-up with Charlie Reid netting him twenty-five goals in the League and eleven in the Shield, apart from his Cup efforts. Although small, he had tremendous pace and an eye for goal which brought the offer of a trial with West Brom, an offer he declined as he was the sole breadwinner for his parents and the other four young children in the family.

Unfortunately, his luck ran out when he was injured while scoring in a League game against Drumcondra a week before the Cup final. Not realising the extent of the ankle injury – of course, there were no substitutes in those days – he hobbled on, making a bad situation worse. It was a race against time whether he would be fit for the following Sunday but, despite intensive treatment all week, time ran out for 'Wagger' on the morning of the final, when he made the difficult decision himself. He had passed the club's fitness test the previous day but still felt the twinges in his ankle and, rather than risk leaving his teammates to carry on with ten men, he cried off.

It was an honourable decision, which was rewarded with a Cup medal when the Gate beat Dundalk 2–1, but it also marked his last chance of playing in a Cup final. Subsequent moves to Dundalk, Shelbourne and Brideville never got him any further than the semi-final stage.

Spare a thought also for Dundalk centre-forward Alf Rigby, who scored on his third Cup final appearance but had to settle for a loser's medal for the third time. His two previous appearances were for St James's Gate in 1934 and 1937, so it was ironic that the Gate should deny him after his move to Dundalk.

It was Dundalk's third time to contest the Cup final in eight years and each time they had lost by a single goal. They could be excused if they thought there was a jinx on their efforts, but this time their defeat had more natural causes. Regular centre-half Bob Moloney broke his leg playing for the League of Ireland against the Irish League just four days after the semi-final defeat of Shamrock Rovers and his replacement, Jimmy Bowden, didn't have a happy Cup final.

First Round

5 February	Bohemians	1	Limerick	2
	Stevenson		Davies, J. Smith	
6 February	Bray Unknowns	4	Shelbourne	1
	Smyth 2, Buchanan, Hughes		Bradley	
	Distillery	2	Cobh Ramblers	1
	Hogan, Martini		Wall	
	Drumcondra	2	Cork Bohemians	1
	M. Farrell, Healy pen.		Curtin	
	St James's Gate	3	Cork	0
	Byrne 2, Geoghegan			
	Sligo Rovers	1	Dundalk	1
	McPherson		McArdle	
	Terenure Athletic	0	Shamrock Rovers	0
	Waterford	3	Brideville	1
	O'Keeffe 2, McGourty		Maxwell	

First Round Replays

9 February	Shamrock Rovers	2	Terenure Athletic	1
	Snowe, Ward		Staunton	
10 Februay	Dundalk	2	Sligo Rovers	0
	Griffiths, McAfee			

Second Round

26 February	Drumcondra	0	Distillery	4
			Molloy, Campbell, Lambert 2	
27 February	Limerick	1	St James's Gate	1
	Mahony		Kennedy	
	Shamrock Rovers	1	Bray Unknowns	1
	Williams pen.		Doran	
	Waterford	2	Dundalk	3
	O'Donnell, Phelan		McArdle, Donnelly, Rigby	

Second Round Replays

2 March	Bray Unknowns	1	Shamrock Rovers	1
	Hughes		Ward	

St James's Gate	5	Limerick	2

Geoghegan 3, Reid,
W. Byrne

Kelly, Davies

Second Round Second Replay

9 March	Shamrock Rovers	2	Bray Unknowns	1

Ward, Snowe

Smyth

Semi-Finals – Dalymount Park

12 March	Distillery	2	St James's Gate	2

Martini, Doyle

Gaskins pen., Balfe

13 March	Dundalk	2	Shamrock Rovers	1

Donnelly pen., Rigby

Dunne

Semi-Final Replay – Shelbourne Park

23 March	St James's Gate	3	Distillery	2

Balfe 2, Gaskins pen.

Byrne, Lambert

Final – Dalymount Park

10 April	St James's Gate	2	Dundalk	1

Comerford (16m),
Gaskins pen. (49m)

Rigby (47m)

St James's Gate: John Webster, Alec Stewart, Larry Doyle, Joe O'Reilly, Peadar Gaskins, Charlie Lennon, Billy Kennedy, Teddy Balfe, Dickie Comerford, Charlie Reid, Mattie Geoghegan

Dundalk: Charlie Tizard, Billy O'Neill, Mick Hoy, Billy McAfee, Jimmy Bowden, Dicky Lunn, Jimmy McArdle, Joe 'Mungo' Patterson, Alf Rigby, Joey Donnelly, Stanley Griffiths

Referee: P. Snape (Manchester)   Attendance: 30,000

1939

'Sacky' Denies 'Dixie'

Nineteen thirty-nine should have been the year of William Ralph 'Dixie' Dean in the FAI Cup, but the former Everton star was denied by another veteran, William 'Sacky' Glen, the former Shamrock Rovers star who was finishing out his career with arch-rivals Shelbourne.

Dean, who had finished his English League career with Notts County, signed for Sligo Rovers in time for the Cup and he made an instant impact both on and off the pitch. In one League game against Waterford he hit five goals, while his appearance in the Sligo shirt was enough to guarantee a full house, such was the public's interest in the man who held the English League record of sixty goals in a season.

Glen, meanwhile, had had an enviable record on the Irish scene, since he made his debut with Rovers in the 1921-22 season as an eighteen-year-old wing-half. He had won seven Cup medals with the Milltown club and was a regular on the Irish team until he had a disagreement with Rovers' boss, Joe Cunninghan, and left for Brideville. From Brideville he came to Shelbourne for the 1938-39 season.

Part of Glen's armoury was his ability to hit a dead ball with more than ordinary power and it was this which proved decisive in the final replay. Dean had scored first in the final only for Sammy Smyth to equalise direct from a corner. Glen's second-minute free kick, variously described as from thirty to forty yards, settled the issue in the replay before many of the vast crowd had passed through the turnstiles.

Shelbourne centre-forward Tom Flynn, who had been signed from Grimsby Town in time for the second round second replay with Bray and scored the winning goal in that game, had a vivid memory of Glen's winner: 'It has often been said that Sacky's goal was a lucky shot but that's not true. It was planned in the dressing-room by our manager Val Harris, the former Everton player. Sean Balfe and I stood in the wall and moved aside when Sacky struck the ball. It worked as well as any that Rivelino ever struck for Brazil.'

Despite their defeat, Sligo Rovers went ahead with their celebrations after the match – with dramatic results. In the course of the evening Dean's runners-up medal was stolen and he had to return to Liverpool empty-handed. However, seven years later, while he was licensee of the Dublin Packet in Chester, he received the medal in a parcel sent anonymously from Ireland.

For two of the winning Shelbourne team the Cup final occasion had a familiar ring. Goalkeeper John Webster and left-half Charlie Lennon were playing in their third consecutive final, having played for St James's Gate in the 1937 and 1938 finals.

Shelbourne's victory was all the more meritorious because they had to line out without Northern Ireland international winger Tom Priestley in the drawn game. Priestley, a Presbyterian, wouldn't play on a Sunday. He returned to action for the replay and played his part in Shels' historic first Cup triumph.

FAI officials were in a happy mood for, quite apart from the double set of receipts, the comparisons with the IFA Cup final put the FAI in a favourable light. While the FAI final attracted a crowd of over 30,000 and receipts of £1,680, the IFA final between Belfast Celtic and Bangor could only attract receipts of £646. The attendance at the final replay – 28,369 – was a record for a mid-week match, and 3,000 more fans gained free admission when a gate crashed under the crush of latecomers.

First Round

5 February	Cobh Ramblers	1	Cork Bohemians	2
	Quaine		T. Byrne, Fitzgerald	
11 February	Shelbourne	2	St James's Gate	0
	Stewart o.g., Sharkey			
	UCD	1	Bray Unknowns	1
	P. Crean		Leeney	
12 February	Bohemians	2	Distillery	5
	Boyle, Fullen		Foy, McNally	
	Brideville	1	Distillery	5
	Jackson		Brazil 3, J. Doyle pen., Maxwell	
	Cork City	1	Sligo Rovers	2
	Davis		Hay pen., Monaghan	
	Dundalk	2	Drumcondra	1
	Hutchinson o.g., Byrne		Litherland	
	Limerick	1	Waterford	1
	Cotter		Paterson	

First Round Replays

15 February	Bray Unknowns	1	UCD	0
	Buchanan			
	Shamrock Rovers	0	Bohemians	1
			O'Kane	
16 February	Waterford	3	Limerick	0
	Paterson 2, Regan			

Second Round

4 March	Bray Unknowns	2	Shelbourne	2
	Doran, Leeney		Weir 2	
5 March	Bohemians	3	Cork Bohemians	1
	K. O'Flanagan 2, O'Kane		Byrne	
	Dundalk	4	Waterford	0
	Morgan 2, Gaughran, McArdle			
	Sligo Rovers	2	Distillery	1
	G. McDaid, Johnstone		Scully	

Second Round Replay

8 March	**Shelbourne**	2	**Bray Unknowns**	2
	Weir, Balfe		Hill pen., Doran	

(After extra time.)

Second Round Second Replay

15 March	**Bray Unknowns**	0	**Shelbourne**	1
			Flynn	

Semi-Final – Milltown

25 March	**Shelbourne**	1	**Bohemians**	0
	Weir			

Semi-Final – Dalymount Park

26 March	**Sligo Rovers**	2	**Dundalk**	1
	O'Connor, Began		McArdle	

Final – Dalymount Park

23 April	**Shelbourne**	1	**Sligo Rovers**	1
	Smyth (80m)		Dean (43m)	

Shelbourne: John Webster, William 'Sacky' Glen, Johnny Preston, Hugh Sharkey, Billy Little, Charlie Lennon, Patrick Drain, Alec Weir, Tom Flynn, Sean Balfe, Sammy Smyth

Sligo Rovers: David Cranston, Gerry McDaid, Daniel Livesley, William Hay, Alf Peachey, John Burns, Matt Began, Hugh O'Connor, William 'Dixie' Dean, William Johnstone, Paddy 'Monty' Monaghan

Referee: H. Hertles (Runcorn)   Attendance: 30,000

Final Replay – Dalymount Park

3 May	**Shelbourne**	1	**Sligo Rovers**	0
	Glen (2m)			

Shelbourne: Tom Priestley for Drain
Sligo Rovers: Grahan for Burns

Referee: H. Hertles (Runcorn)   Attendance: 28,369

1940

Jimmy Dunne's Day

Jimmy Dunne, called 'Snowy' because of his mop of blond hair, had to leave Ireland to establish himself as a first team centre-forward, but he did so with such success that his record is second to none. And when he eventually returned to Shamrock Rovers as player-coach he led the Milltown club to successive League titles, topped off with the FAI Cup in 1940.

A product of Dublin's hot-bed of soccer, Ringsend, Dunne's career was interrupted early on when he was interned in the Tintown camp on the Curragh during the Civil War. Upon his release he was signed by Rovers but couldn't get a first team place due to the brilliance of Billy 'Juicy' Farrell and the Grand Slam team of 1924-25. Instead he played his football in the Leinster Senior League with the reserves, scoring with great regularity and eventually coming to the notice of a scout for English Third Division side New Brighton. The scout wrote to England saying that he had spotted 'a future Irish centre-forward' and Dunne bore out his prophecy.

He made a quick impact at New Brighton and was then signed by First Division Sheffield United, who kept him in their reserves for a number of seasons before giving him his head in the League side. Dunne never looked back after that, establishing a club-record forty-one goals in the 1930-31 season and recording many hat-tricks in a glittering career.

He had no difficulty making his mark in the international arena either, and his fourteen goals in fifteen games bear ample testimony to his ability at the highest level. He was also capped by the IFA, scoring four goals in seven Internationals. A near record fee of £8,000 tempted Sheffield United to sell Dunne to Arsenal, where he won a League medal before moving to Southampton. Everywhere he went he was acclaimed, not only as a great footballer but also as a gentleman. On one of his trips with Ireland after he had left Southampton, the Irish party passed through Southampton docks and the local dock workers gave vent to rousing cheers when they sighted Dunne.

From Southampton he was enticed home by his old club and he quickly helped Rovers to success with League victories in 1937-38 and 1938-39. Cup victory in 1940 was the icing on the cake for Dunne, who contributed a goal in the 3-0 win over Sligo Rovers which attracted a record crowd of almost 40,000 and receipts of over £2,000 for the first time. Dunne was truly one of Dublin's favourite sons at that time.

Two other players had not-so-pleasant memories of that Cup campaign. Drumcondra wing-half Billy Mulville had his leg broken in a tackle with Rovers' centre-half Bob Bryson in the second round tie at Tolka Park. There was no stretcher available – it hadn't returned from its previous hospital visit – and the crowd was so great that Mulville had to be placed on the blackboard used for tactical talks and lifted over the heads of the crowd. 'I was more afraid of falling off the blackboard than of my broken leg,' he recalled.

Sligo Rovers' forward Paddy Barlow had only recently signed from Huddersfield Town, where he had suffered a bad injury. He hadn't played in the Cup but he had done so well in League games that he fancied his chance of a Cup final place. Instead he was told: 'You're our best forward, but Mattie Began has been lucky for us.' Began had scored Sligo's winners in the semi-finals of 1939 and 1940, but his luck ran out against Rovers. For Barlow, Cup glory was only delayed.

First Round

3 February	**St James's Gate**	1	**Shelbourne**	1
	Bradshaw		Burns	
4 February	**Bray Unknowns**	5	**Grattan United**	2
	Leeney 4, Doran		Ring 2 (1 pen.)	
	Brideville	3	**Bohemians**	1
	O'Reilly, Dunn, Reid		P. Morris	
	Drumcondra	W/O	**Cork City**	Scratch

(Cork City expelled by FAI)

	Dundalk	1	**Distillery**	2
	Donnelly		Scully, Reid	
	Limerick	1	**Shamrock Rovers**	3
	J. O'Mahony		Ward, Dunne, Reynolds	
	Sligo Rovers	3	**Cobh Ramblers**	2
	McAleer 2, Burnsides		Quaine 2	
	Waterford	3	**Longford Town**	1
	O'Keeffe 2, Sharkey		Griffin	

First Round Replay

14 February	**Shelbourne**	3	**St James's Gate**	4
	Naughton, Delaney,		Jackson, Rogers,	
	Osborne		Bradshaw, Geoghegan	

Second Round

24 February	**St James's Gate**	2	**Distillery**	0
	Jackson, Smith			
25 February	**Brideville**	0	**Sligo Rovers**	2
			Connor, Prout	
	Drumcondra	0	**Shamrock Rovers**	1
			Ward	
	Waterford	2	**Bray Unknowns**	2
	Coad, O'Keeffe		Leeney, Meehan	

Second Round Replay

28 February	**Bray Unknowns**	2	**Waterford**	0
	Buchanan, Richardson			

Semi-Final – Shelbourne Park

30 March **Shamrock Rovers** **2** **Bray Unknowns** **0**
Clark, Fallon

Semi-Final – Dalymount Park

31 March **Sligo Rovers** **2** **St James's Gate** **1**
Prout pen., Began Kennedy

Final – Dalymount Park

21 April **Shamrock Rovers** **3** **Sligo Rovers** **0**
Ward (38m), Fallon (75m),
Dunne (85m)

Shamrock Rovers: Mick McCarthy, Mattie Clarke, Shay Healy, Harry Finnegan, Bobby Bryson, Joe Creevy, Joe Ward, Jimmy Dunne, Jimmy Clark, Bill Cameron, Billy Fallon

Sligo Rovers: Jimmy Twomey, Denis Thompson, Bill Powell, Jim McCann, Alf Peachey, Tom Arrigan, Matt Began, Bob Gregg, Joe McAleer, Jimmy Connor, Stan Prout

Referee: H. Nattrass (Sunderland) Attendance: 38,509

1941

The Cork All-Stars

Nineteen forty-one saw the emergence of the great Cork United side that was to dominate the League of Ireland scene during the 1940s, but failed to get a regular hold on the FAI Cup. A combination of returned exiles and quality home players who in normal times would have gone to English clubs made Cork one of the most exciting and successful teams in League of Ireland history. However, while they won the League five times in six seasons, they could only manage two Cup triumphs from four finals.

The team that beat Waterford in 1941 to complete the League and Cup double included three returned exiles in goalkeeper Jimmy 'Fox' Foley (ex-Glasgow Celtic and Plymouth Argyle) and wingers Jack O'Reilly (ex-Norwich) and Owen Madden (ex-Birmingham). Also included were two outstanding young talents, centre-forward Sean McCarthy and inside-left Liam O'Neill, plus three former Newry Town players, Paddy Duffy, Jimmy Hooks and Mick McKenna. It's interesting to note that Waterford also relied heavily on Cork talent with goalkeeper Denis Daly, full-back Tommy Myers and wingers Jackie O'Driscoll and Tim O'Keeffe all from Leeside.

Not surprisingly, rivalry was keen and the replay saw Cork's captain Madden and Waterford winger O'Driscoll despatched to the line for fighting – the first time players had been sent off in a Cup final. Madden, who admitted that his expulsion was justified, later had to collect the Cup when Cork finished 3–1 winners of the replay.

The loss of O'Driscoll was a sore blow to Waterford, for he had been having a good game and was their top scorer in the Cup. It was the second blow to their hopes, with inside-left Billy Cameron, a Scotsman who had won a Cup medal with Shamrock Rovers in 1940, missing the final through injury. His replacement, Maurice Hartery, was usually included as a winger. 'We arrived for the final on Saturday and stayed in the Four Courts Hotel,' recalled Paddy Coad, the Waterford star who was to become synonymous with the Cup. 'Our trainer, Davy Christopher, was keen on exercise and walking, so we had to walk the following day from the hotel to Dalymount. The Cork team passed us in their taxis and gave us a razzing. After the drawn game we went home that night but Cork went out to Bray and stayed there preparing for the replay.'

'We were full-time professionals at that time,' recalled Owen Madden, who was a retained Birmingham player and was asked to return after the war but declined. 'That gave us a big advantage. In the summer we got a signing-on fee to tide us over until the following season. With winning the Leagues we were probably over-confident in the Cup. We were so used to winning the League that there was no big bonus for the Cup.'

A second round tie, which contained more than its share of drama, was that between Shelbourne and Dundalk. Three games were needed before Dundalk got through but it was the second game, at Oriel Park, which proved most dramatic. 'The game was stopped when we were losing 2–0 because the crowd invaded the pitch after Tom Crawley laid out Shels' winger Mickey Delaney,' recalled Dundalk captain Joey Donnelly. 'We were in the dressing room changing when Sam Prole and FAI Secretary, Joe Wickham, came in and said we'd forfeit the game if we didn't go out.' When the game resumed Dundalk went a further goal behind before rallying for a 3–3 draw. Dundalk's run ended with a semi-final defeat by Cork United, but the money earned allowed the management to strengthen the team for the following season, when the Cup was won for the first time.

Another player with good reason to remember the 1941 Cup campaign was Peter Farrell, later to become a regular with Everton and the Republic of Ireland. 'I was an eighteen-year-old schoolboy attending Dun Laoghaire CBS when I was picked to play for Shamrock Rovers in the Cup,' he recalled. 'I missed out on junior football because Rovers spotted me in a schoolboys Cup final and signed me after. It's funny because I hated Rovers as a kid. Bray Unknowns were my team – I would have paid money to play for Bray. My debut came about when I turned up for Rovers 'B' on the Saturday and was told I wasn't playing. I thought I had been dropped but I had to go to Milltown on the Sunday and Jimmy Dunne told me he had a sore heel and I was playing inside-right. Joe Ward was playing outside me and he scored four goals as we beat Cork Bohs 8–3.'

First Round

8 February	**Brideville**	2	**Bray Unknowns**	0
	Boland, Dunn			
	Drumcondra	2	**Jacobs**	1
	O'Brien, Kennedy		Martini	
9 February	**Bohemians**	0	**Waterford**	1
			O'Keeffe	
	Dundalk	5	**St James's Gate**	1
	Bryan 2, Barlow 2, Reid		Smith	
	Evergreen	0	**Cork United**	2
			O'Neill, McCarthy	
	Limerick	1	**Distillery**	0
	O'Mahony			
	Longford Town	0	**Shelbourne**	5
			Carroll 2, Delaney,	
			W. Byrne, Fallon	
	Shamrock Rovers	8	**Cork Bohemians**	3
	Ward 4, Clark 2,		Whitenell, Curtin, Byrne	
	Geoghegan, Buchanan			

Second Round

1 March	**Shelbourne**	4	**Dundalk**	4
	Byrne, Doyle,		McArdle, Donnelly,	
	Feenan, Carroll		Barlow, Hirst	
2 March	**Cork United**	4	**Drumcondra**	2
	McCarthy, Nash,		O'Brien, O'Riordan o.g.	
	McFarlane, O'Neill			
	Limerick	3	**Waterford**	5
	Cassidy, O'Mahony pen.,		Cameron, Meek o.g., Coad,	
	McAleer		O'Driscoll 2	
	Shamrock Rovers	3	**Brideville**	1
	Dunne, Geoghegan 2		Cronin	

Second Round Replay

6 March	**Dundalk**	3	**Shelbourne**	3
	Donnelly, McArdle,		W. Byrne, Dinneen,	
	Crawley pen.		J. Doyle	

Second Round Second Replay

12 March	**Dundalk**	2	**Shelbourne**	0
	Reid, Bryan			

Semi-Finals – Dalymount Park

29 March	**Shamrock Rovers**	2	**Waterford**	2
	Ward, Clark		O'Driscoll, Coad	
30 March	**Cork United**	3	**Dundalk**	0
	O'Neill, McFarlane, Madden			

Semi-Final Replay – Dalymount Park

9 April	**Waterford**	1	**Shamrock Rovers**	1
	O'Driscoll		Clark	

Semi-Final Second Replay – Dalymount Park

10 April	**Waterford**	3	**Shamrock Rovers**	2
	O'Keeffe 2 (1 pen.), Johnstone		Dunne 2	

Final – Dalymount Park

20 April	**Cork United**	2	**Waterford**	2
	O'Reilly 2 (29m, 78m)		O'Driscoll (5m),	
			Johnstone (72m)	

Cork United: Jimmy 'Fox' Foley, Johnny McGowan, Paddy Duffy, Jimmy Hooks, Jerry O'Riordan, Mick McKenna, Jack O'Reilly, Bobby McFarlane, Sean McCarthy, Liam O'Neill, Owen Madden

Waterford: Denis 'Tol' Daly, Johnny Hartery, Tommy Myers, Michael O'Mahony, John 'Fatty' Phelan, Waltie Walsh, Jackie O'Driscoll, Paddy Coad, Johnny Johnstone, Maurice Hartery, Tim O'Keeffe

Referee: T. Dwyer (Dublin)   Attendance: 30,132

Final Replay – Dalymount Park

23 April   **Cork United**   **3**   **Waterford**   **1**
McCarthy (20m),   Johnstone (38m)
O'Reilly (63m, 80m)

Both teams unchanged

Referee: T. Dwyer (Dublin)   Attendance: 13,057

It's a Record!

- In 118 FAI Cup Finals so far (including twenty-eight final replays), only eight players have been sent off – Jackie O'Driscoll (Waterford) and Owen Madden (Cork United) in 1941; Eric Barber (Shelbourne) in 1973; Alan Gough (Shelbourne) in 1996; Simon Webb (Bohemians) in 2002; Keith Fahey (St Patrick's Athletic) in 2003; Pat Sullivan (Longford Town) in 2007, and Stephen Bradley (Shamrock Rovers) in 2010. Sullivan was the first player to be sent off after receiving two yellow cards.

1942

Dressing Room Drama

Dundalk finally ended the Cup hoodoo which seemed to affect their earlier efforts when they beat League champions Cork United, chasing their second successive double, in a classic 1942 final in which the drama wasn't confined to the pitch. In fact, the pre-match deliberations in the Dundalk dressing room are the real story of that famous victory.

The drama started at the semi-final stage when Dundalk, up to their old tricks, fielded Bangor inside-forward Couzer against Shamrock Rovers. Dundalk won after a replay but Rovers didn't object. However, one of the Dundalk players, Frank Grice, who was from Northern Ireland and had played for Notts County and Tottenham, told captain Joey Donnelly that Couzer wasn't free to sign for Dundalk and that if there had been an objection Dundalk would have lost it. Donnelly then asserted himself by informing reserve Jimmy McArdle that he would be playing in the final and advising him to do some extra training.

Couzer and McArdle were both present in Dalymount on Cup final day but the Dundalk Committee, while acknowledging that Couzer was illegal and couldn't be played, decided to opt for Dickie Lunn at wing-half, with Grice moving into the attack. This didn't satisfy Donnelly, who knew that Lunn – known as the 'Mighty Atom' and standing at 5' 4" in height – had no chance in the air against Cork's Florrie Burke, a commanding six-footer. The captain asked the Committee to think again and pick the right team!

'They had a second meeting and poor Lunn, who had stripped and been rubbed down, was then dropped and McArdle chosen,' recalled Donnelly. 'Lunn said it was the only time he'd been stripped and rubbed down to sit on the line! Johnny Leathem nearly caused a row over Lunn being dropped but I'm glad to say McArdle had a big part in our win.'

Dundalk's win had an extra-special meaning for Donnelly. Apart from being one of four Dundalk men in the team – along with O'Neill, Crawley and McArdle – 1942 was also his benefit year after years of loyal service to the border club. Donnelly, who shone at wing-half and inside-forward and was capped ten times for Ireland, is reckoned to be the best player Dundalk ever produced.

For Dundalk outside-right Paddy Barlow, the final represented a triumph over adversity for, just three years earlier, he had been told by specialists that he would never play again. A promising career at English First Division club Huddersfield Town was ended but, showing great character, he fought back to fitness and defied the medical profession with his achievements with Dundalk.

One of the surprising features of the final was the size of the attendance. With wartime travel restrictions in force and both teams from the provinces, the crowd of 34,298 must have included many who walked long distances to witness this final between two of the great teams of the 1940s.

The 1942 Cup campaign is also remembered for the outcry among Shamrock Rovers' supporters when player-coach Jimmy Dunne was dropped for the semi-final against Dundalk. (Dunne was dropped for Des Westby and not Paddy Coad, as is often stated.) Some of Dunne's Ringsend fans were so incensed that they dug up Rovers supremo Joe Cunningham's lawn in protest!

First Round

8 February	Cork Bohemians	2	Cork United	5
	Carroll, Whitenell		Fenton, O'Neill,	
			McCarthy 2, Madden	
	Dundalk	2	Distillery	1
	Kelly, Lavery		Cullen	
	Limerick	1	Bohemians	2
	Byrne		Jordan, Breslin	
	Shamrock Rovers	3	Brideville	1
	Dunne, Coad, Cochrane		Smyth	

Byes: Bray Unknowns, Drumcondra, St James's Gate, Shelbourne

Second Round

28 February	Shelbourne	1	Dundalk	2
	Hayden		Barlow, Lavery	
1 March	Bray Unknowns	3	Shamrock Rovers	3
	Brazil 2, O'Brien		Cochrane, Farrell, Dunne	
	Cork United	1	St James's Gate	0
	O'Neill			
	Drumcondra	2	Bohemians	2
	McNamara, Daly		Breslin, Smith	

Second Round Replays

4 March	Bohemians	1	Drumcondra	3
	McGrane		Meehan 2, T. O'Brien	
5 March	Shamrock Rovers	6	Bray Unknowns	1
	Bryson pen., Comerford 2,		Brazil	
	Dunne 2, Coad			

Semi-Final – Dalymount Park

| 5 April | Shamrock Rovers | 1 | Dundalk | 1 |
| | Coad | | McCartney | |

Semi-Final Replay – Dalymount Park

| 8 April | Dundalk | 2 | Shamrock Rovers | 1 |
| | Barlow, Kelly | | Coad | |

Semi-Final – Dalymount Park

12 April	**Cork United**	**4**	**Drumcondra**	**2**
	S. McCarthy 4		Ward 2	

Final – Dalymount Park

26 April	**Dundalk**	**3**	**Cork United**	**1**
	Kelly 2 (57m, 70m),		O'Reilly (52m)	
	Lavery (84m)			

Dundalk: Gerry Matier, Billy O'Neill, Tom Crawley, Joey Donnelly, Johnny 'Hec' Leathem, Frank Grice, Paddy Barlow, Jimmy McArdle, Art Kelly, Johnny Lavery, Sammy McCartney

Cork United: Jimmy 'Fox' Foley, Billy Hayes, Paddy Duffy, Johnny McGowan, Jerry O'Riordan, Richie Noonan, Jack O'Reilly, Florrie Burke, Sean McCarthy, Liam O'Neill, Owen Madden

Referee: T. Dwyer (Dublin)   Attendance: 34,298

It's a Record!

- The original FAI Cup was purchased for £68/10/-, and was retired after the 2006 Cup final.

1943

McNamara's Band

Cork United were among the hottest favourites of all time to beat Drumcondra in the 1943 FAI Cup Final. It wasn't that Drumcondra were a poor team – far from it – but Cork United had just won the League of Ireland title for the third year in succession and, of fifty-six League games in those three years, they had lost only seven. They had won the Cup in 1941 and lost a great final to Dundalk in 1942, so they were expected to make amends against Drumcondra. 'Cork United were 5/1 on to win,' recalled Drums' wing-half Billy Mulville, 'but we raised our game for that match.' Led by centre-forward Tommy McNamara and known as 'McNamara's Band', they confounded the critics to beat Cork 2–1 and take the Cup back to Tolka Park for the second time.

With the League of Ireland reduced to ten teams, the FAI introduced a two-leg system for first round matches and Drumcondra were drawn against non-League Distillery, the Intermediate Cup-holders for the past four years. 'Distillery should have been in the League of Ireland,' said Mulville. 'League teams hated to be drawn against them in the Cup.' The two-leg system probably worked to Drumcondra's advantage as it took some of the pressure off them. At any rate, after a 1–1 first leg, they stormed into the second round with a 4–1 second-leg win.

The second round tie away to Dundalk proved to be very eventful, especially for full-back Tommy O'Rourke: 'I missed a penalty, gave away a penalty and scored a penalty in a 2–2 draw,' he recalled. 'I missed a penalty, hitting it wide off the post, when the score was 0–0. Then I took down Joey Donnelly, who scored from the spot to make it 1–0. When the score was 2–1, Dundalk's goalie Gerry Matier planted Tommy McNamara, who was chasing a ball that was going over the end line and I converted the penalty to earn us a replay.' O'Rourke also scored from the spot in the replay when Dickey McGrane, who had been brought into the side, made his mark with a hat-trick. Billy Mulville also came into the side for the replay – at the expense of Fran O'Brien – and retained his place for the rest of the Cup campaign.

The only other second round tie resulted in a sensational win for re-election candidates Brideville away to Cup specialists Shamrock Rovers. Wearing white shirts the players had bought by pooling their wartime clothing coupons, the hard-up Dublin club reaped a semi-final bonanza of two games against Cork United, which enabled it to pay off its debts.

While Cork United had disposed of Brideville by 31 March, it took Drumcondra three games to get past Limerick – and all three were played in April, proving ideal preparation for the final on 18 April. One of the stumbling blocks as far as Drumcondra were concerned was a young Limerick centre-forward called David Walsh. A Waterford man, he had only one season with the Shannonsiders before moving on to Linfield, where he won IFA Cup medals in 1945 and 1946, and was then transferred to West Bromwich Albion and later Aston Villa, winning international honours from both the FAI and the IFA. He came in the middle of a line of great Limerick centre-forwards, being preceded by Tommy Byrne, who moved on to Belfast Celtic, and being followed by Paddy O'Leary, who later moved to Cork United.

A sad postscript to Drumcondra's win – but a sign of the times – was Tommy O'Rourke's need shortly after to sell his Cup medal in order to raise the balance necessary for a deposit on a house when he was getting married.

First Round

First round ties played on a two-leg basis. Aggregate scores decided winner.

7 February	**Brideville**	**2**	**Jacobs**	**1**
1st Leg	Smyth, Clarke		Hollingsworth	
14 February	**Jacobs**	**3**	**Brideville**	**3**
2nd Leg	Hollingsworth 2, Kirwan		O'Hagan, Shields, Clarke	

(Brideville won 5–4 on aggregate.)

7 February	**Cork United**	**1**	**Shelbourne**	**1**
1st Leg	N. Dunne		Bradshaw	
14 February	**Shelbourne**	**1**	**Cork United**	**2**
2nd Leg	Bradshaw		O'Reilly, McCarthy	

(Cork United won 3–2 on aggregate.)

7 February	**Limerick**	**2**	**Bray Unknowns**	**0**
1st Leg	J. O'Mahony 2 (1 pen.)			
13 February	**Bray Unknowns**	**0**	**Limerick**	**2**
2nd Leg			D. Walsh, McLoughlin	

(Limerick won 4–0 on aggregate.)

7 February	**Drumcondra**	**1**	**Distillery**	**1**
1st Leg	McGrane		Molloy	
14 February	**Distillery**	**1**	**Drumcondra**	**4**
2nd Leg	Ward		O'Rourke pen., McNamara 3	

(Drumcondra won 5–2 on aggregate.)

6 February	**Bohemians**	**0**	**Shamrock Rovers**	**2**
1st Leg			Coad, Grogan	
14 February	**Shamrock Rovers**	**0**	**Bohemians**	**0**

(Shamrock Rovers won 2–0 on aggregate.)

7 February	**St James's Gate**	**3**	**Dundalk**	**3**
1st Leg	Flanagan 2, Rogers		Doran, McDonald, Barlow	
14 February	**Dundalk**	**2**	**St James's Gate**	**2**
2nd Leg	Doran, Donnelly		Flanagan 2	

(Draw: Aggregate score 5–5.)

First Round Play-Off

17 February	**Dundalk**	**2**	**St James's Gate**	**1**
	Barlow, Lavery		J. Matthews	

Second Round

28 February	**Dundalk**	**2**	**Drumcondra**	**2**
	Donnelly pen., Lavery		Shields, O'Rourke pen.	
	Shamrock Rovers	**1**	**Brideville**	**2**
	Delaney		T. Clarke, S. Smyth pen.	

Byes: Cork United and Limerick

Second Round Replay

2 March	**Drumcondra**	**4**	**Dundalk**	**0**
	O'Rourke pen., McGrane 3			

Semi-Final – Dalymount Park

28 March	**Cork United**	**2**	**Brideville**	**2**
	Madden, O'Driscoll		Shields 2	

Semi-Final Replay – Dalymount Park

31 March	**Cork United**	**2**	**Brideville**	**0**
	O'Reilly, McCarthy			

Semi-Final – Dalymount Park

4 April	**Drumcondra**	**0**	**Limerick**	**0**

Semi-Final Replay – Dalymount Park

7 April	**Drumcondra**	**3**	**Limerick**	**3**
	O'Rourke pen., McNamara,		Walsh, McLoughlin,	
	McGrane		M. O'Mahony	

Semi-Final Second Replay – Dalymount Park

10 April	**Drumcondra**	**4**	**Limerick**	**2**
	Daly, Dyer 2, McNamara		McGlynn o.g., Walsh	

Final – Dalymount Park

18 April   **Drumcondra**   **2**   **Cork United**   **1**
                McGrane (11m),   O'Reilly (73m)
                McNamara (61m)

Drumcondra: Ned Flynn, Tommy O'Rourke, Kevin Clarke, Billy Mulville, Fergie McGlynn, Jim O'Mara, Leo Ward, Paddy Daly, Tommy McNamara, Paddy Dyer, Dick McGrane

Cork United: Kevin McAlinden, Billy Hayes, Paddy Duffy, Johnny McGowan, William Curtin, Connie Forde, Jack O'Reilly, Noel Dunne, Sean McCarthy, Owen Madden, Jackie O'Driscoll

Referee: W. Behan (Dublin)   Attendance: 30,549

It's a Record!

- Bill Cleary's six goals for Bohemians against Bray Unknowns at the Carlisle Grounds in January 1930 is an FAI Cup record. It was a re-fixture, which Bohs won 7–3, after the original game had to be abandoned with Bohs leading 1–0.

- Jimmy Turnbull (Cork) scored eleven goals in the 1936 FAI Cup campaign.

1944

Rovers Raise Their Game

The ability of Shamrock Rovers teams to raise their game for Cup finals is well known, and former Shelbourne full-back Johnny Olphert reckoned that Rovers' 3–2 win in the 1944 FAI Cup Final was a classic case of this. 'We won everything bar the Cup that year,' recalled Olphert. 'We won the Shield and the League and we were a certainty in the final because we had beaten Rovers practically every time we played them that year.' Mind you, a little thing called luck, which generally deserted Shelbourne in finals, also had a part to play, with Shelbourne wing-half Eddie Gannon scoring an own goal and centre-half Paddy Kinsella missing a penalty.

Olphert, however, preferred to be hard on himself: 'In the final I never got a kick of the ball, other than kicking it out as goalkeeper Fred Kiernan wasn't too keen on kicking out himself. Rovers just took control and their right-winger Mickey Delaney, who used to play for us, had a blinder. I never got a tackle or anything on him. For the penalty, the ball was in the net when Mattie Clarke got to it and threw it out. It was a goal but the referee gave us a penalty and Paddy Kinsella missed it.'

The 1944 Cup campaign saw the two-leg system extended to semi-final matches, as the loss of Brideville and Bray Unknowns had reduced the League of Ireland to eight teams. In addition, the Intermediate Cup had been suspended, so there were no non-League teams in the competition. Shamrock Rovers disposed of Cup-holders Drumcondra comfortably in their semi-final, but

Shelbourne had a little more trouble with Dundalk. 'I used to dread playing against Dundalk,' recalled Olphert. 'To get over them was a great performance. I always had to play against Paddy Barlow and he and I used train together. He was the best corner-kicker I ever saw. He played for corner-kicks.' Although Barlow scored in the second leg semi-final tie, Olphert had the last laugh as Shelbourne got through on a 4–2 aggregate.

Matt Doherty, Rovers' right-half, was a Derryman who had played in an IFA Cup Final with Derry City in 1936 and returned to that club to win an IFA Cup medal in 1949.

Eddie Gannon may have had the misfortune to put through his own goal in the final but he went on to have a distinguished career. A graduate of Distillery, he joined Notts County after the war and then moved to Sheffield Wednesday before returning to Shelbourne in 1955. He won international and inter-League honours.

Paddy Coad, who was winning his first Cup medal after the disappointment of 1941 with Waterford, gave an interesting insight to the financial incentives offered to Shamrock Rovers players: 'We were never on more than a £5 bonus for a win in a Cup final. Normally it was a £1 bonus in the first round unless the opposition was particularly stiff, then the bonus might be £2, with a further £2 for the second round and £3 and £4 for the semi-final.'

First Round

All ties, except final, over two legs. Aggregate scores decided winner.

26 February 1st Leg	**Bohemians** M. O'Flanagan, Kelly	**2**	**Drumcondra** McGrane, Daly, O'Rourke, Ward	**4**
5 March 2nd Leg	**Drumcondra** McNamara	**1**	**Bohemians** K. O'Flanagan	**1**

(Drumcondra won 5–3 on aggregate.)

27 February 1st Leg	**Dundalk** Flanagan 3, Lavery, Barlow	**5**	**Cork United** McCarthy	**1**
5 March 2nd Leg	**Cork United** McCarthy	**1**	**Dundalk**	**0**

(Dundalk won 5–2 on aggregate.)

27 February 1st Leg	**Shamrock Rovers** Eglington 2, Crowe, Coad 2	**5**	**Limerick** McKenna	**1**
5 March 2nd Leg	**Limerick** Darcy, Cronin	**2**	**Shamrock Rovers** Coad, Crowe	**2**

(Shamrock Rovers won 7–3 on aggregate.)

27 February 1st Leg	**St James's Gate** McAllister	**1**	**Shelbourne** McCluskey, Fallon 2	**3**
4 March 2nd Leg	**Shelbourne** Walsh, Cassidy, Fallon	**3**	**St James's Gate** Matthews	**1**

(Shelbourne won 6–2 on aggregate.)

Semi-Final – Dalymount Park

25 March 1st Leg	**Shamrock Rovers** Eglington, Coad	**2**	**Drumcondra**	**0**
2 April 2nd Leg	**Drumcondra** McNamara, Ward	**2**	**Shamrock Rovers** Coad 2, Rogers 3	**5**

(Shamrock Rovers won 7–2 on aggregate.)

Semi-Final – Dalymount Park

26 March 1st Leg	**Dundalk** D. Flanagan	**1**	**Shelbourne** Cassidy	**1**
1 April 2nd Leg	**Shelbourne** Walsh 2, McCluskey	**3**	**Dundalk** Barlow	**1**

(Shelbourne won 4–2 on aggregate.)

Final – Dalymount Park

16 April **Shamrock Rovers** **3** **Shelbourne** **2**

Rogers (8m), Fallon (18m),
Gannon o.g. (19m), McCluskey (80m)
Crowe (40m)

Shamrock Rovers: Larry Palmer, Joe Nolan, Mattie Clarke, Matt Doherty, Charlie Byrne, Peter Farrell, Mickey Delaney, Paddy Coad, Liam Crowe, Bobby Rogers, Tommy Eglington

Shelbourne: Fred Kiernan, Arthur Whelan, Johnny Olphert, Eddie Gannon, Paddy Kinsella, Charlie Mullally, Billy Kennedy, Joe 'Barreler' Cassidy, Mick McCluskey, Sid Walsh, Willie Fallon

Referee: P. Finnegan (Dublin) Attendance: 34,080

It's a Record!

- Aviva Stadium is the eighth venue to host the FAI Cup Final. Most of the previous finals were held at Dalymount Park, but the old Lansdowne Road stadium, Shelbourne Park, Flower Lodge, Tolka Park, the RDS and Tallaght Stadium have also hosted finals.

1945

Gregg Hits a Winner

It sounds like a trick question, but it isn't: which team lost two FAI Cup ties and still won the Cup? The answer is Shamrock Rovers and the year in question was 1945. At the time only eight teams competed, so first round ties and semi-finals were two-leg affairs. In their first round, first leg tie, Rovers lost 3–2 to Limerick at Milltown, recovering to win the second leg at the Market's Field 3–1. The semi-final was a more dramatic affair, with Dundalk winning the first leg 3–0 and Rovers overcoming that deficit with a 5–0 second leg win, helped by a penalty and an own goal. Rovers' feat of two defeats en route to a Cup win was repeated by Drumcondra in 1946.

Bohemians were confident going into the final, for although they had finished bottom of the League, they had disposed of champions Cork United in the semi-final and their team was laced with talent, which made a mockery of their low rating. Four of their players – Peter Molloy, Pat Waters, Kevin O'Flanagan and Noel Kelly – were destined to experience English League football after the war. The all-Dublin pairing of Cup-holders Rovers and Cup fighters Bohemians attracted a record attendance of 41,238 to Dalymount Park.

Dr Kevin O'Flanagan was captain of Bohemians and the star performer during their Cup run, with three goals in the five games to the final. However, Rovers won 1–0 and O'Flanagan recalled, 'I was very disappointed and especially at having played so badly myself. I couldn't understand why I played so badly but when I got home that night I discovered I had a temperature of 103 and that explained it – I was coming down with 'flu.' Kevin's disappointment is understandable when one considers that, shortly after, Bohemians won the Inter-City Cup, the unofficial All-Ireland title, beating the great Belfast Celtic 1–0 in the final. Kevin missed Bohemians' 1947 Cup final defeat, as he was practising in London at the time.

Podge Gregg was Rovers' hero, scoring the winning goal late in the game when he finished Mickey Delaney's cross to the net. The big Ringsend centre-forward was in his second spell with Rovers, having spent the 1943-44 season with Glentoran, where he enjoyed success in the Gold Cup and the Inter-City Cup. He was also chosen for the North Regional League and scored twice against the League of Ireland in a 4–3 win on St Patrick's Day, 1944 in Dublin. When he was suspended by the Glens early in 1945 for not training, Rovers stepped in and asked him to sign in time for the Cup. 'I would have played for Rovers for nothing,' he recalled, 'so I took a big cut in wages – £3 a week and a £1 a point instead of £9 a week with Glentoran – and signed in February, so that I was only getting match fit when the Cup started in March.'

For the first round tie against Limerick, the Cunninghams dropped one of their occasional bombshells when they left out left-winger Tommy Eglington and replaced him with Larry White. Coach Bob Fullam protested, but to no avail. Rovers were fortunate to escape with a one-goal deficit. The following week, with Gregg getting fitter and notching two goals, Rovers ran in three goals before Limerick replied. Gregg was again the hero in the semi-final second leg, when his hat-trick wiped out Dundalk's first leg lead.

Eglington survived the Cunninghams' poor opinion of him to become one of Rovers' star exports, moving to Everton in 1946 with wing-half Peter Farrell. He enjoyed a long and happy innings at Goodison Park before moving to Tranmere Rovers and then back home to Cork Hibernians, with whom he played in the 1963 Cup final. He was capped twenty-four times by the Republic of Ireland.

First Round

All ties, except final, over two legs. Aggregate scores decided winner.

3 March	Shelbourne	2	Bohemians	2
1st Leg	Hill, Thomas		M. O'Flanagan, Burns	
11 March	Bohemians	4	Shelbourne	0
2nd Leg	Murtagh o.g., Glennon pen.,			
	K. O'Flanagan, Burns			

(Bohemians won 6–2 on aggregate.)

4 March	Drumcondra	0	Cork United	2
1st Leg			McCarthy, Madden	
11 March	Cork United	5	Drumcondra	0
2nd Leg	McCarthy 2, Moroney,			
	Madden 2			

(Cork United won 7–0 on aggregate.)

4 March	Dundalk	2	Brideville	0
1st Leg	Flanagan 2			
10 March	Brideville	2	Dundalk	1
2nd Leg	Smyth, Shields		Fallon	

(Dundalk won 3–2 on aggregate.)

4 March	Shamrock Rovers	2	Limerick	3
1st Leg	Coad 2		P. O'Leary, Dunne pen., Healy	
11 March	Limerick	1	Shamrock Rovers	3
2nd Leg	Dunne		Gregg 2, Coad	

(Shamrock Rovers won 5–4 on aggregate.)

Semi-Final – Dalymount Park

31 March	Shamrock Rovers	0	Dundalk	3
1st Leg			Flanagan 2 (1 pen.), Fallon	
8 April	Dundalk	0	Shamrock Rovers	5
2nd Leg			Coad pen., Gregg 3,	
			Matthews o.g.	

(Shamrock Rovers won 5–3 on aggregate.)

Semi-Final – Dalymount Park

1 April	Bohemians	2	Cork United	1
1st Leg	Glennon 2 (1 pen.)		McCarthy	

The Mardyke, Cork

| 8 April | **Cork United** | 2 | **Bohemians** | 1 |
| 2nd Leg | Madden, Moroney | | K.O'Flanagan | |

(Draw: Aggregate score 3–3.)

Semi-Final Play-Off – Dalymount Park

| 11 April | **Bohemians** | 2 | **Cork United** | 0 |
| | Waters, K. O'Flanagan | | | |

Final – Dalymount Park

| 22 April | **Shamrock Rovers** | 1 | **Bohemians** | 0 |
| | Gregg (55m) | | | |

Shamrock Rovers: Larry Palmer, Mattie Clarke, Jackie Coyle, Matt Doherty, Charlie Byrne, Peter Farrell, Mickey Delaney, Paddy Coad, Podge Gregg, Bobby Rogers, Tommy Eglington

Bohemians: Jimmy Collins, Frank Glennon, Billy Richardson, Ossie Nash, Peter Molloy, Pat Waters, Kevin O'Flanagan, Noel Kelly, Mattie Burns, Frank Morris, Mick O'Flanagan

Referee: T. Butler (Dublin)   Attendance: 41,238 (All-time Record)

1946

Untried 'Robin' Stars

Joseph 'Robin' Lawler set something of a precedent in 1946 when he won a Cup medal with Drumcondra – without ever playing a League of Ireland game for the club. Cup final day was a good one for the Lawler family, with brother Jimmy also on the victorious Drumcondra team, the first time for brothers to win Cup medals on the same day since Jeremiah and Christy Robinson (Bohemians) in 1928.

Robin Lawler was playing Leinster League football with Transport when manager Matt Giles answered his brother Dicky's cry for help. Dicky was assistant manager to Jock McCosh at Drumcondra and, having reached the Cup semi-final, their plans were upset when wing-half and captain Billy Mulville suffered a bad ankle injury. Lawler, an amateur, was transferred to Drums but Matt Giles, thinking of the player's future, got the League of Ireland club to sign an agreement stating that they had no power of retention over their new signing.

This proviso proved crucial after Lawler distinguished himself in the Cup semi-final play-off against Shelbourne and the final against Shamrock Rovers, which Drums won 2–1. Following his appearance in an Inter-City Cup tie shortly after, the scouts were on his trail and Drumcondra were prepared to do a deal.

Everton manager Theo Kelly travelled over to Tolka Park and agreed a fee for Lawler, only to find that Drums had no right to sell him. Belfast Celtic had already nipped in and clinched a deal with the player himself – a deal which was more lucrative to the player, with no transfer fee to be negotiated and no limit to the signing-on fee allowed.

Lawler, who was twenty, had three great seasons with Belfast Celtic, winning an IFA Cup medal in 1947 when the opposition was provided by Glentoran – and included brother Jimmy who, along with centre-forward Tommy McCormack and Rovers' inside-forward Noel Kelly, had been transferred to the Oval around the same time Robin went to Celtic. For Kelly, who later moved to Arsenal, the 1947 final was third time unlucky in successive Cup finals – and each with a different club: Bohemians (1945), Shamrock Rovers (1946) and Glentoran (1947). In each case, defeat was by a one-goal margin.

A classy player who read the game well, Robin Lawler also had a long throw-in and it was one of his throws that led to the second Celtic goal in their famous 2–0 win over the Scotland team during the club's farewell North American tour in 1949. Lawler was transferred to Fulham when Celtic went out of football and won eight Republic of Ireland caps at left-back.

Another Drumcondra player who had reason to be grateful to Matt Giles was left-back Joe Barnwell, who had been playing in St James's Gate's reserves when Giles took him to Distillery, where he won Intermediate Cup medals before signing for Drums for what was to be a fruitful autumn of his career. Drumcondra proved that football had a heart when they struck a special medal for the man who missed the final, their captain Billy Mulville.

Schoolboy team Munster Victoria, who were the great rivals of Home Farm in those days, had no less than seven 'past pupils' playing on Cup final day – Peter Keogh, Con Martin and the two Lawlers with Drumcondra, Kelly, Charlie Byrne and Tommy Eglington with Rovers.

First Round

All ties, except final, over two legs. Aggregate scores decided winner.

2 March	**Shelbourne**	3	**Limerick**	3
1st Leg	Kinsella, Malone 2 (1 pen.)		Byrne 3	
10 March	**Limerick**	0	**Shelbourne**	3
2nd Leg			Keely, Malone, Crowe	

(Shelbourne won 6–3 on aggregate.)

3 March	**Bohemians**	0	**Cork United**	1
1st Leg			O'Leary	
10 March	**Cork United**	0	**Bohemians**	0

(Cork United won 1–0 on aggregate.)

3 March	**Waterford**	3	**Drumcondra**	2
1st Leg	Cronin 2, McCann		Daly, Henderson	
9 March	**Drumcondra**	6	**Waterford**	0
2nd Leg	McCormack 3, Ward,			
	Henderson 2			

(Drumcondra won 8–3 on aggregate.)

3 March	**Dundalk**	2	**Shamrock Rovers**	2
1st Leg	Dykes, Fallon		Delaney, Coad pen.	
10 March	**Shamrock Rovers**	1	**Dundalk**	0
2nd Leg	Coad			

(Shamrock Rovers won 3–2 on aggregate.)

Semi-Final – The Mardyke, Cork

31 March	**Cork United**	2	**Shamrock Rovers**	0
1st Leg	Hayen pen., Noonan			

Dalymount Park

7 April	**Shamrock Rovers**	4	**Cork United**	2
2nd Leg	Delaney 2, Eglington,		O'Leary, Noonan	
	Coad pen.			

(Draw: Aggregate score 4–4.)

Dalymount Park

31 March	Shelbourne	2	Drumcondra	1
1st Leg	Crowe, McCormack		McCormack	
7 April	Drumcondra	1	Shelbourne	0
2nd Leg	McCormack pen.			

(Draw: Aggregate score 2–2.)

Semi-Final Play-Offs – Dalymount Park

10 April	Drumcondra	4	Shelbourne	1
	McCornack 3 (1 pen.), Ward		McGowan	
12 April	Shamrock Rovers	4	Cork United	1
	Coad, Eglington, Delaney, Cochrane		Madden	

Final – Dalymount Park

21 April	Drumcondra	2	Shamrock Rovers	1
	McCormack (12m), Henderson (85m)		Coad (1m)	

Drumcondra: Peter Keogh, Con Martin, Joe Barnwell, Joseph 'Robin' Lawler, Kevin Clarke, Jim O'Mara, Benny 'Rosie' Henderson, Dermot Delaney, Tommy McCormack, Jimmy Lawler, Leo Ward. Manager: J. McCosh

Shamrock Rovers: Jimmy Collins, Mattie Clarke, Frank Glennon, Noel Kelly, Charlie Byrne, Peter Farrell, Davy Cochrane, Paddy Coad, Mickey Delaney, Jimmy McAlinden, Tommy Eglington

Referee: W. Keane (Limerick)   Attendance: 34,248

1947

Return of 'The King'

In 1947 'The King' returned to Cork – and Cork United won the FAI Cup. Sean McCarthy, known as 'The King' in Cork for his goalscoring exploits, had spent the 1945-46 season helping Belfast Celtic win the Irish League title, but his return to his native Cork helped United field what must have been one of the most exciting forward lines ever in League of Ireland football – wingers Jackie O'Driscoll and Owen Madden, inside-forwards McCarthy and Tommy Moroney, and centre-forward Paddy O'Leary. Even in that array of forward talent, it was McCarthy who stood out and it was his goals that were the difference between winning and losing the Cup.

McCarthy was nineteen when he first came to the fore with the Cork United team that won the double of League and Cup in 1940-41, and he helped United to three more League titles before he left for Belfast Celtic. The season before he left, he hit an astonishing twenty-six goals in just fourteen League games – practically two goals a game! While with Celtic, his talent was recognised by the international selectors and he played in a Victory international against England, doing well against Neil Franklin, even though England won 1–0. His return to Cork lasted only one season. He then left for England and played for Dartford in the Southern League before being snapped up by Bristol City where, he admitted, 'I didn't make a big impression because I was losing interest at that time.'

A modest, unassuming man, McCarthy was among a band of players whose best years coincided with the war, and whose international opportunities were limited. He spent thirteen seasons as a full-time professional and, after his sojourn with Bristol City, returned to Cork and helped Evergreen United reach the Cup final in 1953. For all his talent, McCarthy was a bundle of nerves before the 1947 final replay, as he admitted to Bohemians' full-back Billy Richardson. However, it didn't stop him scoring the all-important opening goal to set up United's victory.

Bohemians had their problems when both first-choice full-backs, Richardson and Noel Snell, failed fitness tests for the final. Richardson, who played in the replay, damaged an Achilles tendon in training; Snell twisted his ankle in a Cup final rehearsal League game in the Mardyke the week before. One problem they had sorted out, though, concerned centre-forward Michael O'Flanagan. Earlier in the season he had been turning out only when it suited him, but following a protest by the other players prior to the Leinster Cup semi-final tie against Drumcondra, he agreed to make himself available every week. Bohemians quickly benefited from the healing of the split, winning the Leinster Cup with a record 11–0 win over Grangegorman, to which O'Flanagan contributed six goals.

O'Flanagan was an international in rugby as well as soccer, and in Tommy Moroney Cork United had someone equally talented in both codes. However, following the Cup final, Moroney was transferred to West Ham United, where he had six good years before returning to Cork as player-manager of Evergreen United.

Cork United's team was unique in that it was the first, and so far the only, all-Cork team to win the FAI Cup. The unlucky man in the squad was a name-sake of 'The King', Sean McCarthy, known as 'Small Seanie'. The most versatile player in the team, but the only one not to get representative honours, he missed the final due to a cartilage operation and Paddy Noonan took his place. A medal was struck for 'Small Seanie' and he later won one in his own right in 1953 with Cork Athletic.

First Round

All ties, except final, over two legs. Aggregate scored decided winner.

15 February	Shelbourne	0	Shamrock Rovers	1
1st Leg			Coad	
12 March	Shamrock Rovers	0	Shelbourne	1
2nd Leg			Hanson	

(Draw: Aggregate score 1–1.)

16 February	Bohemians	3	Drumcondra	0
1st Leg	M. O'Flanagan 2, O'Kelly			
5 March	Drumcondra	2	Bohemians	1
2nd Leg	McConkey 2		Kirby	

(Bohemians won 4–2 on aggregate.)

16 February	Cork United	9	Waterford	1
1st Leg	Madden 3 (1 pen.), Moroney 3		Cronin	
	S. McCarthy 2, O'Leary			
23 February	Waterford	1	Cork United	1
2nd Leg	Sergeant		S. McCarthy	

(Cork United won 10–2 on aggregate.)

16 February	Dundalk	1	Limerick	0
1st Leg	J. Kelly pen.			
13 March	Limerick	3	Dundalk	1
2nd Leg	Murphy 2, Venner		Matthews	

(Limerick won 3–2 on aggregate.)

First Round Play-Offs

13 March	Shelbourne	5	Shamrock Rovers	2
	Brennan, Hanson 2,		Coad 2	
	Malone, Peelo			

Semi-Final – The Mardyke, Cork

| 23 March | Cork United | 1 | Limerick | 0 |
| 1st Leg | O'Leary | | | |

Dalymount Park

| 30 March | Limerick | 3 | Cork United | 3 |
| 2nd Leg | Murphy 2, Hartery | | S. McCarthy 2, O'Leary | |

(Cork United won 4–3 on aggregate.)

Dalymount Park

23 March 1st Leg	**Bohemians** M. O'Flanagan, Kirby, Morris	**3**	**Shelbourne** Malone 2	**2**
29 March 2nd Leg	**Shelbourne** Hanson 2, Malone	**3**	**Bohemians** M. O'Flanagan, Halpin pen., O'Kelly	**3**

(Bohemians won 6–5 on aggregate.)

Final – Dalymount Park

20 April	**Cork United** Denning o.g. (12m), McCarthy (29m)	**2**	**Bohemians** M. O'Flanagan (37m), Halpin pen. (70m)	**2**

Cork United: Jimmy 'Fox' Foley, Johnny McGowan, Dave Noonan, Jack O'Reilly, Florrie Burke, Paddy Noonan, Jackie O'Driscoll, Sean McCarthy, Paddy O'Leary, Tommy Moroney, Owen Madden

Bohemians: Leo Denning, Billy Cleary, Eddie Eccles, Danny Cameron, Shay Nolan, Tommy Halpin, Bobby Smith, Frank Morris, Mick O'Flanagan, Brendan O'Kelly, Eugene Kirby

Referee: T. Butler (Dublin)   Attendance: 20,988

Final Replay – Dalymount Park

24 April	**Cork United** McCarthy (24m), Moroney (45m)	**2**	**Bohemians**	**0**

Cork United: Unchanged
Bohemians: Billy Richardson for Cleary

Referee: T. Butler (Dublin)   Attendance: 5,519

1948

Rosie, Oh Rosie!

Benny Henderson played in four FAI Cup Finals and on the first three occasions Jimmy Collins was the opposing goalkeeper. The record books show that Benny came out on top, winning in 1946 and 1954, and losing in 1948, but the strange thing is that each final was decided in a different way – 1946 by a goal that shouldn't have been, 1948 by a penalty that was missed, and 1954 by an own goal!

Henderson was the central figure in the dramatic moments of the 1946 and 1948 Cup finals. 'I take no laurels for the goal that won the Cup in 1946 – it was the goalkeeper's fault. He was trying to be too stylish,' said the Drums favourite about the winner, which he scored from an impossible angle. Still, it's nice to win a Cup medal in your first season of senior football and at the celebration party later in Hollybank Road, Benny obliged with the popular tune 'Rosie O'Grady' – and was ever after stuck with the nickname 'Rosie'.

Outside-right in 1946, Henderson was outside-left in 1948 – a tribute to his skill with either foot. He scored in his second final also, but this time it was a cracker, struck perfectly when the ball fell to him on the edge of the penalty area.

However, with Rovers leading 2–1 and just two minutes to go, fate intervened to add another chapter to the Henderson-Collins saga. Stand-in centre-half Bobby Rogers handled and Drums were awarded a penalty. Henderson was deputed to take it. 'I had a long run up to it and should have smacked it but I tried to be neat and place it and Collins made a great save,' he recalled. 'It came back out to me but I was so disgusted I didn't follow up. If I had I could have buried it. I didn't drink at the time but I went missing for a couple of days after. I was so disgusted, it had an awful effect on me.'

Drumcondra, who were going for the double, having finished the season as League champions, faced a Rovers' team seething with discontent at a decision of club boss Joe Cunningham. With six weeks of the season lost due to the bad winter of 1947, Cunningham brought forward Rovers' first round Inter-City Cup tie to the Wednesday before the Cup final. It was almost a costly decision, for centre-half Charlie Byrne was injured and forward Bobby Rogers had to drop back for the final.

However, it was on the question of pay that Cunningham dropped his bomb-shell. He paid no match fee for the Inter-City Cup tie, only the win bonus. 'Both games were outside our contract time but there was a verbal agreement that we got paid for every game we played out of season,' recalled Podge Gregg. For the next round of the Inter-City Cup, some of the disenchanted players made themselves unavailable and Rovers were eliminated.

The players in dispute left Rovers the following season, with Rogers and Gregg joining ambitious Leinster League side St Patrick's Athletic. They had the last laugh, too, when Pat's knocked Rovers out of the Cup in 1949 – with goals by Rogers and Gregg!

The unlucky man in 1948 was regular Shamrock Rovers goalkeeper, Tommy Godwin. He broke a bone in his leg in the record 8–2 semi-final win over St Patrick's Athletic, but it wasn't discovered until after the game. Jimmy Collins, who took his place, also filled in on the League of Ireland teams against the English and Scottish Leagues. Just over a year later, Godwin won the first of his thirteen international caps and towards the end of 1949 he was transferred to Leicester City.

First Round

8 February	Cobh Ramblers	1	St Patrick's Athletic	4
	Forde		Cassidy 2, McDonald, McCormack	
14 February	Shelbourne	5	Dundalk	1
	Malone 2, Peelo, Durkan o.g., Carroll		P. Walsh	
15 February	Cork United	5	St James's Gate	1
	S. McCarthy 5		Colfer	
	Limerick	1	Drumcondra	3
	O'Grady		Lawlor 2, Delaney	
	Shamrock Rovers	3	Bohemians	0
	Gregg 2, Coad			
	Waterford	3	Transport	1
	Manning, A. Curtin 2		Lester	

Second Round

28 February	Shamrock Rovers	2	Waterford	1
	Gregg 2		A. Curtin pen.	
29 February	Drumcondra	1	Shelbourne	0
	Lawlor			

Byes: Cork United and St Patrick's Athletic

Semi-Final – The Mardyke, Cork

| 21 March | Cork United | 1 | Drumcondra | 1 |
| | Drummond | | Delaney | |

Semi-Final – Dalymount Park

| 21 March | Shamrock Rovers | 8 | St Patrick's Athletic | 2 |
| | Gregg 4, Coad 2, Glennon, Kirby | | Shields, McCormack | |

Semi-Final Replay – Dalymount Park

| 24 March | Drumcondra | 2 | Cork United | 0 |
| | McConkey 2 | | | |

Final – Dalymount Park

11 April   **Shamrock Rovers**   **2**   **Drumcondra**   **1**
Coad (45m), Kirby (75m)   Henderson (18m)

Shamrock Rovers: Jimmy Collins, Mattie Clarke, Jackie Coyle, Ossie Nash, Bobby Rogers, Tommy Dunne, Frank Glennon, Paddy Coad, Podge Gregg, Des Treacy, Eugene Kirby

Drumcondra: Peter Keogh, Johnny Robinson, Joe Barnwell, Tommy Kinsella, Kevin Clarke, Billy Mulville, Christy Giles, John 'Kit' Lawlor, Dermot Delaney, Paddy Daly, Benny 'Rosie' Henderson

Referee: E. Whelan (Dublin)   Attendance: 33,812

It's a Record!

- Dave Mulcahy (St Patrick's Athletic) had the distinction of scoring in the last game at the old Lansdowne Road stadium – the 2006 FAI Cup Final – and in the first game in the Aviva Stadium, when he played for the Airtricity League against Manchester United.

1949

Captain's Reward – A Move

Sunday, 10 April 1949 started just like any other day for Nicholas 'Johnny' Matthews, captain of Dundalk. He had to report for work at the Urney factory in Tallaght to supervise the installation of air-conditioning, work which couldn't be done during the week when production was in full swing. Shortly after one o'clock he finished work in a lather of sweat, made his way home for a lunch of poached egg and toast, had a quick shower and was still tying his shoelaces as his brother drove him to Dalymount Park, where he was due to lead his club in the FAI Cup Final against Shelbourne.

In sharp contrast to Matthews's hurried preparations, the Shelbourne team arrived at Dalymount in a fleet of limousines headed by a brass band. 'I remember Peter Keely waving to me from the back of one of the limousines as I walked across the road from St Peter's Church,' recalled Matthews. It was a nice piece of one-upmanship on the part of Shelbourne, whose young, exciting attack, which included Middlesboro-bound Arthur Fitzsimons and Peter Desmond, made them favourites.

Busy and all as he had been that morning, there was more work for Matthews to do before he got to kick a ball. Some of the Dundalk players had taken note of the crowd at the game and were unhappy with the £8 bonus they were to receive if they won. 'They wanted £10 and gave me an ultimatum that they wouldn't tog out if they didn't get it,' said Matthews. 'I went in to the directors and, with extreme reluctance, they gave in. They said it was costing them money being in the Cup final!'

When the game got under way, Matthews and his teammates found themselves under great pressure and Shelbourne missed a lot of chances. Gradually, however, Dundalk got on top and goals from Jackie Walsh and Scotsman Ronnie Henderson made it 2–0 at half-time, with Jackie Walsh adding another in the second period. So it was a proud and very tired Johnny Matthews who accepted the Cup on Dundalk's behalf.

Shortly after, Dundalk qualified for the Inter-City Cup Final but lost to Shamrock Rovers. It had been a tremendous season for the border club, so captain Matthews got a bit of a shock when he was told, after the Rovers game, that he was being put on the transfer list. While some of the odium of the players' Cup final ultimatum may have stuck to him, there was another factor in the directors' dissatisfaction with Matthews – he had earlier turned down a lucrative move to West Ham United! 'Sam Prole wasn't too pleased when I didn't go to West Ham,' recalled Matthews. 'He offered me £650 and expenses but I had just moved into a new house and didn't consider football a secure livelihood. The fee was in the region of £9,000 and would have been a League of Ireland record. Three weeks after, West Ham signed Frank O'Farrell from Cork United.'

Matthews, who was captain of the League of Ireland team as well as Dundalk, was finally snapped up by Ards, who later transferred him to Glenavon for an Irish League record fee of £1,750. He captained Glenavon when they made history by becoming the first provincial club to win the Irish League title in 1951-52, and he also captained the Irish League on numerous occasions until he returned to League of Ireland football in 1954 with Transport.

First Round

19 February	Shamrock Rovers	1	St Patrick's Athletic	1
	Mullen		Cassidy	
20 February	Drumcondra	2	Limerick	0
	Lawlor, Henderson			
	Dundalk	4	Cork Athletic	1
	McElhinney, Henderson 2, Hamilton		Curtin	
	Freebooters	0	Shelbourne	3
			Malone, Carroll 2	
	Transport	2	Sligo Rovers	0
	Lester pen., Kearns			
	Waterford	4	Bohemians	1
	Murray, Curtin 2 (1 pen.), E. Noonan		Rooney	

First Round Replay

23 February	St Patrick's Athletic	2	Shamrock Rovers	1
	Gregg, Rogers		Higgins	

Second Round

5 March	St Patrick's Athletic	0	Shelbourne	1
			Cranley	
9 March	Drumcondra	4	Transport	0
	Henderson 2, Glynn, Lawlor			

Byes: Dundalk and Waterford

Semi-Final – Milltown

26 March	Drumcondra	2	Dundalk	2
	Ward, Glynn		J. Walsh, Henderson	

Semi-Final – Dalymount Park

27 March	Shelbourne	3	Waterford	1
	Keely, Cranley, Carroll		E. Noonan	

Semi-Final Replay – Dalymount Park

30 March	**Dundalk**	**2**	**Drumcondra**	**1**
	Hamilton, Henderson		Kinsella	

Final – Dalymount Park

10 April	**Dundalk**	**3**	**Shelbourne**	**0**
	J. Walsh 2 (20m, 68m),			
	Henderson (41m)			

Dundalk: Alex Anderson, John Fearon, John Maguire, Philip Murphy, Michael Skivington, Nicholas 'Johnny' Matthews, Peadar Walsh, Danny McElhinney, Ronnie Henderson, Eamonn Hamilton, Jackie Walsh

Shelbourne: Norman Tapkin, John Murphy, Sean Haughey, Dickie Rooney, Shay Nolan, Peter Keely, Martin Colfer, Arthur Fitzsimons, Brendan Carroll, Peter Desmond, Gerry Malone

Referee: E. Boland (Dublin)   Attendance: 28,539

1950

Triumph for Matt Giles

The FAI Cup has twice been won by teams managed by members of the famous Giles family. However, while Johnny Giles's triumph with Shamrock Rovers in 1978 comes readily to mind, not so well known is his Uncle Matt's achievement with Transport in 1950. Due to a bad leg injury suffered in childhood, Matt was unable to follow his brother Dickie (Johnny's father) as a footballer, settling instead for a career as a mentor. While Dickie enjoyed some success as a footballer with Dolphin in the 1930s, Matt had to be content with a role on the sidelines, but he proved to be an astute assessor of football talent. Dickie became coach to Distillery, regarded by many as the greatest non-League team ever seen, and later moved to Drumcondra as assistant manager to Jock McCosh, enjoying Cup success in 1946. By then, however, Matt had found a niche of his own – with Leinster League club Transport.

'I joined Transport in 1945 on condition they got me a job, which they did,' recalled Matt. 'They were in the Leinster League, Division II, and we won it that year. Two years later, in 1947-48, we were runners-up in the Leinster League to St Patrick's Athletic and got to the final of the Leinster Senior Cup, which Pats won 3–1 in a second replay.'

Transport, who had a strong base within the national bus company CIE, were a go-ahead outfit. Playing out of Bray, the club officials practically re-built the Carlisle Grounds pitch with their own voluntary labour to bring it up to an acceptable standard. Their hard work was rewarded when they applied for

League of Ireland membership in 1948 – and got it ahead of their Leinster League and Leinster Cup conquerors, St Patrick's Athletic. In only their second year of League membership, Transport won the FAI Cup after a three-game final marathon with Cork Athletic, which caught the imagination of the public. Remarkably, the two teams were paired in the first round in each of the following two seasons – and it took three games to separate them on each occasion, but with the honours going to Cork both times.

Matt Giles reckons it was Transport's professional approach that won them the Cup in 1950. At the suggestion of club chairman Willie Murphy, who lived in Bray, the team had full-time training from the week before the final, with various local concerns helping out. 'We had lunch every day in the International Hotel after training, and on Friday we played golf at the invitation of Bray Golf Club,' recalled Matt. 'It was originally intended for one week but it went on for two and a half weeks because of the two replays. Of course, we had to get the players off work and pay them for lost time, but our full-time training paid off in the last game when we were very much on top.'

Of all the goals scored in the final, the most remarkable was that which Jim Loughran scored seconds from the end of the first replay. With his back to goal and thirty-five yards out, he hit the ball over his head, up into the air and it dropped like a stone over goalkeeper Tom Healy's head into the net. When you score goals like that you are justified in thinking your name is on the Cup!

One player with an intriguing Cup story was centre-half Mick Collins: 'I was released by Transport two weeks before the final in a dispute over money,' he recalled. 'I paid into the first two games at the stiles and after the second replay I was approached and trained with them from Monday to Friday because I got the terms I wanted. I could have been the subject of a protest, but I was captain for three years afterwards and then manager.' Collins had a decisive influence on the destination of the Cup, as he blotted out Cork danger man Paddy O'Leary in the second replay.

Matt Giles quit Transport the following year but he had further tastes of Cup glory with Drumcondra in 1954 and 1957, having joined the Tolka Park club in 1953 as chief scout for manager Billy Behan.

First Round

18 February	Jacobs	0	Shamrock Rovers	1
			Coad	
19 February	AOH	2	Dundalk	1
	Madden, G. O'Sullivan		Murray	
	Albert Rovers	2	Longford Town	2
	O'Connell, Allen		Clarke, McDaid	
	Drumcondra	2	Cork Athletic	3
	Glynn, Daly		O'Leary, Vaughan 2	
	Limerick	1	Bohemians	2
	Neilan		Healy, Kavanagh	
	St Patrick's Athletic	3	Shelbourne	1
	Cassidy, Haughey o.g., Collins		B. Curtis	
	Sligo Rovers	3	St James's Gate	0
	Waters 2, Kirwan o.g.			
	Waterford	1	Transport	1
	D. McCulloch		P. Doyle	

First Round Replays

22 February	Transport	2	Waterford	0
	Lester, P. Doyle			
23 February	Longford Town	0	Albert Rovers	0

First Round Second Replays

| 1 March | Albert Rovers | 2 | Longford Town | 1 |
| | Allen 2 | | Leavy | |

Second Round

11 March	Bohemians	1	Transport	2
	Kavanagh		Lester, Smith	
12 March	AOH	0	St Patrick's Athletic	1
			Donnelly	
	Shamrock Rovers	1	Cork Athletic	1
	Kirby		O'Reilly pen.	
	Sligo Rovers	2	Albert Rovers	0
	Waters 2			

Second Round Replay

16 March   **Cork Athletic**   2   **Shamrock Rovers**   1
O'Leary, Lennox   O'Connor

Semi-Final – Milltown

1 April   **Transport**   2   **Sligo Rovers**   1
Lester pen., Duggan   Waters

Semi-Final – Dalymount Park

2 April   **St Patrick's Athletic**   1   **Cork Athletic**   1
Comerford   Broderick

Semi-Final Replay – Dalymount Park

5 April   **St Patrick's Athletic**   2   **Cork Athletic**   2
Cassidy 2   Vaughan 2

Semi-Final Second Replay – The Mardyke, Cork

12 April   **Cork Athletic**   4   **St Patrick's Athletic**   2
Vaughan, Cronin   Maher 2
Brokderick, O'Leary

Final – Dalymount Park

23 April   **Transport**   2   **Cork Athletic**   2
Lester (55m),   O'Leary (4m),
Duggan (75m)   Cronin (15m)

Transport: Paddy Carroll, John 'Pip' Meighan, Jim Loughran, Paddy Gibney, Jimmy Woods, John Kennedy, Paddy Doyle, Larry Kearns, Jimmy Duggan, Barney Lester, Bobby Smith

Cork Athletic: Tom Healy, Jack O'Reilly, Dave Noonan, George Warner, Florrie Burke, Frank Cantwell, Johnny Vaughan, Murty Broderick, Paddy O'Leary, Paddy Cronin, Jackie Lennox

Referee: W. H. E. Evans (Liverpool)   Attendance: 27,807

Final Replay – Dalymount Park

26 April **Transport** **2** **Cork Atheltic** **2**
Smith (82m), Loughran (108m) O'Reilly pen. (25m),
Lennox (102m)

Transport: Martin Doyle for Woods, Noel Doyle for P. Doyle
Cork Athletic: Danny O'Connell for Noonan

Referee: W. H. E. Evans (Liverpool) Attendance: 21,123

Final Second Replay – Dalymount Park

5 May **Transport** **3** **Cork Athletic** **1**
Lester 2 (21m, 50m), Vaughan (26m)
Duggan (82m)

Transport: Mick Collins for M. Doyle; Paddy Doyle for N. Doyle
Cork Athletic: Dave Noonan for O'Connell

Referee: T. Seymour (Yorkshire) Attendance: 26,406

It's a Record!

• The first father and son to win FAI Cup-winner's medals were the Buckles, Harry (1926) and Bobby (1934).

1951

Cork on the Double

Nowadays footballers are cosseted so that nothing distracts them for anything up to a week before a Cup final and, even for an ordinary Cup tie, a twenty-four-hour guard is maintained to ensure that their concentration on the game is total. However, in the past, some teams found that a little bit of pre-match panic often got the adrenalin flowing and produced the right result on the pitch. In 1951, for instance, Cork Athletic had an extended first round tie with Transport, with the second replay fixed for Dalymount Park. The Cork train arrived in Dublin only twenty minutes before kick-off, yet Athletic made light of their rushed preparations and recorded a convincing 3–0 win, with Jackie Lennox scoring two of the goals. Just to prove that panic stations motivated him, Lennox managed a repeat the following season. 'I lived in Crosshaven and had a puncture on my way to Cork to link up with the team travelling to Dublin for the second round tie against Shamrock Rovers,' he recalled. 'When the train pulled out one of the directors waited for me and when I arrived, he drove me to Mallow where the train had waited for us.' The result of the game? Shamrock Rovers one, Cork Athletic two, with Lennox scoring the first goal and laying on the second for Paddy O'Leary.

Lennox was from Blackpool in England and, just before the war, had played in Blackpool's A team with future England international Stan Mortenson. After the war, his family moved to Cork and Lennox played for Crosshaven before being signed by Cork Athletic, for whom he played in four Cup finals, winning twice.

A remarkable feature of Cork's Cup run in 1951 was their appearance in Dalymount Park in each round of the competition. Their first round second replay with Transport was played there; a second round re-fixture with Limerick was also played there as, of course, were the semi-final and final. 'In Limerick, the home team's Joe Casey missed a penalty when we were 1–0 up,' recalled wing-half Willie Cotter. 'The English referee abandoned the game after seventy-seven minutes for fear of crowd trouble as the crowd had encroached on the greyhound track around the pitch. In the re-fixture in Dalymount we were lucky as Paddy O'Leary impeded the 'keeper for our equaliser, but we destroyed them in the Mardyke.'

O'Leary and Shelbourne's Tommy Carberry were the stars of the Cup that year, each scoring in every round, and they obliged again in the final. O'Leary hit a cracking goal from a pass by Bobby McAlea, playing his first Cup tie at the expense of Frank Hennessy; and when Cork thought they had done enough, Carberry punished them with an equaliser.

Full-back Dave Noonan chipped a bone in his ankle in the drawn game and a re-shuffle for the replay saw Cotter moving to left-full, Willie O'Mahony to left-half and Danny O'Connell coming in at right-half. Speedy winger Johnny Vaughan scored the only goal and Cork Athletic later went on to clinch the League title, thus emulating their predecessors, Cork United, who had completed the double ten years previously.

First Round

17 February	**St Patrick's Athletic**	1	**Drumcondra**	2
	Cassidy		Glynn, Henderson	
18 February	**Bohemians**	3	**Longford Town**	1
	Jordan, Dunne, Kavanagh		McNamara	
	Cork Athletic	2	**Transport**	2
	Hennessy, O'Leary		Kirby, Gibney	
	Evergreen	1	**Shamrock Rovers**	3
	O'Connell		Bergin 2, Ambrose	
	Jacobs	1	**Dundalk**	2
	Malone		Martin, Ralph	
	Limerick	2	**AOH**	1
	B. Neilan, J. Neilan		G. O'Sullivan	
	Shelbourne	4	**Waterford**	1
	Carberry 2, Colfer, Walsh o.g.		Greene	
	Sligo Rovers	4	**St James's Gate**	1
	McDonagh, Isles, Jackson pen., Millar pen.		Menzies	

First Round Replay

21 February	**Transport**	1	**Cork Atheltic**	1
	Donnelly		Cronin	

First Round Second Replay

28 February	**Cork Athletic**	3	**Transport**	0
	Lennox 2, Hennessy			

Second Round

10 March	**Bohemians**	0	**Drumcondra**	2
			Glynn, Daly	
11 March	**Limerick**	0	**Cork Athletic**	1
			Lennox	

(Abandoned 77m: crowd encroachment)

	Shamrock Rovers	1	**Shelbourne**	2
	O'Callaghan		Carberry 2	
	Sligo Rovers	2	**Dundalk**	0
	Isles, Maguire			

Second Round Re-Fixture: Dalymount Park

| 14 March | Cork Athletic | 1 | Limerick | 1 |
| | Vaughan | | Cunneen | |

Second Round Replay

21 March	Cork Athletic	6	Limerick	0
	O'Leary 3, Lennox,			
	Vaughan, Cronin			

Semi-Finals – Dalymount Park

31 March	Shelbourne	1	Drumcondra	0
	Carberry			
1 April	Cork Athletic	2	Sligo Rovers	0
	O'Leary 2			

Final – Dalymount Park

| 22 April | Cork Atheltic | 1 | Shelbourne | 1 |
| | O'Leary (33m) | | Carberry (82m) | |

Cork Athletic: Ned Courtney, Paddy Noonan, Dave Noonan, Willie O'Mahony, Florrie Burke, Willie Cotter, Johnny Vaughan, Paddy Cronin, Paddy O'Leary, Bobby McAlea, Jackie Lennox

Shelbourne: Hugh Brien, Sean Haughey, Tommy Mulligan, Andy Fitzpatrick, Barney Curtis, Peter Keely, Paddy 'Hitler' Cunningham, George Lynam, Martin Colfer, Gerry Malone, Tommy Carberry

Referee: T. Seymour (Yorkshire)   Attendance: 38,912

Final Replay – Dalymount Park

| 29 April | Cork Athletic | 1 | Shelbourne | 0 |
| | Vaughan (45m) | | | |

Cork Athletic: Danny O'Connell for D. Noonan
Shelbourne: Unchanged

Referee: T. Seymour (Yorkshire)   Attendance: 22,010

1952

Law – and Booze – Beat Cork

The law – and the booze – foiled Cork Athletic in their bid to win a second successive FAI Cup in 1952. They were beaten 3–0 by Dundalk in a replay, but had been only minutes away from victory in the first game. Then-goalkeeper Ned Courtney went down injured. While he was being treated, the referee warned Cork about time-wasting, so left-full Dave Noonan took the goalie's sweater and, in a re-shuffle, Courtney finished the game on the wing. With the defence disorganised, Dundalk centre-forward Joe Martin nipped in for an eighty-seventh minute equaliser.

Cork's preparations for the replay the following Wednesday were chaotic. The team stayed in Dublin overnight, returned home on Monday, 'cured' themselves on Tuesday and, according to Frank Johnstone in the *Irish Times*, 'Cork, even in the pre-match kick-about, displayed none of Dundalk's sprightliness.' In the words of Cork wing-half Johnny Moloney: 'The replay was a farce – our fellows were still too drunk after Sunday.' And Dundalk weren't slow to take advantage, with Johnny Fearon scoring within two minutes following a lovely dummy by Paddy Mullen.

The law also played havoc with Cork's preparations, for director Jimmy Lynch appeared in court on the Monday on an attempted murder charge and club officials and players were among those giving evidence. 'I was involved as a witness,' recalled winger Johnny Vaughan. 'I had been offered a job by Jimmy Lynch on the night of the incident. He had a few drinks with us at home and then went on to his girlfriend. After a disagreement, he apparently tried to strangle her and left her for dead. I was in court both days before the replay. The case was definitely a contributory factor in our defeat.' With director Lynch on trial, Cork's morale for the replay must surely have been at a very low ebb.

Dundalk rode their luck to record their third Cup success. From the very first round, when they were drawn at home to League new-comers and runaway leaders St Patrick's Athletic, it was apparent that Lady Luck was on their side. Dundalk had wiped out a 2–0 deficit when Pat's left-winger Jack Breen headed through. Goalkeeper Walter Durkan got his hands to it but couldn't hold the ball and it dropped over the line. As he stooped to pick it up he looked at the referee, who waved play on. Dundalk eventually won 3–2 but a photograph in the *Irish Independent* the following day clearly showed the ball was about two feet over the line when play was waved on! Photographer Malachy Bellew was banned from Oriel Park as a result.

Dundalk's semi-final replay against Waterford was also decided controversially in favour of the border club. Played at Milltown, Dundalk were losing 3–1 but staged a great rally to equalise and bring the game to extra time. With the light fading, the referee ordered fifteen minutes each way instead of the statutory ten and Dundalk proved strongest, winning 6–4, with the final minutes being played with the aid of car headlights and the Milltown training lights.

Centre-forward Joe Martin believes that a tactical talk given by FAI National coach Dugald Livingstone, at the behest of Dundalk supremo Bob 'Sam' Prole, had a big bearing on the result. 'He told me to stand ten yards off centre-half Florrie Burke. That way he won't know what to do, Livingstone said. It worked like a dream, he didn't know whether he was coming or going. I was using the Revie plan three years before Revie.'

Two of the Dundalk players were transferred to English clubs after the final. Left-full Tommy Traynor signed for Southampton, where he had a long and illustrious career, while wing-half Paddy Gavin moved to Doncaster Rovers. Dundalk were the first Cup-winners who had to apply for re-election to the League of Ireland, finishing second from the bottom of the table.

First Round

16 February	Drumcondra	0	Jacobs	0
17 February	Aer Lingus	0	Shamrock Rovers	3
			Hennessy 2, Burns	
	AOH	2	Evergreen	1
	J. Murphy 2		W. Moloney	
	Dundalk	3	St Patrick's Athletic	2
	Mullen, Fearon, McDonagh		Gibbons 2	
	Shelbourne	1	Bohemians	0
	Malone			
	Sligo Rovers	1	Limerick	1
	O'Connell		A. Neilan	
	Transport	1	Cork Athletic	1
	Lester		Lennox	
	Waterford	2	Pike Rovers	1
	Nelson, D. Fitzgerald		Meaney	

First Round Replays

20 February	Cork Athletic	0	Transport	0
	Jacobs	1	Drumcondra	2
	Duffy pen.		O'Toole 2	
21 February	Limerick	0	Sligo Rovers	2
			Coll pen., Buggy	

First Round Second Replay

27 February	Transport	2	Cork Athletic	3
	Lyons, Reville		O'Mahony, O'Leary, Burke	

Second Round

1 March	Shamrock Rovers	1	Cork Athletic	2
	Burns		Lennox, O'Leary	
2 March	AOH	0	Dundalk	4
			Fearon 2, Martin 2	
	Shelbourne	3	Waterford	3
	Dwyer 2, Malone		D. Fitzgerald, Barry, T. Fitzgerald	
	Sligo Rovers	3	Drumcondra	1
	O'Connell, Buggy, Coll		Coffey pen.	

Second Round Replay

| 13 March | **Waterford** J. Fitzgerald | 1 | **Shelbourne** | 0 |

Semi-Finals – Dalymount Park

| 29 March | **Dundalk** Fearon, Moloney | 2 | **Waterford** D. Fitzgerald, J. Fitzgerald | 2 |
| 30 March | **Cork Athletic** O'Leary 2, O'Sullivan, Lennox | 4 | **Sligo Rovers** Buggy, Miller, Lipper | 3 |

Semi-Final Replay – Milltown

| 2 April | **Dundalk** Moloney 2, McDonagh 2, Martin 2 | 6 | **Waterford** McQuade 2 (1 pen.), Nelson, D. Fitzgerald | 4 |

Final – Dalymount Park

| 20 April | **Cork Athletic** O'Leary (50m) | 1 | **Dundalk** Martin (87m) | 1 |

Cork Athletic: Ned Courtney, Paddy Noonan, Dave Noonan, Johnny Moloney, Florrie Burke, Willie Cotter, Johnny Vaughan, Murty Broderick, Paddy O'Leary, Paddy Cronin, Jackie Lennox

Dundalk: Walter Durkan, Joe Ralph, Tommy Traynor, Paddy Gavin, Mattie Clarke, Jackie McCourt, Leo McDonagh, Johnny Fearon, Joe Martin, Paddy Mullen, Fergus Moloney

Referee: C. Fletcher (Cheshire)   Attendance: 26,479

Final Replay – Dalymount Park

| 23 April | **Dundalk** Fearon (2m), Moloney (67m), Mullen (83m) | 3 | **Cork Athletic** | 0 |

Dundalk: Unchanged
Cork Athletic: Jackie Waters for Courtney; Willie O'Mahony for Broderick

Referee: C. Fletcher (Cheshire)   Attendance: 20,753

1953

Raich Carter's Year

When a rift developed between Hull City's chairman and the club's player-manager Raich Carter, the chairman had the last word, releasing Carter from his contract in January 1953. Cork Athletic, displaying commendable initiative, offered Carter £50 a game plus expenses which, at that time, amounted to another £20. With the £20 ceiling on wages in England, it was an attractive offer and Carter readily agreed to sign.

Carter, who was thirty-nine, had enjoyed a star-studded career, winning English Cup medals with Sunderland (1937) and Derby County (1946), and being capped in such illustrious company as Stanley Matthews, Tom Finney and Tommy Lawton. He was undoubtedly the biggest name to sign for an Irish club since 'Dixie' Dean's spell with Sligo Rovers in 1939.

However, it wasn't all plain sailing for Cork. After Drumcondra had been beaten by a Carter goal in the first round of the Cup, the Tolka Park club objected on the grounds that Carter's signing didn't comply with the rule which stated that a player must be in residence in the Republic two weeks before the tie. It was argued that he had attempted to fly from Manchester on the necessary date but all planes were grounded due to weather conditions and he didn't arrive until the following day. The FAI overruled the objection.

The second round tie against Waterford made history when it was decided to make it the first all-ticket match with a 9,000 limit, which included fans seated all around the touchline. Carter again proved the matchwinner, with two goals in the 3–2 win, but Cork wing-half Johnny Moloney had another reason to remember the game: 'The crowd invaded the pitch when Paddy Noonan clobbered Denny Fitzgerald and I got three teeth knocked out by a spectator.'

Cork winger Johnny Vaughan also recalled the Carter year: 'Raich Carter gave us a tremendous boost. It took two men to mark him all the time. Part of our training was me sprinting from the half-way line to the corner flag. The ball was played from Paddy O'Leary to Carter and he hit it to the corner flag. If I didn't get there in time, you'd hear the roars from him all over the place.'

The semi-final was the only game in which Carter failed to score; another Englishman, Jackie Lennox, got the two goals which beat Limerick. History was made when Evergreen United qualified from the other semi-final to set up the first all-Cork final.

Of the twenty-two players in action in the final, twenty were from Cork. Two of the subs who came in for the replay were also from Cork. Cork Athletic goalkeeper Ned Courtney was from Dublin but had spent most of his life in Cork, while Lennox and Carter were from England. Another twist was supplied by Evergreen centre-half Florrie Burke, who was a retained player of Cork Athletic but was kept out of football for League games only. Cup rules were different, so he was able to line out in the final against his own club!

Johnny and Willie Moloney made history when they became the first brothers to oppose each other in a Cup final. While Johnny had the last laugh, he had the toughest build-up, as he was married and living in Evergreen territory!

In one of its many strange decisions, the FAI decided to play both the Cup final and replay in Dublin – and were rewarded with the absurdly low attendance of 6,000 for the replay in which Carter proved the matchwinner again in Cork Athletic's 2–1 victory. He thus became the first winner of both FA and FAI Cup medals.

First Round

8 February	AOH	2	Longford Town	2
	Dunlea, T. G. Murphy		P. Gilbert 2	
14 February	Drumcondra	0	Cork Athletic	1
			Carter	
	Jacobs	3	Transport	1
	McEvoy, Ward, Keegan		Clements	
15 February	Bohemians	2	Limerick	2
	Carrick, Hutchinson pen.		Collopy 2	
	Dundalk	3	Waterford	3
	Martin, McDonagh, Fearon		J. Fitzgerald 2, Bergin	
	Evergreen	1	Shamrock Rovers	1
	Venner		Coad pen.	
	St Patrick's Athletic	1	Shelbourne	1
	Gibbons		Cunningham	
	Sligo Rovers	3	UCD	3
	Reddy, McDonagh 2		Doris, Cassidy, Lenihan pen.	

First Round Replays

15 February	Longford Town	3	AOH	0
	P. Gilbert 3			
18 February	UCD	2	Sligo Rovers	3
	Lenehan, Cassidy		Ward, Coll, O'Hara	
19 February	Shelbourne	1	St Patrick's Athletic	3
	Dwyer		Gibbons, Boland 2	
	Limerick	3	Bohemians	0
	Collopy 2 (1 pen.), Rochford			
	Waterford	2	Dundalk	2
	T. Fitzgerald, G. Hale		Martin, McDonagh	
25 February	Shamrock Rovers	2	Evergreen	4
	Coad 2		Venner 2, S. McCarthy, Giffney o.g.	

First Round Second Replay

26 February	Waterford	2	Dundalk	1
	McQuade, Bergin		Mullen	

Second Round

8 March	Evergreen	1	Jacobs	1
	Venner		Duffy	
	Limerick	1	Longford Town	1
	Rochford		P. Gilbert	
	St Patrick's Athletic	0	Sligo Rovers	0
	Waterford	2	Cork Athletic	3
	McQuade pen., T. Fitzgerald		Carter 2, O'Leary	

Second Round Replays

11 March	Jacobs	0	Evergreen	1
			S. McCarthy	
	Sligo Rovers	0	St Patrick's Athletic	1
			Collins	
12 March	Longford Town	1	Limerick	1
	P. Gilbert		Bradley	

Second Round Second Replay – Dalymount Park

18 March	Limerick	0	Longford Town	0

(After extra time.)

Second Round Third Replay – Dalymount Park

19 March	Limerick	2	Longford Town	1
	Bradley, Collopy		Collins	

(After extra time.)

Semi-Finals – Dalymount Park

28 March	Cork Athletic	2	Limerick	1
	Lennox 2		Collopy	
29 March	Evergreen	1	St Patrick's Athletic	0
	O'Neill			

Final – Dalymount Park

26 April **Cork Athletic** **2** **Evergreen** **2**
Carter (37m), Venner (55m),
D. Noonan (86m) O'Neill (69m)

Cork Athletic: Ned Courtney, 'Small' Seanie McCarthy, Dave Noonan, Johnny Moloney, Paddy O'Callaghan, Georgie McGrath, Johnny Vaughan, Murty Broderick, Paddy O'Leary, Raich Carter, Willie Cotter

Evergreen United: Derry Barrett, Peter Doolin, Mick Taylor, Seamus Madden, Florrie Burke, Jerry 'Bontv' Lynch, Willie Moloney, Eddie Doran, Sean McCarthy, Liam O'Neill, Billy Venner

Referee: A. E. Ellis (Halifax)   Attendance; 17,396

Final Replay – Dalymount Park

29 April **Cork Athletic** **2** **Evergreen** **1**
Lennox (17m), O'Neill (74m)
Carter (54m)

Cork Athletic: John Coughlan for O'Callaghan; Jackie Lennox for Cotter
Evergreen United: Nicky Hayes for Taylor

Referee: A. E. Ellis (Halifax)   Attendance: 5,940

1954

The £500 Bonus

Big money was at stake when Drumcondra met St Patrick's Athletic in the 1954 FAI Cup Final. Pat's, only in the League of Ireland three years, had placed a substantial bet at generous odds before the first round and the prospect of a big pay-out was used as an incentive for the players. A figure as high as £500 a man was on offer and, to put that into perspective, it would have bought a good house in 1954.

Former Everton and Ireland star inside-forward Alex Stevenson was the popular manager of Pat's. Reckoned to be the best manager Pat's ever had, he was a players' man, giving them a rough time but still earning their respect. However, he was the centre of controversy over his Cup final selection when he left out the club's top scorer Shay Gibbons. 'Shay had been playing but he was not consistent,' he recalled. 'He had bags of speed and could hit a ball with his right foot but he wasn't a great header and lacked heart so I left him out. I took a bit of stick over that. Even the chairman didn't agree with my decision because Gibbons was a big favourite in Inchicore, but I did what I thought was right.'

Stevenson's decision was obviously influenced by the semi-final games with Cup-holders Cork Athletic. After a 0–0 draw, winger Joe Haverty was unavailable for the replay as he was needed for a Youth International in West Germany. Paddy 'Ginger' O'Rourke was introduced and took his chance well, scoring the only goal of the game. For the final, Stevenson decided to stick with O'Rourke and omit Gibbons to make room for Haverty's return.

Ironically, the game was decided by a misunderstanding at the other end, when centre-half Dessie Byrne headed the ball over advancing goalkeeper Jimmy Collins's head and into his own net. Collins was married to Byrne's sister, so there must have been many an interesting family discussion on that goal! Defeat meant the usual £5 match fee instead of the £500 bonus, but for two Pat's players – Haverty and full-back Fergie Crawford – another offer was made, with Arsenal anxious to sign both young players, who were in their first season. Haverty agreed terms and moved to Highbury, where he was a favourite for a number of years, but Crawford turned the London club down as he was anxious to finish his printing apprenticeship.

Drumcondra's success meant a quick return on his investment for club boss Bob 'Sam' Prole, who had only taken over that season after moving from Dundalk. For Drums' manager Billy Behan the Cup final was the last leg of a unique hat-trick of involvement in the Cup finals as a player (1931 and 1936), referee (1943) and manager. Having taken over that season at Prole's request, Behan led Drums to Leinster Cup and FAI Cup success, but his reign was a short one, as a disagreement with Prole led to his resignation during the close season.

It was the first time a Cup final was decided by an own goal, but it wouldn't be the last time for St Pat's to be denied in this fashion.

First Round

27 February	**Bohemians** Jordan	1	**Albert Rovers** Cremin	1
	Jacobs Hutchinson pen.	1	**St Patrick's Athletic** Gibbons	1
28 February	**Cork Athletic** O'Leary 3, Broderick	4	**Botanic** J. Murphy	1
	Drumcondra Lester, Kinsella, Glynn 3, Rowe	6	**Cobh Ramblers**	0
	Evergreen O'Neill pen.	1	**Limerick**	0
	Shamrock Rovers Coad	1	**Sligo Rovers** Bradley	1
	Shelbourne Keely	1	**Waterford**	0
	Transport Lipper	1	**Dundalk** Kelly	1

First Round Replays

3 March	**Albert Rovers** Hackett	1	**Bohemians** Byrne, Dunne	2
	St Patrick's Athletic J. O'Brien	1	**Jacobs**	0
4 March	**Dundalk**	0	**Transport** Tracey, Lipper	2
10 March	**Sligo Rovers**	0	**Shamrock Rovers** Tuohy, Ambrose	2

Second Round

20 March	**Shelbourne**	0	**Drumcondra** Rowe, Fitzpatrick o.g.	2
21 March	**Cork Athletic** D. Noonan, Moloney	2	**Bohemians**	0
	Evergreen	0	**St Patrick's Athletic**	0
	Transport Conroy	1	**Shamrock rovers** Nolan, Quinn o.g.	2

Second Round Replay

24 March	St Patrick's Athletic	1	Evergreen	0
	Fitzgerald			

Semi-Finals – Dalymount Park

3 April	Drumcondra	2	Shamrock Rovers	1
	Glynn, Rowe		Hennessy	
4 April	Cork Athletic	0	St Patrick's Athletic	0

Semi-Final Replay – Dalymount Park

7 April	St Patrick's Athletic	1	Cork Athletic	0
	O'Rourke			

Final – Dalymount Park

25 April	Drumcondra	1	St Patrick's Athletic	0
	D. Byrne o.g. (79m)			

Drumcondra: Paddy Neville, Shay Noonan, Pat Lynch, Tommy Kinsella, Johnny Robinson, Tim Coffey, Tommy Rowe, Paddy Daly, Bob Duffy, Dessie Glynn, Benny 'Rosie' Henderson. Manager: Billy Behan

St Patrick's Athletic: Jimmy Collins, Tommy Desay, Fergie Crawford, Harry Boland. Dessie Byrne, Jimmy Nelson, Joe O'Brien, Tommy 'Longo' White, Christy Fitzgerald, Paddy 'Ginger' O'Rourke, Joe Haverty. Manager: Alex Stevenson

Referee: P. Power (York)   Attendance: 20,000

1955

Tuohy Avails of Reprieve

Liam Tuohy had the sickness of his teammate Paddy Ambrose to thank for his FAI Cup debut in 1954 – at a time when his future with Shamrock Rovers was in doubt. Fortunately, he took his chance so well that he proved Rovers' match-winner in his second Cup campaign in 1955 and went on to win four Cup medals, losing out on another two through sickness at Cup final time.

Tuohy was leading scorer in Rovers' reserves in March 1954, when the club signed left-winger Christy Warren from Pearse Rovers. Warren took over from Tuohy, who had to suffer the ignominy of running the line! It looked like Tuohy's career was over before it had even started, so, the following day being Sunday, he reverted to junior football with his East Wall pals.

Unknown to him, Rovers' centre-forward Ambrose had gone down with 'flu and, while Tuohy was out in the morning helping his mates, Milltown chief Joe Cunningham was calling to his house to notify him of his selection for the first team game against St Patrick's Athletic that afternoon. Fortunately, Tuohy made it to Milltown on time, Rovers drew 0–0 to collect another valuable point on their way to the League title, and the left-winger did well enough to be retained for the mid-week Cup replay away to Sligo Rovers.

Ambrose was back in action for that game and it's history now that Tuohy and Ambrose scored the goals which gave Rovers a 2–0 win. In the remaining twelve seasons he spent at Milltown, Tuohy was never dropped. A winger with pace and an eye for goal, only Paddy Coad scored more Cup goals for Rovers than Tuohy. In his first two full seasons he won Cup medals but he had a particularly spectacular campaign in 1955, when he scored vital goals in each round, including the winner in the final against Drumcondra. 'That final was so bad,' he recalled, 'that the crowd refused to give the ball back at one stage. Eventually another, older ball was produced, the throw-in was taken and I scored the only goal of the game.'

Luck plays a major role in any footballer's career, and Tuohy always felt he was lucky. After a spell with Newcastle United he returned to Rovers in 1963 as captain. 'Rovers hadn't done anything the previous season and yet, with practically the same team, we swept the boards. After that, coach Sean Thomas should have been there for life but he left and I became player-coach and we won the Cup for the following five seasons.' It was only in the later finals of that run that his own luck deserted him when a streptococcal throat infection caused him to miss playing in at least two of the big occasions.

The 1955 Cup also saw a most unusual incident in Shamrock Rovers' 2–2 draw away to Sligo Rovers. The referee awarded Sligo a controversial penalty in the last minute with the score 2–1 in the Dublin club's favour. The pitch was invaded by both sets of supporters but the referee allowed the penalty to be taken even though the crowd was lined up from the uprights right around the penalty spot. If the kick had gone wide it would have hit a spectator! Sligo's Austrian international Albert Straka scored from the spot to make it 2–2.

Rovers' 1955 triumph marked the second occasion that a son emulated his father in winning a Cup medal. Right-full Mickey Burke's father John had been left-back on Rovers' famous five-in-a-row team of the 1930s. For Rovers' player-coach Paddy Coad, the occasion was less memorable, as a septic instep led to hospital treatment two days before the final. He was forced to step down, letting eighteen-year-old Hughie Gannon in for his Cup debut and a winner's medal.

It was a final wing-half Ronnie Nolan almost missed. 'I was waiting for a bus in Leeson Street to take me to Dalymount,' he recalled, 'and they were all going by full. Fortunately, the Milltown golf professional, Christy Greene, was driving past, spotted me in the queue and brought me to the ground. Otherwise, I'd have missed the final.'

First Round

5 March	**Bohemians**	0	**Shelbourne**	2
			D. Curtis 2	
	St Patrick's Athletic	4	**Grangegorman**	0
	O'Rourke 2, White, Gibbons			
6 March	**Drumcondra**	1	**Dundalk**	1
	O'Hara		Geoghegan	
	Evergreen	2	**Albert Rovers**	2
	Moroney, Cronin		Dwan, Cremin	
	Jacobs	0	**Longford Town**	1
			Ward	
	Sligo Rovers	2	**Shamrock Rovers**	2
	Armstrong, Straka pen.		Hennessy, Tuohy	
	Transport	3	**Limerick**	0
	Mangan, O'Brien, Lynam			
	Waterford	6	**Cork Athletic**	1
	J. Fitzgerald 2, Gauld 2,		Horgan	
	McIlvenny, Barry			

First Round Replays

9 March	**Shamrock Rovers**	2	**Sligo Rovers**	1
	Coad, Tuohy		Reddy	
	Albert Rovers	1	**Evergreen**	2
	J. O'Connell		Higgins, Moroney	
10 March	**Dundalk**	0	**Drumcondra**	2
			Healy, O'Hara	

Second Round

26 March	**Transport**	2	**Longford Town**	3
	Mangan, O'Brien		Gilbert 2, Ward	
27 March	**Evergreen**	0	**Drumcondra**	2
			Glynn pen., O'Hara	
	Shamrock Rovers	3	**Shelbourne**	0
	McCann, Tuohy 2			
	Waterford	5	**St Patrick's Athletic**	1
	D. Fitzgerald, J. Fitzgerald,		Gibbons	
	Gauld, McIlvenny, Price			

Semi-Finals – Dalymount Park

9 April **Shamrock Rovers**   3   **Longford Town**   0
Tuohy 2, Coad

10 April **Waterford**   2   **Drumcondra**   2
Barry, McIlvenny   Henderson, Glynn pen.

Semi-Final Replay – Dalymount Park

13 April **Drumcondra**   2   **Waterford**   1
Glynn pen., Rowe   J. Casey

Final – Dalymount Park

24 April **Shamrock Rovers**   1   **Drumcondra**   0
Tuohy (78m)

Shamrock Rovers: Christy O'Callaghan, Mickey Burke, Gerry Mackey, Ronnie Nolan, Shay Keogh, Liam Hennessy, Jimmy 'Maxie' McCann, Noel Peyton, Paddy Ambrose, Hughie Gannon, Liam 'Rasher' Tuohy. Coach: Paddy Coad

Drumcondra: Paddy Neville, Shay Noonan, Pat Lynch, Tommy Kinsella, Johnny Robinson, Dessie Glynn, Benny 'Rosie' Henderson, Tommy Rowe, Bob Duffy, Eddie O'Hara, Stan Pownall

Referee: A. E. Ellis (Halifax)   Attendance: 33,041

1956

Cork's Dietary Problems

Cork Athletic's defeat by Shamrock Rovers in the 1956 Cup final marked the end of an era that stretched back to 1940, when Athletic's predecessors, Cork United, were founded. Between them they won the League title seven times in a sixteen-year period, contested nine Cup finals and emerged victorious on four occasions. And to judge from Jimmy Delaney's experience, the Cork team of 1956 were the authors of their own misfortune. 'I often wondered how they were able to play at all after the feeds they had before games,' he said. 'Soup, spuds, cabbage, meat, was their usual diet while I had a poached egg or something light. They ate too much but they were a grand bunch.'

Delaney, who had helped Derry City win the IFA Cup in 1954 and packed grounds in the process, signed for Cork as player-coach and proceeded to pack grounds in the Republic as well. Even though he was forty-one, he still had a lot to contribute and there was the added attraction of his bid to become the first player with Scottish, English, IFA and FAI Cup medals. His first two medals had been won with Glasgow Celtic and Manchester United.

Apart from their odd ideas about diet, Cork had another problem – goalkeeper Pascal O'Toole was a complete novice. In his first game with Cork, he knew so little about the rules that he went out near the touch-line to pick up the ball! He was learning all the time and, although he had a good semi-final against Waterford, he is often held responsible for one of the late goals by which Shamrock Rovers deprived Cork of the honours in the final.

Cork were so near to victory – 2–0 up with twelve minutes to go – that one of their directors left Dalymount to buy the champagne. While he was away, this is what happened as described by Rovers' hero Ronnie Nolan: 'Cork were 2–0 ahead and we were losing heart when Paddy Coad moved me to left-half with Liam Hennessy going left-full mid-way through the second half. We started going forward a bit more – it was all or nothing – and Tommy Hamilton got a good goal. Then we got a penalty to make it 2–2. At that stage we were all over them and, with two minutes to go, Coad took a corner and I headed it into the top right corner over Dave Noonan's head.' Such were the celebrations it took the Rovers players twenty minutes to get off the pitch.

For Cork, it was an unprecedented disaster of such magnitude that wing-half Johnny Moloney's comment is readily appreciated: 'After the final we listened to the radio in our hotel and we still couldn't believe the result!'

Ronnie Nolan's goal had other repercussions. 'The following day I met an old schoolmate of mine, Jack Kiely, and his leg was in plaster,' recalled Nolan. 'Apparently when I scored the winner he jumped up on the terraces, fell down the steps and broke his ankle!'

One Corkman whose 1956 Cup feat mustn't go unrecorded is Eddie Doran of Evergreen United, who hit three goals in three minutes in the first round tie away to Limerick. In all probability this is a Cup record, although the timing of goals was not common in the early years of the Cup.

First Round

18 February	Transport	1	Bohemians	1
	Reid		Foster	
19 February	Bray Wanderers	2	Longford Town	0
	Duggan, Giles			
	Cork Athletic	3	St Patrick's Athletic	2
	O'Leary 2, W. Moloney		Cassidy 2	
	Limerick	1	Evergreen	5
	Docherty		Doran 3, Vaughan, Cronin	
	Shamrock Rovers	2	Shelbourne	0
	O'Reilly, Fitzpatrick o.g.			
	Sligo Rovers	1	Drumcondra	1
	Armstrong		Glynn pen.	
	Waterford	3	Albert Rovers	0
	Johnstone, O'Grady, Price			
	Workman's Club	3	Dundalk	1
	Millar, Mooney, Hill		Callan	

First Round Replays

22 February	Bohemians	1	Transport	3
	Hoey		Brady, O'Brien, Conroy	
29 February	Drumcondra	2	Sligo Rovers	0
	Lawlor, Pownall			

Second Round

3 March	Drumcondra	0	Shamrock Rovers	3
			Coad, Hamilton,	
			Hennessy pen.	
4 March	Bray Wanderers	0	Workman's Club	0
	Cork Athletic	0	Evergreen	0
	Transport	1	Waterford	1
	Conroy		D. Fitzgerald	

Second Round Replays

7 March	Evergreen	1	Cork Athletic	2
	Lynam pen.		Delaney, Collins	

	Bray Wanderers	0	Workman's Club	1
			Hill
8 March	Waterford	1	Transport	0
	J. Fitzgerald		

Semi-Final – Tolka Park

7 April	Shamrock Rovers	2	Workman's Club	1
	Tuohy, Hamilton		May

Semi-Final – Dalymount Park

8 April	Waterford	0	Cork Athletic	0

Semi-Final Replay – Dalymount Park

11 April	Cork Athletic	5	Waterford	1
	Delaney, Murphy 2, Horgan 2		G. Hale

Final – Dalymount Park

29 April	Shamrock Rovers	3	Cork Athletic	2
	Hamilton (77m),		Delaney (34m),
	Hennessy pen. (80m),		Murphy (43m)
	Nolan (92m)		

Shamrock Rovers: Christy O'Callaghan, Mickey Burke, Ronnie Nolan, Paddy Coad, Gerry Mackey, Liam Hennessy, Jimmy McCann, Noel Peyton, Paddy Ambrose, Tommy Hamilton, Liam Tuohy. Coach: Paddy Coad

Cork Athletic: Pascal O'Toole, Paddy Noonan, Dave Noonan, Johnny Moloney, John Coughlan, Tim Daly, John Horgan, Tommy Collins, Jimmy Delaney, Jimmy Murphy, Donie Wallace

Referee: A. Bond (London)   Attendance: 35,017

1957

Radford's Master Switch

Frank Radford, Drumcondra's coach when they qualified for the FAI Cup Final in 1957, had spent some years with Shamrock Rovers and he put the lessons learned at Milltown to good effect as Rovers provided the opposition in a Cup final that Drums won 2–0. Rovers' inside-forwards Noel Peyton and Paddy Coad were thrown out of gear by the tight marking of Drums' wing-halves Brendan Healy and Tommy Rowe, but the master switch involved wingers Willie Coleman and Stan Pownall. Coleman, usually a right-winger, operated on the left and gave Mickey Burke a torrid time. He proved the difference between the teams on the day, being taken down for the penalty from which Drumcondra took the lead and then adding the second goal himself.

While Rovers surprisingly omitted Tommy Hamilton from their forward line, Drumcondra surprisingly included Mick Gorman in theirs. Signed only two months previously, Gorman had only played one first team game before the final but had been making an impression in the reserves. A bustling centre-forward, he had attracted the attention of Aston Villa but declined their offer. Chosen to unsettle Rovers' centre-half Gerry Mackey, he did his job well. In a brief career in senior football, he won an amateur cap against Holland, apart from his Cup medal, but he returned to his first love – hurling – the following season.

Christy 'Bunny' Fullam was another of Radford's successes. Fullam had won amateur caps with Bohemians and a League medal with Shelbourne in 1952-53, but was then placed on the transfer list and opted for Welsh League football with

Holyhead Town. 'At the start of the 1956-57 season, Frank Radford came in for me,' recalled Fullam. 'He gave me a month's trial and, at the end of the month, I was signed. I was delighted because it put an end to three years of travelling over to Holyhead every Friday night.' Fullam was Drums' penalty-taker and he had his nerve tested in the Cup final. 'Darcy saved my kick,' he said, 'but he had moved before the kick so the referee ordered it to be re-taken. Some of the lads told me not to take it but Radford insisted I take it and I had my mind made up anyway. The second time I just hit it and I knew it had to go in.'

Fullam, who was captain of the Drumcondra team which so nearly completed the double in 1960-61, felt the 1957 team was better. 'The semi-final, when we beat Evergreen United 5–2, was the best we ever played,' he said. 'Kit Lawlor was magic. He gave an exhibition that day, he was like George Best. Every time he got near the goal it was danger.' Lawlor, who had been on the Drums team beaten by Rovers in the 1948 Cup final, was in his second spell at Tolka Park, having had some years in England with Doncaster Rovers.

The up-and-coming players on the team included Coleman, goalkeeper Alan Kelly and centre-half John 'Sonny' O'Neill. The latter two were transferred the following year, after Drums had won the League, to Preston North End, with Kelly going on to become the most-capped Republic of Ireland goalkeeper of his era. As far as Rovers' boss Paddy Coad was concerned, Kelly was the one who got away. 'I was tipped-off about him and I saw him a couple of times,' he recalled. 'He didn't impress me at all, yet he turned out to be an international goalkeeper. You don't win all the time.' 'Sam' Prole, the Drumcondra owner, felt much the same way about winger Coleman. He had a deal lined up with Sunderland but the Dundalk-based youngster didn't want to move to England. Ironically, after he was married, he went to work in England.

One goal from the 1957 Cup campaign which deserves mention was that scored in a first round tie by Shelbourne's Tommy Carberry against Shamrock Rovers at Milltown. 'It was a goal the like of which you'll never see again,' recalled Shels' manager Gerry Doyle. 'His shot hit the cross-bar and flew out over goalie Darcy's head and his own as he was running in. So he did the only thing he could: he threw himself arse over tip, hit the ball flush with his heel and it rocketed into the net!'

First Round

16 February	Workman's Club	1	Transport	0
	Duggan			
17 February	AOH	0	Sligo Rovers	1
			Colton	
	Cork Athletic	4	UCD	2
	Kelly pen., Collins 2,		P. Noonan o.g., Plunkett	
	Welstead			
	Evergreen	1	Dundalk	1
	Lynam		S. Noonan pen.	
	Limerick	2	Bohemians	2
	Kemmy pen., Lipper		Levins pen., Walsh	
	Longford Town	1	Drumcondra	5
	Archbold		Cross 3, Pownall, Coleman	
	Shamrock Rovers	2	Shelbourne	2
	Coad, McCann		Carberry, Dillon	
	Waterford	4	St Patrick's Athletic	0
	J. Fitzgerald 4			

First Round Replays

20 February	Bohemians	1	Limerick	4
	O'Farrell		Lipper, Cunneen, Bergin 2	
21 February	Dundalk	0	Evergreen	3
			Noonan, Leahy 2	
27 February	Shelbourne	0	Shamrock Rovers	1
			McCann	

Second Round

10 March	Cork Athletic	1	Limerick	1
	Coughlan		Johnston	
	Shamrock Rovers	2	Sligo Rovers	1
	Hennessy, Tuohy		Colton	
	Waterford	3	Evergreen	3
	D. Fitzgerald, J. Fitzgerald,		Leahy 2, Noonan pen.	
	Beglin			
	Workman's Club	0	Drumcondra	1
			McCourt	

Second Round Replays

13 March	**Evergreen** O'Leary 3	3	**Waterford**	0
14 March	**Limerick** Johnston 2, Kemmy pen., Cunneen	4	**Cork Athletic** Welstead	1

Semi-Finals – Dalymount Park

30 March	**Shamrock Rovers** Keogh	1	**Limerick** Cunneen	1
31 March	**Drumcondra** Lawlor 2, Fanning, Pownall, Coleman	5	**Evergreen** O'Leary, Lynam	2

Semi-Final Replay – Dalymount Park

3 April	**Shamrock Rovers** McCann, Tuohy, Ambrose	3	**Limerick** Bergin	1

Final – Dalymount Park

28 April	**Drumcondra** Fullam pen. (22m), Coleman (47m)	2	**Shamrock Rovers**	0

Drumcondra: Alan Kelly, Christy 'Bunny' Fullam, George McDonnell, Brendan Healy, John 'Sonny' O'Neill, Tommy Rowe, Stan Pownall, John 'Kit' Lawlor, Mickey Gorman, Jackie McCourt, Willie Coleman. Coach: Frank Radford

Shamrock Rovers: Eamonn 'Sheila' Darcy, Mickey Burke, Shay Keogh, Ronnie Nolan, Gerry Mackey, Liam Hennessy, Jimmy 'Maxie' McCann, Noel Peyton, Paddy Ambrose, Paddy Coad, Liam 'Rasher' Tuohy. Coach: Paddy Coad

Referee: T. H. Cooper   Attendance: 30,000

1958

Glory for Gannon

Hughie Gannon won two FAI Cup medals – in 1955 and 1958 – but, even though it cost him a fractured jaw, he had no hesitation in naming his 1958 medal as the most memorable. Softening the blow was the fact that he received his injury in the best possible manner – while scoring the goal that gave Dundalk a 1–0 victory over his old club, Shamrock Rovers.

'My Cup medal in 1955 with Shamrock Rovers was a gift,' he recalled. 'I had come to Rovers about a month before the final from Johnville, with whom I had been playing minor football even though Rovers were paying me a wage for eighteen months – since I returned from a trial with Manchester United. When I was found out, Rovers took up their option on me and I played about three League games before the Cup final, the first under an assumed name – Behan – because I wasn't properly registered! On the morning of the Cup final, I was playing in Ringsend Park when Paddy Coad called to our house and said I was to report to Dalymount Park without my dinner. I didn't know anything about playing until I arrived there at 2.30. Coad himself was injured – he had a bad instep – but he had obviously wanted me to have a good night's sleep. After the match I offered my medal to Coad but he said no, whoever plays in a Cup final gets a medal.'

When he failed to break into the great Rovers team of 1956, Gannon moved on to Shelbourne for the 1956-57 season and from there to Dundalk in October 1957. With former Drumcondra defenders Shay Noonan and Johnny Robinson and ex-Irish League players Ted McNeill, Vincent Gilmore and George Toner, the Dundalk team had a makeshift look about it and Rovers were 5/2 on favourites to record another Cup triumph.

However, the pundits had reckoned without the Dundalk defence, which hadn't conceded a goal in the Cup and wasn't going to give away any gifts now. 'Ted McNeill didn't have a goal scored against him but he lived dangerously on a couple of occasions,' recalled Dundalk director Jim Malone. 'In the replay against Limerick, the referee gave us a free and McNeill took a quick one to Joe Ralph which was intercepted and put into the net. The referee disallowed it on the grounds that the ball hadn't cleared the eighteen-yard line but even we were amazed at that decision.'

With the final scoreless in the second half, Gannon struck for Dundalk. 'A long ball was kicked on and I sprinted through the middle after it,' he recalled. 'The ball bounced around the penalty spot, Rovers' goalie Christy O'Callaghan was slow off his line and I managed to hit the ball with my head and then was hit on the jaw. I remember Gerry Mackey saying to me, "It's all right, Hughie, the ball is in the net".'

Gannon, not realising he had a broken jaw, was handed a sponge and played out the rest of the game on the wing. He and his colleagues survived a major scare when Tommy Kerr handled but Liam Hennessy drove the resultant penalty wide.

'I think we knew then that Rovers would never score,' said Gannon. 'In the dressing room I started spitting out blood and was brought over to the Mater Hospital. I got out a week later – when the celebrations were all over! That second medal was more important to me because I earned it. The first medal was a gift.'

Rovers didn't help their cause in the final with a controversial selection which saw regulars Shay Keogh and Tommy Hamilton dropped for newcomers Tommy Farrell and Sean Carroll, signed recently from Home Farm. Unhappy player-coach Paddy Coad could only inform Inter-League cap Hamilton that 'selection has been taken out of my hands'. It was a familiar plea at Milltown during the Cunningham family's reign.

First Round

15 February	**Bohemians**	0	**Evergreen**	2
			Coughlan, Moloney	
16 February	**Bray Wanderers**	1	**Shelbourne**	2
	Seerey		O'Brien pen., Kane	
	Drumcondra	1	**Limerick**	1
	Healy		Johnston	
	Dundalk	1	**Cork Hibernians**	0
	Gannon			
	St Patrick's Athletic	2	**Tycor Athletic**	1
	Whelan, Dunne		McEvoy	
	Shamrock Rovers	4	**Chapelizod**	1
	Ambrose, Coad, McCann, Tuohy		O'Connor	
	Sligo Rovers	2	**Cobh Ramblers**	0
	McDonagh, Armstrong		Treacy o.g.	
	Waterford	5	**Transport**	1
	J. Fitzgerald 2, D. Fitzgerald, Hunt, Norris		Garland	

First Round Replay

20 February	**Limerick**	1	**Drumcondra**	0
	Wallace			

Second Round

8 March	**St Patrick's Athletic**	3	**Evergreen**	1
	Mitchell 2, Fitzgerald		Leahy	
9 March	**Limerick**	0	**Dundalk**	0
	Shelbourne	0	**Waterford**	0
	Sligo Rovers	1	**Shamrock Rovers**	1
	Armstrong		Nolan	

Second Round Replays

12 March	**Shamrock Rovers**	3	**Sligo Rovers**	2
	Hamilton, McCann, Tuohy		Bradley, McCaul	
13 March	**Dundalk**	3	**Limerick**	0
	Gannon 2, McGahon			

Waterford	2	Shelbourne	2
Griffin, D. Hale		Webber, Kane	

Second Round Second Replay

19 March	Shelbourne	1	Waterford	0
	Keegan		(At Dalymount Park)	

Semi-Finals – Dalymount Park

29 March	Shamrock Rovers	1	St Patrick's Athletic	0
	Hennessy pen.			
30 March	Dundalk	1	Shelbourne	0
	Gilmore			

Final – Dalymount Park

20 April	Dundalk	1	Shamrock Rovers	0
	Gannon (62m)			

Dundalk: Ted McNeill, Joe Ralph, Ken Finn, Leo McDonagh, Johnny Robinson, Shay Noonan, Niall McGahon, Hughie Gannon, Vincent Gilmore, George Toner, Tommy Kerr

Shamrock Rovers: Christy O'Callaghan, Mickey Burke, Gerry Mackey, Ronnie Nolan, Tommy Farrell, Liam Hennessy, Jimmy 'Maxie' McCann, Sean Carroll, Paddy Ambrose, Paddy Coad, Liam 'Rasher' Tuohy. Coach: Paddy Coad

Referee: D. H. Howell (Birmingham)   Attendance: 27,000

1959

Alex's Fateful Decision

A fateful decision taken by manager Alex Stevenson eleven days before the 1959 Cup final had a vital bearing on Waterford's chances against St Patrick's Athletic. The teams were scheduled to meet each other in a League game at Tolka Park and Stevenson, mindful that it was a 'final rehearsal'. was undecided whether to rest top scorer Alfie Hale or flying winger Jack Fitzgerald. Eventually he decided to rest the older Fitzgerald, a decision which rebounded on him when Hale was carried off with torn knee ligaments following a tackle with St Pat's captain Tommy Dunne. Hale spent the following six months in plaster.

In the absence of Hale, a young local, Seamus Halpin, was introduced for the Cup final but he made little impression as the teams fought out a 2–2 draw and was replaced by another local, Teddy Brett, for the replay which St Pat's won 2–1 to take the FAI Cup to Inchicore for the first time. A crucial factor in the game was a missed penalty by Richard 'Dixie' Hale, the older brother of usual penalty-taker Alfie. Dixie, who was one of the star players in both games, blazed the spot kick over the bar.

Dixie was the youngest player ever to play for Waterford, lining out as a sixteen-year-old in the 1951-52 season. He won a Shield medal the following season and was then signed as a full-time professional by Shamrock Rovers. However, he got tired of life in Dublin and soon moved back to Waterford. At the time of the 1959 final he was unemployed and making plans to emigrate to England and play non-League football the following season when Waterford contacted Swansea Town and a deal was done. Dixie, who had a ten-year career in England in the lower divisions, was one of the best Irish players never capped, but he was honoured by the League of Ireland selectors on a number of occasions.

St Patrick's Athletic goalkeeper, Dinny Lowry, had another player's misfortune to thank for his first Cup medal. 'I was out of favour earlier that season with John Heavey in goal,' he recalled. 'I wasn't even bothering playing for the reserves. Then one Sunday after dinner I got a call to play because Heavey had gone over on his ankle playing on the street. I had a blinder and he never got back, eventually leaving for Shelbourne.' Lowry won a second medal with Pat's in 1961, but Heavey didn't do too badly either, winning League and Cup honours with Shelbourne.

The Cup final occasion had an extra-special meaning for Pat's captain Tommy Dunne, son of the late great Jimmy Dunne. In 1940 he had been part of the Cup final occasion when Shamrock Rovers, managed by his father who also played, beat Sligo Rovers 3–0. Tommy was Rovers' mascot. He later played for the Milltown club before moving to St Pat's, where he enjoyed much success, winning League and Cup medals, inter-League and international honours. Tommy's younger brother Jimmy was also in the winning St Pat's team.

Undoubtedly the biggest shock of the 1959 campaign occurred in the very first match, when bottom-of-the-table Bohemians beat League leaders Shamrock Rovers 3–2. The elements played a part in this game, with Bohs going into a 3–0 half-time lead after having the elements in their favour, and Rovers just not managing the equaliser despite incessant pressure in the second period. It was of such a game that the late Billy Lord's after-match comment, 'Football is a funny game,' was greeted with, 'Yes, and everyone's laughing at us,' by the ready-witted Liam Tuohy!

First Round

14 February	**Bohemians**	3	**Shamrock Rovers**	2
	Webber 2, Moraghan		Lynch, Tuohy	
15 February	**Bray Wanderers**	1	**Chapelizod**	2
	Bennett		Bailey 2 (1 pen.)	
	Cobh Ramblers	0	**Drumcondra**	1
			Forster o.g.	
	Dundalk	3	**Albert Rovers**	3
	Murphy, Hoey, McGahon		T. Collins 2, Hickey	
	Evergreen	1	**Cork Hibernians**	1
	O'Brien		Morley	
	Limerick	3	**Shelbourne**	0
	O'Reilly 2, G. McCarthy			
	St Patrick's Athletic	3	**Sligo Rovers**	1
	J. Dunne, Peyton, T. Dunne		Meldrum	
	Transport	2	**Waterford**	2
	Moore, O'Reilly pen.		P. Fitzgerald 2	

First Round Replays

18 February	**Cork Hibernians**	2	**Evergreen**	1
	Vaughan, Redmond		Leahy	
19 February	**Waterford**	4	**Transport**	1
	D. Hale, P. Fitzgerald, A. Hale 2		Hyland	
25 February	**Albert Rovers**	0	**Dundalk**	0

First Round Second Replay

2 March	**Albert Rovers**	0	**Dundalk**	4
			McDonagh, Gibbons, Murphy, Noonan pen.	

Second Round

7 March	**Chapelizod**	1	**St Patrick's Athletic**	4
	Sherry		Peyton, Whelan, J. Dunne 2 (1 pen.)	
8 March	**Bohemians**	1	**Cork Hibernians**	1
	Webber		Vaughan	

Drumcondra Rowe, Duffy	2	**Limerick** McNamara, Wallace	2
Dundalk Noonan pen.	1	**Waterford** P. Fitzgerald, A. Hale	2

Second Round Replays

11 March	**Cork Hibernians** Cahill o.g., Vaughan, O'Connor	3	**Bohemians**	0
12 March	**Limerick** Wallace	1	**Drumcondra** Coleman	1

Second Round Second Replay

19 March	**Drumcondra** Coleman	1	**Limerick** Lynam	1

Second Round Third Replay – Milltown

24 March	**Limerick** O'Reilly 2	2	**Drumcondra**	0

Semi-Final – Tolka Park

28 March	**St Patrick's Athletic** Curtin	1	**Cork Hibernians**	0

Semi-Final – Dalymount Park

29 March	**Waterford** Coady	1	**Limerick**	0

Final – Dalymount Park

19 April	**St Patrick's Athletic** Hunt o.g. (6m), McGeehan (81m)	2	**Waterford** J. Fitzgerald (25m), O'Brien o.g. (80m)	2

St Patrick's Athletic: Dinny Lowry, Johnny White, Harry O'Brien, Tommy Dunne, Doug Boucher, Vinny O'Reilly, Pascal Curtin, Ronnie Whelan, Johnny McGeehan, Jimmy Dunne, Willie Peyton. Manager: Jimmy Collins

Waterford: Vincent Dunphy, Jack Hunt, Milo Slattery, Richard 'Dixie' Hale, Con Martin, Noel Griffin, Denny Fitzgerald, Jack Fitzgerald, Peter Fitzgerald, Seamus Halpin, Tommy Coady. Manager: Alex Stevenson

Referee: J. Meighan (Dublin)   Attendance: 22,000

Final Replay – Dalymount Park

22 April	St Patrick's Athletic	2	Waterford	1
	McGeehan (2m),		P. Fitzgerald (57m)	
	Peyton (54m)			

St Patrick's Athletic: Paddy 'Ginger' O'Rourke for Whelan
Waterford: Teddy Brett for Halpin

Referee: J. Meighan (Dublin)   Attendance: 22,800

It's a Record!

- Captain Albert Prince-Cox, who refereed the 1930 FAI Cup Final, was an interesting character. After serving in the Royal Flying Corps in World War I, he became a referee, and refereed thirty-two international matches in the 1920s. He was manager of Bristol Rovers from November 1930 until October 1936, and is responsible for them playing in their distinctive blue and white quarters.

1960

Doyle's Babes Triumph

Gerry Doyle, who became manager of Shelbourne mid-way through the 1956-57 season, was a great believer in a youth policy, so it was entirely fitting that he should capture his first major trophy – the FAI Cup in 1960 – with one of the youngest teams ever to represent Dublin's oldest professional club. Doyle, a former Shelbourne player, had been involved with St Finbarr's schoolboy teams and had sent players to Shelbourne before he was appointed manager. A firm believer in the maxim, 'If they're good enough, they're old enough', he held firm to his belief in youth during his successful managerial career. With the exception of winger Ollie Conroy, Shelbourne's 1960 team was under twenty-three, with three players – full-back Tony Dunne and forwards Eric Barber and Jackie Hennessy – winning senior FAI Cup medals just twelve months after winning FAI Youth Cup medals with Shelbourne.

However, for manager Doyle, the star of the side was inside-right Christy Doyle. 'He was the best player I ever had,' he recalled. 'A nephew of the great Jimmy Dunne, he was capped after only two seasons in the League of Ireland. I signed him from Alton of Donnybrook. He had won no honours as a schoolboy or youth, but I was a nervous wreck for six weeks until I got him to sign. He was fast, with a great shot in either foot. He could have gone to England, and it was a tragedy when he gave it up after only three seasons in the League.'

One Shelbourne player who did take his chances in England was right-full Tony Dunne. A fee had been agreed with Manchester United after Shels' League game with Shamrock Rovers on 10 April, but United manager Matt Busby let Dunne stay with Shelbourne for the Cup final. 'Winning the Cup was probably the biggest thing I'd ever won in my life and I was over the moon,' recalled Dunne, 'but I wasn't given a lot of time to be happy about it because I travelled the next day to Manchester.' Dunne subsequently won every honour in the game with United: League, Cup and European Cup medals, plus thirty-two caps. For many years he was rated the best left-back in Europe.

The Sunday before the Cup final, Dunne was in the wars and had to go off when Shelbourne lost 4–3 to Cork Celtic at Turner's Cross in a League game. The game mattered a lot more to Celtic than to Shelbourne – and Shels finished with nine men! Goalkeeper Billy Behan, in because regular 'keeper Finbar Flood had fractured a finger, was also a casualty. As a result, Flood lined out in the final with his fractured finger strapped.

The final against Cork Hibernians was far from memorable, with Shelbourne winning 2–0 after the Cork side had an early Johnny Vaughan 'goal' disallowed – a pattern which was to be repeated when the sides met again in the 1963 final. Shelbourne's best display was undoubtedly that against old rivals Shamrock Rovers in a second round replay. 'We got a bad press after the first game because we couldn't finish off the ten men when Liam Hennessy had to go off injured,' recalled Freddie Strahan. 'For the replay Gerry Doyle used the press criticism to motivate us and we played our best to win 3–0.' Hibernians, who included the legendary Charlie Tully of Belfast Celtic and Glasgow Celtic fame, had a young Jackie Morley at wing-half. Morley was destined to compete in four Cup finals – two with Hibernians and two with Waterford – but a winner's medal eluded him.

First Round

14 February	Cork Celtic	0	Waterford	1
			A. Hale	
	Cork Hibernians	4	Pike Rovers	3
	Lynam, Collins,		Tuite, Lipper, Cunneen	
	Tully, Bailham			
	Dundalk	2	St Patrick's Athletic	1
	Lawlor 2		Peyton	
	Limerick	6	Longford Town	0
	O'Brien, O'Reilly 2, Lynam,			
	Hyland o.g., O'Connor			
	Shamrock Rovers	2	Drumcondra	2
	Cross, Hennessy pen.		Ryan 2	
	Sligo Rovers	4	Bray Wanderers	2
	McGarry 3, Arthurs		Bennett 2 pens.	
	Transport	3	Jacobs	1
	Mitchell 2, Reville		Dixon	
17 February	Shelbourne	5	Bohemians	2
	Hennessy 3, Barber, Doyle		Dalton, O'Brien	

First Round Replay

25 February	Drumcondra	0	Shamrock Rovers	1
			Ambrose	

Second Round

6 March	Cork Hibernians	0	Sligo Rovers	0
	Dundalk	4	Transport	1
	Meldrum, Harte,		Hendricks	
	Munroe, T. Murphy			
	Limerick	1	Waterford	3
	O'Reilly		D. Fitzgerald, S. Coad 2	
	Shamrock Rovers	1	Shelbourne	1
	Hamilton		Hennessy	

Second Round Replay

| 9 March | Shelbourne | 3 | Shamrock Rovers | 0 |

Barber 2, Doyle

| | Sligo Rovers | 2 | Cork Hibernians | 3 |

McGarry, Armstrong · · · Maguire, Lane, Collins

Semi-Finals – Dalymount Park

| 2 April | Shelbourne | 4 | Dundalk | 1 |

Barber, Hennessy, Wilson, · · · Harte
Conroy

| 3 April | Cork Hibernians | 1 | Waterford | 0 |

Dunphy o.g.

Final – Dalymount Park

| 24 April | Shelbourne | 2 | Cork Hibernians | 0 |

Barber (33m), Wilson (75m)

Shelbourne: Finbarr Flood, Tony Dunne, Brendan O'Brien, Theo Dunne, Freddie Strahan, Jackie Kelly, Joe Wilson, Christy Doyle, Eric Barber, Jackie Hennessy, Ollie Conroy. Manager: Gerry Doyle

Cork Hibernians: Sean O'Brien, Jerry Lane, Liam O'Flynn, Tony O'Brien, Patsy Dorgan, Jackie Morley, Johnny Vaughan, Dessie Maguire, Tommy Collins, Charlie Tully, Mick Aherne. Manager: Johnny McGowan

Referee: J. Meighan (Dublin)   Attendance: 32,308

1961

White's Bizarre Goal

Confidence is desirable going into a Cup final, but over-confidence has to be guarded against. Drumcondra fell victim to the latter when, as League of Ireland champions, they lost to St Patrick's Athletic 2–1 in the 1961 FAI Cup Final. 'We thought we had it won,' recalled captain Christy 'Bunny' Fullam. 'We were so confident and playing so well. We hadn't been beaten for a long time and, in ten or eleven weeks, we had hardly had a goal scored against us.' Drums could be forgiven for dismissing St Pat's lightly, for they had completed the double over them in the League, with a 6–0 win at home and a 2–0 win away. Pat's, however, had proved their Cup mettle by twice travelling to Cork and coming away with a win each time. They also beat Cup-holders Shelbourne en route to the final.

When the League's top scorer, Dan McCaffrey, gave Drums the lead after ten minutes it seemed the double was on, but then the game turned around following a bizarre equalising goal. 'St Pat's got a free kick on the half-way line and Sean McCarthy squared it to Johnny White,' recalled Drumcondra goalkeeper Mick Smyth. 'He hit it towards goal, I saw it, came out and caught a glimpse of a red shirt out of the corner of my eye. By the time I looked back the ball was floating over my head into the net – the wind had caught it in that instant when I was distracted. At that moment I wished the ground would open up and swallow me.'

It was a bitter blow for the twenty-year-old goalie but it proved to be the only Cup final blemish in a career that took in seven deciders. Smyth was never subsequently on the losing side in a Cup final, winning five times with Shamrock

Rovers and once with Bohemians. He also went on to earn international and inter-League honours and had a short spell in England with Barrow.

For St Patrick's Athletic, it was their second Cup triumph in three years – each time as underdogs. Manager on each occasion was Jimmy Collins, the only goalkeeper to manage two Cup-winning teams, while the winning goal in both finals was struck by left-winger Willie Peyton. Wing-half Joe Clarke completed a notable double, having won an FAI Junior Cup medal with St Saviour's in 1959.

The 1961 Cup campaign was also notable for the departure of Paddy Coad, whose name had been synonymous with the Cup for more than twenty years. His goal for Waterford in the semi-final against Drumcondra was his forty-first Cup goal, a record which is unlikely to be surpassed. A native of Waterford, most of his goals were scored with Shamrock Rovers between 1942 and 1958, but he had short spells with his local club before and after his Milltown years. His total of eleven caps would have been much greater but for the war, and he was honoured on numerous occasions by the League of Ireland selectors between 1943 and 1955.

Coad played in eight finals, one with Waterford and the rest with Rovers, and missed another final through illness, but he was only on the winning side four times. However, as player-coach at Milltown, he built up a team in the 1950s which became known as 'Coad's Colts' and which was accepted as the team to beat. Coad's Colts set the standard for others to match, and their epic clashes with teams like Waterford, Drumcondra, St Patrick's Athletic, Shelbourne and Evergreen United ensured League of Ireland football a massive following.

First Round

18 February	Transport	0	Jacobs	1
			Sinclair	
19 February	Bohemians	0	Shelbourne	1
			Barber	
	Cork Celtic	1	St Patrick's Athletic	2
	Noonan		Curtin, O'Reilly	
	Cork Hibernians	1	Dundalk	0
	Morley pen.			
	Drumcondra	2	Workman's Club	1
	Connor o.g., Fullam pen.		O'Leary	
	Limerick	0	Shamrock Rovers	0
	Sligo Rovers	0	Waterford	1
			Crawford o.g.	
	Tycor Athletic	2	Albert Rovers	0
	Woods, Quinn			

First Round Replay

22 February	Shamrock Rovers	1	Limerick	0
	Ambrose			

Second Round

11 March	Jacobs	0	Cork Hibernians	0
12 March	St Patrick's Athletic	2	Shelbourne	1
	O'Rourke, McGeehan		Barber	
	Shamrock Rovers	0	Waterford	1
			Nolan o.g.	
	Tycor Athletic	0	Drumcondra	2
			Morrissey, McCaffrey	

Second Round Replay

15 March	Cork Hibernians	2	Jacobs	1
	Mooney, Collins		Murphy pen.	

(After extra time.)

Semi-Final – Dalymount Park

9 April	Drumcondra	4	Waterford	1
	Morrissey, McCaffrey, Pownall, Halpin		P. Coad	

Semi-Final – The Mardyke, Cork

9 April	Cork Hibernian	1	St Patrick's Athletic	2
	Vaughan		O'Rourke, Whelan	

Final – Dalymount Park

23 April	St Patrick's Athletic	2	Drumcondra	1
	White (22m), Peyton (57m)		McCaffrey (10m)	

St Patrick's Athletic: Dinny Lowry, Johnny White, Tommy Dunne, Joe Clarke, Sean McCarthy, Vinny O'Reilly, Pascal Curtin, Paddy 'Ginger' O'Rourke, Jimmy Redmond, Ronnie Whelan, Willie Peyton. Manager: Jimmy Collins

Drumcondra: Mick Smyth, Christy 'Bunny' Fullam, Alf Girvan, Robert Prole, Sean Smith, Tommy Rowe, Ray Keogh, Ned Halpin, Dan McCaffrey, Jimmy Morrissey, Stan Pownall

Referee: S. Spillane (Cork)   Attendance: 22,000

It's a Record!

- Sammy Spillane (Cork) and John Carpenter (Dublin) jointly hold the record for refereeing the most FAI Cup Finals. They each were in charge of three finals, but Carpenter's three involved two replays, while Spillane's involved one.

- The Bohemians–Shamrock Rovers final in 1945 attracted a crowd of 41,238.

1962

Smallpox Scare Hits Shels

Shamrock Rovers are the kingpins where the FAI Cup is concerned, so there is nothing any other team likes better than to lower their colours – especially in the final. While this feeling is true of every team in the League of Ireland, it is even more so in the case of Shelbourne, Rovers' traditional Ringsend rivals. In their early days, Rovers drew their support from the Ringsend side of the bridge, while Shels got their support from the city side. In 1962 that rivalry was as strong as ever and 29 April was a festive occasion in Ringsend as the great rivals met each other in the Cup final for the third time.

Rovers had come out on top in 1925 and 1944 but Shelbourne supporters had good reason to believe that 1962 would be different. Weren't the Reds League champions and hadn't they, nine days previously, hammered Rovers 6–2 in an important League game? With a young, exciting team, most of whom had won Cup medals in 1960, it seemed Shels for once were entitled to be favourites, especially as Rovers were in something of a transition period since the great Paddy Coad had returned to Waterford.

Fate, in the shape of a smallpox scare on the European continent, took a hand. The League of Ireland had arranged a game against the Italian Lega Nazionale for 6 May in Rimini and the players chosen had to be vaccinated against smallpox. Few players suffered any reaction but, unfortunately for Shelbourne, two who did were defenders Freddie Strahan and Tommy Carroll. Strahan spent the week before the final in bed with a high temperature. Another injection on the Saturday failed to bring any relief.

'I got out of bed as we were going for the double,' recalled Strahan, 'but I shouldn't have played. It was a scorching day and I was so weak I didn't have the legs. Even my father, who knew nothing about football, told me I got a roasting.' Ironically, it was revealed after the final that the smallpox injections had been unnecessary.

While Strahan had been suffering his temperature in silence, Rovers' troubles had been given plenty of press space. Tommy Hamilton, who had won a Cup medal in 1956, but was surprisingly omitted for the finals of 1957 and 1958, which Rovers lost, had been enjoying a tremendous season but was left out for the semi-final against Waterford. The press reacted strongly against what seemed another injustice to the likeable Bray man.

The issue was resolved when Tony Byrne, who had just made his way back into the team following an injury sustained on a US tour, injured his knee in training. He failed a fitness test at Milltown on the morning of the semi-final. Hamilton was recalled and promptly made the most of it with a fine display and the goal which earned Rovers a replay.

The Cup final was Hamilton's last competitive game for Rovers and he turned on the style, scoring twice in what he described as 'the best game I ever had with Rovers'. The following night he had a benefit game against Sunderland and then, as his business took him to Cork, he joined Cork Hibernians in an exchange that took Jackie Mooney to Milltown. To round off a great season, Hamilton was voted 'Personality of the Year' by the Soccer Writers' Association of Ireland.

First Round

18 February	Bohemians	1	Transport	1
	J. Boyce		Kane	
	Cork Celtic	3	**Dundalk**	2
	McDonagh o.g., Leahy, O'Leary		Cross, Callan	
	Drumcondra	3	**Ringmahon Rangers**	0
	Kennedy, Girvan, Keogh			
	Limerick	2	**St Patrick's Athletic**	3
	Mulvey 2		Whelan, O'Rourke, Peyton pen.	
	Sligo Rovers	3	**Shamrock Rovers**	3
	Turner, Munns 2		Hamilton, Bailham 2	
	Waterford	2	**Cork Hibernians**	1
	Sinnott, A. Casey		McElroy	
	Workman's Club	0	**Shelbourne**	2
			Hennessy, Hannigan	
25 February	**Pike Rovers**	2	**Longford Town**	1
	P. Hackett, Costelloe		Dodrill	

First Round Replays

21 February	Transport	1	Bohemians	3
	Fottrell		Boyce 2, Dowling	
28 February	Shamrock Rovers	1	Sligo Rovers	0
	O'Neill			

Second Round

11 March	Bohemians	0	Shamrock Rovers	1
			Bailham	
	Pike Rovers	1	**Shelbourne**	2
	Casey		Coleman, Wilson	
	St Patrick's Athletic	1	**Cork Celtic**	0
	Whelan			
	Waterford	2	**Drumcondra**	0
	J. Fitzgerald, D. Fitzgerald			

Semi-Finals – Dalymount Park

13 April	**Shelbourne**	**3**	**St Patrick's Athletic**	**0**
	Hannigan 2, Wilson			
15 April	**Shamrock Rovers**	**1**	**Waterford**	**1**
	Hamilton		Sinnott	

Semi-Final Replay – Tolka Park

18 April	**Shamrock Rovers**	**5**	**Waterford**	**2**
	Bailham 2, Ambrose,		Jimmy O'Neill, Dixon	
	O'Neill 2			

Final – Dalymount Park

28 April	**Shamrock Rovers**	**4**	**Shelbourne**	**1**
	Ambrose 2 (37m, 44m),		Barber (31m)	
	Hamilton 2 (63m, 85m)			

Shamrock Rovers: Paddy Henderson, John Keogh, Pat Courtney, Ronnie Nolan, Tommy Farrell, Eamonn Farrell, Frank O'Neill, Tommy Hamilton, Eddie Bailham, Paddy Ambrose, Tony O'Connell. Coach: Sean Thomas

Shelbourne: John Heavey, Tommy Carroll, Brendan O'Brien, Paddy Bonham, Freddie Strahan, Paddy Roberts, Joey Wilson, Ben Hannigan, Eric Barber, Jackie Hennessy, Ollie Conroy. Manager: Gerry Doyle

Referee: S. Spillane (Cork)   Attendance: 32,000

1963

Holland Puzzles Hammo

English referees have been in charge of many FAI Cup finals and, in 1963, one of the best of them, Arthur Holland, had the whistle for the game between Shelbourne and Cork Hibernians. Controversy surrounded one of his decisions, as Hibernians' inside-right Tommy Hamilton recalled: 'Shelbourne were winning 1–0 when their goalkeeper John Heavey tried a short kick-out to Freddie Strahan and Johnny Kingston nipped in and scored. The referee disallowed it and when I queried him he said the ball wasn't outside the area, but he changed that afterwards and said that he disallowed the goal because our trainer George O'Sullivan was still on the pitch after treating one of our players. We at Hibs always thought it was a good goal.'

Shelbourne were worthy winners on a day when a bus strike affected the attendance, but they had to depend on half-back Paddy Roberts and full-back Paddy Bonham (from a penalty) for their goals. (Bonham made the team because of an injury to regular left-back Brendan O'Brien.) Shelbourne were nearly deprived of another key figure, as centre-half and captain Freddie Strahan played with his right side plastered up from an injury received in the week prior to the final. Right-back Tommy Carroll became the fourth member of Shelbourne's 1959 Youth Cup-winning team to add a senior medal to his collection. He later played in England with Ipswich Town and Birmingham City.

Once again, Shelbourne's best displays came in the rounds before the Cup final. After being held to a draw by Drumcondra in the quarter-final, the return of veteran winger Ollie Conroy inspired a great 2–0 win in the replay, with Conroy laying on both goals. Shelbourne had to play most of the game with ten men, as inside-right Ben Hannigan was sent off. Hannigan, who had taken over after the early retirement of Christy Doyle, was a skillful but controversial figure and, in the final, referee Holland had to warn him early in the game. He quickly made amends, however, when he laid on the opening goal for Roberts. The semi-final was another good day for Shelbourne, as they beat their great rivals, Shamrock Rovers, whose form in the early rounds had given some indication of what was to come in the immediate future.

Shelbourne's win gave manager Gerry Doyle his second Cup win in four years, with a League title in between, but his dedication to the task didn't always meet with the approval of his family. 'The first round game against Jacobs was fixed for the same day as my daughter's wedding,' he recalled, 'so I had to leave the reception to attend the match. Needless to say, I wasn't very popular!'

Tommy Hamilton, who had won two Cup medals with Shamrock Rovers and had been surprisingly omitted from two other Cup final teams, got to the final in his first season with Hibernians, as he had done with Rovers and he repeated that feat in 1966 with Limerick after he had been persuaded to post-pone his retirement by Ewan Fenton, Limerick's player-manager. Tommy Eglington, Hibernians' left-winger, was playing in his fourth final, having won two medals with Shamrock Rovers in the 1940s before he moved to Everton. Although in his forties, Eglington had a marvellous season and scored two great Cup goals – the winner against Dundalk when time was running out and a tremendous left-foot volley in the semi-final against Limerick.

First Round

16 February	Jacobs	1	Shelbourne	3
	Kane		Roberts, Wilson, Dunne	
17 February	Cork Hibernians	2	St Patrick's Athletic	1
	Kingston 2		Whelan	
	Dundalk	2	Waterford	0
	Hasty, Redmond			
	Limerick	3	Home Farm	1
	F. McNamara 2, O'Connor		Dixon	
	Shamrock Rovers	3	Cork Celtic	0
	Mooney, Bailham, O'Connell			
	Transport	5	Cobh Ramblers	0
	Bailey 2, Dixon, Byrne 2			

Byes: Bohemians and Drumcondra

Second Round

10 March	Dundalk	1	Cork Hibernians	2
	Hasty		Eglington, O'Flynn	
	Limerick	2	Transport	2
	O'Connor, Conroy		Bennett, McDonagh	
	Shamrock Rovers	7	Bohemians	3
	Fullam, Mooney 4, O'Neill, Nolan		Boyce, Maguire 2	
	Drumcondra	3	Shelbourne	3
	Dixon 3		Wilson 2, Barber	

Second Round Replays

13 March	Shelbourne	2	Drumcondra	0
	Hannigan, Hennessy			
20 March	Transport	1	Limerick	2
	Bennett		O'Connor, Finucane	

Semi-Final – Flower Lodge

7 April	Cork Hibernians	4	Limerick	1
	Kingston 3, Eglington		O'Brien	

Semi-Final – Dalymount Park

7 April **Shelbourne** 2 **Shamrock Rovers** 0
Hennessy 2

Final – Dalymount Park

21 April **Shelbourne** 2 **Cork Hibernians** 0
Roberts (17m),
Bonham pen. (79m)

Shelbourne: John Heavey, Tommy Carroll, Paddy Bonham, Paddy Roberts, Freddie Strahan, Tony Corrigan, Joe Wilson, Ben Hannigan, Eric Barber, Jackie Hennessy, Ollie Conroy. Manager: Gerry Doyle

Cork Hibernians: Bobby Brohan, Jerry Lane, Jackie Morley, Tony Allen, Noel O'Mahony, Pat O'Callaghan, Mick Aherne, Tommy Hamilton, Johnny Kingston, Donie Wallace, Tommy Eglington. Manager: Tommy Moroney

Referee: A. Holland (Barnsley)   Attendance: 15,000

It's a Record!

- When Dessie and Richie Baker and Stephen and Declan Geoghegan helped Shelbourne defeat Bohemians in the 2000 Cup final, it was the first time that two sets of brothers featured on an FAI Cup-winning team.

1964

Byrne In – Thomas Out

When Shamrock Rovers beat Cork Celtic in a replay to win the 1964 Cup final, they completed the Grand Slam of League, Shield, Leinster Cup and FAI Cup. It should have seen coach Sean Thomas's job secure for another few years. Instead, it meant the parting of the ways because international right-winger Frank O'Neill had been dropped for the replay, utility forward Tony Byrne taking over.

'Worried by the closeness of the first game, the directors took the amazing decision to drop Frank O'Neill for the replay,' recalled Thomas. 'That hurt me more than one could visualise. Frank did not have a great game in the final but his work over the season was nothing short of fantastic. He was truly the architect of many of our victories. For me, O'Neill's omission was the last straw and brought to a head my decision to leave the club. I did not have complete control over team selection but the team picked itself. However, on a couple of occasions prior to the Cup final, players had been left out of the side and, although I disagreed with the directors, it was their club and no amount of arguing from me could change their thinking. In the midst of my disillusionment, Bohemians made me an offer I couldn't refuse. While I was jumping from one end of the League table to the other, I was to become my own man, with complete responsibility for all team affairs at Dalymount Park.'

Fortunately for Rovers, replacement Byrne was fighting fit for his unexpected call-up. 'A good friend of mine, Jim Kavanagh, gave me access to the Guinness gym and so I was doing double training – circuit training with weights, which

Rovers never did, as well as the usual training,' he recalled. 'I was mad fit for the replay even though I hadn't played a lot of games that season.' Byrne, who years later took a controlling interest in Rovers' traditional rivals, Shelbourne, had a good game in the 2–1 replay win.

Ronnie Nolan, the wing-half whose career at Rovers spanned the great side of 1956 as well as the 1964 side, had this to say: 'The 1964 team was more effective than the 1956 team. They couldn't be knocked off their game as easily. They were more professional and could mix it better. They could overcome difficulties the 1956 team couldn't, for example, tight marking, etc. Their record was phenomenal – they played about sixty games and lost only three. The only trophy we didn't win was the Top Four – Dundalk beat us in the final.' Added to their other assets, the 1964 team was prepared to defy pain in order to play, as exemplified by captain Liam Tuohy, who had two ribs cracked in a clash with Celtic's Ray Cowhie and played on in terrible pain. His visit to the hospital had to wait until he collected the Cup!

Rovers' Cup campaign had got off to a sensational start when, drawn against their nearest League rivals Dundalk in what was obviously the match of the first round, they accepted an offer to play Spain's B team in Madrid – just four days before the Cup tie! The Spaniards, who included notables such as Iribar and Ufarte, hammered Rovers 7–2 – the only time the Milltown men were outclassed that season. However, Dundalk suffered the backlash, with Rovers recording a super 7–0 Cup win.

Adding lustre to Rovers' achievements is the comment of Donal Leahy, centre-forward for defeated finalists Cork Celtic: 'The 1964 team was the best Celtic team ever,' he claimed. It can't have helped their morale that manager Liam O'Neill, the former Cork United and Belfast Celtic star, was not in Dalymount Park for the Cup final.

The final replay was notable for the introduction of the first substitute in a Cup final, when Shamrock Rovers' centre-back Tommy Farrell was replaced by Sean Smith after eighteen minutes. The FAI are often criticised, but they were ahead of their rivals in this matter. The first substitute in an English FA Cup Final was in 1968.

First Round

14 February   **TEK United**   3   Shelbourne   7
Giles 2, Johnston   Dunne 2, Barber 2,
Dowling 2, Boyce

Bohemians   2   **Transport**   2
M. Conroy, E. Kinsella   J. Byrne, Bennett pen.

15 February   **Cork Celtic**   2   **St Patrick's Athletic**   1
Noonan, Leahy   Bates

Drogheda   1   Glasheen   0
McCaffrey

Drumcondra   2   Cork Hibernians   0
Lynch, Cowzer

Jacobs   2   Waterford   1
Waters 2   J. Fitzgerald

Limerick   3   Sligo Rovers   1
Doyle 2, O'Brien   Norris

Shamrock Rovers   7   Dundalk   0
Mooney 3, Bailham 3,
Ambrose

First Round Replay

19 February   **Transport**   2   **Bohemians**   3
Bennett, Burke   Conroy, Burke o.g., Kearin

Second Round

6 March   **Drumcondra**   1   Drogheda   0
Lynch

8 March   **Jacobs**   2   **Bohemians**   3
Brennan, W. Young o.g.   L. Gilmore 3

Limerick   0   **Shamrock Rovers**   1
Bailham

Shelbourne   1   **Cork Celtic**   3
Hennessy   McCarthy, O'Mahony pen.,
Casey

Semi-Final – Flower Lodge

5 April   **Cork Celtic**   **2**   **Bohemians**   **0**
Casey, Leahy

Semi-Final – Dalymount Park

5 April   **Shamrock Rovers**   **1**   **Drumcondra**   **0**
Tuohy

Final – Dalymount Park

26 April   **Shamrock Rovers**   **1**   **Cork Celtic**   **1**
Mooney (49m)   Leahy (81m)

Shamrock Rovers: Pat Dunne, John Keogh, Pat Courtney, Ronnie Nolan, Tommy Farrell, Johnny Fullam, Frank O'Neill, Jackie Mooney, Eddie Bailham, Paddy Ambrose, Liam 'Rasher' Tuohy. Manager: Sean Thomas

Cork Celtic: Kevin Blount, Liam O'Flynn, Pat O'Mahony, Ray Cowhie, John Coughlan, Mick Millington, Paul O'Donovan, Austin Noonan, Donal Leahy, Al Casey, Frank McCarthy. Manager: Liam O'Neill

Referee: D. A. Corbett (Wolverhampton)   Attendance: 35,500

Final Replay – Dalymount Park

29 April   **Shamrock Rovers**   **2**   **Cork Celtic**   **1**
Bailham 2 (68m pen., 86m)   Casey (75m)

Shamrock Rovers: Tony Byrne for O'Neill. Sub: Sean Smith for Farrell, (18m)
Cork Celtic: George Lynam for Coughlan

Referee: D. A. Corbett (Wolverhampton)   Attendance: 23,600

1965

Mary Jane Spins A Yarn

On his way to the FAI Cup Semi-Final between Cork Celtic and Shamrock Rovers at Flower Lodge in April 1965, the English referee travelled on the same train as the Rovers' party. Ever one with an eye to the main chance, Mary Jane Cunningham, wife of Rovers' boss Joe Cunningham, entertained the referee with a liberal dose of Irish spirits – and graphic examples of the rough play to be expected from the Cork Celtic team! It was a typical example of gamesmanship by the formidable Mary Jane but, in the event, it proved unnecessary as winger Tony O'Connell gave Rovers the lead as early as the third minute and Celtic subsequently never played up to form. Rovers' 3–0 win was their first at the 'Lodge'.

Down through the years after the Cunninghams took over Rovers in 1936, Mary Jane, the daughter of a former Committee man, exerted a tremendous influence – some say the dominant influence – on club policy. The team was selected over a meal at the Cunningham home in Donnybrook and, rightly or wrongly, Mary Jane was given the blame when a controversial choice was made. For instance, the dropping of player-coach jimmy Dunne for the 1942 Cup semi-final was traced to a game in Cork two weeks previously when Mary Jane's vociferous promptings caused the gentlemanly Dunne to put his fingers to his lips in admonition!

Mercenary matters were another bone of contention at Milltown right from the start of the Cunningham reign, when William 'Sacky' Glen, Charlie Reid and Peadar Gaskins all left the fold after a dispute over financial terms. Here again,

Mary Jane had a singleminded approach as witness her response to Eddie Bailham's late goal which gave Rovers a 1–0 win over Limerick at the Market's Field during the 1964 Cup campaign. 'Weren't we unlucky,' she said, 'we nearly got them to Milltown.'

Rovers' Cup final opponents in 1965 were Limerick, appearing in their first final and led by Scottish player-manager Ewan Fenton, a veteran of Blackpool's win in the 1953 English FA Cup. He had bad news for his team on their train journey to Dublin for the semi-final against League champions Drumcondra. 'We were told that goalkeeper Kevin Fitzpatrick was out because of 'flu,' recalled Al Finucane. 'That was a bad blow to us as no one gave us a chance anyway.'

'Our reserve goalie, Eddie Connelly, had gone home to Dublin but had left his boots in Limerick,' recalled Fenton, 'so I had to chase around for his boots when Kevin went sick. I told Eddie to report but he probably didn't know he was going to play.' Connelly, who had no first team experience, played a blinder, an early save of his being particularly vital. Limerick got through 1–0 but Fitzpatrick was back for the final.

It took Rovers two games to dispose of Limerick in the final but, for most observers, the first game was marred by the tragic broken leg suffered by Limerick winger Michael Doyle. 'His injury was a great tragedy,' said Fenton. 'He was going to be one of the all-time greats in Ireland. He came through with Finucane and Fitzpatrick and he was a natural. He had so much going for him. He had two great feet.' Fortunately, the rule allowing substitutes had been introduced the previous year, so Denis Linnane came in for Doyle. It was a near thing, though, for in those first years subs were only allowed in the first forty-five minutes and Doyle was injured in the forty-first!

First Round

10 February	TEK United	1	Shelbourne	3
	Brock		Barber, Bonham pen., Conroy	
12 February	Belgrove	2	Transport	1
	Sullivan, Reardon		Burke pen.	
14 February	Drogheda	1	Limerick	2
	Lynch		Mulvey, Mitchell	
	Drumcondra	3	Cork Hibernians	0
	Brooks, Kingston 2			
	Glasheen	0	Shamrock Rovers	1
			Dunne	
	St Patrick's Athletic	2	Bohemians	1
	Roche pen., Cheevers		Murray pen.	
	Sligo Rovers	0	Dundalk	3
			McGrath 2, Masterson pen.	
	Waterford	0	Cork Celtic	3
			Casey 2, Noonan	

Second Round

7 March	Cork Celtic	1	Belgrove	1
	Groeger		V. O'Riordan	
	St Patrick's Athletic	1	Limerick	1
	Whelan		Mulvey	
	Shamrock Rovers	3	Dundalk	1
	Nolan, Mooney, Caswell o.g.		Hasty	
	Shelbourne	1	Drumcondra	2
	Hannigan		Kingston, Campbell	

Second Round Replays

10 March	Belgrove	0	Cork Celtic	1
			Casey	
11 March	Limerick	2	St Patrick's Athletic	1
	Keogh o.g., O'Rourke		Peyton	

Semi-Final – Dalymount Park

| 4 April | Limerick | 1 | Drumcondra | 0 |
| | Mitchell | | | |

Semi-Final – Flower Lodge

Shamrock Rovers   3   **Cork Celtic**   0
O'Connell, Mooney,
Fullam pen.

Final – Dalymount Park

25 April   **Shamrock Rovers**   1   **Limerick**   1
Dunne (63m)   Mulvey (70m)

Shamrock Rovers: Mick Smyth, John Keogh, Pat Courtney, Ronnie Nolan, Tommy Farrell, Paddy Mulligan, Frank O'Neill, Jackie Mooney, Noel Dunne, Johnny Fullam, Liam 'Rasher' Tuohy. Manager: Liam Tuohy

Limerick: Kevin Fitzpatrick, Vinny Quinn, Joe Casey, Al Finucane, Ewan Fenton, Dessie McNamara, Dick O'Connor, Eddie Mulvey, Peter Mitchell, Paddy 'Ginger' O'Rourke, Mick Doyle. Sub.: Denis Linnane for Doyle, 41m. Manager: Ewan Fenton

Referee: S. Spillane (Cork)   Attendance: 22,000

Final Replay – Dalymount Park

28 April   **Shamrock Rovers**   1   **Limerick**   0
Fullam (55m)

Shamrock Rovers: Tony O'Connell for Tuohy
Limerick: Denis Linnane for Doyle

Referee: S. Spillane (Cork)   Attendance: 19,436

1966

Tears for Finucane

The laneway at the back of the Dalymount Park stand has hosted many emotional scenes in the aftermath of Cup final day, and 1966 was no exception. Heartbroken Limerick wing-half Al Finucane was in tears as he spoke to his mother and father and to the distraught Limerick fans who had gathered to console their heroes following a second successive defeat by the mighty Shamrock Rovers.

The door of the official entrance opened and the Limerick group turned to see who was coming out. Rovers' captain, Ronnie Nolan, emerged with his kit bag in one hand and the FAI Cup in the other. He walked down to his car, opened the boot, threw in the Cup with his kit and drove home. Familiarity breeds contempt.

The Limerick fans were dumbfounded. What they had witnessed amounted practically to sacrilege. In their hearts they knew that, had it been a Limerick victory, the Cup would have returned to Shannon-side in splendour, bonfires would have burned, the Cup would have been paraded through the town. The blow of defeat wasn't softened by the thought of the Cup bouncing around Nolan's boot on its way to his Kimmage home.

That moment, more than any other, sticks in Finucane's mind when he looks back to the 1966 final. It served to heighten his resolve to bring the Cup back to Limerick some day.

Finucane was the most successful Limerick player ever, but he had player-manager Ewan Fenton to thank for his career in the League of Ireland. An inauspicious spell at inside-forward in his early days had led the Board of Directors to form the view that he wouldn't make the grade, but Fenton persuaded them to retain him, claiming that the experience up front would serve him well in his best position of wing-half. And so it proved, with Finucane being honoured at international and inter-League level and winning every domestic honour apart from a League medal.

Fenton's shrewdness also paid off in the semi-final replay against Sligo Rovers, which was played under lights at Tolka Park. Limerick normally objected to playing under the Tolka lights but, on this occasion, knowing that Sligo centre-half David Pugh was short-sighted, they agreed to the venue – and a match plan of hitting long balls down the middle worked to Limerick's advantage.

Limerick also suffered the unusual fate of having to play their second round home tie against Dundalk at a neutral venue. Their usual home ground, the Market's Field, was unavailable because the greyhound track was being extended; the alternative venue, Thomond Park, which had been used for their first round tie with Bohemians, was also unavailable, so the game eventually went ahead at Dalymount Park, despite Dundalk's best efforts to get the game to Oriel Park.

Fenton was not despondent at Limerick's second Cup final defeat by Shamrock Rovers. 'Rovers were some team,' was his view, 'and for us to compete and get so close was a great feat. We didn't disgrace ourselves in any way. We hadn't even got to a Cup final before 1965.'

First Round

11 February	Dalkey United	3	Transport	1
	F. Byrne, McDonnell, Kane		J. Byrne	
13 February	Cork Hibernians	1	Shamrock Rovers	1
	McCole		O'Connell	
	Drumcondra	0	Cork Celtic	2
			Leahy, O'Donovan	
	Dundalk	1	St Patrick's Athletic	1
	Hasty		Peyton	
	Limerick	3	Bohemians	1
	O'Connor, McNamara,		T. O'Connor	
	T. Hamilton pen.			
	Sligo Rovers	1	Drogheda	1
	Burnside		Gardiner	
	Tramore Athletic	1	Shelbourne	4
	Fitzgerald		Barber, Strahan pen.,	
			Conroy, Walsh	
	Waterford	4	Home Farm	0
	Lynch 3, Casey			

First Round Replays

16 February	Drogheda	1	Sligo Rovers	2
	Dunne		Burnside, Morrisson	
	Shamrock Rovers	3	Cork Hibernians	1
	Tuohy, O'Neill 2 (1 pen.)		Allen	
23 February	St Patrick's Athletic	1	Dundalk	2
	Peyton pen.		Bushe, Hasty	

Second Round

5 March	Limerick	3	Dundalk	0
	Finucane, O'Brien, Mulvey			
	(At Dalymount Park)			
6 March	Cork Celtic	1	Sligo Rovers	1
	Byrnes		Dunne	
	Dalkey United	0	Waterford	2
			O'Neill 2	
	Shamrock Rovers	1	Shelbourne	1
	Tuohy		Barber	

Second Round Replays

9 March	Shelbourne	0	Shamrock Rovers	1
			O'Neill pen.	

(After extra time.)

	Sligo Rovers	3	Cork Celtic	0
	Turner, Dowling, Dunne			

Semi-Final – Dalymount Park

2 April	Shamrock Rovers	2	Waterford	2
	Tuohy, Gilbert		Coad, Casey	

Semi-Final – Tolka Park

3 April	Limerick	0	Sligo Rovers	0

Semi-Final Replay – Dalymount Park

6 April	Shamrock Rovers	4	Waterford	2
	O'Neill 2, Gilbert 2		O'Neill, McGeough	

Semi-Final Replay – Tolka Park

13 April	Limerick	3	Sligo Rovers	0
	Hamilton 2, Curtin			

Final – Dalymount Park

24 April	Shamrock Rovers	2	Limerick	0
	O'Connell (66m), O'Neill (83m)			

Shamrock Rovers: Mick Smyth, John Keogh, Pat Courtney, Paddy Mulligan, Ronnie Nolan, Johnny Fullam, Frank O'Neill, Brian Tyrrell, Bobby Gilbert, Tony O'Connell, Noel Hayes. Manager: Liam Tuohy

Limerick: Kevin Fitzpatrick, Vinny Quinn, Joe Casey, Al Finucane, Ewan Fenton, Dessie McNamara, Dick O'Connor, Tommy Hamilton, Eddie Mulvey, Joe O'Brien, Pascal Curtin. Manager: Ewan Fenton

Referee: P. Graham (Dublin)   Attendance: 26,898

1967

The Fifty-bob TV Money

When the question of live television coverage of the FAI Cup Final came up in 1967, delegates Bart Cummins (St Patrick's Athletic) and Des Cunningham (Shamrock Rovers) were keen supporters of the idea. 'We felt it had to come,' said Cummins. 'Our concern was to propagate the game.' A fee in the lower hundreds was agreed with the national television station, RTÉ, but the immediate effect was a practical halving of the attendance at the game, which featured the all-Dublin pairing of Cup-holders Shamrock Rovers and doughty Cup fighters St Patrick's Athletic. Cummins and Cunningham had their moment of glory, causing quite a stir when, as presidents of their clubs, they led out their teams, a function which it had been felt would be left to the respective managers, as was the practice in England. However, the status of League of Ireland managers was not too high in the 1960s.

For the players there was an extra bonus of £2.10.0 for TV appearance money. Rovers' striker Mick Leech, who had made his debut in the semi-final, recalled that his biggest impression after the final, which was a lacklustre affair, was the neighbours saying, 'We saw you on the telly.' Rovers' players had other things on their minds for, after playing West Ham United in a benefit match, they departed for a seven-week stint in the United States. Still, they managed to beat Pat's 3–2.

A familiar figure was missing from Rovers' line-out in the final – Ronnie Nolan was left out for the first time in almost fifteen years. Pressure of work led to difficulties with training and a resultant loss of form. He was dropped in the reshuffle for the semi-final, which led to the introduction of Mick Leech, and was left out of the squad for the final. Rovers obviously thought he was finished and, the following November, he went to Bohemians as manager, a post which led to him winning a seventh FAI Cup medal.

With Rovers, Nolan had tasted success all the way but, as he recalled, he had been prepared for it: 'When I joined Rovers in the early fifties, a lot of us had been with successful schoolboy teams and we expected success rather than hoped for it. Of the team that won the Cup in 1955, Hughie Gannon, Mickey Burke, Gerry Mackey and I all played with Johnville.' In a fifteen-year career with Rovers, he won six Cup medals, four League medals, ten international caps and was a regular on the League of Ireland team for over ten years. He was versatile, too. Although most often named at right-half, he also filled in at left-full and centre-back, not just for League games, but in Cup finals as well.

According to ace Manchester United scout Billy Behan, Ronnie Nolan was the best League of Ireland player never to leave Ireland. 'Ronnie was the best defensive wing-half that I ever saw in the League of Ireland – he was absolutely brilliant . . . because he could read the game,' said Behan.

Three times Behan was foiled in his attempt to sign Nolan for United. First, because Ronnie's father wanted him to finish his apprenticeship as a fitter; second, because acting manager Jimmy Murphy felt he couldn't sign a part-timer during United's hour of need after the Munich disaster; third, when Matt Busby, recovering from the injuries he received in Munich, was delayed a few weeks in coming over to see Nolan and, in that time, signed Maurice Setters. Nolan was brilliant when Busby was present, but the United manager felt he couldn't sign another right-half, although acknowledging that Ronnie was as good as Setters, if not better!

First Round

12 February	Bohemians	3	Tullamore	0
	O'Sullivan 3			
	Cork Celtic	0	St Patrick's Athletic	1
			Dunne	
	Cork Hibernians	0	Sligo Rovers	0
	Drogheda	1	Bridewell	1
	Whelan		P. O'Connor	
	Dundalk	6	Tramore Athletic	1
	Stokes 3, Hale, O'Connell, Hannigan		Goggin pen.	
	Home Farm	1	Drumcondra	0
	Morrissey o.g.			
	Limerick	1	Waterford	0
	Morrissey o.g.			
	Shamrock Rovers	1	Shelbourne	0
	Kearin			

First Round Replays

15 February	Sligo Rovers	2	Cork Hibernians	3
	Brooks 2		O'Callaghan, Connolly, Noonan	
22 February	Bridewell	0	Drogheda	3
			Kidd, Culligan, O'Reilly	

Second Round

5 March	Bohemians	0	Drogheda	2
			Gardiner, O'Reilly	
	Dundalk	1	Cork Hibernians	1
	Hale		Murphy	
	Limerick	0	St Patrick's Athletic	1
			Peyton	
	Shamrock Rovers	2	Home Farm	1
	Tuohy 2		Daly	

Second Round Replay

8 March	Cork Hibernians	0	Dundalk	1
			Callan	

Semi-Final – Dalymount Park

1 April	Shamrock Rovers	1	Dundalk	1
	Leech		Stokes	

Semi-Final – Tolka Park

2 April	St Patrick's Athletic	1	Drogheda	0
	Bates			

Semi-Final Replay – Tolka Park

5 April	Shamrock Rovers	3	Dundalk	0
	Dixon, Leech 2			

Final – Dalymount Park

23 April	Shamrock Rovers	3	St Patrick's Athletic	2
	O'Neill pen. (39m),		Dunne (31m), Bates (44m)	
	Leech (50m), Dixon (80m)			

Shamrock Rovers: Mick Smyth, John Keogh, Pat Courtney, Johnny Fullam, Paddy Mulligan, Mick Kearin, Frank O'Neill, Billy Dixon, Bobby Gilbert, Mick Leech, Tommy Kinsella. Manager: Liam Tuohy

St Patrick's Athletic: Dinny Lowry, Paddy Dowling, Vinny O'Reilly, Willie Roche, Doug Boucher, Jackie Hennessy, Gerry Monaghan, Noel Dunne, Noel Bates, Johnny Campbell, Willie Peyton. Manager: Gerry Doyle

Referee: P. P. Coates (Dublin)   Attendance: 12,000

1968

The Greaves of Irish Soccer

When Shamrock Rovers' B team manager, Paddy Ambrose, spotted nineteen-year-old Mick Leech in action, he reported back, tongue in cheek, to manager Liam Tuohy: 'You won't like him. All he does is score goals.' By the time he was twenty-one, Leech had won three FAI Cup medals – and he had scored in each final. He was undoubtedly the key man in Rovers' triumphs of 1967, 1968 and 1969. He made his Cup debut in the 1967 semi-final against Dundalk and only played a total of nine Cup games from then until the 1969 final replay, yet his goal tally was an impressive fourteen. No wonder he was dubbed 'the Jimmy Greaves of Irish soccer'!

Perhaps the most memorable of those Cup campaigns was that of 1968, when a young Rovers team got through to a final meeting with League champions Waterford. Rovers were hoping to equal the five-in-a-row Cup success of their predecessors in the 1930s, but Waterford had been so impressive in the League that they were made favourites. Rovers triumphed, thanks to sweeper Johnny Fullam and ace opportunist Leech. Manager Liam Tuohy considered centre-half Frank Brady – an older brother of Republic of Ireland midfielder, Liam – too inexperienced for the task of marking Waterford danger man Mick Lynch, so he experimented with Fullam as a sweeper for the first time. The classy Fullam did a perfect job in marshalling his defence to cancel out the threat of the free-scoring Waterford forward line.

Leech, who missed the first two rounds of the Cup through injury, scored two in the semi-final to put-paid to Dundalk and gave a repeat performance to scupper Waterford's hopes of the double in the final. His second goal was a classic, with Leech calmly taking the ball round the despairing dive of Peter Thomas and pushing it into the net. 'There were only about two minutes to go,' recalled Leech. 'As I was coming out Peter was sitting there dejectedly and I patted him on the head and said, "Hard luck, Thommo, there's always next year".' Little did either player know that it would take Thomas twelve years to win that elusive Cup medal.

Another Rovers youngster, Mick Lawlor, son of the former Drumcondra and Republic of Ireland forward 'Kit' Lawlor, weighed in with a goal in each round of the Cup. Kit had won a medal with Drums in 1957, but Mick did a lot better, winning four medals – two each with Rovers and Dundalk.

Leech, whose philosophy was 'the ball has just got to cross the line', was noted for his quicksilver anticipation in the penalty area and scored most of his goals in or around the six-yard box. 'I never got the jitters before Cup finals or internationals,' he said. 'In fact, I enjoyed playing before big crowds. I reacted to the atmosphere.' In 1968, the Cup final attendance was over 39,000, the second highest ever.

In 1969 Leech missed Rovers' semi-final games with Shelbourne due to damaged knee ligaments. 'My first match back was the final against Cork Celtic,' he recalled. 'I got a big injection in my knee to get me ready, but the hard ground didn't suit me and I was so bad I was taken off. Three days later it was touch and go if I played but it rained, Liam Tuohy put me in and I scored twice. Tuohy left after that final and for me, Rovers was never the same after. He had been a tremendous influence on me. He was the best.'

Leech and Tuohy teamed up again in Brazil in 1972 when Tuohy was manager of the Republic of Ireland team in a mini-World Cup tournament. Once again, Tuohy brought the best out of Leech, who scored two goals in four games and was named in the best eleven from Ireland's group. Paddy Mulligan was the only other Irishman in a 4-2-4 line-up which included the great Portuguese forward Eusebio.

First Round

11 February	Athlone Town	0	Shelbourne	2
			Conroy, O'Connor	
	Bohemians	1	Limerick	2
	J. Doran		J. Murphy, McEvoy	
	Cork Hibernians	3	Drumcondra	4
	Fogarty 2, McSweeney		Hand 2, Brohan o.g., Whelan	
	Shamrock Rovers	2	Cork Celtic	0
	Lawlor, P. O'Mahony o.g.			
	Sligo Rovers	1	Dundalk	1
	Holden		Hannigan	
	Tramore Athletic	0	St Patrick's Athletic	3
			Dunne, Bates, Ryan	
	Waterford	1	Drogheda	0
	J. O'Neill			
14 February	St Brendan's	1	Home Farm	3
	James o.g.		Duffy, McDonnell o.g., Fullam o.g.	

First Round Replay

15 February	Dundalk	4	Sligo Rovers	0
	Hannigan, Hale 2, Burke			

Second Round

3 March	Dundalk	1	Limerick	0
	Murray pen.			
	Home Farm	1	Drumcondra	2
	Daly		Hand pen., Morrissey	
	Shamrock Rovers	1	Shelbourne	0
	Lawlor			
	Waterford	6	St Patrick's Athletic	0
	McGeough, Matthews 2, Lynch 2, O'Neill pen.			

Semi-Final – Tolka Park

30 March	Shamrock Rovers	3	Dundalk	0
	Leech 2, Lawlor			

Semi-Final – Dalymount Park

| 31 March | Waterford | 2 | Drumcondra | 1 |
| | O'Neill, Hale | | Hand pen. | |

Final – Dalymount Park

21 April	Shamrock Rovers	3	Waterford	0
	Leech 2 (64m, 89m),			
	Lawlor (69m)			

Shamrock Rovers: Mick Smyth, Jimmy Gregg, Pat Courtney, Mick Kearin, Frank Brady, Johnny Fullam, Frank O'Neill, Mick Lawlor, Bobby Gilbert, Mick Leech, Damien Richardson. Manager: Liam Tuohy

Waterford: Peter Thomas, Peter Byran, Paul Morrissey, Vinny Maguire, Jackie Morley, Jimmy McGeough, John O'Neill, Alfie Hale, Mick Lynch, Shamie Coad, Johnny Matthews. Manager: Vinny Maguire

Referee: O. McCarthy (Cork)   Attendance: 39,128

It's a Record!

- The highest-scoring finals were those of 1935, when Bohemians beat Dundalk, and 2006, when Derry City beat St Patrick's Athletic. Both had a 4–3 scoreline.

1969

Leahy Drowns His Sorrows

After fifteen years and two FAI Cup Finals but no winner's medal, 1969 was the year when Cork Celtic centre-forward Donal Leahy finally got his hands on the Cup – and received a winner's medal as well.

The 1968-69 season saw Leahy phasing out his own involvement and taking charge of Celtic's reserve team. However, when Cup-time came around, player-manager Billy McCullough, the former Arsenal and Northern Ireland centre-half, persuaded Leahy to make a comeback as the attack was in need of a spearhead. After a couple of League games in which he came on as sub, Leahy lined out in the first round tie against Drumcondra – and scored the winner.

St Patrick's Athletic were disposed of in the second round, and then Celtic were faced with a four-game marathon semi-final against Limerick, in which the dice were eventually loaded in Celtic's favour. The first game was in Cork, the second in Limerick, the third in Cork, but the fourth was in Tolka Park, with the Limerick camp justifiably claiming a raw deal. There was only one goal between the teams in the end – and Leahy supplied it again.

The final was another heartbreak for Leahy and his Celtic teammates. Leading 1–0 for most of the game through a John Carroll goal, time was running out on an ineffective Shamrock Rovers when the Cup-holders got a stroke of luck. Paddy Mulligan tried a header which appeared to be going wide when Celtic right-full John Keogh, a former Rovers' player, deflected it into his own goal. Some of the Celtic players were so convinced they had blown their chance that they stayed in Dublin overnight and had a boozing session! One of the features of the game had been centre-back Eamon Heffernan's dominance of Rovers' ace marksman Mick Leech. For the replay, manager Liam Tuohy introduced Damien Richardson on Heffernan and put Leech on McCullough. Cork fell for it and Leech took McCullough to the cleaners.

After the game, a disconsolate but ever-sporting Leahy went to the Rovers' dressing room to invite the players to Celtic's function in the North Star Hotel, as Rovers had had their function on the Sunday. To his dismay he found the players were all gone but the Cup was still there, in the company of one official. So Leahy brought the Cup to Celtic's party, club officials filled it and the players drowned their sorrows from it!

Later they were joined by some of the Rovers players and Leahy, in conversation with Johnny Fullam, a friend from many inter-League trips, remarked how disappointed he was, after fifteen years in football, to have no Cup medal, just two runners-up. Fullam said nothing but shortly after in the post Leahy received one of the Dubliner's medals with the request that one of Leahy's runners-up medals be sent in return; a nice gesture from one of the greats of League of Ireland football to another great who hadn't got all he deserved from the game. In fact, Leahy's career suffered because he was based in Cork at a time when the power base was solidly in Dublin. Drumcondra boss Bob 'Sam' Prole, an international selector at the time, tried to woo Leahy to Dublin and guaranteed him an international cap if he signed. Leahy, who had been in three World Cup squads without making even one appearance as a sub, declined Prole's offer.

First Round

7 February	Shelbourne	0	Transport	0
9 February	Drumcondra	0	Cork Celtic	1
			Leahy	
	Jacobs	0	Ringmahon Rangers	0
	Limerick	2	Cork Hibernians	1
	O'Brien, McEvoy		Sheehan	
	Longford Town	2	Sligo Rovers	0
	Hogan, Bermingham			
	St Patrick's Athletic	3	Bohemians	1
	McDonnell, Campbell 2 (1 pen.)		Hamill	
	Shamrock Rovers	3	Dundalk	0
	Richardson, Leech 2			
	Waterford	5	Drogheda	2
	Matthews 2, Hale 2, Buck		Whelan, Ennis	

First Round Replays

12 February	Transport	2	Shelbourne	3
	Cowzer, Boyce		Delargy 2, Dempsey	
15 February	Ringmahon Rangers	3	Jacobs	1
	Coleman, Gosnell 2		Keogh	

Second Round

2 March	Cork Celtic	2	St Patrick's Athletic	1
	Calnan, O'Mahony pen.		Brady	
	Limerick	1	Waterford	0
	Mitchell			
	Longford Town	0	Shelbourne	2
			Delargy pen., Murray	
	Shamrock Rovers	4	Ringmahon Rangers	0
	Leech 2, Richardson, O'Neill			

Semi-Final – Flower Lodge

30 March	Limerick	1	Cork Celtic	1
	Bartley		Calnan	

Semi-Final – Dalymount Park

Shamrock Rovers	1	**Shelbourne**	1
O'Neill pen.		Campbell	

Semi-Final Replay – Tolka Park

2 April	**Shamrock Rovers**	1	**Shelbourne**	0
	Lawlor			

Semi-Final Replay – Thomond Park

3 April	**Cork Celtic**	1	**Limerick**	1
	McCarthy		McEvoy	

(After extra time.)

Semi-Final Second Replay – Flower Lodge

10 April	**Cork Celtic**	0	**Limerick**	0

Semi-Final Third Replay – Tolka Park

15 April	**Cork Celtic**	1	**Limerick**	0
	Leahy			

Final – Dalymount Park

20 April	**Shamrock Rovers**	1	**Cork Celtic**	1
	Keogh o.g. (82m)		Carroll (27m)	

Shamrock Rovers: Mick Smyth, Christy Canavan, Pat Courtney, Paddy Mulligan, David Pugh, Mick Kearin, Frank O'Neill, Ben Hannigan, Mick Leech, Mick Lawlor, Tom Kinsella. Sub.: Hugh Brophy for Leech, 79m. Manager: Liam Tuohy

Cork Celtic: Tommy Taylor, John Keogh, Pat O'Mahonv, Liam Ronayne, Eamonn Heffernan, Billy McCullough, Paddy Shortt, John Carroll, Donal Leahy, Les Wilson, Frank McCarthy. Manager: Billy McCullough

Referee: J. Carpenter (Dublin)   Attendance: 28,000

Final Replay – Dalymount Park

23 April **Shamrock Rovers** **4** **Cork Celtic** **1**
Leech 2 (33m, 40m), McCarthy (54m)
Kearin (53m)
Richardson (59m)

Shamrock Rovers: Damien Richardson for Hannigan; Hugh Brophy for Kinsella
Cork Celtic: Unchanged

Referee: J. Carpenter (Dublin) Attendance: 18,000

It's a Record!

- Jack Baylor (Fordsons), Billy Behan (Shamrock Rovers) and John 'Pip' Meighan (Transport) all won FAI Cup-winner's medals, and went on to referee FAI Cup Finals. Derry Barrett (Evergreen United) won a runners-up medal and later refereed a Cup final.

- Athlone Town (1924), Dundalk (1958), Shamrock Rovers (1968) and Sligo Rovers (2010) are the only teams to win the Cup without conceding a goal. Sligo's goal was still intact after a penalty shoot-out in the final.

1970

O'Connell Pays A Dividend

After seventy-nine years as the standard-bearers of amateur football in Ireland, Bohemians finally made the big decision to turn professional in March 1969. Manager Sean Thomas, in his second spell with the Dalymount club, had a stroke of luck when winger Tony O'Connell, unhappy at Dundalk, bought out his own contract and became Bohemians' first professional on 11 March. St Patrick's Athletic goalkeeper Dinny Lowry signed on a free transfer on 13 March. O'Connell and Lowry played without pay for Bohemians for the last five games of the 1968-69 season as the club's articles of association were not altered to permit payment until the annual general meeting in May. However, the move to Dalymount gave both O'Connell and Lowry a new lease of life.

Lowry had won international and inter-League honours and two Cup medals with St Patrick's Athletic but was regarded as a veteran, while O'Connell had won inter-League honours and three Cup medals with Shamrock Rovers before moving to Dundalk, where he had won a League medal, an international cap and further inter-League honours. O'Connell also had a successful spell in North America in 1963-64, where he had Malcolm Allison as his manager and Tony Book, later to make his name with Manchester City under Allison, as a team-mate.

Despite additional signings like Johnny Fullam from Shamrock Rovers, Tommy Kelly from Boston and Ben O'Sullivan from Derry City, Bohemians made a bad start to their first League campaign as professionals. Out of

212

contention for everything bar the FAI Cup, manager Thomas signed left-winger Mick Kelly from Manchester United and moved O'Connell to centre-forward. Ronnie Nolan also agreed to come out of retirement and took his place at centre-back alongside Fullam. It proved a winning combination. From a team struggling at the foot of the table, Bohemians climbed to safety and clinched the Cup thanks to a three-month unbeaten run.

Luck played its part in the Cup, as Bohemians' longest journey was to Tolka Park to play Dundalk in the semi-final. 'Our travelling expenses for the entire tournament amounted to 7/6,' recalled Sean Thomas, adding, 'Without wishing to detract from our own players' performance, in each of the first two rounds we were helped by the early dismissal of a player from the opposing side.' In both instances, Tony O'Connell was the central figure. Cork Celtic goalkeeper Alex Ludzic was sent off for kicking him in the first round and Shelbourne centre-half Brendan Place got his marching orders for a similar offence in the second round.

The Shelbourne game took place on a busy weekend for O'Connell. 'I was manager of the Irish schoolboys team and we played England in Sheffield on the Saturday,' he recalled. 'It was a twenty-four-hour journey, leaving Dublin on Friday at eight o'clock and not arriving at our hotel until half-four on Saturday with the kick-off at seven o'clock. We were stuck in the train for about four hours. No wonder we lost 11–0. I flew back the following day for the game against Shels.'

The final against Sligo Rovers proved a marathon affair, requiring three games before Bohemians came out on top 2–1, with O'Connell striking a beautiful winning goal after charging down an attempted clearance by Sligo player-manager Ken Turner. The club's first professional couldn't have paid a more welcome dividend. O'Connell got a nice bonus when his good form with Bohs was rewarded by international manager Mick Meagan and he won his second cap in September 1970 against Poland. He retired after the Cup-holders were beaten by Limerick in a second round replay in March 1971.

First Round

28 January	Rialto	0	Home Farm	0
	(At Tolka Park)			
30 January	Drumcondra	0	Athlone Town	2
			Mooney 2	
1 February	Bohemians	1	Cork Celtic	0
	O'Connell			
	Drogheda	0	Cork Hibernians	0
	Finn Harps	1	Dundalk	1
	Bradley		Turner	

(Abandoned 57m)

	Limerick	5	TEK United	0
	Doran, Finucane, Turner o.g.,			
	Joe O'Mahony, Leahy			
	Ringmahon Rangers	0	Waterford	7
	(At Flower Lodge)		Power, Dunne 2, O'Neill,	
			Hale 2, Matthews	
	St Patricks's Athletic	0	Sligo Rovers	3
			Pugh 2 pens., Wilson	
	Shamrock Rovers	1	Shelbourne	2
	Barber		Place, Delargy	

First Round Re-Fixture

11 February	Finn Harps	1	Dundalk	1
	McDermott		Turner	

First Round Replays

4 February	Cork Hibernians	1	Drogheda	0
	Wigginton			
	Home Farm	1	Rialto	2
	Daly		Campbell, Farrell	
	(At Tolka Park)			
25 February	Dundalk	4	Finn Harps	0
	Murray 2 (1 pen.),			
	Bartley, Turner			

Second Round

12 February	Waterford	2	Limerick	2
	Matthews 2 (1 pen.)		McEvoy 2 (1 pen.)	

Second Round Replay

19 February	Limerick	0	Waterford	1
			Matthews	

Third Round

8 March	Athlone Town	0	Dundalk	0
	Bohemians	1	Shelbourne	0
	T. Kelly			
	Sligo Rovers	4	Rialto	0
	Brooks, Pugh, Wilson, Mitchell			
	Waterford	1	Cork Hibernians	2
	Casey		Wigginton, Lawson	

Third Round Replay

12 March	Dundalk	2	Athlone Town	0
	Ennis o.g., Brennan			

Semi-Final – Tolka Park

28 March	Bohemians	1	Dundalk	0
	O'Sullivan			

Semi-Final – Dalymount Park

29 March	Cork Hibernians	0	Sligo Rovers	0

Semi-Final Replay – Dalymount Park

1 April	Sligo Rovers	2	Cork Hibernians	1
	Brooks, Mitchell		Davenport pen.	

Final – Dalymount Park

19 April   **Bohemians**   **0**   **Sligo Rovers**   **0**

Bohemians: Dinnv Lowry, John Doran, Johnny Fullam, Ronnie Nolan, David Parkes, John Conway, Tommy Kelly, Fran Swan, Tony O'Connell, Tommy Hamill, Mick Kelly. Manager: Sean Thomas

Sligo Rovers: Tom Lally, Ken Turner, Kevin Fallon, David Pugh, Tony Stenson, Tony Burns, Pat McCluskey, Tony Fagan, John Cooke, Gerry Mitchell, Johnny Brooks. Manager: Ken Turner

Referee: D. Barrett (Cork)   Attendance: 16,000

Final Replay – Dalymount Park

22 April   **Bohemians**   **0**   **Sligo Rovers**   **0**

Both teams unchanged.

Referee: D. Barrett (Cork)   Attendance: 11,000

Final Second Replay – Dalymount Park

3 May   **Bohemians**   **2**   **Sligo Rovers**   **1**
                Fullam (49m)   Cooke (15m)
                O'Connell (62m)

Both teams unchanged. Subs: Bohemians: Ben O'Sullivan and Jackie Clarke for Conway and M. Kelly, 45m. Sligo Rovers: Dick McKiernan for Stenson, 12m

Referee: D. Barrett (Cork)   Attendance: 22,000

The original FAI Cup medal

The famous medal won by the
captain of Belfast team Alton
United in 1923

Drumcondra, 1927. From left, back row: J. Hoare (trainer), Con Coyle, Donie Fleming,
Jim Cleary, John 'Myler' Keogh, Johnny Murray, G. Allen. Front row: Owen McCarney,
George Swan, Joe Grace (captain), Eddie Cullen, Tom Moore, P. Maxwell.

Waterford, 1937. From left, back row: T. J. Corcoran, T. Kiely, C. Henderson, C. Byrne, J. B. Corcoran, E. P. Sillett, M. Mawe, J. Heenan. Second row: J. J. Kearney (Hon Treasurer), T. Newham (Vice Chairman), P. Jackman, E. Noonan, J. Phelan, A. Robinson, W. Walsh, J. McGourty, W. Walsh, J. Holden (Hon Secretary), D. Christopher (Trainer). Front row: H. Foy, J. McDonnell, T. Arrigan (Captain), G. P. Whelan (Chairman), T. Fullerton, S. Gill, T. O'Keeffe

St James's Gate AFC, 1938. From left, back row: H. Kelly, J. Gleeson, F. Culverhouse, T. Keogh, J. Hill. Second row: R. A. McNeile, Dr Delaney, R. McDonald, M. Stokes, A. H. Hughes, C. Sexton. Third row: E. McKay, L. Doyle, A. Stewart, J. O'Reilly, J. Webster, P. Gaskin, R. Comerford, D. Voyles. Front row: J. Walsh, C. Lennon, W. Kennedy, W. Byrne, A. Jackson, Sir John Lumsden, M. Geoghegan, E. Balfe, N. Reid (mascot), C. Reid, M. Richardson

Sean McCarthy, known as 'The King' due to his goalscoring exploits, helped Cork United to victory in the 1941 and 1947 Cup finals.

Shamrock Rovers, 1940. From left, top row: S. Farrelly, 'Marlowe' Dunne, Larry Palmer, J. Smithers, Paddy Doherty, Shay Healy, Mick McCarthy, Podge Gregg, Joe Creevey, Billy Fallon. Second row: 'Ando' Byrne, Mattie Clarke, 'Lowry' Maher, Paddy Reynolds, Tommy Pounce, Billy Cameron, Billy Meek, Paddy Murphy, Harry Finnegan, C Finnegan, Joe Williams, Joe Byrne. Bottom row: Captain Tom Scully, George Price, Jimmy Dunne, Joe Cunningham, Mary Jane Cunningham, Jack McCarthy, Mattie McNevin. Sitting: Kevin Matthews, Joe Ward, Dessie Westby, Paddy 'Sonny' Molloy.

Cork United, 1947. From left, back row: Jackie O'Reilly, Tommy Moroney, Sean McCarthy, Jimmy 'Fox' Foley, Dave Noonan, Johnny McGowan. Front row: Jackie O'Driscoll, Owen Madden, Florrie Burke, Small Seanie McCarthy, Paddy O'Leary.

Transport, 1950. From left, back row: Stephen Murray (trainer), Jim Loughran, John Kennedy, Paddy Carroll, Paddy Gibney, Mick Collins, Matt Giles (manager). Front row: Bobby Smith, Paddy Doyle, John Meighan (captain), Jimmy Duggan, Bernie Lester, Larry Kearns.

St Patrick's Athletic, 1959. From left, back row: Jimmy Collins (manager), Johnny McGeehan, Harry O'Brien, Tommy Dunne, Johnny White, Vinny O'Reilly, Jimmy Dunne, Dougie Boucher, Ronnie Whelan. Front row: Willie Peyton, Pascal Curtin, Dinny Lowry, Paddy 'Ginger' O'Rourke.

Eric Barber takes a shot on goal against Cork Hibernian, 1960.

Mick Leech scoring for Shamrock Rovers in the 1968 FAI Cup final against Waterford, Dalymount Park

Finn Harps, 1974. From left, back row: Patsy McGowan (manager), Gerry McGranaghan, Declan McDowell, Brendan Bradley, Jim Sheridan, Donal O'Doherty. Front row: Jim 'Chang' Smith, Tony O'Doherty, Paul McGee, Gerry Murray, Paddy McGrory, Peter Hutton, Charlie Ferry.

Home Farm's Frank Devlin, who scored the winning goal in the 1975 Cup final against Shelbourne.

The most successful manager in FAI Cup history, Jim McLaughlin

© The Irish Independent

Dundalk, 1979. From left, back row: Jimmy Dainty, Tom McConville, Hilary Carlyle, Richie Blackmore, Sean Byrne, Cathal Muckian, Leo 'Pop' Flanagan. Front row: Paddy Dunning, Liam Devine, Mick Lawlor, Dermot Keely, Martin Lawlor, Vinny McKenna.

Sligo Rovers, 1983. From left, back row: Paul Fielding (player-manager), Mick Savage, Gus Gilligan, Graham Fox, Colin Oakley, Chris Rutherford, Paul Moylan, John Skeffington, Pauric McManus (trainer). Front row: Mick Ferry, Harry McLaughlin, Andy Elliott, Tony Fagan (captain), Mick Graham, Martin McDonnell, Tony Stenson.

UCD, 1984. From left, back row: Frank Devlin, Alan O'Neill, Ken O'Doherty, Brendan Murphy, Joe Hanrahan, Robbie Lawlor. Front row: Aidan Reynolds, John Cullen, Martin Moran, Paddy Dunning, Robbie Gaffney, Paul Roche, Keith Dignam.

Michael O'Connor, who was left out of the Dundalk team in the 1988 Cup final by his brother Turlough.

© Sportsfile

© The Derry Journal

Derry City, 1989. From left, front row: Jonathan Speak, Jack Keay, Jim McLaughlin (manager), Stuart Gauld (captain), Noel Larkin. Middle row: Joe Loughlin (physio), Paul Doolin, John Coady, Liam Coyle, Kevin Brady, Mick Neville, Pascal Vaudequin, Felix Healy. Back row: Herbie Wade (kitman), Paul Curran, Tim Dalton, Paul Hegarty, Paul Carlyle, Kevin Mahon (first-team coach).

Bray Wanderers, 1990. From left, back row: David Kealy, Kevin Reynolds, Josh Moran, Mick Doohan, Derek Corcorcan, Dermot Judge. Front row: Anthony McKeever, Brian Cosgrave, John Finnegan, Martin Nugent, John Ryan, Colm Phillips, Tommy McDermott.

© Sportsfile

Galway United, 1991. From left, back row: George Guest, Adrian Walsh, Derek Rogers, Declan McIntyre, John Cleary, Paul Campbell, Johnny Glynn, Peter Carpenter, Kevin Cassidy, Joey Malone (manager). Front row: Jimmy Nolan, Johnny Morris Burke, Larry Wyse, Tommy Keane, Noel Mernagh, Stephen Lally.

Cork City, 1998. From left, back row: Cormac Cotter, Liam Murphy (assistant manager), Derek Coughlan, Phil Harrington, Noel Hartigan, Noel Mooney, Dave Hill, Gerry Harris (secretary), Dave Barry (manager). Middle row: Ollie Cahill, John Cotter, Gareth Cronin, Jason Kabia, Declan Daly (captain), Mark Herrick, Kelvin Flanagan, Brian Barry-Murphy. Front row: Dominic Iorfa, John Caulfield, Gerald Dobbs, Patsy Freyne, Greg O'Halloran.

Longford Town, who won the Cup for the first time in 2003. From left, back row: Brian McGovern, Barry Ferguson (captain), Sean Francis, Vinnie Perth, Shane Barrett, Stephen O'Brien. Front row: Alan Murphy, Alan Kirby, Sean Prunty, Philip Keogh, Sean Dillon.

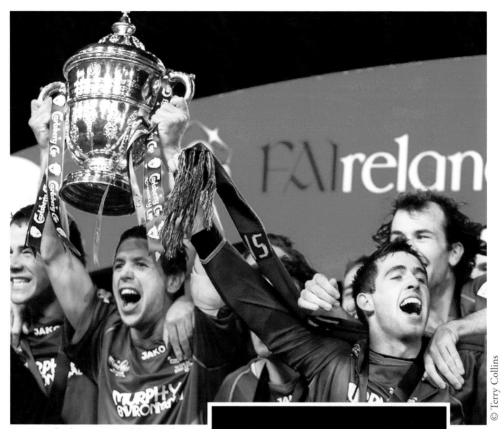

© Terry Collins

Drogheda United celebrate their
first Cup final victory in 2005.

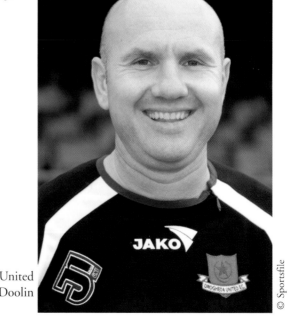

© Sportsfile

Drogheda United
manager Paul Doolin

Stephen Kenny, Derry City manager

Conor Sammon, UCD, in action against Sean Prunty, Longford Town, in the FAI
Ford Cup semi-final, October 2007

Mindugas
Kalonas in
action for
Bohemians in
the FAI Cup
final, 2008

Sporting Fingal
manager Liam
Buckley

Sporting Fingal, 2009. From left, back row: Darren Quigley, Stephen Paisley, Shane McFaul, Conan Byrne, Shaun Maher, Eamonn Zayed. Front row: Collie James, Robert Bayly, Lorcan Fitzgerald, Shaun Williams, Gary O'Neill.

Sligo Rovers manager Paul Cook, with goalkeeper Ciaran Kelly, celebrate their victory over Shamrock Rovers after a tense penalty shoot-out in the 2010 Cup final.

WILLS'S CIGARETTES

J. DELANEY

H. CARTER.

Two legends who featured in the Cup in the 1950s, Jimmy Delaney (1956) and Raich Carter (1953).

1971

A Medal for McEvoy

Down in Limerick they reckon Andy McEvoy was the most skilful player they ever had – and also the shyest. Football was McEvoy's livelihood for ten years while he was with Blackburn Rovers but he never became accustomed to the adulation his talent provoked.

He scored a goal of such brilliance in a League game at Kilcohan Park that the Waterford crowd applauded him for a full three minutes while the game was in progress. His teammates recall that McEvoy practically cringed with embarrassment! He was also fond of juggling with the ball in training, but if he felt that he had an audience he promptly kicked the ball away.

He left his native Bray at the age of eighteen to join Blackburn Rovers, then managed by Jackie Carey. After a settling-in period of about four years he blossomed into one of the most prolific goalscorers in the English First Division, topped only by Jimmy Greaves. However, life in England held little appeal for him and when his wife inherited a farm in Kilmihil, County Clare, he let it be known that he was anxious to return home. Limerick director Jack Tuohy jumped in ahead of the posse and secured the Republic of Ireland striker on the understanding that if he returned to England he would again become Blackburn's player.

One of McEvoy's greatest assets was his ability to place the ball in whichever part of the goal he wanted. In training one day he demonstrated a free kick routine whereby the ball was played off the bar for an inrushing forward to finish off. Three times in succession he hit the bar. Strange to relate, it was a routine he never tried in a match. However, he was quick to spot what was on in a free kick situation as Bohemians found to their cost in this year's second round tie.

'We were winning 2–1 in the second half but finding it a hard slog to get up the field against the elements,' recalls Joe O'Mahony. 'We finally got a free on the edge of their penalty area, Andy said to me, "roll it here" and bang – that was it – 3–1 and the game was over. He saw the gap and that was enough for him.'

Limerick's win in the final gave McEvoy his first medal and he achieved it with practically no training, as manager Ewan Fenton recalled: 'Andy had a problem training because his job took him all around the country delivering Guinness. He was never available, which was difficult because all the other lads were as keen as mustard, but I couldn't leave him out of the side. He was so good he should never have left English football.'

Fenton completed a unique double when leading Limerick to victory, for the previous year he had managed Linfield when they won the IFA Cup. In a three-year spell with the Belfast club, he won the Irish League title in 1968-69, apart from the 1970 Cup win.

The manager was involved in a selection controversy before the final against Drogheda when he was under pressure to choose Scottish forward Hugh Hamilton ahead of Englishman Dave Barrett. However, he stuck to his guns, Barrett got the all-important lead goal in the replay and when he introduced Hamilton at half-time, the Scot responded with another two to clinch an historic first Cup victory for Limerick.

So great was the enthusiasm in the city that, even though the rain never let up, there was a bigger crowd at the railway station to greet the players on their return than was at the match. The crush of people caused two huge concrete pillars to be knocked over and the crowds swarmed onto the railway tracks. As a result, the driver refused to bring the train into the station and the players had to walk the last three miles!

First Round

6 February	Transport	0	Drogheda	3
	(At Tolka Park)		Conroy pen., McEwan, Verity	
7 February	Athlone Town	0	Waterford	6
			McMahon 3 (1 pen.),	
			Hale 2, Matthews	
	Bohemians	2	Drumcondra	0
	Dunne 2			
	Cork Hibernians	2	Dundalk	1
	Davenport, Wigginton		McKeever	
	Limerick	1	Shelbourne	0
	Hamilton			
	St Patrick's Athletic	2	Bluebell United	0
	O'Connor 2			
	Shamrock Rovers	1	Cork Celtic	0
	Leech			
	Sligo Rovers	3	Tullamore	1
	Pugh, Fagan, Mitchell		Geraghty pen.	
	TEK United	1	Finn Harps	5
	Fogarty pen.		Bradley 3 (1 pen.), Coyle,	
	(At Finn Park)		Gaston	

Second Round

24 February	Cork Hibernians	1	Waterford	0
	Marsden			

Third Round

14 March	Cork Hibernians	2	Finn Harps	2
	Connolly, Marsden		Bradley 2	
	Limerick	0	Bohemians	0
	Shamrock Rovers	2	Drogheda	5
	Martin, Richardson		Cullen 3, Conroy, Whelan	
	Sligo Rovers	1	St Patrick's Athletic	2
	Mitchell		O'Connor, Murray pen.	

Third Round Replays

17 March	Bohemians	0	Limerick	0
	(Abandoned 45m)			
	Finn Harps	1	Cork Hibernians	1
	Nicholl		Marsden	
	(After extra time.)			

Third Round Re-Fixture

23 March	Bohemians	1	Limerick	3
	O'Connell		Hamilton 2, McEvoy	

Third Round Second Replay – Dalymount Park

24 March	Cork Hibernians	5	Finn Harps	0
	Wigginton, Dennehy,			
	Young 2, Marsden			

Semi-Final – Tolka Park

27 March	Limerick	1	St Patrick's Athletic	0
	Meaney			

Semi-Final – Dalymount Park

28 March	Cork Hibernians	0	Drogheda	0

Semi-Final Replay – Tolka Park

7 April	Drogheda	2	Cork Hibernians	1
	Shawcross pen., McEwan		Young	

Final – Dalymount Park

18 April	Limerick	0	Drogheda	0

Limerick: Kevin Fitzpatrick, Joe Bourke, Richie Hall, Al Finucane, Sean Byrnes, Joe O'Mahonv, Shamie Coad, Andy McEvoy, Paddy Shortt, David Barrett, Tony Meaney. Sub.: Hugh Hamilton for Coad, 62m. Manager: Ewan Fenton

Drogheda: Cecil Baxter, Paddy Dowling, Mick Meagan, Dave Shawcross, Dick Jacenuik, Andy McSwiney, Mick Cooke, Frank McEwan, Ronnie Whelan, Pat Cullen, Mick Fairclough. Sub: Mick Conroy for Fairclough, 77m. Manager: Mick Meagan

Referee: D. V. Byrne (Dublin)   Attendance: 16,000

Final Replay – Dalymount Park

21 April	**Limerick**	**3**	**Drogheda**	**0**
	Barrett (51m)			
	Hamilton 2 (79m, 83m)			

Limerick: Unchanged. Sub: Hugh Hamilton for Bourke, 45m
Drogheda: Mick Conroy for Fairclough. Sub: Fairclough for Whelan, 62m

Referee: D. V. Byrne (Dublin)   Attendance: 15,000

It's a Record!

- Corkmen Pat and Alan Kelly are the only father and son who have refereed FAI Cup Finals.

- In 2003, Corkman Alan Kelly became the youngest Cup final referee. He was twenty-eight when he took charge of the Longford Town–St Patrick's Athletic game.

1972

McMenemy's Gift

Dave Bacuzzi, the former Arsenal, Manchester City and Reading full-back, didn't know what to expect when he was appointed manager of Cork Hibernians. Coming straight from a full-time set-up, he discovered Hibs were a half-way measure with about six full-time professionals training in the mornings and the part-timers training at night. In League of Ireland terms it was a good set-up, but one which, because of the outlay, needed to be successful.

Appointed in 1970, when Cup-time drew close at the end of the year, Bacuzzi got on to Doncaster Rovers manager Lawrie McMenemy looking for players. McMenemy was preparing for a second round English Cup tie, and if Doncaster lost he would be trimming the wage bill. They lost, so Bacuzzi got on again and spoke to four players McMenemy was prepared to release. Only one, striker Tony Marsden, was prepared to leave England. He went to Cork on a month's trial and scored a goal per game. 'At the end of the month I got back on to Lawrie and asked him about Marsden,' recalled Bacuzzi. 'I didn't want to boost him up too much but I could have dropped through the floor when he said he was free.' Hibs went on to win the League title in Bacuzzi's first season.

Marsden scored three important Cup goals in 1971, when Hibs made a brave bid for the double, losing to Drogheda in a semi-final replay. The following season, with one of Bacuzzi's home-grown products alongside Marsden, Hibs recorded their first Cup success.

Miah Dennehy had played mainly in Hibs' reserves as a winger in Bacuzzi's first season and he wasn't a very confident player. Tried up front, he began to score regularly, revelling in a free role and earning a first team place. He scored two of the goals with which Hibs beat Shamrock Rovers in the play-off for the League title in 1970-71, with Marsden getting the other. 'Miah's main assets were stamina and speed,' said Bacuzzi. 'He was the fittest player I ever came across at any club. We played with three up front – Marsden, Dave Wigginton and Dennehy – and they were the fittest players in the club. Our policy was to put the ball into space for them to run on to and cause havoc.'

Hibs and Waterford were the top two teams in the League of Ireland in 1971-72 and the League race boiled down to a last match meeting between them at Flower Lodge. Hibs, two points behind, needed to win to force a play-off. The game was played a week before the Cup final, for which both teams had qualified.

'We lost 3–2 after leading 2–0 with eleven minutes to go before a record Cork crowd of over 25,000,' recalled Bacuzzi. 'I went home seething and went straight to bed, barely grunting at my in-laws who had just arrived! We got it out of our systems at training in the Quarry on Tuesday night and then looked forward to Sunday.'

Cup final day turned out to be Dennehy's day, as the blond striker hit a hat-trick – the first in an FAI Cup Final – to end Waterford hopes of the double. By the time the Cup came around again in 1973, Dennehy had been transferred to Nottingham Forest. He was also a Republic of Ireland international, and in the space of a couple of years he had made a big impact on Irish soccer. In contrast, Hibs' centre-back, Noel O'Mahony, had thirteen years' League experience before he won his Cup medal.

First Round

13February	CYM (At Whitehall)	0	Cork Celtic Davenport	1
	Drogheda Buck, Cooke, Cullen	3	TEK United	0
	Drumcondra Place, Martin pen.	2	Sligo Rovers Conlon, Gallagher	2
	Limerick McGlynn o.g., Meaney, McEvoy	3	Bohemians Mooney	1
	Longford Town	0	Dundalk Rogers, Turner, Kelly	3
	Rialto Dempsey (At Kilcohan Park)	1	Waterford Hale 5 (1 pen.), Kirby 3, Matthews, Humphries 2	11
	St Patrick's Athletic Murray, Burkett	2	Finn Harps Bradley	1
	Shamrock Rovers	0	Athlone Town	0
	Shelbourne McNaughton (At Dalymount Park)	1	Cork Hibernians Wigginton, Marsden	2

First Round Replays

16 February	Sligo Rovers Campbell	1	Drumcondra Hamill	1
17 February	Athlone Town	0	Shamrock Rovers Martin 2, Lawlor, Richardson, Quinn o.g.	5

First Round Second Replay

23 February	Drumcondra McArdle, Martin pen. (At Dalymount Park)	2	Sligo Rovers	0

Second Round

1 March	Drumcondra Martin	1	Cork Celtic	0

Third Round

12 March	**Cork Hibernians** Dennehy 3, Bacuzzi, Wigginton, Marsden pen.	6	**Drumcondra**	0
	Drogheda Cullen 2	2	**Waterford** Humphries 2, O'Neill, House	4
	Limerick	0	**Dundalk**	0
	St Patrick's Athletic Murray	1	**Shamrock Rovers**	0

Third Round Replay

17 March	**Dundalk** Rogers	1	**Limerick** Finucane	1

Third Round Second Replay – Dalymount Park

22 March	**Dundalk** O'Connor, Rogers	2	**Limerick** McEvoy	1

Semi-Finals – Dalymount Park

8 April	**Cork Hibernians** Sweeney	1	**St Patrick's Athletic**	0
9 April	**Waterford** O'Neill 2, B. McConville o.g., Kirby	4	**Dundalk** Turner	2

Final – Dalymount Park

23 April	**Cork Hibernians** Dennehy 3 (65m, 70m, 83m)	3	**Waterford**	0

Cork Hibernians: Joe Grady, Dave Bacuzzi, Noel O'Mahony, Martin Sheehan, John Herrick, John Lawson, Walter 'Sonny' Sweeney, Gerry Finnegan, Tony Marsden, Dave Wigginton, Miah Dennehy. Manager: Dave Bacuzzi

Waterford: Peter Thomas, Peter Bryan, Tony Cottle, Jackie Morley. Vinny Maguire, John O'Neill, Jimmy McGeough, Johnny Matthews, Alfie Hale, Dave Kirby, Carl Humphries. Manager: Shay Brennan

Referee: C. O'Leary (Dublin)   Attendance: 22,500

1973

FAI Insensitivity

The insensitivity of FAI officialdom to the needs of players was never better illustrated than during the 1973 Cup campaign. By sticking rigidly to the dates set for second round and quarter-final ties, they effectively killed off Shamrock Rovers' chances. Rovers, who had proved their Cup mettle in the first round by coming out on top against Dundalk after three games, needed a further four games to see off the challenge of Athlone Town in the second round. The last three games were played on consecutive days and involved periods of extra time. When the tie was finally decided it left Rovers with just two days to prepare for a quarter-final tie away to Limerick! The FAI, obviously taking no account of the fact that the game in Ireland is part-time, turned down Rovers' appeal for a postponement. Rovers – minus three of their regular back four after the Athlone marathon – went down gallantly at the Market's Field, but justice was not seen to be done. Rovers, who didn't even reach the semi-final, played eight Cup ties in the space of three weeks. Cork Hibernians, who won the Cup, needed only six games to do so, which were spread over a ten-week period.

Hibernians became only the second team, after Rovers, to retain the FAI Cup when they beat Shelbourne 1–0 in a final replay at Flower Lodge, the first time the final was played outside Dublin. A wet day restricted the crowd to 11,000, making the occasion a bit of an anti-climax. 'We had won everything in the space of three seasons and the crowd had become too used to success,' said centre-half Noel O'Mahony. 'The place to win the Cup was in Dalymount Park.' In their two Cup-winning campaigns, Hibernians conceded only two goals, one in the first round in 1972 to Shelbourne and one in the first round in 1973 to non-League Rialto. Only two Cork-born players, O'Mahony and fellow centre-half Martin Sheehan, played in both finals.

O'Mahony, whose brother Declan was goalkeeper in 1973, was a very relieved man when Carl Humphries shot the winning goal in the replay. 'I had stuck my head where I shouldn't early on and got a boot for my trouble,' he recalled. 'I got a few stitches in it and came back to watch the last twenty minutes, but if it had gone to a third match I wouldn't have made it.' Between playing for Cork Hibs and managing Cork Alberts, O'Mahony was involved in six semi-finals during the 1970s but, apart from 1972 and 1973, success eluded him. More fortunate was Denis Allen, who got into the team when Miah Dennehy was transferred to Nottingham Forest just before the 1973 Cup started.

Hibernians, who had four full-time professionals in their side – two less than in 1972 – had to overcome a Shelbourne team which was badly hit by injuries following a very tough game in Ballybofey against League runners-up Finn Harps. 'We were plagued with injuries following that League game,' said manager Gerry Doyle. 'We lost Paddy Dunning; Billy Newman had to go up to Bobby McGregor in Belfast for treatment and Tony McDonnell and Paul McNaughton had to take tests before the replay.' Left-back Ray O'Brien was another player who suffered rough treatment, something which he had a special reason to avoid as, like Tony Dunne in 1960, he was Manchester United-bound as soon as the Cup final was over. Despite injury problems and the sending-off of striker Eric Barber, Shelbourne made it tough for Hibernians, who had to endure some nail-biting moments after Humphries scored. 'In those last minutes as Shelbourne put on the pressure we just gave the ball to Humphries,' recalled player-manager Dave Bacuzzi. 'He was so skilful at retaining possession they couldn't get it off him.'

First Round

16 February	Home Farm-Drumcondra	1	Dalkey United	2
	O'Grady		Byrne, Wildes	
18 February	Cork Hibernians	3	Rialto	1
	Sheehan, Wigginton 2		Norton	
	Drogheda	0	Bohemians	2
			O'Connor, Turner	
	Finn Harps	1	Athlone Town	1
	Minnock o.g.		Parke	
	Limerick	2	Sligo Rovers	1
	Marlowe 2		Moore	
	Shamrock Rovers	1	Dundalk	1
	Leech		Kavanagh	
	Shelbourne	4	St Patrick's Athletic	0
	Barber, McKenna, Rogers, McNaughton			
	Swilly Rovers	2	Cork Celtic	2
	Ludzic o.g., Cassidy		O'Neill, McCarthy	
	Waterford	3	Wembley Rovers	1
	Parr, Matthews pen., Hale		Long pen.	

First Round Replays

21 February	Cork Celtic	6	Swilly Rovers	0
	O'Neill 4, Brooks, Ludzic pen.			
22 February	Athlone Town	1	Finn Harps	0
	Parke			
	Dundalk	0	Shamrock Rovers	0

First Round Second Replay

26 February	Shamrock Rovers	3	Dundalk	0
	Lawlor, Leech, Daly			
	(At Dalymount Park)			

Second Round

1 March	Athlone Town	1	Shamrock Rovers	1
	Parke		Daly	

Second Round Replay – Dalymount Park

7 March   **Shamrock Rovers**   0   **Athlone Town**   0
(After extra time.)

Second Round Second Replay – Dalymount Park

8 March   **Shamrock Rovers**   0   **Athlone Town**   0
(After two periods of extra time.)

Second Round Third Replay – Dalymount Park

9 March   **Shamrock Rovers**   3   **Athlone Town**   1
Davis 2, Lawlor   Wood

Third Round

11 March   **Cork Celtic**   3   **Bohemians**   0
Kelly o.g., Notley, McKenna

Cork Hibernians   0   **Waterford**   0

Limerick   1   **Shamrock Rovers**   0
Kennedy

Shelbourne   0   **Dalkey United**   0

Third Round Replays – Tolka Park

14 March   **Dalkey United**   0   **Shelbourne**   1
                                   Hannigan

15 March   **Waterford**   0   **Cork Hibernians**   2
                               Lawson 2 (1 pen.)

Semi-Final – Flower Lodge

1 April   **Cork Hibernians**   2   **Limerick**   0
Lawson pen., Coyne

Semi-Final – Dalymount Park

1 April   **Shelbourne**   0   **Cork Celtic**   0

Semi-Final Replay – Flower Lodge

4 April   **Cork Celtic**   2   **Shelbourne**   2
Carroll, Brooks   R. Mulhall 2

Semi-Final Second Replay – Dalymount Park

| 11 April | Shelbourne | 1 | Cork Celtic | 0 |
| | Hannigan | | | |

Final – Dalymount Park

| 22 April | Cork Hibernians | 0 | Shelbourne | 0 |

Cork Hibernians: Declan O'Mahony, Dave Bacuzzi, Noel O'Mahony, Martin Sheehan, John Brohan, Walter 'Sonny' Sweeney, John Lawson, Denis Allen, Dave Wigginton, Carl Humphries, Gerry Coyne. Manager: Dave Bacuzzi

Shelbourne: Paddy Roche, Mick Gannon, Brendan Roche, Tony McDonnell, Ray O'Brien, Billy Newman, John Rogers, Ben Hannigan, Vinny McKenna, Paul McNaughton, Eric Barber. Sub: Paddy Mulhall for McDonnell, 19m. Manager: Gerry Doyle

Referee: W. A. O'Neill (Dublin)   Attendance: 12,500

Final Replay – Flower Lodge

| 29 April | Cork Hibernians | 1 | Shelbourne | 0 |
| | Humphries (83m) | | | |

Cork Hibernians: Unchanged. Sub: Frank Connolly for N. O'Mahony, 20m
Shelabourne: Unchanged. Subs: Paddy Dunning for Rogers, 59m; Shay Doyle for Newman, 59m

Referee: W. A. O'Neill (Dublin)   Attendance: 11,000

1974

Harps' £100-a-Head Ace

Finn Harps' success in the FAI Cup in 1974 was a personal triumph for chairman Fran Fields and manager Patsy McGowan, who had guided the Donegal club into the League of Ireland from junior ranks in 1969. Fields, however, gave the credit for Harps' success to the club's costliest signing, Northern Ireland international Tony O'Doherty.

'Tony hadn't kicked a ball for two months because of a groin injury but we kept it quiet and he was our trump card,' said Fields. 'He inspired the whole team. When it was announced the night before that he was in the team, it gave everybody confidence.' Worried about O'Doherty's fitness, Harps started the former Coleraine player at the back, but he was moved to midfield when St Patrick's Athletic scored an early goal and he proceeded to organise Harps' revival.

Fields, who rated O'Doherty as 'one of the greatest players ever in the League of Ireland', was largely instrumental in securing the Derryman's signature. 'We paid £4,000 for him,' he recalled. 'I held a meeting in Jackson's Hotel in Ballybofey and got £100 a head from forty people.' Thanks to Fields' initiative, Harps won the race for the classy utility player ahead of a posse of wealthier clubs.

In 1968, Harps won the FAI Junior Cup with Fields doing the coaching, but when they went out of the Intermediate Cup the following season in the first round to Belgrove, he decided to do something to ensure football right through the season for the Donegal lads. 'On our way home from the Belgrove game we stopped for a meal in Ashbourne and it came to my head then that we should go for League of Ireland football,' said Fields.

Once the decision was taken, the race was on to prepare Finn Park for a League inspection. Here again, Fields was a big help as he was in the plant hire business at the time. Three months' voluntary work constructed a pitch worthy of senior football . . . and then there was the League's annual general meeting to attend, which meant a long day for Fields as he was there from ten in the morning canvassing the delegates.

The League expanded to admit Harps and Athlone Town, and 17 August 1969 was the red-letter day when Cup-holders Shamrock Rovers arrived for the City Cup tie which marked Harps' senior debut. Rovers went home with a 10–2 win under their belts and Harps probably felt they were back at square one.

However, the turning point came when Fields and McGowan put the Rovers' lesson to good use and went talent-spotting. Jim Nicholl was signed from Coleraine, Brendan Bradley from Derry City and Peter Hutton from Crusaders and these players formed the backbone of the new Harps who gradually came to terms with League of Ireland football and eventually earned the club its first senior trophy, the FAI Cup in 1974.

For winger Paul McGee, the Cup was won the day Harps drew their third round tie with Bohemians. 'We were 1–0 down and being run off the park,' he recalled. 'With a few minutes to go, the ball broke to me and I tried a first time shot. It was going for the corner flag when Charlie Ferry stuck his head out and headed it in.' Ferry, who scored the goals that won the replay, had a great Cup campaign, scoring six goals and laying on as many more for his teammates. He and wing-half Paddy McGrory were the sole survivors of Harps' senior debut.

First Round: Oriel Park

31 January	CIE	1	Dundalk	5
	Corcoran		Watson, McManus	
			Waddell 2, Coyne	
2 February	Sligo Rovers	2	Wembley Rovers	1
	Fagan, Logan		Long pen.	

Second Round

17 February	Athlone Town	5	Sligo Rovers	1
	Nicholl 4, Larkin		Fagan	
	Bohemians	2	Dundalk	2
	O'Connor, Flanagan		Coyne, Cobbe	
	Drogheda	0	Cork Celtic	0
	Finn Harps	4	Home Farm	1
	Smith, Forbes, Ferry, Bradley		Devlin	
	Limerick	0	Transport	1
			Leavy	
	Shelbourne	0	Cork Hibernians	3
			F. Murphy. Sweeney 2	
	TEK United	0	St Patrick's Athletic	2
	(At Carlisle Grounds)		Dempsey, O'Sullivan	
	Waterford	1	Shamrock Rovers	1
	Matthews		Fagan	

Second Round Replays

20 February	Cork Celtic	1	Drogheda	1
	Hannigan		Stephens	
	(Abandoned 90m by Ref. J. Carpenter: missiles thrown)			
	Shamrock Rovers	0	Waterford	1
			Leech	
21 February	Dundalk	0	Bohemians	4
			Flanagan 3, O'Connor	

Second Round Re-Fixture

27 February	Drogheda	1	Cork Celtic	0
	Beckett			
	(At Dalymount Park)			

Third Round

10 March	Athlone Town	2	Transport	1
	Healy, Campbell		Conroy	
	Bohemians	1	Finn Harps	1
	Brophy		Ferry	
	Cork Hibernians	1	St Patrick's Athletic	2
	Lawson		O'Sullivan, Dempsey	
	Drogheda	0	Waterford	0

Third Round Replays

13 March	Finn Harps	2	Bohemians	0
	Ferry 2			
14 March	Waterford	3	Drogheda	4
	Macken, Leech 2		Clarke, O'Halloran,	
			Brammeld 2	

(After extra time.)

Semi-Final – Oriel Park, Dundalk

31 March	Athlone Town	0	Finn Harps	5
			Bradley 2, Ferry pen.,	
			Harkin, McGrory	

Semi-Final – Dalymount Park

31 March	St Patrick's Athletic	1	Drogheda	0
	Flanagan			

Final – Dalymount Park

21 April	Finn Harps	3	St Patricks' Athletic	1
	Ferry (4m)		Byrne (19m)	
	Bradley 2 (79m, 88m)			

Finn Harps: Gerry Murray, Gerry McGranaghan, Jin Sheridan, Tony O'Doherty, Peter Hutton, Paddy McGrory, Declan McDowell, Jimmy 'Chang' Smith, Paul 'Skl' McGee, Brendan Bradley, Charlie Ferry. Sub: Donal O'Doherty for Smith, 84m. Manager: Patsy McGowan

St Patrick's Athletic: Tom Lally, Jack Burkett, Ernie Reynolds, Paul Doyle, Brendan Myles, Sean Byrne, Leo 'Pop' Flanagan, Paddy Munroe, Ben O'Sullivan, Paul Smith, Dermot 'Mo' Shields. Sub: Mick Dempsey for Smith. 55m. Manager: Jack Burkett

Referee: E. A. Farrell (Dublin)   Attendance: 14,000

It's a Record!

- The highest scoring semi-finals were in 1948 (Shamrock Rovers 8, St Patrick's Athletic 2), and 1952 (Dundalk 6, Waterford 4, after extra time). Rovers' 8–2 was the biggest winning margin in a semi-final.

- The 1950 (Transport–Cork Athletic), 1970 (Bohemians–Sligo Rovers) and 1999 (Bray Wanderers–Finn Harps) finals each required three games to reach a conclusion.

1975

Bacuzzi's Sacrifice

When Home Farm won the FAI Cup in 1975, with a 1–0 win over Shelbourne, they became the first amateur team to do so in forty years. However, amateurism had changed so much in the intervening period that part of the build-up to Farm's big day involved the players' appeal for some form of win bonus! The suggestion of a clothes voucher was mooted, thirty pounds or more in value, but this was emphatically rejected by Home Farm's officers, some of them survivors from the club's foundation in 1928. Shelbourne's players, meanwhile, stood to gain five hundred pounds if they won the final. Although Home Farm won the game, the rejection of the voucher scheme was instrumental in breaking up the team. Eventually, after losing several players to professional clubs, Farm offered their players a holiday in Spain – on condition that they first signed on for the following season.

Amateurs have always made sacrifices, but the man who made one of the biggest sacrifices for Home Farm was manager Dave Bacuzzi who, at thirty-four, retired to the sidelines when he took over the club, as their rules at the time didn't permit them to play professionals. 'It took a long time to make that decision,' he said. 'I probably would have had a few more years in the League of Ireland but I think I made the right decision.' It was the challenge to his coaching ability that won him over.

Bacuzzi, who had guided Cork Hibernians to Cup success in 1972 and 1973, was let go by Hibs when his second two-year contract ended in 1974. Although

Hibs later changed their minds, by then he had given his word to Home Farm, and so he moved to Dublin.

Despite the club's triumph, he was soon shown the other side of the coin. 'After the Cup final we had to play two League games and needed one point to avoid having to apply for re-election,' he recalled. 'We played Shamrock Rovers at home the following Friday – and there was nobody at the game. That really disillusioned me.'

The captain of Home Farm was long-serving centre-back Jack Dempsey, who only came into the team when regular defender Tom O'Dea emigrated to the United States. However, Dempsey proved an inspiring father-figure to Farm's young side. Director of a fruit company, he brought a box of oranges to the Saturday training sessions and this became the team's lucky mascot. After the semi-final against St Patrick's Athletic, he came off the pitch with his head covered in bruises from his aerial duels with former Leicester City striker Peter Jackson. When the idea of flying O'Dea home from the States for the final was raised, it was shot down by the players.

Among Home Farm's victims on the way to the final were some very well-known names from English football. Second round victims Dundalk had just appointed former Northern Ireland international Jim McLaughlin as player-manager; third round victims Cork Celtic included former Chelsea and England international Bobby Tambling in their lineout and even his goal – rated the best of the tournament by Home Farm administrator Brendan Menton – couldn't deny the Farm; and semi-final victims St Patrick's Athletic were managed by Jack Burkett, the former West Ham United defender who won an English Cup medal in 1964.

First Round

5 February	Drogheda	0	Cobh Ramblers	1
			P. Meade	
6 February	Limerick	2	Belgrove	0
	Duggan, Doyle pen.			

Second Round

16 February	Cobh Ramblers	1	St Patrick's Athletic	3
	G. Ward		Jackson 2, Flanagan	
	Cork Hibernians	4	Finn Harps	0
	Wigginton 2, Sweeney, Marsden			
	CYM	1	Waterford	0
	G. Garvan			
	(At Milltown)			
	Home Farm	1	Dundalk	0
	J. Smith			
	Limerick	1	Bohemians	3
	Duggan		T. O'Connor, Ryan 2	
	Parkvilla	0	Shamrock Rovers	0
	(At Oriel Park)			
	Shelbourne	2	Athlone Town	1
	McNaughton, Lawlor		Healy	
	(At Dalymount Park)			
	Sligo Rovers	1	Cork Celtic	3
	L. McCool		Tambling 2, Hale	

Second Round Replay

| 20 February | Shamrock Rovers | 5 | Parkvilla | 1 |
| | Lyons, Murphy 3 (1 pen.), McEwan | | Kennedy | |

Third Round

7 March	Shelbourne	1	Shamrock Rovers	0
	Hannon			
	(At Dalymount Park)			

9 March	Bohemians	1	Cork Hibernians	1
	T. O'Connor		Wigginton	
	Home Farm	3	Cork Celtic	2
	Devlin 2, Courtney		Allen, Tambling	
	St Patrick's Athletic	1	CYM	0
	Whelan			

Third Round Replay

12 March	Cork Hibernians	1	Bohemians	0
	Lawson			

Semi-Final – Flower Lodge

6 April	Cork Hibernians	1	Shelbourne	1
	Finnegan		Lawlor	

Semi-Final – Dalymount Park

6 April	Home Farm	3	St Patrick's Athletic	2
	Higgins 2, Doyle o.g.		Baker, O'Sullivan	

Semi-Final Replay – Dalymount Park

9 April	Shelbourne	1	Cork Hibernians	0
	Barber			

Final – Dalymount Park

27 April	Home Farm	1	Shelbourne	0
	Devlin (7m)			

Home Farm: Jim Grace, Joe Smith, Brian Daly, Dermot Keely, Michael Brophy, Jack Dempsey, David Hughes, Joe Keely, Tony Higgins, Frank Devlin, Martin Murray. Manager: Dave Bacuzzi

Shelbourne: Willie Byrne, Mick Gannon, Vincent McKenna, Tony McDonnell, Paddy Dunning, John Cervi, Terry Byrne, Albert Hannon, Paul McNaughton, Mick Lawlor, Eric Barber. Manager: Gerry Doyle

Referee: P. Mulhall (Dublin)   Attendance: 10,000

1976

Bohs Ride Their Luck

After a shakey start to their campaign, which saw them survive against non-League opposition with a suspiciously offside goal, Bohemians took the FAI Cup to Dalymount Park for the fourth time in 1976. 'Joe Burke was definitely offside when he scored the winner against Ringmahon Rangers in the first round,' recalled manager Billy Young. 'They defended against us but they would have beaten us if they had taken us on, as we played badly.' Young, who had guided Bohemians to the League title the previous season, had further problems to overcome in the second round against Cork Celtic. 'Centre-forward Terry Flanagan had a great first year with us in 1974-75, but he had a terrible second year and I tried everyone and anyone to replace him,' said Young. 'For the game away to Cork Celtic I tried John Doran, who had been displaced at left-back by Fran O'Brien. He had an inspired game and that was the difference on the day, but he couldn't keep up that form.' Celtic included England World Cup star Geoff Hurst in their lineout and he wasn't the only England star to play in the FAI Cup that season. Bobby Charlton lined out with Waterford but didn't get past the first hurdle, losing 3–0 away to Finn Harps.

Cork Hibernians were another club to invest in English talent, including Rodney Marsh for their first round tie with Drogheda. However, it was Drogheda who came out on top after a four-game marathon that had plenty of talking points. In the first replay in Cork, Drogheda had to come back from a 2–0 half-time deficit, while the third game saw Drogheda striker Cathal

Muckian dismissed after twenty-eight minutes. Yet the Boynesiders' ten men survived the ninety minutes, plus two periods of extra time, to earn a gallant 0–0 draw. Muckian proved the hero of the third replay, hitting two goals as Drogheda advanced on a 3–0 scoreline. Drogheda, under manager Jimmy McAlinden, had their players split between Dublin, Drogheda and Belfast, but they used their experience to deliver the goods and reach the Cup final.

Bohemians, meanwhile, were glad to call on experienced players too, with captain Johnny Fullam proving an inspiring leader as he bid for his seventh Cup medal, while goalkeeper Mick Smyth was in search of his sixth. Up front, Turlough O'Connor saved the day with a late equaliser in the semi-final against Sligo Rovers, but Bohs hit top form in the replay and won easily 5–0. O'Connor also played a key role in the final, laying on the winning goal for Niall Shelly, the utility player who got the nod from Billy Young for the troublesome centre-forward role.

'The 1976 final was the only one I enjoyed,' recalled Mick Smyth. 'I was very confident at that stage. I always felt I was a good goalkeeper but I was never a confident one. Any nightmare match I had was at Milltown, but at Bohs I felt I was one of the stars. I was actually being given a release by Sean Thomas but he left first and then I had a three-month trial under Billy Young and started to play well, with trainer Mick Byrne constantly telling me I was the greatest.' In gratitude to Byrne, Smyth presented him with his medal after the final.

With left-winger Gerry Ryan doubtful with hamstring trouble before the final, manager Young included Ashley Grimes as his reserve and brought him on at half-time. Grimes hit a cracker of a goal only fifteen minutes after coming on, but it was disallowed for offside against Shelly, who didn't appear to be interfering with play. Grimes and Ryan later moved to English football, with Manchester United and Derby County respectively.

Preliminary Round

22 January	Limerick	0	Dalkey United	1
			Devlin	
28 January	Sligo Rovers	3	CIE Transport	0
	Leonard, Smyth o.g.,			
	Doyle o.g.			

First Round

15 February	Bohemians	1	Ringmahon Rangers	0
	Burke			
	Cork Celtic	3	Dundalk	0
	McCarthy pen.,			
	McSweeney, Myers			
	(At Flower Lodge)			
	Dalkey United	0	Athlone Town	0
	(At Carlisle Grounds)			
	Drogheda	1	Cork Hibernians	1
	Stephens		Trainor	
	Finn Harps	3	Waterford	0
	Carlyle, Bradley 2			
	St Brendan's	1	Sligo Rovers	3
	Kennedy		Pugh, Wood, Fagan pen.	
	(At Tolka Park)			
	St Patrick's Athletic	1	Shamrock Rovers	1
	Flanagan		Magee	
	Shelbourne	1	Home Farm	1
	Lawlor		F. Devlin	

First Round Replays

18 February	Cork Hibernians	2	Drogheda	2
	Wigginton, Sweeney		Muckian, Donnelly	
		(After extra time.)		
	Home Farm	0	Shelbourne	3
			Devine, Shields pen., Roche	
19 February	Athlone Town	4	Dalkey United	1
	Whelan, Minnock,		Heffernan	
	Daly, Martin			

Shamrock Rovers Cooke pen.	1	**St Patrick's Athletic** Conway, Bridges, Byrne	3

First Round Second Replay

26 February	**Drogheda**	0	**Cork Hibernians**	0

(At Dalymount Park, after two periods of extra time.)

First Round Third Replay

1 March	**Drogheda** Muckian 2, Tully (At Tolka Park)	3	**Cork Hibernians**	0

Second Round

7 March	**Cork Celtic**	0	**Bohemians** Doran	1
	Drogheda O'Halloran	1	**St Patrick's Athletic**	0
	Shelbourne	0	**Finn Harps** Harkin, Bradley	2
	Sligo Rovers McGee, Leonard 2, Fagan	4	**Athlone Town** Davis 2	2

Semi-Final – Tolka Park

2 April	**Sligo Rovers** McGee	1	**Bohemians** O'Connor	1

Semi-Final – Dalymount Park

4 April	**Drogheda** Muckian	1	**Finn Harps**	0

Semi-Final Replay – Tolka Park

7 April	**Bohemians** Ryan, Kelly, Gregg, T. O'Connor 2	5	**Sligo Rovers**	0

Final – Dalymount Park

18 April	Bohemians	1	Drogheda	0
	Shelly (81m)			

Bohemians: Mick Smyth, Eamonn Gregg, Fran O'Brien, Tommy Kelly, Joe Burke, Johnny Fullam, Pat Byrne, Pádraig O'Connor, Turlough O'Connor, Niall Shelly, Gerry Ryan. Sub: Ashley Grimes for Ryan, 45m. Manager: Billy Young

Drogheda: Leo Byrne, Christy Campbell, Ray McGuigan, Martin Donnelly, Willie Roche, Tony Brunton, George O'Halloran, Denis Stephens, Damien Byrne, Brendan Tully, Cathal Muckian. Sub: Jerome Clarke for Campbell, 75m. Manager: Jimmy McAlinden

Referee: W. A. Attley (Dublin)   Attendance: 10,400

It's a Record!

- Bohemians and Shamrock Rovers have played in the Cup each year since 1922.

- Pat Courtney (Shamrock Rovers, 1964-69) is the only player to play in six successive Cup-winning teams.

1977

St Brigid Intervenes

Jim McLaughlin is a quick learner. The Derryman, who had a good innings in English football with Swansea, Shrewsbury and Peterborough and won twelve Northern Ireland caps, suffered a severe setback on his FAI Cup debut as a manager in 1975. Yet the following season he produced practically a new team to win the League and, in 1977, he guided his team to Cup glory. 'Defeat in the first round by the amateurs Home Farm in 1975 was one of the greatest learning experiences I ever had,' he recalled. 'It was my first FAI Cup tie and I had been lured over from England with talk of about eight full-time professionals. After the game, there were meetings going on all over the town and I was told we couldn't afford this or we couldn't afford that. Douggie Devlin and John Coyne were let go. After that experience I realised it was all about success.'

Dundalk didn't make an impressive start to the 1977 Cup campaign as – shades of Home Farm! – they scraped through 2–1 against amateurs Pegasus. It was in this game that Kevin Moran convinced Manchester United scout Billy Behan that he was English First Division material. 'Pegasus considered that Dundalk's danger man was outside-right Jimmy Dainty, so they put Kevin at left-back to mark him,' said Behan. 'I thought he was outstanding and I realised he could make it to the top.'

After a good 1–0 win away to Cork Celtic, Dundalk were in more trouble in the semi-final against St Patrick's Athletic, whose player-manager was former Chelsea and England star Barry Bridges. 'We should have lost to St Pat's as Neil

Martin caused havoc in the drawn game but, for the replay, I put Tom McConville on him and he dominated him,' recalled McLaughlin. 'Tom may not be better than him in the air but he ensured that if he wasn't going to get the ball, Martin wasn't getting it either!

'When the score was 0–0, Brian McConville gave a bad pass back that put Barry Bridges straight through but he missed the chance. Brian was lying down and it took us a while to persuade him that Bridges had missed and it was time to get up. "I was praying to St Brigid that he'd miss it," he said. Brian was from Faughart and they have great devotion to St Brigid out there.

'We didn't lose from January, after we had a three-hour meeting in Gormanston on a Saturday. I wasn't happy. We weren't on the same wavelength and hadn't got our act together. After that we went about thirteen matches unbeaten. That meeting was very important. Without it we couldn't have done what we did.'

One of the benefactors of that meeting was centre-forward Terry Flanagan, who was obliged to put in extra training stints to combat a weight problem. Having shed a half-stone in the month before the Cup final against Limerick, he proved the match-winner on the day with two goals, the first laid on by player-manager McLaughlin after a run down the left wing.

Limerick were the surprise packet of the Cup. They had been struggling until Frank Johnson was appointed manager and a shock first round win away to League champions Sligo Rovers gave them the boost they needed. In the final, they played the more attractive football without getting any reward and their hopes were also hit by an early injury to influential midfielder Johnny Walsh.

Fate intervened on Dundalk's behalf before a single ball was kicked in the Cup. For the first time ever there was a re-draw of the first round. In the original draw Dundalk were away to Cork Celtic; in the re-draw they were home to Pegasus or Home Farm. St Patrick's Athletic versus Finn Harps was the only tie re-drawn the same.

First Round

27 January	**Pegasus**	2	**Home Farm**	2
	Dolan 2 (At Belfield)		Williams, Dolan o.g.	
2 February	**Wembley Rovers**	0	**Bohemians**	6
	(At Turner's Cross)		Cooke, T. O'Connor 2 (1 pen.), Ryan, P. Byrne, Kelly	

First Round Replay

2 February	**Home Farm**	1	**Pegasus**	2
	Cervi		Travers, Henry	

Second Round

13 February	**Albert Rovers**	0	**Drogheda**	2
			Muckian, Tully	
	Bohemians	2	**Shamrock Rovers**	2
	T. O'Connor 2		Leech, Fullam pen.	
	Cork Celtic	3	**Athlone Town**	0
	Carroll, Tambling, Madden			
	Dundalk	2	**Pegasus**	1
	Lawlor, Flanagan		McGrath	
	St Patrick's Athletic	2	**Finn Harps**	1
	N. Martin, Byrne		Smith	
	Shelbourne	2	**Bray Wanderers**	0
	Delamere, Bailey			
	Sligo Rovers	1	**Limerick**	4
	Leonard		Kirby, Duggan 2, Walsh	
	Waterford	3	**TEK United**	3
	Carey 2, Dunphy		Bell pen., Heffernan, Monaghan	

Second Round Replays

16 February	**TEK United**	1	**Waterford**	2
	Monaghan		Wallace, Matthews	
	(At Tolka Park)			
23 February	**Shamrock Rovers**	0	**Bohemians**	4
			P. Byrne, Cooke, Ryan, Grimes	

Third Round

6 March	Bohemians	1	St Patrick's Athletic	1
	Cooke		S. Byrne	
	Cork Celtic	0	**Dundalk**	1
			Lawlor	
	Drogheda United	1	**Shelbourne**	1
	D. Byrne		Gannon	
	Limerick	0	**Waterford**	0

Third Round Replays

9 March	St Patrick's Athletic	1	Bohemians	0
	N. Martin			
10 March	**Shelbourne**	2	**Drogheda United**	3
	Devine, Finnegan		Muckian 2, Donnelly	
	(At Dalymount Park)			
	Waterford	0	**Limerick**	1
			Kirby	

Semi-Final – Tolka Park

1 April	St Patrick's Athletic	1	Dundalk	1
	N. Martin		Flanagan	

Semi-Final – Dalymount Park

3 April	Limerick	0	Drogheda United	0

Semi-Final Replay – Dalymount Park

6 April	Dundalk	1	St Patrick's Athletic	0
	Braddish			

(After extra time.)

Semi-Final Replay – Tolka Park

7 April	Drogheda United	1	Limerick	1
	Byrne		Nolan	

(After extra time.)

Semi-Final Second Replay – Dalymount Park

14 April   **Limerick**   **2**   **Drogheda United**   **1**
        Duggan, Kirby   Stephens

Final – Dalymount Park

1 May   **Dundalk**   **2**   **Limerick**   **0**
        Flanagan 2 (33m, 87m)

Dundalk: Richie Blackmore, Brian McConville, Jackie McManus, Tom McConville, Jim McLaughlin, Synan Braddish, Seamus McDowell, Jimmy Dainty, Mick Lawlor, Terry Flanagan, Tony Cavanagh. Manager: Jim McLaughlin

Limerick: Kevin Fitzpatrick, Pat Nolan, Tony Fitzgerald, Joe O'Mahony, John Herrick, Eamonn Deacy, Tony Meaney, Johnny Walsh, Des Kennedy, Ger Duggan, Dave Kirby. Sub: Denis Lymer for Walsh, 31m. Manager: Frank Johnson

Referee: N. Breen (Waterford)   Attendance: 17,000

1978

Sligo Revolver Backfires!

Steve Lynex had a very eventful summer in 1977. For a start, the eighteen-year-old winger was given a free release by manager Johnny Giles at West Brom. With his dreams of First Division football in ruins, he was glad to accept an offer of a month's trial from League of Ireland champions Sligo Rovers.

He was given digs above a pub in the town and after some pre-season training and a friendly against an Irish League team in which he did well, he was feeling pleased with himself. His chance of getting a contract appeared bright. However, his prospects were again shattered when, on coming down the stairs from his digs one day, a revolver was thrust into his side and he was bluntly informed, 'We don't want your kind here.' That was enough for Lynex. He packed his bags and left.

Meanwhile, Giles had returned to his native Dublin as player-manager of Shamrock Rovers, taking with him another West Brom colleague, Ray Treacy. When they were discussing possible signings, Treacy suggested that Lynex might do a good job in the League of Ireland; he had the pace to cause defenders problems. It was agreed to offer him a month's trial.

The negotiations that followed required all the tact and diplomacy that Giles could muster. He had to re-assure Lynex on two counts: first, because he was the one who had let him go at West Brom, and second, that Dublin wasn't Sligo. He succeeded – and Sligo's Cup fate was sealed.

After an encouraging trial, Lynex was signed on and he proceeded to come good, especially during Rovers' Cup run when he scored vital goals against

Dundalk and Waterford and proved the matchwinner in the final – against Sligo Rovers, whose fans' chant of 'Sligo reject' had a hollow ring about it after the ninety minutes. It was Lynex's blinding pace that led to him being taken down in the penalty area, and Treacy stepped up to shoot the only goal of the game. It was a neat twist of fortune for Lynex – and Sligo.

Lynex later moved to Birmingham City and then to Leicester City, where his fine wing play brought him to the fringe of the England team. He had no hesitation in naming Giles and Rovers as the making of him.

'Giles is a football genius. I owe him everything,' he said. 'Rovers was a great experience for me. I played in Europe and experienced a Cup final and Rovers gave me the confidence to make a go of it the second time around in England. If I hadn't gone there I probably would have been playing in the reserves somewhere in front of five hundred people and getting nowhere.'

Another player who had Giles to thank that season for his breakthrough to senior ranks was Pierce O'Leary, brother of Republic of Ireland defender David. He made his debut in December at left-back and held his place to win a Cup medal in his first season. In 1985, he managed a repeat with another Green-and-White-Hooped team when, in his first season with Glasgow Celtic, he won a Scottish Cup medal.

It was in this final that Johnny Fullam equalled the record, set in 1939 by William 'Sacky' Glen, of eight Cup-winner's medals. This was his sixth with Shamrock Rovers, while he won two with Bohemians.

First Round

25 January	**AIB** (At Milltown)	**0**	**Waterford** Matthews	**1**
	Avondale United (At Turner's Cross)	**0**	**Galway Rovers** Tom Murphy, Martin	**2**
	St James's Gate Dunne	**1**	**Home Farm** Cervi, Eviston 2, Balcombe 2	**5**
26 January	**Dalkey United** (At Belfield)	**0**	**Finn Harps** Harkin	**1**

Second Round

18 February	**Shelbourne**	**0**	**Cork Alberts**	**0**
19 February	**Athlone Town**	**0**	**Limerick**	**0**
	Finn Harps	**0**	**Shamrock Rovers**	**0**
	Home Farm Nelligan pen.	**1**	**Galway Rovers** McLoughlin	**1**
	St Patrick's Athletic	**0**	**Sligo Rovers** Delamere	**1**
	Thurles Town	**0**	**Drogheda United** Donnelly, Muckian 2	**3**
23 February	**Bohemians**	**0**	**Waterford** Wallace, McCarthy	**2**
1 March	**Cork Celtic** J. Carroll pen.	**1**	**Dundalk** Lawlor 2, Dainty pen.	**3**

Second Round Replays

22 February	**Galway Rovers** O'Connor o.g.	**1**	**Home Farm** Hughes, Eviston	**2**
23 February	**Limerick** Collins	**1**	**Athlone Town** Devlin	**1**
	(After extra time.)			
28 February	**Cork Alberts** C. McCarthy	**1**	**Shelbourne**	**0**
	(Declared void by FAI.)			
1 March	**Shamrock Rovers** Megan, Treacy 2	**3**	**Finn Harps** Ferry, Healy pen.	**2**
	(After extra time.)			

Second Round Second Replay

2 March	Limerick	1	Athlone Town	0
	O'Mahony			
	(At Dalymount Park)			

Re-Fixture

8 March	Cork Alberts	1	Shelbourne	0
	C. McCarthy			

Third Round

12 March	Cork Alberts	1	Sligo Rovers	2
	Morley pen.		Tobin 2	
	Drogheda United	1	Limerick	0
	Clarke			
	Home Farm	0	Waterford	2
			Dunphy, Wallace	
15 March	Dundalk	0	Shamrock Rovers	0

Third Round Replay

22 March	Shamrock Rovers	1	Dundalk	0
	Lynex			

Semi-Final – Dalymount Park

9 April	Shamrock Rovers	2	Waterford	1
	Meagan, Lynex		Wallace	

Semi-Final – Dundalk

9 April	Sligo Rovers	1	Drogheda United	0
	Gilligan			

Final – Dalymount Park

30 April	Shamrock Rovers	1	Sligo Rovers	0
	Treacy pen. (48m)			

Shamrock Rovers: Alan O'Neill, Mick Gannon, Pierce O'Leary, Noel Synnott, Johnny Fullam, Eamonn Dunphy, John Giles, Mark Meagan, Larry Murray, Ray Treacy, Steve Lynex. Sub: Eddie O'Sullivan for Gannon, 63m. Manager: John Giles

Sligo Rovers: Alan Patterson, Paul Fielding, Chris Rutherford, Tony Stenson, Graham Fox, John Gilligan, Tony Fagan, Don Tobin, Tony Cavanagh, Gary Hulmes, John Delamere. Sub: Harry McLoughlin for Delamere, 77m. Manager: Billy Sinclair

Referee: J. Carpenter (Dublin)   Attendance: 12,500

It's a Record!

- Dolphin beat St James's Gate 10–0 away in the first round in 1932.

- William 'Sacky' Glen played in ten FAI Cup Finals.

- Bohemians and Shamrock Rovers have played in the FAI Cup each year since its inception in 1922.

1979

Hump and Twitch Hit it Off

When Jim McLaughlin asked Dermot Keely to sign for Dundalk, centre-back Keely got quite a shock because it was the first time they had spoken a civil word to each other! As opponents – Keely with St Patrick's Athletic – they had hurled abuse at each other on the field. Keely's references to the humpty-back style of running for which McLaughlin was noted were not exactly designed to endear him to the Derryman, while McLaughlin wasn't slow to remind Keely of the nervous twitch that developed in his eye when he got excited.

'Jim played mainly at left-full but when the going got tough he went mad,' recalled Keely. 'The forwards would disappear as they usually do and McLaughlin would come up the field and hurl abuse at me, trying to unsettle me, and I'd tell him to get back in his box, with a few well chosen expletives. So you could have knocked me down when he called and asked me to sign.' The signing wasn't all plain sailing either, as Dundalk director Jim O'Reilly, who sat in on the negotiations, strongly advised McLaughlin to have nothing to do with Keely. However, the manager knew what he wanted, the deal was concluded and a trophy-winning partnership was begun.

Keely, who had won a Cup medal with Home Farm in 1975 before moving to St Patrick's Athletic, soon rewarded McLaughlin's faith, proving the linch-pin of the defence as Dundalk marched to the club's first League and Cup double in 1978-79. The Dundalk defence of Richie Blackmore in goal, Tom McConville and Martin Lawlor at full-back, and Keely and Paddy Dunning at centre-back was the best the League of Ireland had seen for a number of years. 'They were ruthless – they wouldn't give you a sausage,' commented McLaughlin.

As has happened on a number of occasions, the Cup finalists were scheduled to meet in a League game the week before the final. On this occasion, the game was at Oriel Park and Dundalk were hosting Waterford. 'The game meant nothing to us because we had the League wrapped up but they beat us 3–0 and took too much pleasure out of it,' recalled McLaughlin. 'Sid Wallace got two goals and gave Dermot Keely the V sign after he stuck in the second. Keely told him he wouldn't get two kicks never mind two goals the following week!

'When I went into the dressingroom on Cup final day I had a lot of things written on a page but I put a match to the paper and said, "Right, lads, so much for what I was going to say, now go out and do what you're capable of." It was the best team talk I ever gave.'

Dundalk, who went in front after four minutes when a Sean Byrne shot completely fooled Waterford goalkeeper Peter Thomas, had to soak up a lot of pressure before Hilary Carlyle wrapped up the game in injury time when he ran on to a ball from defence, seemed to push Tommy Jackson out of the way and delivered a beautiful shot well out of Thomas's reach.

'That Cup final was a great occasion,' recalled Keely, whose father Peter was a losing finalist with Shelbourne in 1949 and 1951. 'When we got back to Dundalk that night, huge crowds welcomed us. It was fantastic compared to Home Farm when there was nothing after we won in 1975. But that was the last time they got excited in Dundalk. The next time we won, in 1981, it was nothing like that – they had got used to winning.'

First Round

11 February	Athlone Town	1	Sligo Rovers	0
	Bradley			
	Crofton Celtic	0	Drogheda United	2
	(At St Colman's Park)		Brammeld 2	
	Dundalk	1	St Patrick's Athletic	0
	Carlyle			
	Galway Rovers	4	Cork Celtic	1
	Proctor, Collins 2, McGrain		O'Brien	
	Home Farm	1	Finn Harps	2
	Moran		P. McGuinness, McGrory	
	Shamrock Rovers	2	Shelbourne	1
	Byrne 2		Barber	
	Thurles Town	0	Limerick	0
	Waterford	1	Bohemians	1
	Finucane		Kelly	
18 February	Tramore Athletic	0	Swilly Rovers	1
	(At UCC Grounds)		O'Keefe	
28 February	Cork Alberts	3	Wembley Rovers	0
	McCarthy, Lane, Murphy			

First Round Replays

15 February	Limerick	4	Thurles Town	1
	Meaney 2 (1 pen.), Duggan, Fitzgerald		Flanagan	
22 February	Bohemians	1	Waterford	1
	T. O'Connor		Finucane	

First Round Second Replay

1 March	Waterford	1	Bohemians	0
	Hall			

Second Round

28 February	Galway Rovers	1	Swilly Rovers	0
	French			
1 March	Athlone Town	0	Drogheda United	1
			Brammeld	

Third Round

11 March	**Drogheda United**	1	**Cork Alberts**	1
	Leech		Lane	
	Dundalk	2	**Finn Harps**	0
	Dainty pen., Muckian			
	Galway Rovers	0	**Waterford**	1
			McCarthy	
	Shamrock Rovers	2	**Limerick**	0
	Byrne, Gaffney			

Third Round Replay

15 March	**Cork Alberts**	2	**Drogheda United**	0
	Hutchinson, Lane			

Semi-Finals – Dalymount Park

1 April	**Dundalk**	2	**Cork Alberts**	1
	Byrne, Dunning		Murphy	
8 April	**Shamrock Rovers**	1	**Waterford**	2
	Giles pen.		Wallace 2	

Final – Dalymount Park

22 April	**Dundalk**	2	**Waterford**	0
	Byrne (4m), Carlyle (90m)			

Dundalk: Richie Blackmore, Tom McConville, Dermot Keely, Paddy Dunning, Martin Lawlor, Leo 'Pop' Flanagan, Mick Lawlor, Sean Byrne, Jimmy Dainty, Hilary Carlyle, Cathal Muckian. Manager: Jim McLaughlin

Waterford: Peter Thomas, Ger O'Mahony, Tony Dunphy, Al Finucane, Brian Gardiner, Mick Madigan, Tommy Jackson, Vinny McCarthy, John Smith, Sid Wallace, Johnny Matthews. Manager: Tommy Jackson

Referee: P. Daly (Dublin)   Attendance: 14,000

1980

Jackson Changes his Mind

Limerickman Al Finucane is one of only two players – Johnny Fullam (Shamrock Rovers and Bohemians) is the other – to have captained two different clubs to FAI Cup success, but his 1980 triumph with Waterford was almost denied him.

Although Waterford's manager, Tommy Jackson, the former Northern Ireland international, often asked Finucane's advice on League of Ireland players, there was a personality clash between the two from the day he took over. Blows were almost struck when this disagreement surfaced at Brian Gardiner's wedding in Kilkenny, when former Manchester United full-back Shay Brennan moved in to smooth things over.

Waterford had enjoyed a lot of success in the League but, apart from a lone win in 1937, the Cup had eluded them. At times it seemed there was a jinx over their efforts and this opinion was fuelled when goalkeeping errors by the normally reliable Peter Thomas proved costly in a 1978 semi-final tie against Shamrock Rovers and in the 1979 final against Dundalk. However, the harder the task became the more the Waterford club wanted to achieve that second Cup success.

Good wins over Thurles Town, Cork United and Athlone Town put Waterford into a semi-final against Limerick, the club Finucane had captained to Cup glory in 1971. By a strange twist, the League fixtures paired the two clubs at Kilcohan Park the week before the semi-final – in a repeat of 1979 when the Blues played Dundalk in the League the week before they met in the Cup final.

In 1979 Dundalk had lost the League game but won the Cup tie. History was about to repeat itself.

Waterford lost the Kilcohan clash 4–3 in what Finucane described as 'the greatest League of Ireland game I ever played in'. He scored one of the Blues' goals and was involved in another. The following Tuesday, when the manager rang him to arrange a meeting in Tipperary, Finucane thought he was looking for some advice on the Limerick players he knew so well. Instead, he was told he was being dropped for the Cup semi-final. 'The manager thought I hadn't put it in the previous Sunday,' recalled Finucane. 'I was naturally stunned but I said, "You're the manager, it's your decision."'

When the news broke the following day, Waterford Chairman Joe Delaney was on the phone to Finucane asking him what was going on. When Finucane said he had been dropped, Delaney replied, 'If you're not playing on Sunday, he'll be sacked on Saturday,' indicating how highly Finucane was rated among Blues fans. At training in Waterford the day before the game, Jackson informed Finucane that he was playing.

However he arrived at his decision, it proved a good one on Jackson's part, for Finucane had a vital role to play in the Cup final against St Patrick's Athletic. Waterford were leading St Pat's from early on with a goal by left-full Brian Gardiner, but gradually the Dublin side were getting on top and centre-forward Jackie Jameson, in particular, was causing his marker, Tony Dunphy, a lot of problems. Eventually, Jackson told Finucane to switch with Dunphy and mark Jameson and from then on the game went away from St Pat's. 'Jameson liked to be right up against his marker, to know exactly where he was,' explained Finucane, 'and Tony was doing this. When I marked him, I stood off him so that he didn't know where I was and he didn't like that and eventually got booked for taking a swipe at me!'

First Round

10 February	**AIB** O'Reilly (At Belfield)	1	**Athlone Town** Devlin 3, Clarke	4
	CIE Transport Smith, Cassidy (At Richmond Park)	2	**St Patrick's Athletic** Wright, Barron	2
	Cobh Ramblers	0	**Home Farm**	0
	Cork United McCarthy 2, Allen, Punch	4	**UCD** Moran	1
	Drogheda United	0	**Limerick United** Walsh, Delamere, Ferguson o.g.	3
	Dundalk Braddish, Duff, Harkin	3	**Finn Harps** Minnock	1
	Shamrock Rovers	0	**Bohemians** Lawless, Whelan	2
	Shelbourne	0	**Galway Rovers** Cooke pen.	1
	Sligo Rovers	0	**Tramore Athletic**	0
	Thurles Town	0	**Waterford** Kirk 2, Finucane, Gardiner, O'Mahony	5

First Round Replays

13 February	**St Patrick's Athletic** Carthy 2, Daly	3	**CIE Transport** Cassidy, O'Brien	2
14 February	**Home Farm** Archbold, Williams	2	**Cobh Ramblers**	0
20 February	**Tramore Athletic** (At Flower Lodge)	0	**Sligo Rovers** Skeffington 2	2

Second Round

28 February	**Athlone Town** P. O'Connor, McCue	2	**Sligo Rovers**	0
	Waterford Madigan, Murray 2 (1 pen.)	3	**Cork United**	0

Third Round

9 March	Bohemians	2	Galway Rovers	1
	Byrne, Lawless		Quinlivan	
	Dundalk	0	Limerick United	1
			Morris	
	St Patrick's Athletic	1	Home Farm	1
	Carthy		Archbold	
	Waterford	1	Athlone Town	0
	Gardiner			

Third Round Replay

| 12 March | Home Farm | 1 | St Patrick's Athletic | 2 |
| | King | | Carthy 2 | |

Semi-Finals – Dalymount Park

30 March	St Patrick's Athletic	1	Bohemians	0
	Malone			
6 April	Waterford	1	Limerick United	1
	Jackson pen.		Walsh	

Semi-Final Replay – Milltown

| 10 April | Waterford | 3 | Limerick United | 2 |
| | Wallace, Dunphy, Kirk | | Kennedy, Walsh | |

Final – Dalymount Park

| 20 April | Waterford | 1 | St Patrick's Athletic | 0 |
| | Gardiner (22m) | | | |

Waterford: Peter Thomas, Ger O'Mahony, Tony Dunphy, Al Finucane, Brian Gardiner, Mark Meagan, Mick Madigan, Vinny McCarthy, Larry Murray, Sid Wallace, Paul Kirk. Subs: Tommy Jackson for McCarthy, 73m; Eamonn Coady for Wallace, 83m. Manager: Tommy Jackson

St Patrick's Athletic: Jim Grace, Tony Higgins, Willie Roche, Barry Murphy, George Munnelly, Niall O'Donnell, Joey Malone, Tommy Hynes, Derek Carthy, Jackie Jameson, Paul Kirwan. Subs: Mick Wright for Carthy, 70m; Aidan Daly for Munnelly, 77m. Manager: Charlie Walker

Referee: K. O'Sullivan (Cork)   Attendance: 18,000

1981

The Courage of Fairclough

Mick Fairclough, who clinched the 1981 FAI Cup for Dundalk with a superbly taken goal after a run from the half-way line, shouldn't have been playing that day. Six years earlier, he had been the victim of a brutal tackle from a Watford player during an English Third Division game for Huddersfield Town. The resulting knee injury finished his English League career at the age of twenty-two. Fairclough had been transferred to Huddersfield from Drogheda where, as a youth, he had lined out in the 1971 FAI Cup Final against Limerick. With Huddersfield he played First, Second and Third Division football before his injury, was capped at under twenty-three level and also travelled with the international squad to Brazil in 1972. He attempted a comeback with Dundalk in 1978 but found his knee wasn't up to it. 'Jim McLaughlin then put me in touch with Bobby McGregor in Belfast and it was like a miracle after that, as four or five specialists had said I'd never play again,' he recalled.

'Mick was playing for CIE against Telephones when I saw him again,' said McLaughlin. 'It was a very physical game and he was throwing himself around even though he was a cripple. I said why not risk it at a higher level if you're prepared to do that. He was dying to have a go so it only took two seconds to persuade him to sign.'

Fairclough made his League comeback in February 1980 as a sub against Shamrock Rovers at Milltown – and scored the equaliser. It was a dream comeback and when he returned just over a year later to the same ground for the FAI

Cup Semi-Final against Finn Harps he was on the mark again, scoring the only goal of the game. 'When I go out on the pitch I just throw caution to the winds – I was always like that,' he said. 'I never did think of my injury; there wouldn't be any point in going out there if I did. As far as I'm concerned I'm as fit as anyone else out there.'

Dundalk centre-half Dermot Keely was concussed for most of the first half of the final against Sligo Rovers following a collision with teammate Tom McConville. He recalled that Dundalk departed from normal pre-match procedure to discuss the opposing star man, Charlie McGeever. 'We rarely spoke about the opposition, but we spent about ten minutes talking about picking up McGeever in midfield,' he said. 'Then, when I saw him lining up in defence I knew we would win. Still, he was great in that game. He leaped like a kangaroo and there was no marking him at the corners.' Sadly, McGeever's promising career was halted shortly after when he suffered a bad knee injury.

Another star for Sligo that year was winger Harry McLoughlin, whose rocket shot beat Waterford in the semi-final replay at Tolka Park. However, his lack of experience of the big occasion showed in the final. 'I should have scored after about four minutes,' he recalled. 'The ball came out and broke to me. With only Richie Blackmore to beat I should have taken it around him but I hit it first time and he saved it with his legs.'

The game got away from Sligo when Dundalk winger John Archbold opened the scoring direct from a corner kick. It was one more blow to add to the catalogue of misfortune that has befallen Sligo in Cup finals. As veteran supporter Fraser Browne put it, 'In 1939 the goals we conceded in the final against Shelbourne came direct from a corner kick and a free kick; in 1978 the goal came from a penalty kick in mysteriously added-on time; in 1981 the first goal came direct from a corner kick. Can any other club have been so unlucky in Cup finals?' Fortunately, Sligo's run of misfortune was to end soon.

First Round

8 February	**Ballyfermot United**	2	**Cork United**	5
	Cleary, Al Farrell pen.		McSweeney, McCarthy,	
	(At Milltown)		Allen, Waters 2	
	Cobh Ramblers	3	**Galway Rovers**	1
	O'Leary, McDaid, F. O'Neill		Herrick pen.	
	Dundalk	1	**Hammond Lane**	0
	Lawlor			
	Finn Harps	3	**Athlone Town**	0
	McIlwaine 2, Logan			
	Home Farm	1	**Bohemians**	0
	Thomas			
	Limerick United	2	**Thurles Town**	2
	Matthews, Kennedy		Doran, Cooke	
	Tramore Athletic	0	**Drogheda United**	3
	(At Turner's Cross)		Murray 2, Byrne	
	St Patrick's Athletic	4	**Shelbourne**	1
	Mahon 2, Jameson, Carthy		Donnelly pen.	
	Sligo Rovers	1	**UCD**	1
	McLoughlin		Doyle	
	Waterford	2	**Shamrock Rovers**	1
	Gardiner, Madden		Buckley	

First Round Replays

| 11 February | **Thurles Town** | 1 | **Limerick United** | 1 |
| | Sheehy | | Meaney | |

(After extra time.)

| 12 February | **UCD** | 1 | **Sligo Rovers** | 2 |
| | Doyle | | Fagan, McGeever | |

First Round Second Replay

| 19 February | **Limerick United** | 2 | **Thurles Town** | 0 |
| | Murphy, Morris | | | |

Second Round

| 18 February | **Cork United** | 0 | **Drogheda United** | 1 |
| | | | Nugent | |

St Patrick's Athletic	1	Dundalk	1
Mahon pen.		Duff	

Second Round Replay

26 February	Dundalk	2	St Patrick's Athletic	0
	T. McConville, Archbold			

Third Round

8 March	Cobh Ramblers	1	Finn Harps	4
	P. O'Neill		Logan 2, McLoughlin, McGonagle	
	Drogheda United	0	Dundalk	0
	Limerick United	1	Waterford	1
	Jackson o.g.		Dunphy	
	Sligo Rovers	3	Home Farm	0
	McGroarty, Patton, McGeever			

Third Round Replays

12 March	Dundalk	1	Drogheda United	0
	Duff			
19 March	Waterford	3	Limerick United	1
	Madden 2, Jackson		Matthews	

Semi-Final – Dalymount Park

4 April	Sligo Rovers	2	Waterford	2
	Patton, Sheridan		Finucane, Madden	

Semi-Final – Milltown

5 April	Dundalk	1	Finn Harps	0
	Fairclough			

Semi-Final Replay – Tolka Park

9 April	Sligo Rovers	1	Waterford	0
	McLoughlin			

Final – Dalymount Park

26 April   **Dundalk**   **2**   **Sligo Rovers**   **0**
Archbold (52m)
Fairclough (79m)

Dundalk: Richie Blackmore, Tom McConville, Dermot Keely, Paddy Dunning, Martin Lawlor, Sean Byrne, Leo 'Pop' Flanagan, Vinny McKenna, John Archbold, Mick Fairclough, Willie Crawley. Subs: Tony O'Doherty for Lawlor, 66m; Brian Duff for Crawley, 80m. Manager: Jim McLaughlin

Sligo Rovers: Declan McIntyre, Mick Ferry, Paddy Sheridan, Donal O'Doherty, Charlie McGeever, Jimmy McGroarty, Tony Fagan, Gerry Doherty, Harry McLoughlin, Brendan Bradley, Liam Patton. Subs: Pat Coyle for Patton, 81m; Martin McDonnell for O'Doherty, 83m. Manager: Patsy McGowan

Referee: P. Mulhall (Dublin)   Attendance: 12,000

It's a Record!

- The oldest FAI Cup-winner was Harry Buckle, who was eleven days past his forty-fourth birthday when he captained Fordsons to victory in 1926.

- Apart from player-manager Liam Tuohy, Damien Richardson was the only member of Shamrock Rovers' six-in-a-row squad of the 1960s who went on to manage a team to FAI Cup glory. In contrast, from the Rovers' three-in-a-row squad of the 1980s, Dermot Keely, Pat Byrne and Paul Doolin all managed that feat.

1982

Ward's Successful Switch

Tony Ward is synonymous with rugby, having been a regular member of the Irish team for a number of years and two-time winner of the coveted Golden Boot award. However, he has had a life-long love affair with soccer and played it as often as he could, winning a schoolboy cap in the company of Liam Brady and lining out with Shamrock Rovers in the League of Ireland and the FAI Cup. As a member of a particularly good Rangers schoolboy side, he had received offers of trials with English League clubs. Until 1982, his only senior soccer award was a Leinster Senior Cup medal won with Rovers. 'I would love to have been able to play soccer and rugby but you can't – you fall between two stools,' he said.

He was based in Limerick when Eoin Hand, the former Portsmouth and Republic of Ireland defender, was appointed manager of the Market's Field Club. Hand tried to woo Ward over to soccer, but Ward made it clear that rugby came first. At the start of the 1980-81 season, he played in friendlies against Tottenham and Newport County, but was unavailable then due to his Garryowen commitments. When Garryowen were knocked out of the Munster Cup early in 1981, he played a few more games for Limerick and at the start of the 1981-82 season, he played in some League Cup ties and also lined out against Southampton in the UEFA Cup.

In 1982 Garryowen was knocked out of the Munster Cup early on again, allowing Ward to play in Limerick's opening FAI Cup tie away to Bluebell United. Limerick scrambled an unimpressive win, but subsequent good wins over Shelbourne and Aer Lingus clinched a semi-final tie against Athlone Town. Rugby took over then, as Garryowen had a League final engagement, but Ward was available for the replay and played in the 1–0 win even though he was 'dying with the 'flu'.

'The final was one of the most enjoyable games I played in,' he recalled. 'It was a great team; there was great camaraderie. We stayed in the Burlington for the weekend. Everything was as it should be – done professionally. I remember driving up in the coach to Dalymount and seeing Bohemians' full-back, Dave Connell, walking up with his bag in his hand. I thought that could be the difference between us, our preparation compared to theirs.'

While Ward didn't play many games for Limerick, he was involved in training sessions on the morning of every home game and these sessions concentrated on set pieces. This paid off in the final, with Ward driving over a low corner centre-half Brendan Storan shot to the net for the only goal of the game.

Joe O'Mahony played a captain's part as Limerick held on to their lead. 'With just over ten minutes to go, I fell heavily and banged my head,' he recalled. 'Although it rained right through the game, the ground was still hard and I suffered double vision but I wouldn't go off – I wanted to lift that Cup. Just after that, Mick Shelly shot, I threw myself at it and it hit the side of my throat. I knew then that our name was on the Cup. It was very satisfying for me and more than made up for losing in 1977.'

About Ward's involvement, O'Mahony said, 'Tony played a big part in our win. He gave us great width on the right and whenever we gave him the ball he made great ground. He had great pace and balance and could have been the difference between us going the whole way or not.'

First Round

5 February	Shelbourne	2	Waterford	1
	Joyce 2		Madden	
6 February	Bluebell United	0	Limerick United	1
	(At Iveagh Grounds)		Gaynor	
7 February	Bohemians	4	Finn Harps	0
	McDonagh, O'Brien			
	Jameson 2			
	Cork United	1	Home Farm	1
	McCarthy		Connolly	
	Drogheda United	1	Shamrock Rovers	1
	Martin		Hankin	
	Dundalk	1	Thurles Town	0
	Flanagan			
	Galway United	2	Tramore Athletic	1
	Morley, Mannion		O'Regan	
	St Patrick's Athletic	1	Athlone Town	1
	Mahon		Carroll	
	UCD	1	Sligo Rovers	1
	Reynolds		Bradley	
	Workman's Club	0	Aer Lingus	1
			Burnett	

First Round Replays

10 February	Sligo Rovers	1	UCD	3
	Bradley		Dignam, Norman pen.,	
			Saundh	
	Home Farm	1	Cork United	2
	Burke		C. McCarthy 2	
11 February	Shamrock Rovers	0	Drogheda United	0
	(After extra time.)			
	Athlone Town	2	St Patrick's Athletic	2
	M. O'Connor pen., McCue		Mahon 2	
	(After extra time.)			

First Round Second Replays

17 February	**Drogheda United**	1	**Shamrock Rovers**	4
	Treacy		Buckley 2, Campbell, Gaffney	
	St Patrick's Athletic	0	**Athlone Town**	3
			Carroll, Davis 2	

Second Round

17 February	**Dundalk**	4	**Cork United**	3
	Kehoe, Fairclough, Flanagan 2 (1 pen.)		McConville o.g., O'Mahony, McSweeney	
	Shelbourne	1	**Limerick United**	2
	Joyce		Hand 2	

Third Round

7 March	**Athlone Town**	1	**Shamrock Rovers**	0
	Devlin			
	Dundalk	2	**Galway United**	0
	Crawley 2			
	Limerick United	4	**Aer Lingus**	0
	Gaynor, Storan, Hulmes, Walsh			
	UCD	1	**Bohemians**	2
	O'Doherty pen.		Eviston, Doolin	

Semi-Final – Tolka Park

| 2 April | **Bohemians** | 3 | **Dundalk** | 3 |
| | King, Jameson, O'Brien | | Flanagan pen., Ralph, Kehoe | |

Semi-Final – Dalymount Park

| 4 April | **Athlone Town** | 1 | **Limerick United** | 1 |
| | Devlin | | Gaynor | |

Semi-Final Replay – Milltown

6 April   **Bohemians**   **0**   **Dundalk**   **0**

(After extra time.)

Semi-Final Replay – Tolka Park

8 April   **Limerick United**   **1**   **Athlone Town**   **0**
Gaynor

Semi-Final Second Replay – Tolka Park

14 April   **Bohemians**   **1**   **Dundalk**   **1**
O'Brien   Crawley

Semi-Final Third Replay

21 April   **Bohemians**   **2**   **Dundalk**   **1**
Shelly, Reynor   Kehoe

Final – Dalymount Park

2 May   **Limerick United**   **1**   **Bohemians**   **0**
Storan (34m)

Limerick United: Kevin Fitzpatrick, Pat Nolan, Brendan Storan, Joe O'Mahony, Al Finucane, Eoin Hand, Jimmy Nodwell, Johnny Walsh, Tony Ward, Tommy Gaynor, Gary Hulmes. Subs: Ger Duggan for Hand, 71m; Des Kennedy for Hulmes, 83m. Manager: Eoin Hand

Bohemians: Dermot O'Neill, Dave Connell, Jacko McDonagh, John McCormack, Gino Lawless, Paul Doolin, Tommy Kelly, Noel King, David 'Rocky' O'Brien, Jackie Jameson, Mick Shelly. Subs: John Reynor for Kelly, 79m; Alan Kinsella for Reynor, 91m. Manager: Billy Young

Referee: S. Kinsella (Dublin)   Attendance: 12,000

1983

Local Hero Harry

When Sligo Rovers won the FAI Cup for the first time in 1983 – after five previous unsuccessful attempts – even the players were caught on the hop! Regarded as one of the worst sides ever to represent the Connacht club, and firmly stuck at the bottom of the League table, none of the players bothered to have the usual bet at the start of the Cup. 'If we thought we had even half an average team, we always had a bet,' said captain Tony Fagan, 'but we weren't a good side in 1983.'

One factor that didn't help Sligo's League form was the absence of star winger Harry McLoughlin for the best part of four months. 'I was out sick with high blood pressure and spent some time in St Vincent's Hospital in Dublin,' he recalled. 'They put me on tablets but told me I couldn't play football while I was on the tablets. That was too much for me so eventually I threw away the tablets and went back training. I made my comeback in the first round of the Cup away to Home Farm. I thought I was terrible in the second half and I wanted to come off but Paul Fielding wouldn't take me off. Obviously he felt I needed the match practice.'

Player-manager Fielding's decision was justified a month later in the second round of the Cup when McLoughlin hit a superb goal to give Sligo the best possible start against Cup specialists Shamrock Rovers, with captain Tony Fagan completing the job with a free kick 'special'. 'That win put us back on our feet,' said Fagan. 'The club was able to borrow money on the strength of being in the semi-final.'

Sligo, drawn against non-League Cobh Ramblers in the semi-final, thought they had got the easier half of the draw – but that was far from the case. It took a goal in the last three minutes from sub Mick Graham to save Sligo in the first game at Flower Lodge. A 2–2 draw followed at the Showgrounds, then a 0–0 draw at Flower Lodge. At half-time in the third replay at the Showgrounds, Cobh led 2–0 and it looked all over for the men from the West. However, a quick goal on the resumption from centre-half Chris Rutherford and the backing of an enthusiastic crowd kept the pressure on Cobh. Rutherford struck again and then sub Gus Gilligan, who had only made a comeback the previous day in the reserves following a cartilege operation, netted the winner.

Sligo's luck seemed to have run out in the final when Rutherford had to be replaced in the first twenty minutes. Then Barry Murphy headed Bohemians into the lead and Sligo's centre-half, Tony Stenson, received a nasty cut on his leg that threatened to end his involvement. The intervention of former trainer James Tiernan, who came down from the stand and insisted that Stenson would be in no danger if he played on, was vital. 'A normal fellow would have come off,' said captain Fagan, 'but Stenson got about five stitches at half-time and played on. Being the Cup final, he wasn't going to go off – and then he hit the equaliser. After that, Bohs lost all their rhythm and Harry scored a goal worthy of winning any Cup final.'

McLoughlin's winning goal was straight from the coaching manual. He switched from the right wing to the left, ran on to a ball Martin McDonnell had pushed down the wing and, as the Bohemians defenders backed off, he looked up, saw Dermot O'Neill slightly off his line, looked down and struck the ball with stunning accuracy into the far corner. It was third-time lucky for McLoughlin, who had been signed from Sligo Boys' Club in 1977 as a twenty-one-year-old and had suffered the disappointments of Cup final defeats in 1978 and 1981. For Tony Fagan it was even sweeter, as he had also been on the losing side in 1970.

First Round

5 February	Home Farm	0	Sligo Rovers	1
			Elliott pen.	
6 February	Athlone Town	2	Bluebell United	0
	Wyse, Byrne			
	Cobh Ramblers	2	Dundalk	1
	McDaid, O'Halloran		Archbold	
	Finn Harps	0	CIE Mosney	0
	Galway United	1	Drogheda United	1
	Duff		Dillon	
	Shamrock Rovers	2	Ringmahon Bangers	0
	Synnott, Campbell			
	Shelbourne	0	Bohemians	0
	UCD	0	Limerick United	2
			Duggan, Kennedy	
	Waterford	2	St Patrick's Athletic	2
	Gardiner, Coady		Davis, Cleary	

First Round Replays

9 February	Bohemians	2	Shelbourne	1
	Gannon o.g., O'Brien pen.		McCabe pen.	
	Drogheda United	1	Galway United	0
	Dillon			
10 February	St Patrick's Athletic	2	Waterford United	2
	McKeon, Mahon pen.		O'Mahony, Browne	
	(After extra time.)			
16 February	CIE Mosney	0	Finn Harps	0
	(At United Park)			
	(After extra time.)			

First Round Second Replays

15 February	Waterford United	1	St Patrick's Athletic	1
	Breslin		Hennebry	
	(After extra time.)			
25 February	Finn Harps	2	CIE Mosney	0
	Bradley, Sheridan			

First Round Third Replay

| 17 February | St Patrick's Athletic
Cleary, Mahon, Tierney | 3 | Waterford United
Coady, Madigan | 2 |

Second Round

| 23 February | St Patrick's Athletic | 0 | Limerick
Morris | 1 |

Third Round

6 March	Athlone Town	0	Bohemians O'Brien, Walker	2
	Cobh Ramblers F. O'Neill	1	Finn Harps	0
	Limerick United	0	Drogheda United Murray	1
	Sligo Rovers McLoughlin, Fagan	2	Shamrock Rovers Buckley	1

Semi-Final – Tolka Park

| 3 April | Bohemians | 0 | Drogheda United | 0 |

Semi-Final – Flower Lodge

| 3 April | Cobh Ramblers
O'Halloran pen. | 1 | Sligo Rovers
Graham | 1 |

Semi-Final Replay – Oriel Park, Dundalk

| 6 April | Bohemians | 0 | Drogheda United | 0 |
| | (After extra time.) | | | |

Semi-Final Replay – Showgrounds, Sligo

| 6 April | Sligo Rovers
McLoughlin, Graham | 2 | Cobh Ramblers
Crowley, O'Flynn | 2 |
| | (After extra time.) | | | |

Semi-Final Second Replay – Tolka Park

13 April   **Bohemians**   **3**   **Drogheda United**   **0**
Jameson, Murphy, Doolin

Semi-Final Second Replay – Flower Lodge

13 April   **Cobh Ramblers**   **0**   **Sligo Rovers**   **0**

Semi-Final Third Replay – Showgrounds

17 April   **Sligo Rovers**   **3**   **Cobh Ramblers**   **2**
Rutherford 2, Gilligan   F. O'Neill 2

Final – Dalymount Park

24 April   **Sligo Rovers**   **2**   **Bohemians**   **1**
Stenson (58m),   Murphy (35m)
McLoughlin (77m)

Sligo Rovers: Colin Oakley, Mick Ferry, Chris Rutherford, Tony Stenson, Graham Fox, Mick Savage, Tony Fagan, Martin McDonnell, Harry McLoughlin, Gus Gilligan, Andy Elliott. Sub: Paul Fielding for Rutherford, 19m. Manager: Paul Fielding

Bohemians: Dermot O'Neill, Dave Connell, Barry Murphy, Alan Kinsella, Gino Lawless, Paul Doolin, Pat Walker, John Reynor, David 'Rocky' O'Brien, Jackie Jameson, Terry Eviston. Subs: Donal Murphy for Eviston, 66m; Mick Shelly for Reynor, 81m. Manager: Billy Young

Referee: R. Finn (Waterford)   Attendance: 8,500

1984

Tony O'Neill Vindicated

By his own admission, Tony O'Neill was a 'brutal' player, so it is to his credit that he decided early on to channel his love of football in other directions. Career-wise, he qualified as a doctor and specialised in sports medicine, while hobby-wise, he became involved in the running of University College Dublin's soccer club. Gradually the two complemented one another so well that it was hard to see where one began and the other ended.

O'Neill's early experience as an administrator was as club secretary for five years in the 1960s. Later, he ran the club's Amateur League team for six years with some success and he was heavily involved in a succession of foreign tours to places like Australia, the United States, the Middle East, the Far East, and a history-making trip to China in 1976.

Meanwhile, the club had become a member of the League of Ireland's B Division in 1970 but had never managed anything better than a mid-table position. However, the feeling within the committee was that the club should aspire to full League status. 'In terms of facilities and participation, we thought we could make a go of it, because we had seen it done in other countries,' explained O'Neill, 'but we didn't think it would happen so quickly.'

In fact, League membership was sprung on the club in 1979, after their application had been turned down at the annual general meeting, when Cork Celtic failed to get their house in order and were thrown out on 19 July. As UCD's was the only application to hand, they were elected to take Celtic's place.

'I was expecting to be appointed in charge of the League of Ireland B team – and it turned out to be the League of Ireland team, with Theo Dunne,' recalled O'Neill.

Once in, UCD and O'Neill were never short of ideas to make up for their lack of players. An arrangement with Vancouver Whitecaps helped get the club over a tricky patch for a couple of years, while the soccer scholarship scheme was gradually producing players of League-of-Ireland ability. In their first and fourth seasons, the club had to apply for re-election; the latter occasion prompted them to sign their first professionals.

It was a brave decision but one that brought quick reward, as O'Neill appointed Dermot Keely player-manager and Keely signed goalkeeper Alan O'Neill, defenders Robbie Lawlor and Paddy Dunning, midfielder Robbie Gaffney and forward Frank Devlin. Even though Keely left in mid-season for Shamrock Rovers, the foundations had been laid that would yield FAI Cup glory, ironically at the expense of Keely and Rovers.

While their style of play may not have been attractive – dour defence allied to breakaway attacks – it was effective and was a case of the team playing to its strengths. Everton found this out later in the Cup-winners' Cup when they scraped through on a 1–0 aggregate and their manager, Howard Kendall, paid the UCD defence a nice compliment when he stated later in the campaign that the Bayern Munich defence could hardly be any better than UCD's!

UCD ended Shamrock Rovers' long-running invincibility in Cup final replays but they almost lost the Cup as soon as they won it: shortly after the game it was stolen along with vice-chairman Tony Dunne's car. It was returned twenty-four hours later – but Dunne's car was found burnt-out.

Both final goals for UCD were scored by players who had been on soccer scholarships and, to complete the double, they both graduated the same year. Ken O'Doherty, scorer of the winning goal, became the club's first big-money transfer when he moved to Crystal Palace the following season, while Joe Hanrahan later moved to Manchester United.

First Round

3 February	**Ballyfermot United** (At Milltown)	0	**Bank Rovers** Cooke o.g.	1
5 February	**Drogheda United**	0	**Waterford United** Bennett	1
	Finn Harps Bradley, Travers McLoughlin pen.	3	**Bohemians**	0
	Galway United Cassidy 2, Laffey, Duff	4	**Crofton Celtic**	0
	Limerick City Kennedy	1	**Athlone Town** Collins	1
	St Mary's, Athlone (At St Mel's Park)	0	**Shamrock Rovers** O'Brien, Campbell, McDonagh pen.	3
	St Patrick's Athletic Baddish, Malone	2	**Home Farm** Swift, Conway 2	3
	Shelbourne Delamere	1	**Dundalk**	0
	Sligo Rovers O'Sullivan o.g., McGee, Savage	3	**UCD** Dignam, O'Doherty, Lawlor	3

First Round Replays

8 February	**UCD** O'Sullivan 2, Devlin, O'Doherty pen., Hanrahan	5	**Sligo Rovers**	0
9 February	**Athlone Town** Collins, M. O'Connor pen.	2	**Limerick City** Kennedy, P. O'Connor o.g., Hulmes	3

Second Round

23 February	**Bank Rovers** (At Oriel Park)	0	**Waterford United** Bennett 2, Sutton, Coady, Reid	5

Third Round

11 March	Home Farm	1	UCD	2
	Duffy		Martin o.g., Gaffney	
	Limerick City	0	Shamrock Rovers	1
			Eviston	
	Shelbourne	1	Galway United	0
	Joyce			
	Waterford United	2	Finn Harps	1
	Coady, Reid		McGroarty	

Semi-Final – Dalymount Park

6 April	Shamrock Rovers	1	Shelbourne	1
	Eccles		Joyce	

Semi-Final – Tolka Park

8 April	UCD	1	Waterford United	0
	Hanrahan			

Semi-Final Replay – Dalymount Park

11 April	Shamrock Rovers	1	Shelbourne	0
	Buckley			

Final – Dalymount Park

29 April	UCD	0	Shamrock Rovers	0

UCD: Alan O'Neill, Robbie Lawlor, Ken O'Doherty, Paddy Dunning, Martin Moran, Robbie Gaffney, Keith Dignam, John Cullen, Aidan Reynolds, Frank Devlin, Joe Hanrahan. Sub: Brendan Murphy for Reynolds, 78m. Joint Managers: Dr Tony O'Neill, Theo Dunne

Shamrock Rovers: Jody Byrne, Anto Whelan, Jacko McDonagh, Dermot Keely, John Coady, Neville Steedman, Noel King, Pat Byrne, Mick Neville, Alan Campbell, Liam Buckley. Sub: Terry Eviston for Whelan, 78m. Manager: Jim McLaughlin

Referee: J. Carpenter (Dublin)   Attendance: 8,000

Final Replay – Tolka Park

4 May **UCD** 2 **Shamrock Rovers** 1
Hanrahan (41m), McDonagh pen. (75m)
O'Doherty (95m)

UCD: Brendan Murphy for Reynolds
Shamrock Rovers: Unchanged

Referee: J. Carpenter (Dublin) Attendance: 6,500

It's a Record!

- On 15 February 1976, Mick Meagan and his son Mark became the first father and son to play on the same team in the FAI Cup. They helped Shamrock Rovers draw 1–1 with St Patrick's Athletic.

- Jack O'Reilly (Cork United and Cork Athletic) scored seven FAI Cup Final goals.

- In 1932 there were no replays in any round of the Cup.

1985

McGuill Helps Rovers

Dundalk director Enda McGuill helped smooth Shamrock Rovers' path to their twenty-second FAI Cup success in 1985 – by writing a letter to Athlone Town centre-forward Noel Larkin! Following a disagreement with manager Turlough O'Connor, Larkin decided he wasn't enjoying his football anymore and announced his retirement. 'I was out for three weeks and never did any training, let alone play a game, during that time,' he said. 'Then I got a letter from Enda McGuill which helped persuade me to come back. He said that it would be time enough for me to watch matches when I was forty but while I was still able to play I should be out there playing. That got me thinking and then Jim McLaughlin came on and asked me to sign for Rovers. It was the right team at the right time.'

McLaughlin, who had earlier recommended Larkin to his old club Dundalk, needed a striker when close season signing Paul McGee decided to have another go at cross-channel football with Preston North End. Fortunately for McLaughlin, Larkin had turned down Dundalk's approach and he had also turned down Galway United. Ironically, Galway provided the opposition to Rovers in the Cup final – and Larkin hit the winner. An FAI Cup medal was the only domestic award missing from Larkin's collection from his spell with Athlone Town and, as Rovers completed the double, he added another League medal to his trophy haul.

For the Bonner twins, Denis and Packie, 1985 was a special year. Denis lined

283

out at centre-half for Galway United in the FAI Cup Final, while Packie was in goal for Glasgow Celtic in the Scottish Cup Final.

Unfortunately, Noel Larkin's goal spoiled a unique double, as Packie duly collected a winner's medal at Hampden Park. Both brothers attended their twin's Cup final but, whereas Packie's trip was paid for by the FAI as he was in Dublin for an international match, Denis had to travel to Scotland at his own expense.

Galway's march to the final was a success story for a number of people in particular. Eamonn Deacy, for instance, their rugged midfielder, had turned his back on a full-time career with Aston Villa in the English League to return to his native city. He had played for Limerick in their unsuccessful Cup final bid in 1977 and his experience was vital, as Galway surprised many pundits with their Cup run, the highlights of which were undoubtedly the semi-final games with Limerick. Directors Joe Hanley and Mattie Greaney also deserve a lot of credit, having taken over a debt-ridden club and revived it mainly by introducing an all-Galway policy. Player-manager Tom Lally, who had kept goal in the 1970 and 1974 finals for unsuccessful Sligo Rovers and St Patrick's Athletic respectively, was the man who put that policy into operation with a playing style that won Galway United a lot of friends. Unfortunately, his Cup final luck was out for the third time.

Success for Shamrock Rovers brought more problems than accolades for manager Jim McLaughlin, as the close season saw him lose influential midfielder and coach Noel King and international central defender Jacko McDonagh to French Second Division clubs. While McDonagh moved because he was unable to secure employment in Ireland, King was able to take a leave of absence from his job to give full-time football and coaching a try.

First Round

7 February	Dundalk	1	St Patrick's Athletic	0
	B. Wright			
10 February	Avondale United	0	Galway United	4
	(At St Colman's Park)		Dowling o.g., Murphy,	
			Gardiner pen., S. Lally	
	Bohemians	0	Shamrock Rovers	0
	Cork City	2	Bank Rovers	0
	Keane, Woodruff			
	Drogheda United	2	Finn Harps	0
	Byrne, Dillon			
	Limerick City	0	Home Farm	0
	Mervue United	1	UCD	2
	Collins		Hanrahan, Lawlor	
	(At Terryland Park)			
	Shelbourne	2	Longford Town	1
	Joyce 2		Mahon	
	Sligo Rovers	1	Athlone Town	1
	Moylan		Clarke	
	Waterford United	4	Hammond Lane	0
	Madigan 2, McGee, McCarthy			

First Round Replays

20 February	Shamrock Rovers	0	Bohemians	0
	Athlone Town	1	Sligo Rovers	1
	M. O'Connor		McLoughlin	
21 February	Home Farm	0	Limerick City	2
			Gaynor 2	

First Round Second Replay

27 February	Sligo Rovers	0	Athlone Town	3
			P. O'Connor, Carroll, Clarke	
28 February	Bohemians	0	Shamrock Rovers	1
			M. Byrne	

Second Round

20 February	**Drogheda United**	5	**Cork City**	3
	Collins 2, Fairclough,		McDermott 2, Parr	
	Dillon, Martin			
7 March	**Athlone Town**	2	**Dundalk**	2
	M. O'Connor, Coll		Laryea, McNulty	

Second Round Replay

| 13 March | **Dundalk** | 0 | **Athlone Town** | 1 |
| | | | Clarke | |

Third Round

17 March	**Drogheda United**	2	**Shamrock Rovers**	3
	Dillon 2		Larkin 2, M. Byrne	
	Limerick City	3	**Waterford United**	1
	Gaynor 2, Hulmes		Morley	
	Shelbourne	0	**Galway United**	0
	UCD	1	**Athlone Town**	3
	Dignam		M. O'Connor 2, Malone	

Third Round Replay

| 21 March | **Galway United** | 4 | **Shelbourne** | 1 |
| | Bonner 2, Cassidy, Glynn | | Mullen pen. | |

Semi-Final – Dalymount Park

| 12 April | **Shamrock Rovers** | 2 | **Athlone Town** | 1 |
| | O'Brien, M. Byrne | | Clarke | |

Semi-Final – Tolka Park

| 14 April | **Galway United** | 2 | **Limerick City** | 2 |
| | Glynn, McDonnell | | Walsh 2 | |

Semi-Final Replay – St Mel's Park, Athlone

| 17 April | **Galway United** | 1 | **Limerick City** | 0 |
| | Mannion | | | |

(After extra time.)

Final – Dalymount Park

28 April **Shamrock Rovers** **1** **Galway United** **0**
Larkin (57m)

Shamrock Rovers: Jody Byrne, Mick Neville, Dermot Keely, Jacko McDonagh, Kevin Brady, Liam O'Brien, Pat Byrne, Noel King, John Coady, Noel Larkin, Mick Byrne. Manager: Jim McLaughlin

Galway United: Tom Lally, Gerry Daly, Brian Gardiner, Denis Bonner, Jimmy Nolan, Eamonn Deacy, John Mannion, Martin McDonnell, Paul Murphy, Kevin Cassidy, John Glynn. Sub: Noel Mernagh for Glynn, 76m. Manager: Tom Lally

Referee: W. Wallace (Donegal) Attendance: 7,000

It's a Record!

- Waterford beat Rialto 11–1 at Kilcohan Park in the first round in 1972.
- Pat Courtney (Shamrock Rovers, 1964-69) is the only player to play in six successive Cup-winning teams.

1986

Doolin is Reassured

When a player moves club there is always a settling-in period, and so it proved for Shamrock Rovers' Paul Doolin after his move from Bohemians for the 1985-86 season. 'I didn't start the season well,' he recalled, 'but then Jim McLaughlin spoke to me. He had Dermot Keely with him and they asked me what was wrong. I said I was used to being taken off when I was not playing well, and Jim said, "That's not what it's like here. Go out and enjoy yourself and if you make mistakes don't worry." He gave me a great belief in myself.'

McLaughlin's reassurance paid off, as Doolin went on to finish as the leading scorer for the Hoops as they completed a League and Cup double – and Doolin was named Man of the Match in the final.

As far as McLaughlin was concerned, the main thing was to get Doolin's head right, 'because he was very hard on himself. I spent more time reassuring him, I didn't have to be critical, because he was very critical of himself.'

McLaughlin, the most successful manager in League of Ireland history, was renowned for his man-management and his ability to get the best from his players. He in turn credits his management success to a trainer he had while playing for Shrewsbury Town.

'When it comes to feeling down, I can say I was that soldier,' he said. 'When I played in England the man who saved my career was Tommy Seymour, the trainer at Shrewsbury, and one of the brightest men I ever met football-wise. He was the one who lifted you up, and there wasn't one player in the club he didn't

288

lift. He always had time for you . . . He taught me more than any other person I ever met. While he could be hard as they come, he was also there if you needed a shoulder to cry on. I realised how important his role was. Anybody can slag a player, but not everybody can help. He was a fabulous man.'

While Rovers' success at this time appeared to be seamless, midfielder Pat Byrne revealed that this wasn't so. 'At the start of the '85-'86 season we were playing badly because of a clique developing within the team. There were three players passing to each other, looking after each other, and then not to blame if anything went wrong. I asked Jim McLaughlin to have a chat about it and I started off the meeting saying that what these three players were doing was not acceptable. We were getting bad results not because we were playing badly but because we were not together. The other players joined in then, and the matter was settled.'

The 1986 Cup campaign saw the re-introduction of two-legged semi-finals for the first time since 1947, but they didn't pass without incident. A group of visiting hooligans caused the second leg between St Patrick's Athletic and Waterford United to be delayed as referee John Spillane took the players off the pitch until calm had been restored. At the time of the stoppage, Pat's were leading 1–0, but they eventually lost 3–1 and 4–2 on aggregate.

In the final, Waterford had no answer to Shamrock Rovers' class, and the game was all over after thirteen minutes when the Hoops led 2–0. It was the last hurrah for their brilliant midfield quartet of Doolin, Pat Byrne, Liam O'Brien and John Coady, as O'Brien was transferred to Manchester United and Coady to Chelsea.

It was also a fitting end to McLaughlin's reign at Milltown. The following month he was persuaded to move to Derry City as General Manager by his former player Noel King, who was City's manager. Derry, of course, were the good-news story for Irish soccer, with their ability to attract huge crowds on their return to senior football after years in the wilderness. Their tie against Finn Harps attracted gate receipts of £23,000, whereas the next best was the £12,700 returned for the Waterford–St Patrick's Athletic semi-final at the RSC, which was a ground record.

First Round

31 January	**Ballyfermot United** Howell (At Tolka Park)	1	**Longford Town** Kavanagh o.g., O'Sullivan	2
2 February	**Athlone Town**	0	**Dundalk** Shelley, Gorman	2
	Cobh Ramblers O'Halloran pen.	1	**Everton (Cork)**	0
	Cork City	0	**Bray Wanderers**	0
	Crosshaven	0	**Newcastle United** Cussen, Meade o.g., Freyne	3
	Finn Harps McNutt, M. Bradley, M. O'Kane	3	**Drogheda United** Maher	1
	Garda (Dublin) (At Brandywell)	0	**Derry City** Mahon, Gauld pen., Da Gama, Bradley, O'Neill	5
	Limerick City Gaynor, McDaid, Kennedy pen., Morley	4	**Rockmount**	0
	St Patrick's Athletic Carty	1	**UCD** Lysaght	1
	Shamrock Rovers M. Byrne 2, Eccles, Coady	4	**Home Farm**	0
	Shelbourne Toner	1	**EMFA** P. Madigan, Walsh	2
	Sligo Rovers	0	**Bohemians** Wyse, Davis	2
	Valeview (Dublin) (At Carlisle Grounds)	0	**Monaghan United** Conlon 2	2
	Waterford United Bennett, Donnelly	2	**Galway United** McGonigle	1
9 February	**Crofton Celtic (Cork)** (At Killeady)	0	**Bluebell United**	0
	TEK United T. McGuirk	1	**Parkvilla (Navan)**	0

First Round Replays

5 February	Bray Wanderers	1	Cork City	3
	D. O'Brien		Whelan 2 (1 pen.), Hennessy	
12 February	UCD	1	St Patrick's Athletic	2
	Murphy		Kavanagh o.g., Cleary	
16 February	Bluebell United	0	Crofton Celtic	1
			L. Neville	

Second Round

23 February	Crofton Celtic	0	Cobh Ramblers	0
	(At Turner's Cross)			
	Derry City	3	Finn Harps	0
	McCreadie, Bradley 2			
	Dundalk	4	TEK United	0
	McNulty, Joyce, Cunningham, McCue			
	EMFA	0	Bohemians	0
	Limerick City	1	Cork City	1
	Gaynor		Kearney	
	Monaghan United	0	Waterford United	2
			Kearns 2	
	St Patrick's Athletic	1	Longford Town	1
	Cassidy		Smyth	
	Shamrock Rovers	2	Newcastle United	1
	Larkin, O'Brien		Daly	

Second Round Replays

26 February	Cork City	2	Limerick City	1
	Hughes 2		Kennedy	
27 February	Bohemians	2	EMFA	1
	Wyse, Conway pen.		Leahy	
	Cobh Ramblers	1	Crofton Celtic	0
	O'Connor			
	Longford Town	0	St Patrick's Athletic	1
			Dillon	

Quarter-Finals

15 March	Cobh Ramblers	1	St Patrick's Athletic	3
	O'Neill		Dillon, O'Reilly, Morrison	

16 March	**Bohemians**	1	**Shamrock Rovers**	2
	Lawless		Larkin, O'Brien	
	Cork City	1	**Derry City**	0
	Hennessy			
	Waterford United	2	**Dundalk**	1
	Bennett, Grace		Shelly	

Semi-Finals First Leg

6 April	**Shamrock Rovers**	4	**Cork City**	1
	O'Brien, Doolin, Larkin 2		Whelan	
	Waterford United	1	**St Patrick's Athletic**	1
	Bennett		Cleary	

Semi-Finals Second Leg

13 April	**Cork City**	2	**Shamrock Rovers**	4
	Hughes, Whelan		M. Byrne, O'Brien 2, Doolin	
	(Shamrock Rovers won on 8–3 aggregate.)			
	St Patrick's Athletic	1	**Waterford United**	3
	Dillon		Kearns, Reid, Bennett	
	(Waterford United won on 4–2 aggregate.)			

Final – Dalymount Park

27 April	**Shamrock Rovers**	2	**Waterford United**	0
	Brady (7m), Synnott o.g. (13m)			

Shamrock Rovers: Jody Byrne; Harry Kenny, Mick Neville, Peter Eccles, Kevin Brady; Paul Doolin, Pat Byrne, Liam O'Brien, John Coady; Noel Larkin, Mick Byrne. Manager: Jim McLaughlin

Waterford United: Dave Flavin; Derek Grace, Kevin Power, Noel Synnott, Duncan Burns; Jimmy Donnelly, Tony Macken, Kieran McCabe, Martin 'Mock' Reid; Terry Kearns, Mick Bennett. Subs: Vinny McCarthy for McCabe, HT; Noel Bollard for Grace, 64m. Manager: Alfie Hale

Referee: E. Farrell (Dublin)   Attendance: 11,500

1987

Keely's Seamless Change

Taking over from a legend is never easy, but Dermot Keely made it appear to be when he took over from Jim McLaughlin as Shamrock Rovers' manager and proceeded to guide the club to its third League and FAI Cup double on the trot. In many ways, Keely was a natural successor to McLaughlin: he was the Derryman's on-field enforcer and a strong voice in the dressing room. His cause was helped by the respect he had from his teammates, many of whom were leaders in their own right.

Keely was still a player when he was appointed and played most of the season, including the three semi-final games against Sligo Rovers, but he was suspended and confined to the dugout when the Hoops played Dundalk in the FAI Cup Final. 'McLaughlin had an air of stature within the group,' explained Alan Mathews, who was at Rovers that year and later served as assistant to Keely. 'Dermot was much more in-your-face as a manager, but the team continued on in the same vein and played some lovely football.'

Keely proved his shrewdness when it came to the transfer market, as two of his signings – UCD's Keith Dignam and Brendan Murphy – slotted in perfectly for the English League-bound pair of Liam O'Brien and John Coady. In the final, it was the athletic Murphy, playing on the left wing, who caused havoc, tormenting the experienced Gino Lawless, winning the penalty that gave Rovers the lead after thirty-five minutes, and generally proving too pacey for the Dundalk right-back.

Coady, who was one of the quickest players on the team, was still at Rovers when Murphy was signed and he recalled, '[Murphy] was a great athlete. He had just arrived and we were doing sprints – two by two – and I was paired with Brendan. Keely and [Paddy] Dunning, his assistant, must have had a bet on because they kept us at them until Brendan won after about six sprints and I was knackered!'

It wasn't only the new signings that helped Rovers to the Cup that season. It was also the year that the extremely talented striker, Mick Byrne, blossomed. Signed for a record fee of £7,000 from Shelbourne in 1984, Byrne's haul of trophies included three FAI Cups, four Leagues and representative honours. Renowned for the 'Byrne turn', which left defenders flat-footed, sometimes it worked so well that it even surprised himself. 'I did it against Waterford one season, and the whole goal opened up,' he recalled, 'but then I put the ball wide.'

Never a prolific goal scorer, he hit thirty goals this season, including five in the FAI Cup. Of the latter, the goal that beat St Patrick's Athletic in the quarter-final replay was typical Byrne. He struck the ball sideways on from the edge of the penalty box into the top right-hand corner. Goals of this quality attracted the attention of French club St Etienne. 'The Cup final was supposed to be my last game for Rovers,' he said, 'but I wasn't going to play in it. I had ankle and groin injuries, but I got a jab before the game. Afterwards I spoke to the St Etienne chairman, but the deal was off because I wasn't fit. I went later to Den Haag in Holland, came back to Rovers after four months, and then signed for Huddersfield Town, where I stayed for two and a half years.'

Rovers also lost the services of Brendan Murphy, as the USA native returned to the States for employment. Meanwhile, 1987 saw the swan song of Sligo Rovers' veteran midfielder Tony Fagan. Aged forty, and a survivor of Sligo's 1970, '78, '81 and '83 Cup final teams, he scored the winner in Sligo's quarter-final victory over Galway United in what was his fifty-second FAI Cup tie. The drawing power of Derry City was also a notable feature, with receipts of £25,000 and £28,000 for their games at Shelbourne and Bohemians respectively, dwarfing anything else recorded. The second leg of Shamrock Rovers' semi-final with Sligo Rovers was the club's last home game at Glenmalure Park, Milltown. The attendance was 4,126, with receipts of £11,000.

FIRST ROUND

29 January	**Bank Rovers (Dundalk)** P. Cunningham (At Oriel Park)	1	**Bohemians** B. Murphy, R. Murphy	2
30 January	**Shamrock Rovers** Larkin 2, Murphy, Doolin, Neville, M. Byrne	6	**Tullamore**	0
31 January	**Mervue United** Collins (At Terryland Park)	1	**Longford Town**	0
	Railway Union (At Milltown)	0	**St Patrick's Athletic** Morrison, Byrne, Dillon	3
1 February	**Dundalk** McCue, Wyse	2	**Drogheda United**	0
	EMFA	0	**Bray Wanderers**	0
	Home Farm R. Kelly	1	**Tramore Athletic** Jackson	1
	Finn Harps McLoughlin	1	**Waterford United** Reid 3 (1 pen.), Kearns, Bennett 2	6
	Galway United O'Flaherty	1	**Fanad United** Ashton o.g.	1
	Monaghan United Kelly pen.	1	**Rockmount** Hinchin, Lawless, O'Sullivan	3
	Newcastlewest	0	**Limerick City** Hamilton 2, Hyde, King	4
	Shelbourne McDermott, Tierney	2	**Derry City** Krstic, Tierney o.g.	2
	Sligo Rovers Edwards, Burke, O'Kelly 2	4	**Crofton Celtic** Neville, McCarthy	2
	Swilly Rovers O'Neill	1	**Colepark United**	0
	UCD P. Hanrahan	1	**Athlone Town** Walsh 2 (1 pen.), Duff	3
5 February	**Cork City** Healy, Caulfield, O'Keeffe, Barry	4	**Cobh Ramblers** Van Wijnen	1

First Round Replays

11 February	**Bray Wanderers** Nugent, Hancock	2	**EMFA** Coady	1
	Fanad United	0	**Galway United** Mernagh, Ashton, Lally	3
	Tramore Athletic	0	**Home Farm** Kelly 2, Murray 2 (1 pen.), McGroggan	5
12 February	**Derry City** Da Gama 3, Krstic	4	**Shelbourne**	0

Second Round

1 March	**Athlone Town**	0	**St Patrick's Athletic**	0
	Bohemians Flynn	1	**Bray Wanderers**	0
	Cork City Caulfield	1	**Derry City** Krstic 3	3
	Dundalk Wyse, Gorman 2	3	**Swilly Rovers**	0
	Home Farm Crowe pen.	1	**Galway United** Mernagh, McGonigle 2	3
	Limerick City Walsh, Hamilton	2	**Shamrock Rovers** P. Byrne 2, Larkin	3
	Mervue United Farragher, Fallon (At Terryland Park)	2	**Rockmount** Gallagher o.g., Philpott pen.	2
	Waterford United Reid	1	**Sligo Rovers** McLoughlin	1

Second Round Replays

4 March	**Sligo Rovers**	0	**Waterford United**	0
	(After extra time.)			
5 March	**Rockmount** Philpott pen.	1	**Mervue United**	0
	St Patrick's Athletic	0	**Athlone Town**	0
	(After extra time.)			

Second Round Second Replays

10 March	Waterford United	0	Sligo Rovers	1
			O'Kelly	
12 March	Athlone Town	0	St Patrick's Athletic	1
			Nolan o.g.	

Quarter-Finals

15 March	Bohemians	2	Derry City	1
	Flynn, Byrne		Da Gama	
	Galway United	0	Sligo Rovers	1
			Fagan	
	Rockmount	0	Dundalk	2
	(At Turner's Cross)		Murray pen., Wyse	
	St Patrick's Athletic	0	Shamrock Rovers	0

Quarter-Final Replay

| 25 March | Shamrock Rovers | 1 | St Patrick's Athletic | 0 |
| | M. Byrne | | | |

Semi-Finals First Leg

5 April	Dundalk	1	Bohemians	2
	Lawless		Jameson, Swan	
	Sligo Rovers	0	Shamrock Rovers	0

Semi-Finals Second Leg

| 10 April | Bohemians | 0 | Dundalk | 1 |
| | | | Wyse | |

(Aggregate 2–2)

| 12 April | Shamrock Rovers | 1 | Sligo Rovers | 1 |
| | M. Byrne | | O'Kelly | |

(Aggregate 1–1)

Semi-Final Replays

| 15 April | Sligo Rovers | 0 | Shamrock Rovers | 1 |
| | | | Larkin | |

16 April	Dundalk	3	Bohemians	0

Eviston, Malone 2 pens.

Final – Dalymount Park

26 April	Shamrock Rovers	3	Dundalk	0

Kenny pen. (35m), Larkin (82m),
M. Byrne (90m)

Shamrock Rovers: Jody Byrne; Harry Kenny, Peter Eccles, Mick Neville, Kevin Brady; Paul Doolin, Pat Byrne, Keith Dignam, Brendan Murphy; Noel Larkin, Mick Byrne. Manager: Dermot Keely

Dundalk: Alan O'Neill; Gino Lawless, Harry McCue, Joey Malone, Martin Lawlor; Larry Wyse, Martin Murray, Barry Kehoe, Terry Eviston; Dessie Gorman, Tom McNulty. Manager: Turlough O'Connor

Referee: P. Kelly (Cork)   Attendance: 8,569

It's a Record!

- In 2003, Irish football moved to a summer set-up. As a result, an interim season was played in the second half of 2002, with two FAI Cup Finals contested in the same year.

1988

No Place for the Brother

Cup final managers have to make difficult decisions when it comes to team selection, but not many are faced with a decision like the one Dundalk manager Turlough O'Connor made when he left his brother Michael out of the team for the 1988 final. 'That was one of the hardest decisions I have ever had to make,' he recalled. 'Michael was a very good player, and he possibly suffered because he was my brother. But I was used to making decisions like that as Michael and Padraig played for me when I was manager of Athlone. I broke it to him the day before and he didn't take it too well. We get on great, but I don't think he has ever forgiven me!'

That Cup campaign started in sensational fashion when, in the opening game, holders Shamrock Rovers were dumped out of the Cup by UCD, the last team to beat them in the Cup, in the 1984 final replay. After that, the story of the competition was Derry City, whose massive following boosted attendances up and down the country. Their first round game against St Joseph's Boys returned receipts of £6,000stg, which would have been greater but for one of their officials being robbed as he was taking cash to the bank. It was reckoned the robbers got away with at least £1,000stg. For Derry City's game against Bohemians, a full house at the Brandywell returned receipts of £21,000stg, with the next-best returns that day being £2,258 for the Waterford–Limerick game. In the quarter-finals, Derry attracted a gate of £19,960 to Tolka Park for their win over Home Farm, while the next-best on the day was £4,300 for St Patrick's Athletic v. Limerick.

That 1988 campaign also featured notable comings and goings. Al Finucane, who had graced the competition since 1961, played his last Cup tie for Newcastlewest at Cobh, while Pat Fenlon, who was to become synonymous with the Cup as player and manager for the next twenty-plus years, marked his Cup debut with a goal for St Patrick's Athletic in their second round win over Bluebell United at Richmond Park.

Jim McLaughlin, who had taken over at Derry City from Noel King, brought the Candystripes to their first FAI Cup Final. As a native of Derry, he understood the fans' fascination with Cup football. 'Ever since I was a child,' he recalled, 'we were brought up on the Cup because of three memorable final matches with Glentoran in 1954. Derry were more Cup-oriented probably because they didn't have much chance of winning the Irish League in those days against the Big Two from Belfast, Linfield and Glentoran.' As for his own philosophy, he said, 'The Cup is not about winning – it's about not losing. That's the thing that sticks in my mind.'

While Derry signed Calvin Plummer from Nottingham Forest for the Cup run-in, Dundalk, having won the League, took the final in their stride. 'I have never been involved with a team so relaxed in a Cup final,' said manager O'Connor. 'Because we had been battling for the League, we didn't have time to think about the Cup.' The game was decided by a controversial penalty, of which O'Connor said, 'I'm not sure if it was a penalty or not. If it had been given against us we'd be disappointed. But the calmness of penalty-taker John Cleary was unbelievable. When he went to celebrate behind the goal, he was putting up his hands when he realised he was facing a sea of red and white and he quickly turned away. The Dundalk fans were at the other end.'

Among the medal-winners were some notable firsts: Terry Eviston, Gino Lawless and Joey Malone had all suffered finals heartbreak on a number of occasions. Martin Lawlor, the only survivor of the 1981 team, was winning his third Cup medal with Dundalk, while Martin Murray bridged a thirteen-year gap between his first medal in 1975 with Home Farm.

First Round

11 February	**Shamrock Rovers**	0	**UCD**	2
			Kavanagh, McKenna	
14 February	**Athlone Town**	1	**Limerick City**	1
	Duff		Lynch	
	Avondale United	0	**Tramore Athletic**	2
			J. Hayes o.g., P. Griffin	
	Ballyfermot United	1	**Longford Town**	1
	Foley		Hackett pen.	
	Bluebell United	3	**St Mary's Cork**	2
	Marsh, Cassidy, Browne		Long pen., O'Brien	
	Bohemians	1	**Fanad United**	0
	Jameson			
	Bray Wanderers	1	**EMFA**	1
	O'Neill		T. Craven	
	Cork City	4	**Galway United**	0
	Caulfield 2, M. O'Keeffe, Freyne			
	Drogheda United	1	**Cobh Ramblers**	1
	Ryan pen.		Myers	
	Home Farm	5	**Culdaff**	0
	Gill 3, R. Kelly 2			
	Mervue United	1	**Monaghan United**	2
	McDonnell		Kelly, Finnegan	
	Pegasus	1	**Newcastlewest**	2
	Skelly		Coll 2	
	Shelbourne	1	**St Patrick's Athletic**	2
	McDermott		Ennis	2
	Sligo Rovers	1	**Dundalk**	1
	Spring		M. O'Connor	
	St Joseph's Boys	0	**Derry City**	6
	(At Brandywell)		Curran, McDaid, Healy, Da Gama 2, Carlyle	
	Waterford United	3	**Finn Harps**	2
	Bennett, Morley, McNally o.g.		McLoughlin 2 pens.	

First Round Replays

17 February	Cobh Ramblers	2	Drogheda United	0
	Crowley pen., Kearns			
	Limerick City	3	Athlone Town	1
	Lynch 2 (1 pen.), McGonigle		Fitzgerald	
18 February	Dundalk	3	Sligo Rovers	2
	Eviston 2, Newe		Lynch, Savage	
	EMFA	0	Bray Wanderers	3
			Devlin 2 pens., Cullen	
	Longford Town	1	Ballyfermot United	0
	O'Neill			

Second Round

6 March	Bluebell United	0	St Patrick's Athletic	3
	(At Richmond Park)		P. Byrne 2, Fenlon	
	Cobh Ramblers	1	Newcastlewest	1
	Myers		Coll	
	Cork City	1	Monaghan United	0
	Caulfield			
	Derry City	0	Bohemians	0
	Dundalk	2	Bray Wanderers	0
	Cleary, Newe			
	Home Farm	2	Tramore Athletic	1
	Gill 2		O'Sullivan	
	UCD	1	Longford Town	2
	O'Brien		O'Neill 2	
	Waterford United	2	Limerick City	2
	Jones, Bennett		Lynch pen., Hyde	

Second Round Replays

9 March	Limerick City	2	Waterford United	0
	Hamilton, Behan			
10 March	Bohemians	1	Derry City	4
	McGee		Speak 3, Cunningham	

Newcastlewest	4	Cobh Ramblers	2

Earls 3, Kennedy — Myers, Crowley pen.

(After extra time; Match declared void: ineligible player)

Re-Fixture

27 March

Newcastlewest	1	Cobh Ramblers	0

Daly

Quarter-Finals

27 March

Dundalk	0	Cork City	0
Home Farm	0	Derry City	3

(At Tolka Park) — Speak, Da Gama, Cunningham

St Patrick's Athletic	2	Limerick City	2

P. Byrne, Dillon — Walsh 2

3 April

Longford Town	1	Newcastlewest	0

Malone

Quarter-Final Replays

30 March

Cork City	0	Dundalk	1

Murray

Limerick City	1	St Patrick's Athletic	2

Behan — Dillon, O'Driscoll

Semi-Finals First Leg

10 April

Dundalk	1	St Patrick's Athletic	0

Gorman

Longford Town	0	Derry City	2

(At St Mel's Park) — Gauld pen., Curran

Semi-Finals Second Leg

17 April

St Patrick's Athletic	0	Dundalk	3

Kehoe, Gorman, Murray

(Dundalk won on 4–0 aggregate.)

Derry City	4	Longford Town	2

Speak, Da Gama, Vaudequin, Cunningham — Morris-Burke, Quigley

(Derry City won on 6–2 aggregate.)

Final – Dalymount Park

1 May   **Dundalk**   **1**   **Derry City**   **0**
                   Cleary pen. (20m)

Dundalk: Alan O'Neill; Gino Lawless, Joey Malone, John Cleary, Harry McCue, Martin Lawlor; Larry Wyse, Martin Murray, Barry Kehoe; Dessie Gorman, Terry Eviston. Sub: Michael O'Connor for Wyse, 70m. Manager: Turlough O'Connor

Derry City: Stuart Roberts; Pascal Vaudequin, Paul Curran, Stuart Gauld, Ray McGuinness; Paul 'Storky' Carlyle, Patrick Joseph 'Felix' Healy, Calvin Plummer, Martin Bayly; Owen Da Gama, Jonathan Speak. Sub: John Cunningham for Healy, 63m. Manager: Jim McLaughlin

Referee: John Spillane (Cork)   Attendance: 21,000

It's a Record!

- Mick Byrne's opening goal for Shamrock Rovers in their semi-final second leg, against Cork City at Flower Lodge on 13 April 1986, may have been the quickest FAI Cup goal ever – he scored after twelve seconds.

1989

Imports Help Derry To Treble

When Jim McLaughlin replaced Noel King as manager of Derry City in what was a less than amicable takeover, he set about dismantling the side King had built, which had delivered Premier Division football to the Maiden City, and an FAI Cup Final appearance. In King's view, Derry players should be full-time and based in Derry, but McLaughlin was more pragmatic. 'I believe first of all in ability,' he said, 'so it doesn't matter whether players are part-time or full-time. The stability in life that goes with a good job can be a help. I'm not all that convinced of full-time football.'

He retained only four of King's full-timers (Tim Dalton, Stuart Gauld, Jack Keay and Pascal Vaudequin) and bolstered them with a group of players signed from his former club, Shamrock Rovers, including Mick Neville, Kevin Brady, Paul Carlyle, Paul Doolin, John Coady and Noel Larkin. With these proven performers, and locals Paul Curran, Felix Healy and Liam Coyle, plus Ballymena's Jonathan Speak, McLaughlin had an unbeatable formula. In 1988-89 they made a clean sweep of the major trophies: League, League Cup and FAI Cup. They were the first, and so far the only, club to complete that treble.

Yet, as often happens, Derry almost fell at the first hurdle in the FAI Cup, as John Coady recalled: 'At Dalymount in the first round, Bohs took the lead and then they got a penalty. Tim Dalton made a great save from Derek Swan, but if that penalty had gone in we were gone. Instead, that took the wind out of their sails and everything changed. The lesson was learned.'

Pat Byrne, who was manager of Shelbourne, had a role to play in Derry's success. 'Jim (McLaughlin) had the ex-Rovers players training with us,' he recalled.

'The four best players in the country, and they were a great help to us. It was a great introduction to our young players to what the League was all about, so I was delighted to have them. Our players saw how professional they were in their training, and how they took pride in the work they put in to things likes crosses and shooting.' The custom was for the Dublin-based players to train with Shelbourne, while Larkin trained in Athlone. They travelled to Derry on Saturday morning, trained and stayed overnight for the game on Sunday.

One of the key figures in Derry's success was local youngster Liam Coyle, whose father Fay was on the Derry team that won the IFA Cup in 1964. Liam turned down the offer of £40 a week from Finn Harps to play for Derry for nothing. He didn't get his chance in the first team until November, and he grabbed it with a hat-trick against Cobh Ramblers. His arrival provided McLaughlin with an embarrassment of riches for the two striking roles – Coyle, Speak and Larkin.

He chose Speak and Coyle for the Cup final against Cork City, which ended in a 0–0 draw. 'On the morning of the replay,' he recalled, 'I went for a walk on Portmarnock strand to think about my team selection. It resulted in one of the hardest jobs I ever had to do – to leave Speak out. I looked to Larkin for his aerial power to counteract Brian Carey. Speak was gutted when I told him. Carey got his move to Manchester United, but we got the medals.' United manager Alex Ferguson had been sufficiently impressed with Carey's display in the drawn game to sign him. It was Larkin's last match in Ireland, as he had only postponed his emigration to Australia because of the replay. The honour of scoring the winning goal fell to local hero Felix Healy, who later became a successful Derry manager. Scoring Cup final goals was nothing new to him, as he had scored for Coleraine in the 1982 and 1986 IFA Cup Finals, which were lost in controversial circumstances to Linfield and Glentoran respectively.

For Cork's Dave Barry, that season was one of fighting relegation with Cork City and enjoying National Football League and All-Ireland success with Cork. He missed the first leg of the NFL final in New York because of the replay. Combining soccer and Gaelic at the highest level was exhausting, as he recalled: 'After the All-Ireland final, I played in the county final for St Finbarr's and I didn't play well. The fans were all disappointed with my performance, while I'm thinking "I don't know how I even walked out on the pitch, never mind play."'

First Round

29 January	Bohemians	1	Derry City	3
	R. Murphy		Doolin, Curran, Coyle	
2 February	Garda	1	Shelbourne	1
	Hennebery		Cullen	
	(At Tolka Park)			
5 February	AIB	0	Limerick City	2
	(At Tolka Park)		Hyde, Hamilton	
	Athlone Town	2	Buncrana Hearts	1
	Duff 2		Smith	
	Brendanville	1	Dundalk	3
	Marshall		Cleary, M. O'Connor, Murray	
	(At Oriel Park)			
	Cobh Ramblers	3	St James's Gate	0
	McDaid, N. O'Rourke, Mulcahy			
	Culdaff	0	Shamrock Rovers	3
			Murray, Donnelly, Kenny	
	Galway United	0	Drogheda United	1
			Braddish	
	Monaghan United	4	EMFA	2
	O'Callaghan 2, Lynch 2		O. Walsh 2	
	Newcastlewest	3	Finn Harps	4
	Earls, McGettigan pen., Duggan		D. Cunningham, Grier, McLoughlin 2	
	Parkvilla	1	Midleton	1
	N. Conway pen.		A. O'Keeffe	
	St Patrick's Athletic	0	Home Farm	1
			L. Devlin	
	Sligo Rovers	0	Cork City	1
			Madden	
	TEK United	2	Longford Town	3
	Carroll pen., Smith		Gilligan, Dempsey pen., O'Neill	
	(At Carlisle Grounds)			
	UCD	2	Rockmount	0
	Tilson, P. Hanrahan			
	Waterford United	1	Bray Wanderers	1
	Ritchie		Judge	

First Round Replays

8 February	Bray Wanderers	1	Waterford United	0
	Davis			
	Shelbourne	2	Garda	1
	Whelan, Cullen		Flynn pen.	
12 February	Midleton	0	Parkvilla	0

(After extra time.)

First Round Second Replay

14 February	Parkvilla	3	Midleton	2
	P. O'Neill, B. McCabe, N. Conway		A. O'Keeffe, J. Daly	

Second Round

19 February	Cobh Ramblers	1	Cork City	2
	O'Halloran pen.		Caulfield, Freyne	
	Derry City	4	Monaghan United	1
	Gauld pen., Miller o.g., Coyle, Neville		O'Callaghan	
	Finn Harps	1	Bray Wanderers	1
	D. Cunningham		Davis	
	Parkvilla	0	Home Farm	2
			Whelan, L. Devlin	
	Shelbourne	1	Dundalk	3
	Cullen		Newe 2, Cleary pen.	
	UCD	0	Shamrock Rovers	1
			Murray	
23 February	Longford Town	2	Athlone Town	1
	Drummond 2		Duff	
28 February	Limerick City	0	Drogheda United	0

Second Round Replays

22 February	Bray Wanderers	1	Finn Harps	1
	Finnegan		McNulty	
2 March	Drogheda United	3	Limerick City	1
	Kelly 2, O'Toole		Hyde	

Second Round Second Replay

5 March	Finn Harps	0	Bray Wanderers	1
			Davis	

Quarter-Finals

5 March	Dundalk	2	Cork City	2
	Wyse, Shelly		Murphy, Murray o.g.	
	Derry City	3	Longford Town	0
	Speak, Doolin, Coyle			
	Home Farm	1	Shamrock Rovers	1
	O'Brien		Murray	
9 March	Bray Wanderers	0	Drogheda United	0

Quarter-Final Replays

14 March	Shamrock Rovers	1	Home Farm	0
	Mumby			
15 March	Cork City	1	Dundalk	0
	Freyne			
	Drogheda United	0	Bray Wanderers	1
			Smith	

Semi-Finals First Leg

9 April	Cork City	0	Bray Wanderers	1
			Davis	
	Derry City	3	Shamrock Rovers	0
	Speak 2, Coyle			

Semi-Finals Second Leg

16 April	Bray Wanderers	0	Cork City	1
			Long pen.	

(Aggregate 1–1 after extra time)

	Shamrock Rovers	1	Derry City	1
	Mumby		Speak	

(Aggregate 1–4)

Semi-Final Replay

19 April	**Cork City**	**4**	**Bray Wanderers**	**0**

Phillips o.g., Barry 2, Nugent

Final – Dalymount Park

30 April	**Cork City**	**0**	**Derry City**	**0**

Cork City: Phil 'Biscuit' Harrington; Liam Murphy, Noel Healy, Brian Carey, Philip Long; Paul Bowdren, Mick Conroy, Dave Barry, Patsy Freyne; Kevin Nugent, John Caulfield. Manager: Noel O'Mahony

Derry City: Tim Dalton; Stuart Gauld, Jack Keay, Mick Neville, Kevin Brady; Paul 'Storky' Carlyle, Paul Doolin, Patrick Joseph 'Felix' Healy, John Coady; Jonathan Speak, Liam Coyle. Sub: Noel Larkin for Coady, 58m. Manager: Jim McLaughlin

Referee: P. Daly (Dublin)   Attendance: 20,100

Final Replay – Dalymount Park

7 May	**Derry City**	**1**	**Cork City**	**0**

Healy (12m)

Derry City: Pascal Vaudequin for Coady; Larkin for Speak. Subs: Speak for Coyle, 82m; Coady for Healy, 88m

Cork City: Ciaran Nagle for Bowdren. Sub: Pat Duggan for Nagle, 53m

Referee: P. Daly (Dublin)   Attendance: 10,800

1990

Devo Slips One Over Derry

This was the year the underdogs made it to the final, with Bray Wanderers representing the First Division and St Francis representing the Leinster Senior League. They each overcame massive odds – and teams with much bigger budgets – to make this first Lansdowne Road final a special occasion, attracting the biggest crowd since 1968.

A change in the rules saw the introduction of the penalty shoot-out, after extra time in replays, and Bray made history when they eliminated Premier Division Shelbourne in the FAI Cup's first shoot-out. Manager Pat Devlin couldn't look, so he went into the dressing room, but there was nowhere to hide for Shels' player-manager Pat Byrne, who was one of the penalty-takers – he missed – as Bray went through to the quarter-finals 4–1.

Bray benefited from another rule change in the semi-final. The two-legged system was dropped in favour of home advantage for first out of the hat, and Bray came out first against favourites Derry City, who had come through the quarter-finals with a shoot-out win over League champions St Patrick's Athletic. With their huge travelling support, Derry weren't pleased with the 6,000-capacity Carlisle Grounds and were of the opinion that it wasn't a suitable venue for a semi-final.

However, Devlin had other things on his mind, and spent the week before the game coaching centre-back Mick Doohan on how to handle Derry danger man Jonathan Speak. When a defensive lapse let Speak in for the lead goal after twenty-five minutes, Devlin had to do some quick thinking. On his way to the dressing room at half-time, he discussed how they were going to wake up the team with his assistant, John Holmes.

'I said to John, "You stand between me and Mick Doohan and I'll make a run at him and you can stop me." So I made to run at Mick and slipped on the winter green that was on the floor and ended up with Mick standing over me. It was comical, but it seemed to do the trick. We played much better in the second half and deserved to win. Afterwards I said to John, "Weren't you supposed to stand between me and Mick?" and he said, "Yeah, but you didn't tell me you were going to slip."'

St Francis, meanwhile, had more mundane problems in their bid to reach the final. Between qualifying rounds and the Cup proper, they had to play ten games to make the final, while their success meant that, after their semi-final win over Bohemians, they had to play a further eleven Leinster Senior League games and possibly five Cup ties before the end of the season. For Bohemians, that semi-final defeat was a particularly bitter pill to swallow, as the club was celebrating its centenary.

In their ten FAI Cup games before the final, St Francis scored twenty-four goals and conceded only four, but one such concession proved to have special significance: it was scored by Roy Keane for Cobh Ramblers in a 2–2 draw in St Colman's Park. Nottingham Forest scout Noel McCabe watched Keane in action in the replay at Baldonnel and recommended him to manager Brian Clough. A successful trial followed, launching the career of Ireland's most successful export.

For the final, though, it was Bray striker John Ryan's turn to take the lime-light. On loan from St Patrick's Athletic, he scored a hat-trick, including two penalties, only the second player to do so in an FAI Cup Final. 'I got him on loan from Brian Kerr, on a gentleman's agreement that I would make sure he returned at the end of the season,' recalled Devlin. 'But he wanted to stay. We were in Europe and he wanted to play in Europe. I returned the favour to Brian some years later when I got Eddie Gormley for him from Drogheda.'

First Round

9 March	**Shamrock Rovers**	2	**Drogheda United**	1
	Kenny pen., B. O'Connor		D. Cunningham	
	Ballyfermot United	0	**Bohemians**	1
	(At Tolka Park)		Whelan	
10 March	**Cobh Wanderers**	0	**Limerick City**	2
	(At St Colman's Park)		Mullane, Tuite pen.	
	College Corinthians	1	**Newcastlewest**	3
	O'Leary		Hogan, Glynn, Kavanagh	
	(At Mardyke)			
11 March	**Athlone Town**	3	**Temple United**	0
	Byrne, Dully 2			
	Ballina Town	0	**Shelbourne**	4
			Keenan, Haylock 2, Whelan	
	Bluebell United	2	**UCD**	2
	T. Cullen, O'Brien		Timmons 2	
	Bray Wanderers	3	**Rockmount**	0
	Nugent 2, Finnegan			
	Cobh Ramblers	1	**Monaghan United**	0
	Cullimore			
	Cork City	1	**Waterford United**	0
	Bannon			
	Derry City	1	**Longford Town**	0
	Doolin			
	Finn Harps	0	**Home Farm**	1
			Glennon	
	Galway United	3	**Moyle Park**	0
	Cooke o.g., Keane, McGee			
	Kilkenny City	0	**St Francis**	1
			Kerr	
	St Patrick's Athletic	1	**Dundalk**	0
	D. Byrne			
	Sligo Rovers	1	**Boyne Rovers**	1
	Hitchcock		McGroggan	

First Round Replays

14 March	**UCD**	4	**Bluebell United**	1
	Cullen 4		Swift	

| 15 March | Boyne Rovers | 0 | Sligo Rovers | 1 |
| | (At United Park) | | Savage | |

Second round

25 March	Bohemians	3	Home Farm	0
	Murray pen., Carroll, Whelan			
	Cobh Ramblers	2	St Francis	2
	R. Keane, O'Halloran		Kerr, Toner	
	Cork City	1	Shamrock Rovers	1
	Caulfield		Eccles	
	Derry City	2	UCD	0
	Krstic 2			
	Galway United	1	Athlone Town	1
	Dolan		Byrne	
	Limerick City	1	St Patrick's Athletic	4
	J. Hanrahan		McDonnell 3, Lawless	
	Shelbourne	1	Bray Wanderers	1
	Haylock pen.		Cosgrave	
	Sligo Rovers	0	Newcastlewest	2
			Hogan 2	

Second Round Replays

29 March	Athlone Town	1	Galway United	2
	Byrne		Mullen, Dolan	
	Bray Wanderers	0	Shelbourne	0
	(After extra time; Bray won 4–1 in penalty shoot-out.)			
	Shamrock Rovers	0	Cork City	1
			Long	
	St Francis	3	Cobh Ramblers	0
	T. Coleman, Toner, Byrne			

Quarter-Finals

8 April	Bohemians	2	Cork City	0
	Swan, Tilson			
	Bray Wanderers	1	Galway United	0
	Ryan			

Derry City	1	St Patrick's Athletic	1
Doolin		Moody	
Newcastlewest	0	St Francis	3
Hilliard, Connolly, Ryan o.g.			

Quarter-Final Replays

| 11 April | St Patrick's Athletic | 1 | Derry City | 1 |
| | Osam | | Byrne o.g. | |

(After extra time; Derry City won 4–3 in penalty shoot-out.)

Semi-finals

22 April	Bray Wanderers	2	Derry City	1
	Reynolds, Smith		Speak	
	St Francis	1	Bohemians	0
	(At Tolka Park) Murphy			

Final – Lansdowne Road

| 13 May | Bray Wanderers | 3 | St Francis | 0 |
| | Ryan 3 (pen. 20m, 65m, pen. 79m) | | | |

Bray Wanderers: Josh Moran; Tony 'Bo' McKeever, Mick Doohan, Colm Phillips, Brian Cosgrave; Martin Nugent, Dermot Judge, Kevin Reynolds, John Finnegan; John Ryan, Tommy McDermott. Subs: David 'Dax' Kealy for Finnegan, 88m; Derek Corcoran for McDermott, 88m. Manager: Pat Devlin

St Francis: Gary Matthews; Stephen O'Reilly, Ken Gibbons, Martin Kerr, Trevor Coleman; Greg Coleman, Terry Hilliard, Bernard Connolly, John Murphy; Brendan Toner, Ben Byrne. Sub: John Nugent for Murphy, 72m; Stephen McGivern for Byrne, 86m. Manager: Pete Mahon

Referee: K. O'Sullivan (Cork)   Attendance: 25,000

1991

Tommy's Weird Feeling

It was a year of shocks in the FAI Cup, with non-League clubs defeating five of their League brethren, but Galway United's Tommy Keane had a feeling that something good was going to happen to his team. 'I knew something good would happen because Joey Malone, our manager, was brilliant at man-management and he developed this fantastic spirit within the group,' he recalled. 'After our first round win against Cobh Ramblers I wondered, could this be our year for the Cup? It was a weird sort of feeling – I can't explain it.'

Keane, who had been introduced to the game by Mike Corbett at Corrib Rangers, tested Malone's management skills from the start of that season when newly signed Larry Wyse was handed the number 8 jersey. 'I told Joey, "If you don't give me number 8, I'm not playing." I had to wear number 8, but I didn't know that Larry liked it too.' A stand-off ensued, Joey did nothing, and Larry gave the jersey to Tommy. Crisis averted – and the two number 8s became great friends.

Harry Redknapp was an admirer of the silky skills of Keane. He spotted the Galway lad while on a pre-season tour with Bournemouth and signed him for a two-year apprenticeship and then as a professional. 'He was very good to young people and very helpful,' recalled Keane. 'After training the first team, he'd come across to the young players and give us advice and, even as a manager, he was still able to play. He improved my game an awful lot.'

A bad knee ligament injury, which left him in plaster for nine months, halted

Keane's progress at Bournemouth, and after a short spell with Colchester United, he returned to Galway United. Little did he know that another injury – a chipped bone in his ankle received in a youth game in Bournemouth – had not healed, and he played for a further six years before it was properly diagnosed.

With Ashtown Villa accounting for Dundalk and Derry City, Midleton knocking out Cup-holders Bray Wanderers, and Elm Rovers and Portlaoise eliminating Monaghan United and Home Farm, the way was clear for a new name on the Cup – and Galway made the most of their opportunity. With Malone assigning a roaming role to Keane, the little (5'5") Galway man proceeded to wreak havoc on defences, scoring in every round of the Cup leading to the final.

'When we qualified for the final, I couldn't wait to play at Lansdowne Road, which I associated with the Irish team,' recalled Keane. 'But I was never more nervous before a game as I was before that final. I was literally shaking until the whistle blew. But, then, if I didn't get nervous I knew I wasn't going to play well. Barry Murphy was marking me and he would say to me, "Tommy, would you ever stop running?" but I had got it into my head to keep running and knacker him out. When he started talking I knew I was getting to him.'

When Keane chipped Shamrock Rovers' goalkeeper, Paul Kavanagh, after eleven minutes, he had visions of becoming the first player to score in every round since Charlie Ferry in 1974, but Dave Connell appeared from nowhere to head clear. Stalemate ensued, and with minutes to go the announcement was made that, 'In the event of a replay it will be held in Tolka Park next Sunday.' That got Keane going. 'I turned to Stephen Lally and Noel Mernagh and said, "Next time you get the ball give it to me, I'm not coming back for a replay." Thirty seconds later, Noel passed to me, I ran down the wing and knew where John Glynn would be. I crossed and he scored, exactly how we had been doing it in training.'

Keane was presented with the Man of the Match award, but in 2010 his former club, West United, presented him with a DVD of the game. 'I had never looked at it, but when I did I reckoned Peter Carpenter should have got the Man of the Match award,' was his candid conclusion.

First Round

10 March	**Carndonagh**	**0**	**Limerick City**	**0**

(After extra time.)

Cork City	**2**	**Bohemians**	**3**
Caulfield, Barry		Tilson 3	

(After extra time; 1–1 after 90m)

Drogheda United	**4**	**Parkvilla**	**1**
Toal, Scully, S. Geoghegan 2		M. Rogers pen.	
Dundalk	**0**	**Ashtown Villa**	**1**
		Murphy	
Edenmore	**1**	**Sligo Rovers**	**2**
T. Craven		Keegan, Conway	
Galway United	**3**	**Cobh Ramblers**	**1**
Campbell, Mernagh, Keane		Hogan	
Longford Town	**0**	**Shelbourne**	**3**
		De Khors, Whelan, McCormack o.g.	
Mallow United	**0**	**Athlone Town**	**1**
		Frawley	
Midleton	**2**	**Bray Wanderers**	**0**
K. Quinn, R. O'Connor			
Monaghan United	**1**	**Elm Rovers**	**2**
McGee		Hilliard, Higgins	
Portlaoise	**3**	**Home Farm**	**1**
Comerford, Conroy, Burke		Duff	
Shamrock Rovers	**4**	**Finn Harps**	**3**
Swan 3, Arkins		McLoughlin, Slevin, O'Donnell	
St Patrick's Athletic	**0**	**Derry City**	**0**

(After extra time.)

UCD	**1**	**Kilkenny City**	**1**
O'Gara		Dunne	

(After extra time.)

Waterford United	**2**	**St Joseph's Boys**	**1**
Owens o.g., J. Browne		Knight	
Wayside Celtic	**0**	**St James's Gate**	**2**
		P. Nolan, Ennis	

First Round Replays

13 March	**Derry City**	1	**St Patrick's Athletic**	0
	D. Gorman			

(After extra time; 0–0 after 90m)

14 March	**Kilkenny City**	2	**UCD**	0
	B. Walsh pen., Dunne			
	Limerick City	3	**Carndonagh**	0
	Ryan, Walsh, Fitzgerald			

Second Round

24 March	**Athlone Town**	2	**Bohemians**	0
	O'Neill, Morrison			
	Drogheda United	0	**Waterford United**	2
			J. Browne 2	
	Limerick City	1	**Elm Rovers**	0
	Ryan pen.			
	Portlaoise	2	**Kilkenny City**	3
	McCormack, Griffey		Best 2, Walsh	
	Derry City	1	**Ashtown Villa**	2
	Speak		Murphy, E. Hannigan	
	Galway United	2	**Shelbourne**	0
	Wyse, Keane			
	Midleton	0	**St James's Gate**	1
			Ennis	

(After extra time; 0–0 after 90m)

	Sligo Rovers	2	**Shamrock Rovers**	2
	J. Byrne, Hitchcock		Campbell pen., Arkins	

(After extra time; 2–2 after 90m)

Second Round Replay

3 April	**Shamrock Rovers**	0	**Sligo Rovers**	0

(After extra time; Shamrock Rovers won 4–2 in penalty shoot-out)

Quarter-Finals

7 April	**Athlone Town**	0	**Shamrock Rovers**	0

(After extra time.)

Kilkenny City	1	**Ashtownvilla**	0
Dunne			
Limerick City	1	**Galway United**	2
Fitzgerald		Mernagh, Keane	
Waterford United	0	**St James's Gate**	1
		Ennis	

Quarter-Final Replay

10 April	**Shamrock Rovers**	1	**Athlone Town**	0
	Devine			

Semi-Finals

28 April	**Kilkenny City**	0	**Shamrock Rovers**	1
			Swan	
	St James's Gate	1	**Galway United**	3
	McGlynn		Glynn, Campbell, Keane	
	(At Tolka Park)			

Final – Lansdowne Road

12 May	**Galway United**	1	**Shamrock Rovers**	0
	Glynn 86m			

Galway United: Declan McIntyre; John Morris-Burke, Derek Rogers, John Cleary, Jimmy Nolan; Paul Campbell, Larry Wyse, Peter Carpenter, Tommy Keane; Noel Mernagh, Johnny Glynn. Subs: Stephen Lally for Morris-Burke, 60m; Kevin Cassidy for Wyse, 87m. Manager: Joey Malone

Shamrock Rovers: Paul Kavanagh; John Devine, Peter Eccles, Barry Murphy, Wayne Cooney; Dave Connell, Neil Poutch, David Campbell, Derek Treacy; Vinny Arkins, Derek Swan. Subs: Barry O'Connor and Sean Byrne for Devine and Poutch, 87m. Manager: Noel King

Referee: J. Purcell (Dublin)   Attendance: 15,257

1992

Gregg's Double Switch

David Tilson can remember the day his fortunes changed at Bohemians. It was 4 November 1990, and he was sitting in the stand in Waterford as Bohs played out a 1–1 draw with the Blues. 'Eamonn Gregg had brought Ollie Walsh with him from Kilkenny and Ollie was one card away from a suspension,' Tilson recalled. 'He's blown for offside but hits the ball over the bar – and that's how I got my chance for two games against Derry and St Pat's, the top two. I managed to play very well, and that stopped me going to Kilkenny on loan as Eamonn had intimated, and started me off as a striker.'

Gregg may have been fortunate in switching Tilson, who had been signed as a left-winger from UCD, but he knew what he wanted when he signed Pat Fenlon, who had been operating on the left-wing for St Patrick's Athletic. 'He said he wanted me to play in the centre of midfield,' recalled Fenlon. 'I liked playing under Eamonn; he was very straight and honest. Him and Maurice Price were a great partnership and should have won a lot more before they broke up.'

Gregg had re-modelled the team from the one that lost in the Cup semi-final in 1990, to such an extent that there were only three survivors – captain Paul Whelan, Alan Byrne and Tilson – but ultimately it was the switching of Tilson and Fenlon that landed the FAI Cup for Bohemians in 1992, right down to the decisive moment in the final.

It was route-one football – a long kick by goalkeeper John Connolly, which was headed on by two of the smallest players on the pitch, Tommy Byrne and

Fenlon, for Tilson to latch on to and smash the ball past Cork City goalkeeper Phil Harrington. 'I'd had a similar chance after about five minutes and made a heavy touch and Harrington got to it,' recalled Tilson. 'So this time I said I'd hit it early and I kicked it over his head, as he had come off his line, expecting something similar to the first time.'

The following day there was a reception for both teams in the Mansion House, and they adjourned to O'Donoghue's on Merrion Row to continue the party. 'There were fellows standing on the bar singing, and the bus outside waiting to bring them back to Cork,' said Tilson. 'Gerry McCabe was the joker in the pack and he made off with the Cup, but it didn't get as far as Cork. The bus was stopped and a committee member brought it back.'

There was always a bus story connected with that Bohemian team, and not all of them ended as happily. 'Before that final we were in the Royal Dublin Hotel waiting for a Garda escort to Lansdowne and there was a breakdown in communication because it never arrived. In the end we made it to the ground twenty-five minutes before the kick-off,' recalled Tilson. 'As we were going out for our warm-up, the Cork players were coming in. Then back to the dressing room for ten minutes, and it was time for the kick-off. It was a presage of what was to come the following year when our bus broke down en route to Dundalk, when we only needed a draw to win the League and we lost to a Tom McNulty goal.'

For captain Paul Whelan, lifting the Cup was special; his father, Ronnie Sr, had won it in 1959 and 1961 with St Pat's and was in hospital that weekend. It was almost a Cup double for the Whelans, but injury caused Ronnie Jr to miss Liverpool's win over Sunderland in the FA Cup.

It was a special year for Sam Allardyce, who guided Limerick to the First Division title and to the quarter-final of the Cup. It was his first honour as a manager after his appointment in 1991 by Fr Joe Young. That season ended on a high for Pat Fenlon also, as he was voted PFAI Player of the Year. Fenlon enjoyed further Cup success when he left Bohs in 1995 for Linfield. He won the treble of League, Cup and League Cup in that year, and won the IFA Cup again in '96, when he scored in a 2–0 win over Bangor. Tilson won a second FAI Cup medal with Shelbourne in '96, before a persistent groin injury forced him to retire.

First Round

14 February	Bohemians	2	Bluebell United	1
	Lawless 2		D. O'Brien	
15 February	Pegasus	0	Limerick City	1
	(At Dalymount Park)		Fitzgerald	
	Shelbourne	2	College Corinthians	0
	Rutherford, Haylock			
16 February	Bray Wanderers	2	Ashtown Villa	1
	Notaro, Campbell		Dillon	
	Cobh Ramblers	0	Monaghan United	0
	Cork City	3	Edenmore	0
	Caulfield 2		Bannon	
	Derry City	1	Sligo Rovers	1
	J. Hanrahan		McGee	
	Home Farm	0	Fanad United	2
			Grier 2	
	Galway United	3	Fermoy	1
	Keane, Mernagh 2		Lawlor	
	Glenmore Celtic	0	Moyle Park	0
	(At Stradbrook)			
	Kilkenny City	1	Dundalk	1
	Madden pen.		Eviston	
	Longford Town	1	Drogheda United	1
	Kelly pen.		Weldrick	
	St James's Gate	1	Athlone Town	0
	Reilly			
	St Patrick's Athletic	3	Shamrock Rovers	1
	Osam, Scott, Ennis		McDonnell	
	UCD	3	Finn Harps	1
	Cullen, Colwell, Keogh		McLoughlin	
	Waterford United	0	Wayside Celtic	1
			Mooney	

First Round Replays

18 February	Moyle Park	1	Glenmore Celtic	0
	Burns			
	(At Red Cow)			

323

20 February	Drogheda United	2	Longford Town	1
	Brogan, Reynolds		M. Devlin	
	(After extra time; 1–1 after 90m)			
	Dundalk	1	Kilkenny City	0
	Irwin			
	(After extra time; 0–0 after 90m)			
	Monaghan United	2	Cobh Ramblers	1
	Power 2		J. O'Rourke	
	(After extra time; 1–1 after 90m)			
	Sligo Rovers	1	Derry City	1
	McGee		O'Brien	
	(After extra time; 1–1 after 90m)			

First Round Second Replay

| 27 February | Derry City | 2 | Sligo Rovers | 1 |
| | Mannion, O'Brien | | Gorman | |

Second Round

6 March	Dundalk	0	Bohemians	2
			Tilson 2	
7 March	Moyle Park	1	Limerick City	2
	Condron		Hill, Fitzgerald	
	(At Red Cow)			
8 March	Bray Wanderers	1	Galway United	0
	Doohan			
	Derry City	0	Shelbourne	1
			Haylock	
	Drogheda United	1	Cork City	1
	Brogan		Bannon	
	St James's Gate	1	Fanad United	1
	Kavanagh		Harkin	
	St Patrick's Athletic	2	UCD	1
	Ennis, Scott		Kavanagh	
	Wayside Celtic	2	Monaghan United	2
	Duignan pen., Keating		Reynor, Murray	
	(At Belfield)			

Second Round Replays

11 March	**Cork City**	3	**Drogheda United**	1
	Napier, Morley, Caulfield		Toal pen.	
	Fanad United	1	**St James's Gate**	1
	McGeever		Kavanagh	

(At Trialough; After extra time; 1–1 after 90m)

12 March	**Monaghan United**	1	**Wayside Celtic**	0
	Power			

Second Round Second Replay

24 March	**Fanad United**	2	**St James's Gate**	3
	Harkin, McIlwaine		Kavanagh, Seville 2	

(At Trialough; After extra time; 2–2 after 90m)

Quarter-Finals

27 March	**Bohemians**	1	**Shelbourne**	1
	Tilson		Howlett	
29 March	**Cork City**	2	**Limerick City**	0
	Barry, Cotter			
	St James's Gate	2	**Monaghan United**	1
	Reilly, Seville		Murray pen.	
	St Patrick's Athletic	1	**Bray Wanderers**	0
	Byrne			

Quarter-Final Replay

1 April	**Shelbourne**	0	**Bohemians**	1
			Tilson	

Semi-Finals

19 April	**Bohemians**	0	**St James's Gate**	0
	Cork City	1	**St Patrick's Athletic**	0
	Bannon			

Semi-Final Replay

23 April	**Bohemians**	3	**St James's Gate**	1
	Lawless 2, Fenlon pen.		Seville pen.	
	(At Dalymount Park)			

Final – Lansdowne Road

| 10 May | Bohemians | 1 | Cork City | 0 |
| | Tilson (78m) | | | |

Bohemians: John Connolly; Donal Broughan, Robbie Best, Paul Whelan, Paul Byrne; Lee King, Pat Fenlon, Alan Byrne, Tommy Byrne; Joe Lawless, Dave Tilson. Manager: Eamonn Gregg

Cork City: Phil Harrington; Liam Murphy, Declan Daly, Paul Bannon, Stephen Napier; Declan Hyde, Dave Barry, Cormac Cotter, Gerry McCabe; Pat Morley, John Caulfield. Subs: John Glynn for Cotter, 80m; Philip Long for Napier, 85m. Manager: Noel O'Mahony

Referee: M. Caulfield (Dublin)   Attendance: 17,000

It's a Record!

- The first penalty shoot-out in the FAI Cup occurred in 1990 when the second round replay between Bray Wanderers and Shelbourne at the Carlisle Grounds remained scoreless after extra time. Shelbourne's Philly Power missed the first penalty, and his side eventually lost 4–1.

1993

Haylock Redeems Himself

There were no giant-killing feats for a change this year, when the teams that beat the previous year's finalists succeeded them in the season's showpiece. However, the logic of that didn't hold all the way, as the team that had beaten the Cup-holders eventually lost out in the decider.

It was a final that featured a veritable raft of former Cup-winners – with Shelbourne fielding five of the great Shamrock Rovers' winners of the 1980s, and Dundalk retaining the same number from their great team of '88. One of those players, Shels' Paul Doolin, was nearly put out of contention by one of his own players. 'In the quarter-final against Glenmore Celtic, I broke my jaw after running into Gary Haylock,' he recalled. 'I cracked it in three places. I had said to Haylock to stop running offside, but he scored a hat-trick and was on the goal hunt. It happened in the first half and at half-time Pat Byrne said "I don't want to risk (Padraig) Dully," but he had to as I was taken off to hospital.'

It says something about Doolin's powers of recovery that not only did he play in the final, but he also played in the semi-final and replay against Derry City a mere three weeks after the Haylock incident. Haylock, originally sent over on loan from Huddersfield Town by former Republic of Ireland manager Eoin Hand, became a great favourite at Tolka Park, and he redeemed himself for the Doolin injury with two match-winning goals in the Brandy-well replay. In the Lansdowne Road final, he linked up with Doolin before crossing the ball for Greg Costello to head the only goal of the game and earn the Reds the FAI Cup for the first time in thirty years.

For two players, this Cup final was the start of a run of bad luck when it came to the FAI decider. Shelbourne midfielder Gary Howlett missed out because of injury, and missed two further finals with the Reds, while Dundalk full-back Thomas Dunne missed out because of international duty. 'I played for Dundalk in the second round at home to Bohs, which ended 0–0,' he recalled. 'But two days later I played for Ireland U-21s in a European Championship match against Germany in Dalymount. The Cup replay was the following night, and Turly left me out, and I didn't get back in. For the final, Ronnie Murphy was struggling with injury and shouldn't have played. I wasn't even on the bench; he brought a local in instead and that's why I left Dundalk.' Dunne only started one more game for Dundalk that season, but ironically it was in an away-win over Shelbourne. His subsequent moves to Shelbourne and Derry City resulted in two more Cup final heartbreaks.

For Turlough O'Connor, the Cup final defeat brought an end to his eight-year reign at Oriel Park. During that time he had restored the club to its former greatness and delivered two League titles, the FAI Cup, two League Cups and twice runners-up in all three major competitions. However, the fans had not responded in kind, and the lack of support didn't augur well.

Apart from the trophies, O'Connor was also an astute wheeler-dealer for the club. 'In my time in Dundalk,' he recalled, 'we sold about nine players to English clubs. The first was Roddy Collins to Mansfield for £20,000, and the next was Steve Staunton, who was playing in the second team. We sent him over to Liverpool and they were delighted with him. Steve was an amateur with us at the time. Liverpool came over on pre-season to Cork, and Steve signed pro forms for us and then for Liverpool the same day. The initial fee was £30,000, then £20,000 after twenty-five games, £25,000 after fifty, and another £25,000 for his first cap. I was on holidays in Kelly's of Rosslare when I got a telegram saying "Congrats, Villa signed Steve and we got £85,000 from the fee." Then Dessie Gorman went to a French club for £40,000, Jim Gannon to Sheffield United for £60,000, Tony Cousins to Liverpool for £70,000 and John Smyth also went to Liverpool. The money received was always used just to keep the club going.' Such are the harsh economic facts of life for League of Ireland clubs.

First Round

14 February	Bray Wanderers	0	Shelbourne	0
	Cork City	7	Dale United	0
	Carr, McCabe, Glynn, Buckley 2, Morley, Barry			
	Derry City	3	Temple United	0
	O'Brien, Ennis, Murray			
	Drogheda United	0	Bohemians	3
			Whelan, Lawless 2	
	Monaghan United	0	Home Farm	0
	Galway United	2	Athlone Town	3
	Devlin, Carpenter		Rogers o.g., Morris-Burke, O'Connor	
	Longford Town	1	Limerick City	2
	McCormack		H. King 2	
	Shamrock Rovers	3	College Corinthians	0
	McGrath, Gallen, Tracey			
	Sligo Rovers	1	Bluebell United	0
	McDonnell			
	St James's Gate	1	Dundalk	2
	Kavanagh		P. Hanrahan 2	
	St Patrick's Athletic	3	Finn Harps	0
	Campbell, Ryan, Dunne			
	Tramore Athletic	0	Bank Rovers	0
	(At Turner's Cross)			
	UCD	2	Castleview	0
	O'Brien, Timmons			
	Waterford United	2	Kilkenny City	2
	Hale, Kearns		O'Brien, Power pen.	
	Wayside Celtic	0	Cobh Ramblers	0
21 February	Glenmore Celtic	4	Ashtownvilla	4
	Brien, Masterson, Dooney, G. Kelly pen. (At Belfield)		Donnelly, D. Kelly 2, Lynch pen.	

First Round Replays

18 February	Cobh Ramblers	3	Wayside Celtic	1
	J. O'Rourke 2, O'Callaghan		Mooney	

	Home Farm	2	**Monaghan United**	0
	Coyle, Reynor o.g.			
	Kilkenny City	1	**Waterford United**	2
	Kelly		Keane 2	
	Shelbourne	4	**Bray Wanderers**	1
	Rutherford 3, Whelan		Douglas	
21 February	**Bank Rovers**	0	**Tramore Athletic**	3
	(At Oriel Park)		Morgan, O'Connor, Hoare	
23 February	**Ashtownvilla**	0	**Glenmore Celtic**	1
	(At Dalymount Park)		M. Byrne	

Second Round

7 March	**Derry City**	1	**Athlone Town**	0
	Bacon			
	Dundalk	0	**Bohemians**	0
	Limerick City	1	**Home Farm**	1
	Walsh		Keddy	
	Shamrock Rovers	3	**Waterford United**	0
	S. Geoghegan, Brazil, McGrath			
	Shelbourne	0	**Cork City**	0
	Sligo Rovers	5	**Cobh Ramblers**	1
	Moran 4, Hastie		O'Callaghan	
	Tramore Athletic	1	**Glenmore Celtic**	3
	Leahy		Flynn pen., Byrne, Masterson	
	(At Turner's Cross)			
	UCD	1	**St Patrick's Athletic**	1
	Palmer		Kelch	

Second Round Replays

10 March	**Bohemians**	2	**Dundalk**	4
	O'Connor, Tilson		Eviston, Lawless, McNulty, P. Hanrahan	
	Cork City	1	**Shelbourne**	2
	Buckley		Rutherford, Doolin	
	(After extra time; 1–1 after 90m)			
	St Patrick's Athletic	1	**UCD**	0
	Hill			

| 11 March | Home Farm | 0 | Limerick City | 0 |

(After extra time.)

Second Round Second Replay

| 17 March | Limerick City | 1 | Home Farm | 0 |

Mumby

Quarter-Finals

| 28 March | Derry City | 2 | Shamrock Rovers | 1 |

Ennis, Trainor — Cullen

| | Dundalk | 2 | Limerick City | 0 |

Irwin, Eviston

| | Glenmore Celtic | 0 | Shelbourne | 6 |

(At Tolka Park) — Haylock 3, Dully 2, Doolin

| | Sligo Rovers | 1 | St Patrick's Athletic | 2 |

Bonner — O'Brien, Dolan

Semi-Finals

| 18 April | Dundalk | 1 | St Patrick's Athletic | 0 |

Lawlor

| | Shelbourne | 0 | Derry City | 0 |

Semi-Final Replay

| 21 April | Derry City | 2 | Shelbourne | 3 |

Carlyle, Ennis — Whelan, Haylock 2

Final – Lansdowne Road

| 16 May | Shelbourne | 1 | Dundalk | 0 |

Costello (59m)

Shelbourne: Jody Byrne; Peter Coyle, Mick Neville, Anto Whelan, Kevin Brady; Gary Haylock, Paul Doolin, Greg Costello, Mark Rutherford; Padraig Dully, Ken O'Doherty. Sub: Bobby Browne for O'Doherty, 71. Manager: Pat Byrne

Dundalk: Alan O'Neill; Richie Purdy, James Coll, Ronnie Murphy, Martin Lawlor; Peter Hanrahan, Tom McNulty, Gino Lawless, Wayne Cooney; Terry Eviston, Brian Irwin. Subs: Alan Doherty for Eviston, 79m; Mick Shelley for Murphy, 88m. Manager: Turlough O'Connor

Referee: O. Cooney (Dublin)   Attendance: 11,000

1994

Lights Go On For Sligo

The 1993-94 season was a slow burner for Sligo Rovers. With only two wins from their first ten First Division games, things were not going according to plan for new manager, Willie McStay, with his team a lowly seventh in the ten-team League. Then everything changed – with the flick of a switch – on 26 November.

'Turning on the floodlights was the turning point of the season for us,' recalled winger Johnny Kenny. 'We couldn't buy a win before that and were about fourteen points behind Athlone. The games were switched from Sunday afternoon to Saturday night, we beat Home Farm 4–0 the first night, and the place was packed after that. There was always a good atmosphere, the results went with us and things took off. We managed to squeeze by Athlone in the end.' Of their remaining seventeen League games, they won twelve and only lost two – a winning form they carried over to their FAI Cup campaign.

Ex-Celtic player-manager Willie McStay, had introduced some fellow Scots to strengthen his squad – notably goalkeeper Mark McLean, midfielder Willie Hastie and striker Eddie Annand – yet it was the contribution of a number of local players that was so important to their success in the Cup.

Kenny, known as the 'Riverstown Flyer', had been introduced to First Division football the previous season when a friend, Gerry Ballintine, mentioned him to Galway United manager Tony Mannion. Kenny ended the season with First Division and First Division Shield winners' medals, and an enhanced reputation. 'Sligo were relegated the same year,' he recalled, 'and when Willie

McStay came to me I jumped at the chance of playing for my home team. I had grown up with Rovers' Cup exploits in '83. I developed a great understanding with Willie on the right side – I did the running and he stayed tight. He did a great job. A lot of the team were full-time professionals, all those Scots lads were training every day. Only Marty McDonnell – the sole link with the '83 team – Declan Boyle, Gavin Dykes and myself were part-time. But he didn't break the bank. These were players who had been let go and were trying to get back into the game.'

Sligo's FAI Cup campaign got off to a less than impressive start, rescued by a freak goal. 'We were playing non-League Glenmore Celtic at home on a ferocious night of wind and rain,' recalled Kenny. 'They scored and, from a free ten yards inside his own half, Declan Boyle's kick caught in the wind and ended up in the net. It was one of those games where we were never going to score otherwise.' A goal from another McStay signing, former Coventry City and Republic of Ireland U-21 cap Gerry Carr, saw Sligo safely through the replay in Dalymount Park. A centre-back, Carr operated in midfield due to the successful partnership of Boyle and Dykes.

The luck of the draw then kicked in, with successive home games against Cork City, Cobh Ramblers and Limerick City. Crucial to Sligo's success in the latter two games was Armagh footballer Ger Houlahan, who combined his Gaelic football duties with a striking role at the Showgrounds. He proved the big loser though, when the final pairing, which saw Sligo take on northwest rivals Derry City, was moved from Tolka Park to Lansdowne Road to accommodate the crowds. Originally fixed for 24 April, the final was moved to 15 May because of Lansdowne Road's rugby schedule. Houlahan, who was captain of the Armagh team that lost the National League final on 1 May to Meath, was unavailable on 15 May due to a clash with Armagh's opening Ulster Championship game. This led to a recall for Padraig Moran, who played on the right wing, with Kenny moving to the left.

It was a wet day, reducing the expected crowd, but Sligo looked on it as a good omen. 'Nineteen eighty-three was a bad day too,' explained Kenny, and they were also facing the same goalkeeper, Dermot O'Neill. In a game rated the best final since 1983, chances were missed by both sides before Carr headed the winner from Annand's corner. When Mark McLean's brilliant save denied Kevin McKeever, Sligo's bid for the treble of First Division, First Division Shield and FAI Cup was realised, trumping Derry's hopes of an FAI and League Cup double. For Kenny, it meant that his first two seasons in the League had yielded five winners' medals. Not so lucky was Dermot O'Neill who, after fifteen years in the League, was still waiting for his first winner's medal.

While Sligo Rovers' floodlights proved the catalyst for their changing fortunes, it didn't turn out quite that way for Finn Harps, who lit up for the first time for their first round FAI Cup tie against UCD. The result was a 1–1 draw, but a dressing room bust-up between manager Patsy McGowan and goalkeeper Declan McIntyre – a Cup-winner with Galway in 1991 – led to McIntyre's departure from the club.

For Derry striker Liam Coyle, 1994 was the start of an amazing Cup run. He played in four successive Cup finals – '94 and '95 with Derry City, '96 in the IFA Cup final with Glentoran and '97 with Derry City. At the end of that run, he possessed a winner's medal from each association.

First Round

4 February	Shelbourne	0	Limerick	1
			G. Ryan	
5 February	Finn Harps	1	UCD	1
	Dunleavy		Griffin	
	St Patrick's Athletic	3	Garda	0
	Dunne, O'Neill, Treacy			
	Sligo Rovers	1	Glenmore Celtic	1
	Boyle		Hannigan	
6 February	Athlone Town	0	Home Farm	0
	Bluebell United	0	Fermoy	0
	Bohemians	1	Shamrock Rovers	1
	Cousins		Geoghegan	
	Bray Wanderers	1	Cherry Orchard	1
	Farrell		Glynn pen.	
	Cork City	4	Elm Rovers	1
	Glynn 2, Morley, Caulfield		Curry	
	Derry City	2	Drogheda United	1
	Vaudequin, O'Brien		Ryan	
	Galway United	0	Dundalk	0
	Kilkenny City	4	Casement Celtic	2
	Kelly 3, Donnelly		Luxford 2	
	Monaghan United	1	Longford Town	0
	Coady			
	St James's Gate	3	College Corinthians	1
	Farrell 2, McAvenue		Abbott	
10 February	Waterford United	0	Cobh Ramblers	1
			Francis	
13 February	Whitehall Rangers	0	Glebe North	0

First Round Replays

9 February	Cherry Orchard	1	Bray Wanderers	2
	Glynn		D. Smith	
	(At Richmond Park; After extra time; 1–1 after 90m)			
	Shamrock Rovers	2	Bohemians	2
	Geoghegan, Burke		T Byrne, O'Connor	
	(After extra time; 1-1 after 90m)			

10 February	Dundalk	0	Galway United	0
	(Abandoned at half-time: pitch unplayable)			
	Glenmore Celtic	1	Sligo Rovers	2
	(At Dalymount Park) Flynn		Annand pen., Carr	
	Home Farm	2	Athlone Town	1
	Keddy, Vaughan		O'Connell	
	UCD	1	Finn Harps	3
	O'Brien		B. Lafferty, Gallagher, Dunleavy	
13 February	Fermoy	2	Bluebell United	0
	McMahon, Myers			
20 February	Glebe North	1	Whitehall Rangers	0
	Durran			

First Round Replay Re-Fixture

17 February	Dundalk	4	Galway United	3
	Coll, J. Hanrahan, Donnelly, Doohan		Brennan, Nolan, Farragher	
	(After extra time; 3–3 after 90m)			

First Round Second Replay

16 February	Bohemians	1	Shamrock Rovers	0
	Cousins			

Second Round

25 February	St James's Gate	0	St Patrick's Athletic	5
			D. Campbell 2 (1 pen.), Ennis,	
			John Byrne, Gormley	
26 February	Finn Harps	0	Monaghan United	0
	Sligo Rovers	2	Cork City	0
	Dykes, Gabbiadini			
27 February	Cobh Ramblers	2	Kilkenny City	1
	Cragoe, K. Kelly		Buttner	
	Derry City	3	Bray Wanderers	1
	O'Brien 2, Coyle		Gormley	
	Fermoy	0	Limerick City	1
			Kerley	
3 March	Dundalk	0	Bohemians	2
			Crawford, Cousins	

336

| 9 March | Glebe North | 0 | Home Farm
Vaughan, Bayly pen. | 2 |

Second Round Replay

| 10 March | Monaghan United
M. Byrne | 1 | Finn Harps | 0 |

Quarter-Finals

19 March	Sligo Rovers Houlahan	1	Cobh Ramblers	0
20 March	Derry City Heaney	1	St Patrick's Athletic	0
	Home Farm (At Tolka Park) Gannon	1	Bohemians H. King	1
	Limerick City Walsh, Minihan	2	Monaghan United Newe	1

Quarter-Final Replay

| 24 March | Bohemians
H. King, Broughan pen., Cousins 2 | 4 | Home Farm
Vaughan | 1 |

Semi-Finals

| 13 April | Bohemians | 0 | Derry City
O'Brien | 1 |
| | Sligo Rovers
Annand | 1 | Limerick City | 0 |

Final – Lansdowne Road

| 15 May | Sligo Rovers
Carr (72m) | 1 | Derry City | 0 |

Sligo Rovers: Mark McLean; Willie McStay, Declan Boyle, Gavin Dykes, Martin McDonnell; Padraig Moran, Will Hastie, Gerry Carr, John Kenny; Ricardo Gabbiadini, Eddie Annand. Manager: Willie McStay.

Derry City: Dermot O'Neill; Pascal Vaudequin, Paul Curran, Stuart Gauld, Paul McLaughlin; Peter Hutton, Kevin McKeever, Donal O'Brien, Paul Kinnaird; Joe Lawless, Liam Coyle. Sub: Gary Heaney for Coyle, 85m. Manager: Tony O'Doherty.

Referee: D. McArdle (Dundalk)   Attendance: 13,800

1995

Felix's Philosophy Pays Off

When Felix Healy was asked to take over as manager of Derry City, he said no. It was December 1994, five years after he had won the treble with City and scored the winning goal in the FAI Cup Final. It was a job he coveted, but he was hoping Jim McLaughlin would take it, as he was busy restoring Coleraine to full health. 'When I took over at Coleraine, they had won four games in eighteen months,' he recalled. 'It was a shambles, but I had put together a really good side who finished second in the Irish League the following season, losing out on the last day. However, when Jim decided he didn't want to come back, I said I better take the job as it might be my only shot at it.'

Derry were sixth in the table when he took over, having won only six of their sixteen games, but a number of shrewd signings soon changed all that. Harry McCourt, brother of current Celtic star Paddy, was the first, arriving from Ards and scoring two goals in a 4–1 win away to Galway. In the remaining seventeen games, Derry only lost twice, McCourt finished top-scorer with eleven goals, and they were a missed-penalty away from completing the League and FAI Cup double.

Apart from McCourt, Healy signed two of his Coleraine players – former Derry winger Paul Carlyle and former Bohemians winger Paul Kinnaird. 'It's a case of realising what you need, and then being lucky with the players available,' he said. 'I was fortunate to get those guys in. McCourt was a runner, unbelievably quick over ten to one hundred yards. We had a race one night between him and Paul Curran, and for the last ten yards he was running backwards waving at

Curran – and Curran wasn't slow! With Liam Coyle, who liked to drop off, they made a great pair. Liam would play the ball over the top or down the channels and Harry was on to it like lightning. Then I was lucky to get Paul Doolin from Portadown. I had played with him and, as Jim McLaughlin used say, he was a real dog. He would never be found wanting in a battle, and he did really well for me.'

Doolin's battling qualities were needed, too, especially in a three-game semi-final marathon with Bohemians, which Derry finally won 3–2 in extra time. It was as a result of that epic contest, with the three games (which included two periods of extra time) played over eight days, that Derry were denied the League title. 'It impacted on our game in Cobh, which was played two days later,' Healy recalled. 'Harry McCourt could have scored six that day, and their only shot in the ninety minutes hit the only tuft of grass in the penalty area and wrong-footed Dermot O'Neill. It ended up 1–1, but in the last twenty minutes they were hoofing the ball anywhere and we didn't have the legs to make them pay.'

The following week, Derry had a League decider in Athlone. 'We kicked off, and they scored after fifteen seconds, a deflected shot that hit Stuart Gauld on the shoulder,' said Healy. 'It wasn't his day, as he missed a penalty later that would have won us the title. It was ironic that, in the Cup final, he had to take a penalty, but he was a brave lad and stuck it away well. I just wish he had done so two weeks earlier. At least when we had the disappointment of Athlone we had the Cup final to look forward to. It would have been worse if we'd had three months to dwell on it. In the final, we were 2–0 up and cantering when they got a penalty, and the last five or six minutes were like the Alamo.'

As a manager, Healy's philosophy was an unusual one: 'I didn't talk a great deal about football,' he said, 'it looks after itself, and no two periods are the same. The ability the players have they will always have. I never talked about the opposition. You have enough to do to get your own team to play, without thinking about the opposition. The key questions are: How badly do you want it? Are you up for the fight? How hungry are you?

'Sometimes I'd tell them fairy stories to get them to perform. One time before a game against St Pat's, I came into the dressing room and the boys were all sitting around and I got a sense they were all right and didn't need my intervention, so I said, "Right, I'm off for a cup of tea with my mother," and they went out and won 3–0. I never raised my voice in the dressing room and never ranted or raved. I was there to help the players. Any donkey in the stand can shout at the players.'

The Cup final victory was special for two players in particular – goalkeeper Dermot O'Neill, who was winning his first medal at the fourth attempt, having lost the 1982, '83 and '94 finals, and Peter Hutton, scorer of the first goal in the 2–1 final win over Shelbourne, who was emulating his father's success with Finn Harps in 1974. 'The game was played on my mother's birthday,' Hutton recalled. 'I backed myself to score the first goal and also predicted the correct result. I had a fiver at 25/1, which rounded off the day nicely.'

Hutton had been a doubt to start due to an ankle ligament injury. 'I had a cortisone injection and wore two different boots, one with studs and one with a moulded sole for the bad ankle, as it gave extra comfort on the hard ground. I got thumped in the first minute of the game and the effects of the cortisone wore off straight away, but the adrenaline got me through.'

First Round

29 January	Avondale United	1	Fermoy	1
	O'Connell		Van Wijnen pen.	
	Belgrove	1	Ashtownvilla	2
	Daly		Reilly, Kearney	
	Bluebell United	4	CIE Ranch	2
	Reilly, Behan 3		Dempsey, Horne	
	Bohemians	2	Limerick	2
	Broughan, P. Hanrahan		Keane, McMahon	
	Cobh Ramblers	1	Shelbourne	3
	J. O'Rourke		Rutherford 2, S. Geoghegan	
	Derry City	1	Finn Harps	0
	Coyle			
	Kilkenny City	0	Dundalk	5
			M. Byrne, J. Hanrahan,	
			B. Byrne 2, Loughlin	
	Longford Town	2	Drogheda United	0
	Buttner 2			
	UCD	1	Cork City	1
	Sherlock		Woods	
1 February	Athlone Town	0	Home Farm	0
	Glebe North	0	Shamrock Rovers	1
	(At United Park, Drogheda)		Whelan	
	Sligo Rovers	1	St Patrick's Athletic	0
	Small			
	Galway United	2	Waterford United	2
	Clery, Herrick		Kelly pen., Cashin	
2 February	College Corinthians	1	Bray Wanderers	0
	Clifford			
5 February	Douglas Hall	1	Monaghan United	1
	Leahy		Smyth	
	(At Turner's Cross)			
8 February	St James's Gate	1	Fanad United	0
	Crowley			

First Round Replays

5 February	Fermoy	0	Avondale United	2
			Healy, Downey	
7 February	Waterford United	1	Galway United	1
	Kelly		Reilly	

(Abandoned 58m: pitch unplayable)

8 February	Limerick	0	Bohemians	2
			Cousins 2	
19 February	Home Farm	2	Athlone Town	0
	Bayly pen., Power			
26 February	Cork City	1	UCD	1
	Morley pen.		O'Byrne pen.	

(At Turner's Cross; After extra time; 0–0 after 90m)

	Monaghan United	2	Douglas Hall	0
	Douglas 2			

First Round Replay Re-Fixture

25 February	Waterford United	1	Galway United	1
	R. Hale		O'Flaherty	

(After extra time; 1–1 after 90m)

First Round Second Replays

1 March	Cork City	1	UCD	0
	Morley			

(At Turner's Cross)

11 March	Galway United	2	Waterford United	0
	Neary, O'Flaherty			

Second Round

24 February	Shelbourne	3	Ashtownvilla	0
	Rutherford, S. Geoghegan, Devereaux			
26 February	Avondale United	2	Longford Town	1
	Downey 2		Donnelly	
	College Corinthians	1	Bluebell United	1
	Burke		Maher o.g.	

	Derry City	3	Home Farm	1
	Doolin 2, Coyle		Kelly	
	Dundalk	5	St James's Gate	0
	Doohan, Kelly pen., M. Byrne 2,			
	J. Hanrahan			
28 February	Bohemians	3	Monaghan United	1
	Swan 2, Tilson		McElligott	
12 March	Shamrock Rovers	3	Cork City	1
	Gannon 2, McGrath		Caulfield	
14 March	Sligo Rovers	0	Galway United	0

Second Round Replays

5 March	Bluebell United	1	College Corinthians	0
	Devereaux			

(After extra time; 0–0 after 90m)

22 March	Galway United	0	Sligo Rovers	2
			Carr, Kenny	

Quarter-Finals

9 March	Dundalk	0	Derry City	1
			Coyle	
12 March	Avondale United	0	Shelbourne	4
			Duffy, Mooney, Rutherford,	
			Mahon o.g.	
	Bluebell United	0	Bohemians	4
	(At Richmond Park)		Murray, Cousins 2, O'Driscoll	
2 April	Shamrock Rovers	0	Sligo Rovers	0

Quarter-Final Replay

5 April	Sligo Rovers	2	Shamrock Rovers	0
	Annand 2 pens.			

Semi-Finals

7 April	Bohemians	0	Derry City	0
9 April	Sligo Rovers	1	Shelbourne	3
	Carr		Devereaux, Arkins, S. Geoghegan	

Semi-Final Replay

| 11 April | Derry City | 0 | Bohemians | 0 |

(After extra time.)

Semi-Final Second Replay

| 14 April | Derry City | 3 | Bohemians | 2 |
| | McLaughlin, Hutton 2 | | Swan, O'Connor | |

(After extra time; 2–2 after 90m)

Final – Lansdowne Road

| 7 May | Derry City | 2 | Shelbourne | 1 |
| | Hutton (9m), Gauld pen. (72m) | | Costello pen. (75m) | |

Derry City: Dermot O'Neill; Pascal Vaudequin, Paul Curran, Stuart Gauld, Paul McLaughlin; Paul 'Storky' Carlyle, Paul Doolin, Peter Hutton, Paul Kinnaird; Harry McCourt, Liam Coyle. Manager: Patrick Joseph 'Felix' Healy

Shelbourne: Alan Gough; Greg Costello, Mick Neville, Ray Duffy, Tommy Dunne; Brian Mooney, Alan Byrne, Brian Flood, Mark Rutherford; Vinny Arkins, Stephen Geoghegan. Sub: Trevor Vaughan for Arkins, 89m. Manager: Colin Murphy

Referee: M. Tomney (Dublin)   Attendance: 14,200

1996

A Little Magic From Shero

Sometimes a club can get lucky with the draw in the Cup; other times, like Shelbourne in 1996, it's one hard battle after another. They faced Premier Division opposition all the way, and only once played at home, when they beat Shamrock Rovers in a first round replay.

In the end, though, they needed a little luck to register their fifth win in the Cup. This occurred most notably in the final against League champions St Patrick's Athletic in Lansdowne Road. Goalkeeper Alan Gough was sent off and, without a substitute goalkeeper, midfielder Brian Flood took over. So unaccustomed was he to his new surroundings that, at one stage, he caught the ball and then went to place his cap in the net, unwittingly carrying the ball over his line. To the dismay of the Pat's supporters, and the relief of Shelbourne, neither referee Pat Kelly nor his linesmen spotted the 'own goal' offence.

While he regarded the Flood incident as one of the most extraordinary things he had ever seen, St Pat's manager Brian Kerr graciously accepted that 'over the two games, Shels were better than us and they got the bit of luck you need with that Flood incident. I was upset, but winning the League in our Inchicore home for the first time was so precious that I didn't feel as bad as I might.' He also pointed out that the Cup final 'was match forty-seven for us. In a part-time situation you can extract so much from the players and they had nothing left in the end.'

Shelbourne had one trump card that season – the mercurial Tony Sheridan.

Hailed at one time as the next Liam Brady because of his talented left foot, the Irish youth and U-21 star turned his back on Coventry City and signed for Shels. 'He was the most naturally gifted player I ever worked with,' said manager Damien Richardson. 'You could play him anywhere and he would do a good job. I saw him playing as a fifteen-year-old for Lourdes Celtic in Sundrive Park, and he ran the show from outside-right and, at half-time, he gave the team talk. I eavesdropped and everything he said made sense.'

In the semi-final, final and final replay, Sheridan scored vital goals at crucial times. 'The goal against Sligo in the semi-final was uniquely Shero,' recalled Richardson. 'Alan Gough caught a cross and threw the ball to Shero on the half-way line, where he was being marked by Robbie Brunton. He gets past him and runs with the ball, the defenders backing all the way, and from about twenty-five yards, without even looking up, he flicked the ball with the outside of his foot and chipped the goalkeeper. The ball seemed to take an eternity to fall into the net. It was a stunning goal.'

To show that that chip was no fluke, Sheridan repeated it in the more exacting surroundings of the Cup final. With Shels down to ten men and Pat's a goal up after Dave Campbell scored on seventy-six minutes, it looked like the Reds' luck had finally run out. But, with four minutes to go, Sheridan struck again with the outside of his left foot, a chip that went in off the crossbar. 'It was a piece of skill that only he could have manufactured,' said Richardson. 'It was something he did in training all the time. "Off the crossbar," he would say, and he'd do it.'

The final replay in Dalymount Park provided a number of interesting storylines. Campbell once again opened the scoring, Sheridan hit the equaliser with his right foot, Gough saved a penalty from Eddie Gormley, and the League's top marksman, Stephen Geoghegan, finished a flowing Shels' left-wing move with a beautiful dink over Pat's goalkeeper Gareth Byrne for an eighty-first minute winner. In addition, unsung centre-back hero Ray Duffy proved unbeatable as Pat's went gung-ho for a late equaliser. It was his head which seemed to get to every ball. His reward? He was released at the end of the season and replaced by Campbell and Pat Scully.

Spare a thought, too, for Shels' midfielder, Gary Howlett, who broke an ankle bone in the semi-final win in Sligo and missed his third final in four seasons. While with Brighton in 1983, he had replaced broken leg victim Gerry Ryan for the FA Cup Semi-Final and Final, and he mused, 'I must have used up all my luck then.'

St Patrick's Athletic's defeat in the final replay was their first in twenty-six games that season.

First Round

11 January	**Dundalk**	1	**Drogheda United**	1
	Doohan		Tresson	
12 January	**Athlone Town**	2	**Monaghan United**	1
	Collins, B. Frawley		Ennis pen.	
	Bohemians	2	**Moyle Park**	0
	O'Driscoll, Swan			
	St Patrick's Athletic	3	**Workman's/Dunleary**	1
	O'Flaherty 2, Glynn		Allen	
13 January	**Cobh Ramblers**	1	**Sligo Rovers**	2
	Cregoe		Gilzean 2	
	Finn Harps	5	**Longford Town**	2
	Murphy, Walsh 2 (1 pen.), Devenney, Dunleavy		Fitzgerald, Devlin	
14 January	**Avondale United**	3	**CYM Terenure**	1
	Downey, O'Connell, Smith		Nolan	
	Bray Wanderers	0	**Fanad United**	4
			Grier 2, McElwaine pen., Harkin	
	UCD	1	**Kilkenny City**	2
	Palmer		B. Arrigan pen., Cooney	
	Tek United	0	**Cork City**	1
			Hill	
	Derry City	0	**St James's Gate**	0
	Shamrock Rovers	0	**Shelbourne**	0
17 January	**Temple United**	2	**Home Farm**	3
	Kearney, Elliott (At Turner's Cross)		Woods, Gough, Hitchcock	
	UCC	0	**Limerick**	1
			McMahon pen.	
	Waterford United	3	**Galway United**	2
	Kelly 2 (1 pen.), Barry		J. Brennan, Killian	
18 January	**Wayside Celtic**	2	**Cherry Orchard**	1
	Geraghty 2		V. Perth	

First Round Replays

16 January	**Shelbourne**	1	**Shamrock Rovers**	0
	Flood			

18 January	**Drogheda United**	2	**Dundalk**	1
	Sullivan, Crolly		M. Byrne	

(After extra time; 1–1 after 90m)

	St James's Gate	0	**Derry City**	1
			G. Heaney	

Second Round

9 February	**Bohemians**	4	**Kilkenny City**	0
	Hanrahan 2, Broughan, Swan			
	Drogheda United	0	**Shelbourne**	2
			Sheridan, S. Geoghegan	
	St Patrick's Athletic	3	**Fanad United**	0
	Morrisroe 2, D. Campbell			
10 February	**Finn Harps**	1	**Athlone Town**	1
	Dunleavy		Parkes	
11 February	**Derry City**	2	**Avondale United**	0
	McCourt, Mohan			
	Home Farm	1	**Cork City**	1
	J. Kelly		Hindmarch	
	Waterford United	0	**Wayside Celtic**	0
14 February	**Limerick**	1	**Sligo Rovers**	3
	H. King		Ramage, A. Rooney, Gilzean	

Second Round Replays

13 February	**Athlone Town**	1	**Finn Harps**	4
	Gaynor		Dunleavy, McGettigan, Speak, Minnock	
14 February	**Cork City**	1	**Home Farm**	0
	Caulfield			
20 February	**Wayside Celtic**	2	**Waterford United**	1
	Simpson, F. Byrne		Carthy	

Quarter-Finals

9 March	**Finn Harps**	0	**Bohemians**	0
10 March	**Cork City**	1	**Sligo Rovers**	2
	Morley		Ramage, Mulligan	

Derry City	**0**	**Shelbourne**	**3**
		Hutton o.g., Howlett, Costello pen.	
Wayside Celtic	**0**	**St Patrick's Athletic**	**3**
		O'Flaherty 3 (1 pen.)	

Quarter-Final Replay

12 March	**Bohemians**	**2**	**Finn Harps**	**0**
	Swan, Cousins			

Semi-Finals

5 April	**Bohemians**	**0**	**St Patrick's Athletic**	**0**
6 April	**Sligo Rovers**	**0**	**Shelbourne**	**1**
			Sheridan	

Semi-Final Replay

16 April	**St Patrick's Athletic**	**0**	**Bohemians**	**0**
	(After extra time.)			

Semi-Final Second Replay

22 April	**Bohemians**	**1**	**St Patrick's Athletic**	**2**
	(At Dalymount Park) Cousins		O'Flaherty 2	

Final – Lansdowne Road

6 May	**Shelbourne**	**1**	**St Patrick's Athletic**	**1**
	Sheridan (86m)		D. Campbell (76m)	

Shelbourne: Alan Gough; Greg Costello, Ray Duffy, Mick Neville, Declan Geoghegan; Tony Sheridan, John O'Rourke, Darren Kelly, Brian Flood, Dave Tilson; Stephen Geoghegan. Subs: Henry McKop for Kelly, 66m; Mark Rutherford for Duffy, 81m. Manager: Damien Richardson

St Patrick's Athletic: Gareth Byrne; Willie Burke, John McDonnell, Dave Campbell, Peter Carpenter; Paul Campbell, Noel Mernagh, Eddie Gormley, Paul Osam; Liam Buckley, Ricky O'Flaherty. Subs: Martin Reilly for Buckley, 70m; John Glynn for O'Flaherty, 79m. Manager: Brian Kerr

Referee: P. Kelly (Cork)   Attendance: 14,000

Final Replay – Dalymount Park

12 May   **Shelbourne**   **2**   **St Patrick's Athletic**   **1**
              Sheridan (71m),   D. Campbell (58m)
              S. Geoghegan (81m)

Shelbourne: Unchanged. Sub: Rutherford for Kelly, 64m

St Patrick's Athletic: Brian Morrisroe for Paul Campbell. Subs: P. Campbell for McDonnell, 30m; Reilly for Osam, 45m; Glynn for Mernagh, 82m

Referee: W. Wallace (Donegal)   Attendance: 11,000

It's a Record!

- In the first round in 1993, Glenmore Celtic produced one of the most sensational comebacks of all time in the FAI Cup. They were 4–0 down with twenty minutes left against Ashtownvilla and salvaged a 4–4 draw in Belfield. They won the replay in Dalymount Park 1–0.

- The lowest attendance for an FAI Cup Final was the 4,100 at the Bray Wanderers–Finn Harps 1999 replay.

1997

Tragedy Blindsides Derry

When it comes to sporting setbacks, 'tragedy' is a word too-often used and far removed from its true meaning. But Derry City experienced the full force of the word in the run-up to the FAI Cup Final, in which they met the holders Shelbourne. Derry were attempting to complete the double, having won the League by a clear ten-point margin from Bohemians, with Shelbourne a distant third. Clearly they were firm favourites – until tragedy struck on the Thursday before the final.

Tommy Dunne, Derry's left-back, recalled the events of that week: 'We [the Dublin-based players] trained with a junior team, but the problem was their season was over. So we split up. Myself, James Keddy and Richie Purdy trained in Tymon North and Tony O'Dowd trained with his brothers in Stewart's Hospital. While training that Thursday, Tony's younger brother, Conor, collapsed and died. It turned out he had an enlarged heart and it just gave out. That summer I had Conor working for me on the truck for Ballygowan, so it really affected me. Tony was so distraught that he couldn't play in the final, and our manager Felix Healy put it well when he said, "Derry are travelling to Dublin, not for a Cup final, but for a funeral." There was a different atmosphere in the dressing-room. Conor's death affected a number of players apart from myself.'

Goalkeeper O'Dowd, who was replaced in goal by Declan Devine, wasn't the only player to miss the final. Derry winger Tom Mohan and Shelbourne striker Pat Morley were injured, with Morley's cruciate injury the latest in a line of Cup final hoodoos that seemed to target his family. Pat and his father Jackie both won the League on a number of occasions, but never had any luck when it came to the Cup.

The final hinged on Shels manager Damien Richardson's plan, which was designed to cover for the absence of Morley and also reduce the effectiveness of Derry's central midfield duo of Paul Hegarty and Peter Hutton. Instead of his usual 4-4-2 formation, he opted for 4-5-1, with Stephen Geoghegan up front and the midfield reinforced by John O'Rourke, whose season was the reverse of Morley's; he had missed most of the season through injury and was making his first start in the FAI Cup.

'The morning before the game at training I told the players the team,' recalled Richardson. 'But I told them to keep it quiet because I wanted to tell Greg Costello he wasn't playing. He was working at the *Sunday World*, but by the time I got over to him he knew and he wasn't happy.' Another person was also disappointed with the team selection, as Richardson revealed: 'The morning of the Cup final, Fred Davis took Alan Gough down to Tolka Park to do some training, and Ollie Byrne wouldn't let them on the pitch, saying we were all going to be sacked. He was incensed over Costello's omission and he let it be known.' Fortunately for Richardson and his staff, O'Rourke had a fine game, Shelbourne won 2–0, and their jobs were safe for another year.

For Tommy Dunne, whose father Theo had won the Cup as a player and manager, it was third-time unlucky, but he did have another League medal – and memories of Felix Healy's team talks. 'They were, to say the least, interesting,' he recalled. 'When we played St Pat's to win the League he gave us a story of a nephew who was on the dark side and he [Healy] was trying to get him right, and he died tragically. The moral was don't have any regrets, leave nothing behind on the pitch. A lot of the time we'd be wondering where he got the stories from. Another time it was about a fellow in the IRA and us Dub lads were wondering should we just get in the car and head home!'

Healy wasn't only a storyteller, he was an activist as well. In the League that season at the Brandywell against Bohemians, James Coll was giving Gary Beckett grief and, at half-time, Healy went onto the pitch, punches were thrown and Coll was sent off. Coll subsequently got a High Court injunction against his suspension.

A rule change this season decreed extra time in the event of a draw and, as a result, only one game went to a replay. The big losers, though, were Limerick, who held Shamrock Rovers to a 3–3 draw after ninety minutes in the first round. Instead of a money-spinning replay at home, they were edged out 5–4 in extra time.

For the third successive final, Dave Campbell opened the scoring, having backed himself to do so each time. Mick Neville won his seventh FAI Cup medal, leaving him just one short of the record held jointly by William 'Sacky' Glen and Johnny Fullam.

First Round

January 10	**Shelbourne**	4	**Everton**	2
	Rutherford, Morley, S. Geoghegan, D. Baker		Nagle, Giltenan	
	St Patrick's Athletic	1	**Athlone Town**	0
	Gormley			
	Waterford United	4	**Monaghan United**	0
	Bowman, Browne 2, Sinnott			
January 11	**Cobh Ramblers**	0	**Sligo Rovers**	3
			Oates, Birks, Moran	
	Derry City	5	**Crumlin United**	0
	Mohan, Curran, Keddy, Cleary o.g., R. Coyle			
	Dublin University	4	**Parkvilla**	0
	Dowling 2, Battigan, Fanning			
	Home Farm	2	**Glenmore Celtic**	1
	Place 2		Dodd	
	Longford Town	0	**St Francis**	1
			Connolly pen.	
	UCD	0	**Bray Wanderers**	1
			K. O'Brien pen.	
January 12	**Cork City**	2	**Galway United**	0
	Coughlan, Hill			
	Garda	0	**Drogheda United**	2
			Sheedy o.g., Tresson	

(After extra time; 0–0 after 90m)

	Kilkenny City	1	**Bohemians**	2
	Cooney		Doolin, McGrath	
	Shamrock Rovers	5	**Limerick**	4
	Tracey 2, Fenlon pen., Cousins, Williams		King, Ryan, Carr, Tobin	

(After extra time; 3–3 after 90m)

	Valeview Shankill	0	**Rockmount**	1
			Martin	
	Wayside Celtic	2	**Finn Harps**	1
	Martin, Geraghty		Dowling	
	(At Carlisle Grounds)			

| Whitehall Rangers | 0 | Dundalk | 0 |

(After extra time.)

First Round Replay

| January 15 | Dundalk | 5 | Whitehall Rangers | 1 |
| | Markey, Gallen 3, B. Byrne | | Doyle | |

Second Round

February 7	Bohemians	2	Wayside Celtic	0
	T. Byrne pen., Swan			
	Waterford United	1	Shamrock Rovers	0
	Golden			
February 8	Derry City	2	Home Farm	1
	L. Coyle 2		Place	
	Drogheda United	2	Rockmount	1
	N. Reid, Tresson		Martin	
	Dublin University	0	Bray Wanderers	3
			O'Hanlon, Coyle 2	
	Sligo Rovers	0	St Patrick's Athletic	1
			Reilly	
February 9	Cork City	4	St Francis	1
	O'Connell, Caulfield, Hartigan, Coughlan		Patton	
	Shelbourne	4	Dundalk	2
	S. Geoghegan 2, Fridge o.g., Rutherford		B. Byrne, Gallen	

Quarter-Finals

March 7	Bohemians	1	St Patrick's Athletic	0
	Parkes			
	Waterford United	1	Drogheda United	0
	Power pen.			
March 9	Bray Wanderers	0	Shelbourne	1
			Morley	
	Derry City	1	Cork City	0
	Beckett			

Semi-Finals

April 4	Bohemians	0	Derry City	2
			Hargan, Mullen o.g.	
	Waterford United	1	Shelbourne	2
	Browne		Campbell, Rutherford	

Final – Dalymount Park

May 4	Shelbourne	2	Derry City	0
	Campbell (80m),			
	S. Geoghegan (87m)			

Shelbourne: Alan Gough; Mick Neville, Pat Scully, Dave Campbell, Declan Geoghegan; Pascal Vaudequin, Tony Sheridan, Brian Flood, John O'Rourke, Mark Rutherford; Stephen Geoghegan. Subs: Greg Costello for Vaudequin, 88m; Dessie Baker for Rutherford, 90m. Manager: Damien Richardson

Derry City: Declan Devine; Declan Boyle, Paul Curran, Gavin Dykes, Tommy Dunne; Sean Hargan, Paul Hegarty, Peter Hutton, James Keddy; Liam Coyle, Gary 'Bing' Beckett. Sub: Ryan Coyle for Boyle, 81m. Manager: Patrick Joseph 'Felix' Healy

Referee: R. O'Hanlon (Waterford)   Attendance: 11,000

1998

Hard Lesson For Rico

Managers Damien Richardson and Dave Barry were both faced with difficult decisions in the 1998 FAI Cup Final. Richardson, faced with a situation not of his making, made the wrong decision; Barry, faced with a problem largely of his own making, took corrective action and brought the Cup back to Cork for the first time in twenty-five years.

Shelbourne boss Richardson was preparing for the final League game of the season – away to Dundalk – and needing only a draw to win the title, when the FAI Disciplinary Committee dropped a bombshell. 'Five days before the Dundalk game, they told us that Pat Fenlon and Dessie Baker were suspended,' he recalled. 'We kicked up because we were supposed to be given two weeks' notice, and they backed down to the extent that they gave us the option of deciding which game – the Dundalk game or the Cup final the following week – the players would play in. I spoke to both players and decided to keep them for the Cup final, which turned out to be the wrong decision. We were beaten 2–1 in Dundalk and lost the Cup after a replay. It's a decision I regret, as the next game should always be the most important game.'

Richardson's decision was probably influenced by the fact that Shels were going for an unprecedented three-in-a-row in the FAI Cup, but defeat meant that his team had failed on the final day in each of the three majors – League, FAI Cup and League Cup. His days in the demanding Tolka Park hot-seat were numbered.

For Dave Barry, meanwhile, Cork City's Cup success was a result of two years of careful grooming of staff. 'When I took over in '96,' he recalled, 'there were twenty-two players on the books and I got rid of sixteen and signed six. We played Waterford Glass in the Munster Cup Final and lost 1–0. That was a wake-up call that the players were not good enough for the Premier Division.'

Barry lost his first four games as manager, but in his four years at the helm the team qualified for Europe each season, won the FAI Cup and the League Cup, and young players like Noel Mooney, Derek Coughlan, Ollie Cahill and Noel Hartigan were introduced, as the club was built back up to top Premier standards.

In the final, which finished 0–0, Shels had the upper hand. For the replay, Barry had to make changes, one enforced, when full-back Stephen Napier was admitted to hospital with an irregular heartbeat, and the other – his big decision – dropping strikers John Glynn and Jason Kabia and calling up veteran John Caulfield as well as nineteen-year-old Noel Hartigan. 'Kabia was so hyper and the occasion probably got to him,' recalled Barry. 'He was caught offside ten or twelve times, and we couldn't get any momentum in our play. It was too easy for Shels' back four; we needed someone cuter for the replay. So I went for John who, even without the ball, upsets people with his talking, and Noel, who I knew wouldn't be fazed by the occasion. We caused them problems, won 1–0, and it could have been 2–0 at least.'

The one moment when the Cork bench had a flutter of nerves came when their former striker, Pat Morley, was introduced with ten minutes to go. He had spent the entire season recovering from a cruciate injury, and his first appearance was a last throw of the dice on Shels' part, but his tough-tackling former team-mates ensured there was no happy ending. In fact, Pat, like his father Jackie (Cork Hibernians and Waterford), had no luck when it came to the FAI Cup, losing all six finals they were involved in.

For Barry, Caulfield and Philip Long it was third-time lucky, having been involved in Cork City's failed bids in 1989 and 1992, while Patsy Freyne, a veteran of the 1989 team, gave a masterclass in midfield, earning the Man of the Match award.

First Round

9 January	Bohemians	0	Cork City	1
			Broughan o.g.	
	Drogheda United	1	Shamrock Rovers	1
	Gallen		Francis	
	Waterford United	2	St Patrick's Athletic	2
	Dully, Mark Reid		P. Campbell, Osam	
10 January	Athlone Town	3	College Corinthians	0
	Martin o.g., Buckley, Carberry			
	Cobh Wanderers	0	Galway United	2
			Lavine 2	
	Derry City	7	Rockmount	0
	Beckett, Keddy 2, Hargan 3, Gallagher			
	Home Farm Everton	3	Home Farm	1
	Moore 2, Place		Campbell	
	Kilkenny City	0	UCD	4
			Kavanagh, Sherlock 2, Bolger	
11 January	Dundalk	5	Swilly Rovers	0
	Doohan, Withnell, Melvin, B. Byrne, McCoy			
	Fanad United	0	Whitehall Rangers	3
			Herron 2, O'Kelly	
	Finn Harps	2	Bray Wanderers	0
	Johnson, Mulligan			
	Monaghan United	0	Cobh Ramblers	3
			O'Connor, Coughlan, Izzi	
	St Francis	1	Cherry Orchard	0
	Gormley			
	Shelbourne	4	Limerick City	1
	Rutherford 2, L. Kelly, D. Baker		O'Donnell	
	Sligo Rovers	1	Mervue United	1
	Hallows		Joyce	
	Wayside Celtic	0	Longford Town	0

First Round Replays

12 January	St Patrick's Athletic	3	Waterford United	0
	Gilzean, Reilly, Devereaux			
14 January	Longford Town	1	Wayside Celtic	1
	Doherty		Callaghan	

(After extra time; 1–1 after 90m)

	Mervue United	0	Sligo Rovers	2
	(At Terryland Park)		Moran 2	
	Shamrock Rovers	2	Drogheda United	0
	M. Kenny, Morrisroe			

First Round Second Replay

21 January	Wayside Celtic	0	Longford Town	1
			D. Gannon	

(After extra time; 0–0 after 90m)

Second Round

5 February	Dundalk	0	Shelbourne	0
7 February	Athlone Town	2	Shamrock Rovers	1
	Kelly, Lee		Tracey	
	Cobh Ramblers	1	St Patrick's Athletic	3
	Coughlan		Gilzean, Braithwaite, Gormley	
	Galway United	2	Finn Harps	2
	Carter, Lavine		Dowling, O'Brien	
	Longford Town	1	Whitehall Rangers	0
	Darby			
	Sligo Rovers	2	St Francis	0
	Flannery, Moran			
8 February	Cork City	1	Derry City	1
	Coughlan		Taggart	
	UCD	1	Home Farm Everton	1
	Martin		Gill	

Second Round Replays

8 February	Shelbourne	2	Dundalk	0
	L. Kelly, Rutherford			

10 February	Derry City	0	Cork City	1
			Brunton o.g.	
	Home Farm Everton	0	UCD	1
			Gifford o.g.	
18 February	Finn Harps	3	Galway United	1
	Minnock, Mulligan, Cullen		Forde	

Quarter-Finals

6 March	St Patrick's Athletic	2	Shelbourne	2
	Gormley, P. Campbell		L. Kelly, S. Geoghegan	
8 March	Cork City	2	Sligo Rovers	0
	Freyne, Flanagan			
	UCD	0	Finn Harps	1
			S. Bradley	
10 March	Athlone Town	1	Longford Town	1
	Rogers pen.		Rooney	

Quarter-Final Replays

| 9 March | Shelbourne | 1 | St Patrick's Athletic | 1 |
| | McCarthy | | Braithwaite | |

(After extra time; 1–1 after 90m)

| 17 March | Longford Town | 1 | Athlone Town | 2 |
| | Silke o.g. | | Hogan, Carberry | |

Quarter-Final Second Replay

| 16 March | Shelbourne | 2 | St Patrick's Athletic | 2 |
| | S. Geoghegan 2 | | Hawkins, Devereaux | |

(After extra time; 2–2 after 90m; Shelbourne won 5–3 on pens.)

Semi-Finals

4 April	Athlone Town	1	Cork City	3
	Carberry		Hartigan, Kabia 2	
	Finn Harps	0	Shelbourne	0

Semi-Final Replay

| 7 April | Shelbourne | 1 | Finn Harps | 0 |
| | S. Geoghegan pen. | | | |

Final – Dalymount Park

10 May   **Cork City**   **0**   **Shelbourne**   **0**

Cork City: Noel Mooney; Stephen Napier, Derek Coughlan, Declan Daly, Gareth Cronin; Kelvin Flanagan, Patsy Freyne, Dave Hill, Ollie Cahill; John Glynn, Jason Kabia. Sub: John Caulfield for Kabia, 60m. Manager: Dave Barry

Shelbourne: Alan Gough; Greg Costello, Tony McCarthy, Pat Scully, Declan Geoghegan; Dessie Baker, Pat Fenlon, Dean Fitzgerald, Mark Rutherford; Stephen Geoghegan, Liam Kelly. Sub: Dave Smith for Costello, half-time. Manager: Damien Richardson

Referee: G. Perry (Dublin)   Attendance: 12,600

Final Replay – Dalymount Park

16 May   **Cork City**   **1**   **Shelbourne**   **0**
                Coughlan (75m)

Cork City: Fergus O'Donoghue for Napier; Caulfield and Noel Hartigan for Glynn and Kabia. Subs: Glynn for Hartigan, 56m; Philip Long for O'Donoghue, 76m

Shelbourne: Smith for Costello. Subs: Tony Sheridan for Rutherford, 80m; Pat Morley for S Geoghegan, 80m; Mick Neville for Fitzgerald, 85m

Referee: G. Perry (Dublin)   Attendance: 6,400

1999

Waitin' For Jason

In the end, there seemed to be an inevitability about it: the 1999 FAI Cup Final wouldn't be decided until Jason Byrne was fit and ready to play. After breaking his ankle in a stormy League game against Sligo Rovers in the Showgrounds in January, it was a long road back for Byrne. The date of the Cup final, 9 May, was too soon for him, but when the final turned into a saga, he was ready to step in and decide the issue on 20 May.

The previous year, when Bray manager Pat Devlin sent Martin Nugent to vet Byrne, who was playing with junior club St Colmcille's, the report concluded that 'he wasn't great, he was strolling around the park, seemed to have the wrong attitude.' However, the fact that Byrne had scored four goals in a 4–0 win was enough for Devlin. 'We put him in the team for a friendly against Peterborough and he was rotten, but he scored,' recalled Devlin. 'We worked on him week in, week out after training every night with Kieran O'Brien on the back pitch, and I can say that Jason became the player he is from his time at Bray.' What he became was the League's most prolific scorer after the legendary Brendan Bradley.

It was a strange season for the Seasiders, who started their League campaign well, moving into third place in the Premier Division after first-time away wins over Bohemians and Shamrock Rovers. A run of eight successive defeats saw them drop to the bottom by Christmas and, although they fought back, they eventually finished second-last and were relegated to the First Division. However, in tandem with their poor League results, they put together a great Cup run, which saw them reach their second final after a three-game marathon quarter-final against Sligo Rovers and a shock semi-final victory over '90s Cup specialists, Shelbourne.

In the other half of the draw, Finn Harps, who were enjoying a good season under Charlie McGeever, knocked out title-holders Cork City, and then received a walk-over in a quarter-final replay from Kilkenny City, who pleaded inability to field a team in Ballybofey on 9 March. This was prompted by a clash of fix-tures, which saw their young striker Michael Reddy called up for UEFA Youth Championship duty in Belfast the same night. It was a first of its kind for the FAI Cup, and Kilkenny were fined £2,500. In 1940, an earlier Cork City had been expelled by the FAI before the first round of the Cup and had to concede a walk-over to Drumcondra.

Harps were favourites for the final and, when Jonathan Speak gave them the lead in the replay, it looked like it was going to be their day. However, Barry O'Connor bought Bray extra time – and more drama. 'In the extra time,' Devlin recalled, 'Harps were winning 2–1 and they were wasting time, trying to run the clock down. They were even bringing on players to give them a medal, and the blue ribbons were on the cup, when we got a penalty in the last minute.' Devlin, as usual, couldn't watch it. Harps' goalkeeper Brian McKenna saved Colm Tresson's kick, but Kieran 'Tarzan' O'Brien was first to the rebound to bring the game to a second replay.

Bray's lengthy injury list was clearing up just in time. Apart from Byrne, who made a substitute appearance in the replay, full-backs Ray Kenny and Maurice Farrell were available after long spells of absence due to injuries. It was a stronger, more compact Bray team in the second replay and, even though Speak put Harps ahead again, the cutting edge of Byrne, a cousin of Republic of Ireland record-goalscorer Robbie Keane, proved the difference between the sides, with two well-taken goals.

First Round

8 January	Athlone Town	0	Sligo Rovers	1
			Hare	
	Bray Wanderers	5	St Francis	0
	K. O'Brien 2, Doohan, Fox, Tresson			
9 January	Cobh Ramblers	2	Garda	2
	Kenneally, Izzi		Coogan, O'Brien	
	Finn Harps	0	Belgrove	0
	Glenmore Celtic	0	St Patrick's Athletic	3
			Molloy 2, Gormley	
	Kilkenny City	3	Swilly Rovers	2
	Vaughan pen., P. Walsh, Goodwin		Heaney, Porter	
	Limerick FC	0	Dundalk	0
10 January	Ashtownvilla	0	Cherry Orchard	2
			Madden 2 pens.	
	Drogheda United	0	Galway United	0
	Longford Town	0	Derry City	1
			Kelly	
	Monaghan United	0	Cork City	2
			Caulfield 2	
	Rockmount	1	UCD	1
	Oldham		Kilmurray	
	St Mary's	1	Bangor Celtic	0
	McAuliffe			
	Shamrock Rovers	0	Shelbourne	3
			S. Geoghegan, Scully 2	
	Waterford United	0	Bohemians	4
			Swan, Doyle 2, Kelly	
	Workman's Club/Dunleary	1	Home Farm Everton	3
	Byrne		Farrell, McGauley, Moore	

First Round Replays

12 January	Dundalk	2	Limerick	2
	Brennan 2		Lynch pen., Doyle	
	(After extra time; 2-2 after 90m)			
	Galway United	1	Drogheda United	0
	Lavine			

	UCD	2	**Rockmount**	0
	Mahon, O'Byrne			
13 January	**Garda**	1	**Cobh Ramblers**	6
	Coogan		Izzi 4, O'Connor, Francis	
27 January	**Belgrove**	0	**Finn Harps**	6
			S. Bradley, Mulligan 2, Speak, F. Harkin, Mohan	

First Round Second Replay

19 January	**Limerick**	0	**Dundalk**	1
			Martin	

Second Round

5 February	**Bohemians**	0	**Shelbourne**	1
			S. Geoghegan	
	Bray Wanderers	3	**Cherry Orchard**	0
	Parsons, B. O'Connor 2			
	Galway United	1	**Home Farm Everton**	0
	Thornton			
6 February	**Sligo Rovers**	2	**Cobh Ramblers**	1
	Hoecks, Shannon		Francis	
7 February	**Cork City**	0	**Finn Harps**	0
	Derry City	2	**Dundalk**	0
	Gallogly o.g., L. Coyle			
	St Mary's	0	**Kilkenny City**	3
			Reddy 2, Cashin	
	St Patrick's Athletic	1	**UCD**	0
	Molloy			

Second Round Replay

17 February	**Finn Harps**	1	**Cork City**	0
	O'Brien			

Quarter-Finals

5 March	**Galway United**	1	**St Patrick's Athletic**	0
	Lavine			

6 March	**Kilkenny City**	2	**Finn Harps**	2
	D. Walsh, Rea		Mulligan, Speak	
	Sligo Rovers	1	**Bray Wanderers**	1
	Hallows		J. Lynch	
7 March	**Derry City**	0	**Shelbourne**	2
			S. Geoghegan 2	

Quarter-Final Replays

9 March	**Finn Harps**	W/O	**Kilkenny City**	
10 March	**Bray Wanderers**	0	**Sligo Rovers**	0

(After extra time.)

Quarter-Final Second Replay

16 March	**Bray Wanderers**	1	**Sligo Rovers**	0
	Tresson pen.			

Semi-Finals

2 April	**Shelbourne**	1	**Bray Wanderers**	2
	Scully		Doohan, Tresson	
4 April	**Galway United**	1	**Finn Harps**	2
	M. Keane		O'Brien, Speak	

Final – Tolka Park

9 May	**Bray Wanderers**	0	**Finn Harps**	0

Bray Wanderers: John Walsh; Mick Doohan, Colm Tresson, Jody Lynch; Ray Kenny, John Ryan, Dom Tierney, Alan Smyth, Philip Keogh, Maurice Farrell, Stephen Fox. Sub: Glen Brien for Ryan, 28m. Manager: Pat Devlin

Finn Harps: Brian McKenna; Trevor Scanlon, Gavin Dykes, Declan Boyle, Jonathan Minnock; Tom Mohan, Donal O'Brien, Fergal Harkin, Eamonn Kavanagh; Jonathan Speak, James Mulligan. Manager: Charlie McGeever

Referee: J. McDermott (Dublin)

Attendance: 7,000

Final Replay – Tolka Park

15 May **Bray Wanderers**   **2**   **Finn Harps**   **2**

B. O'Connor (87m),   Speak (58m), Mohan (102m)

K. O'Brien (120m)

(After extra time; 1–1 after 90m)

Bray Wanderers: Kieran 'Tarzan' O'Brien for Ryan. Subs: Brien for Tierney, 27m; Barry O'Connor for Farrell, 40m; Jason Byrne for Smyth, 68m

Finn Harps: Paddy McGrenaghan for Kavanagh. Subs: Shane Bradley for Harkin, 108m; Eamonn Sheridan for Speak, 112m; John Gerard McGettigan for Mohan, 115m

Referee: J. McDermott (Dublin)   Attendance: 4,100

Final Second Replay – Tolka Park

20 May **Bray Wanderers**   **2**   **Finn Harps**   **1**

Byrne (38m, 73m)   Speak (11m)

Bray Wanderers: Byrne and O'Connor for Smyth and Tierney. Sub: Smyth for Farrell, 87m

Finn Harps: Unchanged. Subs: Ruairi Boyle for Scanlon, 63m; Sheridan for McGrenaghan, 77m; Bradley for Mohan, 83m

Referee: J. McDermott (Dublin)   Attendance: 4,350

2000

Comeback Hero Fenlon

When you suffer a compound dislocation of your ankle and break the tibia and fibia of your left leg, and are then told by a consultant in the Mater Hospital that you won't play again, for most players that would be that. But Pat Fenlon was different. He wasn't yet thirty, he felt he had unfinished business, and even if the 1998-99 season was a write-off, he targeted 1999-2000 for his comeback. 'I was out for six months,' he recalled, 'and I went to Middlesbrough for rehab. My Dad used to scout for them, and Curtis Fleming and Alan Moore were there. Larry Byrne, the Shelbourne physio, was also fantastic – we used to run on Portmarnock beach. It was walking first, then light jogging, then walking in the sea to bring the swelling down.'

By the time the FAI Cup began in 2000, Fenlon was ensconced again in Shels' midfield – this time with a new ally. Manager Dermot Keely, despite the disapproval of club CEO Ollie Byrne, had signed Paul Doolin. 'Ollie probably thought Paul was coming to the end of his career,' recalled Fenlon, 'but he was a great signing for us. He had changed his game to a more defensive midfield role, and that allowed me to get on, and I scored a good few goals.'

The pick of those goals, of course, was the one he scored in the Cup final replay against Bohemians in Dalymount Park on 5 May. It earned Shelbourne their seventh FAI Cup triumph, and also clinched the club's first League and Cup double. It crowned a marvellous comeback, which was duly acknowledged by his fellow professionals when he was voted PFAI Player of the Year. Doolin was completing his fifth League and Cup double, which is a record, while the inclusion of two sets of brothers on the winning team – the Geoghegans and the Bakers – set another Cup record.

Following the three-game final of 1999, the rules were changed to eliminate second replays and penalty shoot-outs were reinstated. There was also controversy in the first round, when FAI Junior Cup-holders Fairview Rangers were forced to play the last thirteen minutes against College Corinthians with ten men, after the referee wrongly sent off Philip Purcell. They won their appeal to have the game declared null and void, but the Appeals Committee overturned that decision and ruled that the game, which had finished 0–0, should be replayed in Cork. Fairview won the replay before going out to title-holders Bray Wanderers, who made a brave defence of their crown before losing in controversial circumstances to Bohemians in the semi-final.

Bray, whose leading scorer, Jason Byrne, was due to serve a one-match ban, thought they had circumvented this by playing a Leinster Senior Cup tie against St Francis in mid-week. In 1990, they had been successful in reinstating striker John Ryan before their quarter-final tie against Galway United by playing a President's Cup match in mid-week. However, when Bohemians protested on this occasion, the FAI Chief Executive, Bernard O'Byrne, advised Bray not to play Byrne in the semi-final. Bray's resentment deepened when a series of decisions went against them in the course of the game. And when the issue subsequently went to arbitration, the FAI were ordered to pay Bray €40,000 in compensation on the basis that the Chief Executive had no authority to interfere with the rules of the competition. The first round was also notable for the achievements of Leinster Senior League clubs, Bangor Celtic and Bluebell United, who eliminated Premier Division sides Drogheda United and Sligo Rovers respectively. Bluebell subsequently took Cup-winners Shelbourne to two games in the quarter-finals. A second round replay worth noting was Finn Harps' 7–1 demolition of Longford Town, when five of Harps' goals came in an eight-minute spell.

For the first time, the final featured the League's two oldest clubs – Bohemians, founded in 1890, and Shelbourne, founded in 1895. As members of the IFA, they had contested the IFA Cup Final in 1908 and 1911, with

Shelbourne coming out on top on the latter occasion. In an act of gamesmanship after the drawn game, Bohs' manager Roddy Collins, aware that Shels' goalkeeper Steve Williams was on loan from Dundalk, put in a bid for him. 'I offered €25,000 that I didn't have,' he admitted. It caused such a furore that, when Collins walked over to the stand after the replay for the presentation, he was greeted with a right-hand to the face from Shels CEO Ollie Byrne!

First Round

7 January	**Athlone Town** Clarke, Parkes 2, Moylan	4	**Limerick City** D. Whyte	1
	Drogheda United	0	**Bangor Celtic** Stout	1
	Galway United Burke o.g.	1	**St Patrick's Athletic** Russell	1
	St Francis	0	**Shelbourne** Doolin	1
8 January	**Derry City** Beckett	1	**Bray Wanderers** Dutton	1
	Kilkenny City Prizeman	1	**Dundalk** Hoey	1
	Longford Town K. O'Connor, Zellor	2	**Waterford United** Iorfa, Sterling	2
	Sligo Rovers	0	**Bluebell United** Fitzpatrick	1
9 January	**Clonmel Town** Boland	1	**Rockmount** Oldham	1
	Cobh Ramblers	0	**Bohemians** O'Hanlon	1
	Fairview Rangers	0	**College Corinthians**	0
	Monaghan United	0	**UCD** P. Hanrahan 2, Martin, O'Byrne	4
	St Mochta's Fitzpatrick 2, Hughes	3	**Evergreen** Conroy	1
	Shamrock Rovers Francis	1	**Cork City** L. O'Brien	1
	Swilly Rovers Heaney 3, Doherty, Donaghy	5	**Parkvilla**	0
18 January	**Finn Harps** Mulligan, Speak	2	**Home Farm Fingal**	0

First Round Replays

11 January	**St Patrick's Athletic** Prenderville, Croly	2	**Galway United** Dolan, Gorman, Malee	3

(After extra time; 2–2 after 90m)

	Waterford United	0	**Longford Town**	1
			Zellor	
12 January	**Cork City**	3	**Shamrock Rovers**	1
	Freyne, Coughlan 2		Woods	
	Dundalk	1	**Kilkenny City**	1
	Sharkey		Breen	

(After extra time; 1–1 after 90m; Kilkeeny won 3–2 on pens.)

19 January	**Bray Wanderers**	2	**Derry City**	1
	J. Byrne 2		McLaughlin	
23 January	**College Corinthians**	1	**Fairview Rangers**	3
	Morley		Kelly, Phelan, Sheehan	

(After extra time; 1–1 after 90m)

	Rockmount	1	**Clonmel Town**	3
	Lynch		Conway, Moroney 2	

Second Round

4 February	**Athlone Town**	0	**Galway United**	0
	Bohemians	3	**UCD**	3
	Kelly, Mullen, Brunton		Mooney, O'Byrne 2	
5 February	**Bangor Celtic**	2	**Shelbourne**	3
	O'Driscoll, Fogarty		S. Geoghegan, Keddy, D. Baker	
	(At Richmond Park)			
	Longford Town	2	**Finn Harps**	2
	K. O'Connor, Parsons		Mulligan 2	
6 February	**Clonmel Town**	1	**Bluebell United**	1
	Conway		Duffy	
	Cork City	0	**Kilkenny City**	2
			Rea, Kerley pen.	
	Fairview Rangers	0	**Bray Wanderers**	2
			Keogh, B. O'Connor	
	Swilly Rovers	1	**St Mochta's**	2
	Heaney		Cummins, Fitzpatrick	

Second Round Replays

8 February	**Finn Harps**	7	**Longford Town**	1
	Kenny, D. Boyle, Mulligan 2,		V. Perth	
	Turner 2, McHugh			

	Galway United	1	**Athlone Town**	1
	Ogden		Clarke	

(After extra time; 1–1 after 90m; Galway won 4–2 on pens.)

	UCD	0	**Bohemians**	3
			Caffrey, Crowe, Kelly	
13 February	**Bluebell United**	2	**Clonmel Town**	0
	Reilly, Dunning			

Quarter-Finals

3 March	**Bohemians**	2	**St Mochta's**	0
	Kelly 2			
4 March	**Bluebell United**	0	**Shelbourne**	0
	(At Tolka Park)			
	Finn Harps	1	**Galway United**	3
	Turner		Keane, Keogh, Lavine	
	Kilkenny City	0	**Bray Wanderers**	2
			J. Byrne, Tresson	

Quarter-Final Replay

7 March	**Shelbourne**	2	**Bluebell United**	1
	Keddy, McCarthy		McGovern	

Semi-Finals

31 March 31	**Galway United**	0	**Shelbourne**	2
			Keddy, D. Baker	
2 April	**Bohemians**	2	**Bray Wanderers**	1
	Hunt, Kelly		Tresson	

Final – Tolka Park

30 April	**Shelbourne**	0	**Bohemians**	0

Shelbourne: Steve Williams; Owen Heery, Pat Scully, Tony McCarthy, Declan Geoghegan; Richie Baker, Paul Doolin, Pat Fenlon, James Keddy; Dessie Baker, Stephen Geoghegan. Manager: Dermot Keely

Bohemians: Michael Dempsey; Tony O'Connor, Shaun Maher, Avery John, Robbie Brunton; Paul Byrne, Kevin Hunt, Stephen Caffrey, Mark Dempsey; Gareth O'Connor, Derek Swan. Subs: Ray Kelly for Byrne, 55m; Graham Doyle for Hunt, 60m; Glenn Crowe for Swan, 80m. Manager: Roddy Collins

Referee: J. Stacey (Athlone) Attendance: 8,428

Final Replay – Dalymount Park

5 May **Shelbourne** **1** **Bohemians** **0**
Fenlon (39m)

Shelbourne: Unchanged. Sub: Dave Campbell for Doolin, 90m

Bohemians: Kelly for Swan. Subs: Swan for Byrne, 51m; Crowe for Kelly, 63m; Doyle for Brunton, 87m

Referee: J. Stacey (Athlone) Attendance: 6,400

It's a Record!

- Usually, when finals result in a replay or multiple replays, the same referee is appointed to the subsequent games. However, this didn't happen in 1996 because Pat Kelly had agreed that, in the event of a replay, Wilfrid Wallace would be in charge, as both of them were retiring that year. It was the second final for both whistlers.

2001

Roddy's Revolution

When he was appointed manager of Bohemians in October 1998, Roddy Collins made a promise to the fans: 'Give me a bit of time and I'll deliver the League title.' In less than three years at the helm of the club he supported as a boy, he led them to a League and Cup double – their first in seventy-three years – and another FAI Cup Final, which they lost after a replay. He had kept his promise. However, within weeks of his double success, while on holidays in Florida, he was informed that he had been sacked, due no doubt to the harsh words he had directed at the club's management committee following the League triumph.

The transformation that Collins brought about at Dalymount involved moving from a part-time to a full-time set-up. This meant a complete overhaul of playing and backroom staff, so that when the double was completed with the winning of the FAI Cup this season, there was only one surviving player left on the staff he had inherited. By a strange twist of fate, it was that player, Tony O'Connor, who scored the goal that won the Cup. 'He was the only part-time player, but a consummate professional,' recalled Collins. 'He took time off work to maintain his fitness levels, he gave great service to the club, and was a great ally to his teammates. It was a fitting tribute to his years of service that he should score the goal.'

In Collins's first season in charge, Bohs had lost the Cup final and were pipped for second place in the League on the last day. 'When I told the board that I was releasing eight players, they said, "Are you sure? We nearly won the double," and I said, "Nearly is not good enough."' O'Connor was one of the players he tried to move on, as he as he attempted to fulfil his plans for a full-time squad. His policy won swift approval when, fielding the first full-time League of Ireland team, Aberdeen were beaten in the UEFA Cup; no Irish club had ever beaten Scottish opposition in Europe before.

Running second in the League in January, Collins made three key signings that pushed Bohs over the line – Mark Rutherford, Alex Nesovic and Paul Byrne. While Rutherford and Nesovic also helped win the FAI Cup, Byrne was Cup-tied after playing in the first round for St Patrick's Athletic.

If Collins was instigating a revolution at Dalymount, Stephen Kenny was doing something similar with Longford Town. Appointed in June 1998, when they finished bottom of the First Division with a meagre twelve points and had to apply for re-election, Kenny restored pride and belief and achieved promotion to the Premier Division in 2000. In their first season in the Premier, they took the FAI Cup by storm, recording thrilling replay wins over Cork City, St Patrick's Athletic and Waterford United to reach their first final. Also, by virtue of Bohs winning the League, Longford qualified for the UEFA Cup. It was a fairytale that attracted record crowds to Strokestown Road.

For the final, Collins lined out without left-back Simon Webb, who had been sick and didn't train all week, and winger Dave Morrison, who was married in Shropshire the day before, but he had to call on both of them to see-off the Longford challenge. It was Morrison's cross which led to veteran O'Connor's winning goal.

The foot and mouth scare caused havoc with Cup fixtures. The second round tie between FAI Junior Cup-holders Portmarnock and Dundalk, originally fixed for 3 February, was postponed five times until 1 April due to the Government's restrictions on Louth clubs. Another delay proved timely for Longford. Their second round replay with St Patrick's Athletic was fixed for 4 March, but was eventually played on 23 March. Keith O'Connor, Longford's match-winner, would have missed the earlier date due to injury.

First Round

4 January	**Home Farm Fingal**	0	**Athlone Town**	0
5 January	**Bohemians**	2	**Drogheda United**	0
	Maher, Nesovic			
	Bray Wanderers	5	**Sligo Rovers**	0
	Keegan 2, Gormley, J. Byrne 2			
	St Patrick's Athletic	4	**Wayside Celtic**	1
	Russell 2, Foley, Holt		McHugh	
	Waterford United	1	**St Francis**	1
	Reynolds		Tighe	
6 January	**Cobh Ramblers**	4	**St Michael's**	0
	Coughlan, Bruton, Golden 2			
	Dundalk	3	**Limerick**	0
	Hoey, Flanagan, Reilly			
	Galway United	0	**Kilkenny City**	2
			Parkes, McAreavey	
	Longford Town	1	**Cork City**	1
	V. Perth		Morley	
8 January	**Home Farm**	0	**Finn Harps**	3
			Tierney, Kenny o.g., Harkin	
	Moyle Park	0	**Cherry Orchard**	1
			Kenny	
	Portmarnock	3	**Rockmount**	0
	Feeney, McDonald, Cummins			
	(At AUL Complex)			
	Rathcoole Boys	0	**Derry City**	3
			Beckett, E. Doherty 2	
	Shamrock Rovers	3	**Dublin Bus**	0
	Grant, Robinson, Palmer			
	Shelbourne	2	**Monaghan United**	0
	Doolin 2			
	UCD	3	**Youghal United**	1
	McAuley, Martin, Martyn		Murphy	

First Round Replay

8 January	**Athlone Town** E. Molloy	1	**Home Farm Fingal**	0

(After extra time.)

10 January	**St Francis**	0	**Waterford United** Scully, Kirby	2
14 January	**Cork City** Coughlan	1	**Longford Town** S. Byrne, N. Byrne	2

Second Round

2 February	**Bohemians** Morrison, Crowe	2	**Bray Wanderers** Campbell	1
	Cherry Orchard Horan (At Richmond Park)	1	**Kilkenny City** Rocha	1
3 February	**Cobh Ramblers** Wolfe	1	**Athlone Town** E. Molloy	1
	Derry City Hutton	1	**Shelbourne** D. Baker	1
	Finn Harps	0	**Shamrock Rovers** Grant, B. Byrne, Deans	3
	Longford Town	0	**St Patrick's Athletic**	0
4 February	**UCD** Swan, Grogan pen.	2	**Waterford United** Bradley, K. Whittle	2
1 April	**Portmarnock** Bruen (At Baldonnel)	1	**Dundalk**	0

Second Round Replays

6 February	**Athlone Town**	0	**Cobh Ramblers** Bruton	1
	Shelbourne Scully	1	**Derry City**	0
13 February	**Kilkenny City** Wilkinson	1	**Cherry Orchard**	0

(After extra time; 0–0 after 90m)

20 February	Waterford United	0	UCD	0

(After extra time; Waterford won 7–6 on pens.)

23 March	St Patrick's Athletic	1	Longford Town	2
	Russell		Gavin, K. O'Connor	

Quarter-Finals

25 March	Cobh Ramblers	0	Waterford United	1
			Kirby pen.	
	Kilkenny City	2	Bohemians	7
	O'Byrne, Jackson		Crowe 2, G. O'Neill, Molloy 2 (1 pen.), Hill, Rutherford	
26 March	Shelbourne	1	Shamrock Rovers	1
	Fenlon		Deans	
15 April	Portmarnock	1	Longford Town	2
	Feeney		K. O'Connor, McNally pen.	
	(At Tolka Park)			

Quarter-Final Replay

29 March	Shamrock Rovers	3	Shelbourne	0
	Grant 2, Woods			
	(At Tolka Park)			

Semi-Finals

13 April	Bohemians	1	Shamrock Rovers	0
	Crowe			
22 April	Waterford United	1	Longford Town	1
	Gavin o.g.		McNally pen.	

Semi-Final Replay

26 April	Longford Town	1	Waterford United	0
	S. Kelly pen.			

Final – Tolka Park

| 13 May | Bohemians | 1 | Longford Town | 0 |

T. O'Connor (62m)

Bohemians: Wayne Russell; Tony 'Toccy' O'Connor, Stephen Caffrey, Shaun Maher, Dave Hill; Trevor Molloy, Jimmy Fullam, Kevin Hunt, Mark Rutherford; Glenn Crowe, Alex Nesovic. Subs: Simon Webb for Fullam, 27m; Dave Morrison for Nesovic, 48m. Manager: Roddy Collins

Longford Town: Stephen O'Brien; Alan Murphy, Eric Smith, Paul McNally, Wesley Byrne; Stephen Gavin, Stuart Byrne, Stephen Kelly, Sean Prunty; Shay Zellor, Keith O'Connor. Subs: Colm Notaro for Zellor, half-time; Stuart Holt for Gavin, 59m; Vinny Perth for Smith, 87m. Manager: Stephen Kenny

Referee: H. Byrne (Dublin)   Attendance: 9,500

It's a Record!

- Aaron Callaghan was the first player to score an FAI Cup goal in December, when he netted after five minutes for Dundalk in their 1–1 first round meeting with Galway United in Oriel Park on 13 December 2001. Dundalk went on to win the Cup that season.

2002 (A)

Gary's the Missing Link

Winning the League, according to Stephen McGuinness, brings a sense of relief, whereas winning the FAI Cup is more exhilarating, more euphoric. The League is a marathon where the Cup is a sprint and, in the case of the latter, even a slight change to a team's line-up can make all the difference.

So it was for Dundalk this season, as McGuinness recalled: 'When we beat Kilkenny in the second round, I got the feeling that we might do something, and Gary Haylock was the key to that. He had just signed for us, and before that, if we conceded a goal, as we did in Kilkenny, we never looked like getting it back. With a goalscorer like him in the side it breeds confidence, and from then on we always felt we would score.'

It was a strange season for Dundalk. The Premier Division was restructured into a ten-team league, which meant that three teams were automatically relegated, and Dundalk spent the season in the relegation zone. The arrival of Haylock, however, provided a boost, as McGuinness recalled: 'Our form in the last eight or nine games would have been good enough to win the League. Eventually we lost out by just one point.'

That form carried over into the Cup, with a quarter-final win away to Finn Harps earning them a home semi-final against Shamrock Rovers, who had spent the season challenging for the title and who had thrashed Dundalk 4–1 in the League seven weeks earlier. When Rovers manager Damien Richardson said on radio before the Cup tie that it would be a great leg-up for his club to win the

383

Cup this year, he provided all the motivation Dundalk needed. 'There was a cockiness about Rovers,' McGuinness recalled, 'and then Sean Francis, who had given us the run-around in the League game, was dropped for Tony Cousins. That suited us.' In the event, Dundalk surpassed themselves in front of the TV cameras and a packed Oriel Park, with a resounding 4–0 win that featured two more Haylock specials. The only sour note on the night was provided by the Rovers' fan who hit Dundalk manager Martin Murray on the head with a coin as he was being interviewed after the game.

The appeal of the Cup to the Dundalk fans was evident by the huge crowds who followed them at home and away on that campaign, but it didn't translate into their League attendances. 'After the Rovers game, the following Tuesday we played Derry City in the League and there was no one at it,' said McGuinness. 'I couldn't understand that, as the League game was relatively more important.'

The run-up to the Cup final was a fraught time for Dundalk. On the Sunday before the final, they were relegated, and their two attacking aces, Haylock and James Keddy, were both doubtful because of injury. On the morning of the game, Keddy failed a fitness test, but Haylock was available after taking a pain-killing injection.

With the Port Tunnel being built, there was traffic chaos in Dublin, yet Dundalk decided to have their pre-match meal in Donabate. The coach was delayed on its return, so the players only arrived in time to see their opponents, Bohemians, out on the pitch warming-up. 'For us, it was in and out, we had so little time,' recalled McGuinness, 'and I remember the referee, Paul McKeon, pulling Donal Broughan and myself aside as we were coming off the pitch after our short warm-up. We were both very physical, and he said to us, "Just remember this is my day as well, so make sure we all enjoy it." I had never really thought of it like that.'

Assistant manager Ollie Ralph had the holy water and blessed each of the players as they went out, but it didn't seem to be working when they went a goal behind after forty minutes to Tony O'Connor's second Cup final goal in eleven months. 'Before the arrival of Haylock that would have killed us,' said McGuinness. 'But four minutes later David Hoey went down the wing and crossed the ball to Haylock, who turned on a sixpence and stuck it in the net.'

Four minutes into the second half, McGuinness met a Ciaran Kavanagh corner and headed it down to Haylock who chested it, spun and knocked in the winner. Bohs' fate was sealed when full-back Simon Webb was sent off for a professional foul.

The first round had seen a repeat of the 2001 final, with holders Bohs drawn away to Longford Town. The game was overshadowed by the move of Town manager Stephen Kenny to Bohs. Longford took out a High Court injunction, claiming he was breaking his contract, and he had to sit in the stand as Bohs beat Longford 4–1, a quick reversal of the 2–0 win to which Kenny had guided Longford in the League the previous week.

First Round

13 December	Derry City	2	Mervue United	0
	Moran, E. Doherty			
	Dundalk	1	Galway United	1
	Callaghan		M. Keane	
	Workman's Club/Dunleary	0	Shelbourne	3
	(At Carlisle Grounds)		Heary, Burns 2	
14 December	Drogheda United	1	UCD	1
	Cummins		McNally	
	Glenmore Dundrum	0	Dublin City	0
	(At Whitehall)			
	St Patrick's Athletic	0	Bray Wanderers	1
			Keogh	
15 December	Longford Town	1	Bohemians	4
	Kirby		Folan, Molloy, Crowe 2	
16 December	Cherry Orchard	2	Garda	0
	Kennedy pen., O'Brien			
	Cork City	0	Shamrock Rovers	1
			Bennett o.g.	
	CYM Terenure	0	Cobh Ramblers	1
			Bruton	
	Glebe North	1	Limerick	2
	Kerr		D. McCarthy, J. Whyte	
	Kilkenny City	2	Waterford United	1
	Revins, Whelehan		Dempsey	
	Monaghan United	2	Athlone Town	1
	McKenna 2		Mullen	
	Sligo Rovers	2	Leeds AFC	0
	Feeney, Cretaro			
	St Kevin's Boys	1	Rockmount	1
	Maher		Downey pen.	
	(At AUL Complex)			
19 December	Finn Harps	5	Greystones	1
	J. Kenny, Devenney, Bonner 2, McGrenaghan		Wallace	

First Round Replays

18 December	Galway United	0	Dundalk	1
			Reilly	
	UCD	2	Drogheda United	0
	McNally, Finn			
20 December	Dublin City	5	Glenmore Dundrum	1
	Sheridan 2, Farrell 2, C. O'Connor		B. Archbold	
23 December	Rockmount	2	St Kevin's Boys	3
	D. Foley, Downey		O'Sullivan, Griffin, O'Hara	

Second Round

11 January	Bohemians	2	Cobh Ramblers	0
	Crowe, Molloy			
	Dublin City	0	Bray Wanderers	2
			J. Byrne 2	
	Shamrock Rovers	4	Monaghan United	1
	T. Grant, Woods 2, Cousins		Murphy	
12 January	Finn Harps	2	Shelbourne	1
	Cooke, McHugh		Minnock	
	Sligo Rovers	2	Limerick	1
	Hutchinson, Flannery		Foley	
13 January	Cherry Orchard	0	UCD	3
			R. Martin, O'Donnell, Grogan	
	Kilkenny City	2	Dundalk	3
	Hughes, Brennan		Prizeman, Haylock, Kavanagh	
	St Kevin's Boys	0	Derry City	0
	(At Whitehall)			

Second Round Replay

20 January	Derry City	1	St Kevin's Boys	0
	Higgins o.g.			

Quarter-Finals

7 February	Dundalk	1	Finn Harps	1
	Reilly		Mohan	
8 February	Bohemians	1	Bray Wanderers	1
	Caffrey		Doohan	

	Shamrock Rovers	2	**Sligo Rovers**	0
	Woods, Francis pen.			
10 February	**UCD**	2	**Derry City**	2
	T. O'Connor, O'Donnell		Hargan, Coyle	

Quarter-Final Replays

12 February	**Bray Wanderers**	0	**Bohemians**	4
			Morrison, G. O'Neill 2, Crowe	
	Derry City	1	**UCD**	0
	E. Doherty			

(After extra time.)

	Finn Harps	0	**Dundalk**	2
			Keddy 2	

Semi-Finals

8 March	**Dundalk**	4	**Shamrock Rovers**	0
	Haylock 2, Reilly, Keddy			
10 March	**Bohemians**	2	**Derry City**	1
	Molloy, Crowe pen.		Coyle	

Final – Tolka Park

7 April	**Dundalk**	2	**Bohemians**	1
	Haylock (44m, 49m)		T. O'Connor (40m)	

Dundalk: John Connolly; John Whyte, Donal Broughan, Stephen McGuinness, David Crawley; David Hoey, Ciaran Kavanagh, John Flanagan, Chris Lawless; Martin Reilly, Gary Haylock. Subs: Cormac McArdle for Lawless, 70m; Cormac Malone for Haylock, 86m. Manager: Martin Murray

Bohemians: Wayne Russell; Tony 'Toccy' O'Connor, Colin Hawkins, Stephen Caffrey, Simon Webb; Fergal Harkin, Kevin Hunt, Dave Morrison, Mark Rutherford; Glen Crowe, Trevor Molloy. Subs: Dave Hill for Morrison, 72m; Paul Byrne for Harkin, 80m; Gary O'Neill for Molloy, 85m. Manager: Stephen Kenny

Referee: P. McKeon (Dublin)   Attendance: 9,200

2002 (B)

Mahon Makes the Right Call

They say it's the little details that make the difference – and the second of the 2002 FAI Cup Finals proved a case in point. Derry City, coming out of a financial crisis, didn't spare on the little details; Shamrock Rovers, on the verge of a crisis, treated it as just another game – and paid the price.

'There were no suits, no pre-match meal,' said Rovers' centre-back Stephen McGuinness. 'It was the first sign that things weren't so good, that the finances were tight. We weren't happy. Instead of being special, it just felt like any other game.'

'We saw them coming in their tracksuits,' recalled Derry's Peter Hutton, 'and that created a bit of a stir in the dressing room and it was used in the team talk. The Cup final is a massive occasion and clubs should make that bit of fuss about it. For a lot of players it could be their one and only final.'

Derry's manager, Kevin Mahon, was associated with City from the time they joined the League of Ireland in 1985. 'I played for the reserves when I was sixteen in 1970, and made my first team debut when I was thirty,' he recalled. He had learned from the master, Jim McLaughlin, how to handle players before a Cup final. 'We took it very seriously,' he said. 'Blazers, shirts and ties for the players, and we stayed in a hotel the night before. We did it properly. It was very noticeable because we had told our players how they should behave, and then Rovers came in very casual, blasé, and they were favourites, and that helped us a little bit.'

With no money to spend, Mahon was depending on a practically all-local squad, and even had to let good players like Paul Curran and Stuart Gauld go. When striker Gary Beckett failed a fitness test, he had some big calls to make, but he got them right. He could have played Peter Hutton anywhere at the back, but instead selected him on the right wing, 'because I saw James Keddy as a major threat.' Behind him, he gambled on Joe Harkin, even though he had only played one game in eighteen months because of a cruciate injury. 'In the month before, he [Harkin] was training really well and I decided if he can do it in training he can do it in the final. I was very lucky because he didn't play very much after.'

Mahon was also fortunate that former Republic of Ireland striker David Kelly was in his team. Kelly, who was assistant manager at Tranmere Rovers, had been approached by a committee man and had signed until the end of the Cup run. 'While he was with us he worked his socks off,' said Mahon. 'He was so modest. Sometimes you get a guy with a big name and he's trying to make an impression, but David just did whatever was necessary. In the semi-final in Cork, because we had injury problems, he volunteered to play on the right wing. He didn't try to be the star, he was such a nice guy – no ego.'

On the morning of the final, though, Kelly's flight from Birmingham was cancelled. He made a dash to Heathrow, where he was fortunate to board a delayed flight to Dublin. Arriving at 2 PM, he received a Garda escort, which brought him to Tolka Park with forty minutes to spare.

Also fortunate to make kick-off was Peter Hutton, who had snapped a ligament in the sole of his foot in a game in Bray, and received intensive treatment in Donegal from former Borussia Mönchengladbach physio Thomas Siegfried. 'I found out about him through Jim McLaughlin,' he recalled. 'I had a few treatment sessions, very hands-on and they definitely worked, but I still got a cortisone injection before the match.'

Not so lucky was Rovers' centre-back McGuinness. 'I could have been the first player to play in two Cup finals in the same year, having won with Dundalk in April, but I was sent off in an early round, Terry Palmer got in and I couldn't get back,' he recalled. 'For the final I wasn't even on the bench, as the manager decided to go with another forward.'

The game was decided by a classic Liam Coyle goal. The Derry legend latched on to a mis-hit shot by Ciaran Martyn in the penalty area to the right of the goal, and hooked the ball over his shoulder into the far corner past a bewildered Tony O'Dowd, Rovers' goalkeeper. Coyle, thirty-three, a veteran of Derry's previous four FAI Cup Finals, said, 'To get the winner was the icing on the cake for me. It was about time I scored in a final. It took me three decades.' He was also full of praise for Mahon's achievement. 'He did an extraordinary job because he had no money to spend. It was probably the greatest achievement that Derry have had in a considerable time. Only Alan Gough and David Kelly were outsiders, and even the bench was all young local lads.'

However, Mahon's success didn't secure his position, and he was let go early into the following season. He blames his own lack of managerial nous for that: 'The club had collected a fortune from top teams like Barcelona visiting the Brandywell, thanks to John Hume, but I was more like a board member than a manager and I couldn't spend the money,' he explained. 'I had attended all these meetings with supporters and promised that we would never be in financial crisis again, but if I was a manager I probably would have spent. Four managers came in after me and they spent a fortune.'

First Round

25 July	Dundalk	2	Shamrock Rovers	2
	Reilly, Ward		Kenny, T. Grant	
	Limerick FC	1	**Waterford United**	1
	S. O'Flynn pen.		K. O'Brien	
26 July	**Athlone Town**	0	**Kilkenny City**	0
	Bohemians	6	**Garda**	0
	Crowe 3 (1 pen.), Ryan,			
	Caffrey, Morrison			
	Bray Wanderers	2	**Glebe North**	0
	Doohan, O'Hanlon			
	Drogheda United	1	**Derry City**	3
	M. Dempsey		Coyle pen., McLaughlin, Martyn	
	Glenmore Dundrum	0	**Cork City**	9
	(At Turner's Cross)		Woods 2, O'Callaghan 2,	
			O'Flynn 3 (1 pen.), Warren,	
			O'Brien	
	St Patrick's Athletic	2	**Galway United**	2
	Russell pen., Osam		Herrick, Sheridan	
	UCD	2	**Kildare County**	1
	Doyle 2		Ryan pen.	
27 July	**Finn Harps**	1	**Leeds AFC**	0
	Mohan			
	Monaghan United	1	**Midleton**	0
	Parsons			
	Shelbourne	8	**Rockmount**	0
	Molloy, R. Baker 2, Cahill,			
	S. Byrne, Hoolahan, S. Geoghegan,			
	Prenderville			
28 July	**CIE Ranch**	1	**Longford Town**	5
	P. Nolan pen.		Sheridan, Prunty, Kirby, Lavine,	
	(At Richmond Park)		Mulvihill	
	Fairview Rangers	4	**Dublin City**	1
	Purcell pen., Harmon,		McGrath	
	B. Heffernan, C. Heffernan			
	Greystones AFC	0	**Sligo Rovers**	1
	(At Carlisle Grounds)		Cretaro	

| Malahide United | 0 | Cobh Ramblers | 1 |
| | | Kabia | |

First Round Replays

| 29 July | Kilkenny City | 3 | Athlone Town | 0 |
| | Mooney, Murphy, O'Connor pen. | | | |

(After extra time.)

| | Waterford United | 2 | Limerick FC | 2 |
| | Fitzgerald, Flanagan pen. | | O'Flynn, Leahy o.g. | |

(After extra time; 1–1 after 90m; Waterford won 4–2 on pens.)

| 30 July | Shamrock Rovers | 2 | Dundalk | 1 |
| | N. Hunt, T. Grant | | Reilly | |

(After extra time; 1–1 after 90m)

| 31 July | Galway United | 0 | St Patrick's Athletic | 1 |
| | | | Maguire | |

(After extra time.)

Second Round

15 August	Derry City	3	Waterford United	0
	Friars, Kelly, Beckett			
16 August	Bohemians	2	UCD	0
	Keegan, Rutherford			
	St Patrick's Athletic	2	Shelbourne	1
	Russell pen., Osam		Cahill	
	Sligo Rovers	0	Bray Wanderers	2
			O'Connor, Byrne	
17 August	Kilkenny City	1	Longford Town	0
	Murphy			
18 August	Fairview Rangers	0	Finn Harps	2
			McGrenaghan, Speak	
	Monaghan United	1	Cork City	1
	Lester		O'Halloran	
	Shamrock Rovers	2	Cobh Ramblers	0
	Keddy, Francis			

Second Round Replay

| 20 August | Cork City | 3 | Monaghan United | 0 |
| | O'Halloran, O'Flynn, Woods | | | |

Quarter-Finals

5 September	Derry City	3	St Patrick's Athletic	1
	Griffin o.g., Martyn 2		Bird	
6 September	Bray Wanderers	0	Bohemians	4
			Keegan, Crowe, McNally, O'Neill	
	Kilkenny City	0	Shamrock Rovers	1
			Hunt	
7 September	Finn Harps	1	Cork City	1
	Minnock		O'Callaghan	

Quarter-Final Replay

10 September	Cork City	2	Finn Harps	0
	O'Flynn, O'Brien			

Semi-Finals

4 October	Cork City	0	Derry City	1
			Friars	
6 October	Shamrock Rovers	2	Bohemians	0
	Palmer, Keddy			

Final – Tolka Park

27 October	Derry City	1	Shamrock Rovers	0
	Coyle (47m)			

Derry City: Alan Gough; Joe Harkin, Eddie McCallion, Paddy McLaughlin, Sean Hargan; Peter Hutton, Ciaran Martyn, Eamonn Doherty, Sean Friars; Liam Coyle, David Kelly. Subs: Tommy McCallion for Coyle, 58m; Darren McCreadie for Friars, 66m. Manager: Kevin Mahon

Shamrock Rovers: Tony O'Dowd; Greg Costello, Pat Scully, Terry Palmer, Richie Byrne; Stephen Grant, Jason Colwell, Luke Dimech, James Keddy; Tony Grant, Noel Hunt. Subs: Shane Robinson for Byrne, 69m; Derek Tracey for Colwell, 69m; Sean Francis for Stephen Grant, 82m. Manager: Liam Buckley

Referee: J. O'Neill (Waterford)   Attendance: 9,500

2003

Longford Make History

After the departure of Stephen Kenny, the manager who had revolutionised Longford Town, the club went into a bit of a slide and just avoided relegation from the Premier Division in 2002 by winning a penalty shoot-out against Finn Harps in Ballybofey. In the summer of 2002, they appointed Alan Mathews, former assistant to Dermot Keely at Home Farm and Shelbourne, as manager. It proved a happy return for Mathews, whose footballing career had ended seven years earlier when he broke his hip playing for Longford. He steadied the ship, with Longford finishing fifth in the Premier, but there was no sign of what was to come when they went out to Kilkenny City in the first round of the FAI Cup.

Instigating a major overhaul of the squad, Mathews opted for 'a bargain-basement team with experience and a lot of hungry young fellows.' It proved a winning combination, with only four survivors from the team that had contested the club's first FAI Cup Final in 2001 – Stephen O'Brien, Alan Murphy, Sean Prunty and Vinny Perth. A mid-table team, they showed a special aptitude for Cup football, reaching the finals of both the League Cup and the FAI Cup. On each occasion, their opponents were St Patrick's Athletic. In the League Cup Final, played on St Pat's home ground, Longford lost, with centre-back Barry Ferguson missing a penalty to equalise in the last minute. 'The players were in tears after that match, so I picked them up by telling them that we still had the FAI Cup,' recalled Mathews. Six weeks later came the re-match in the FAI Cup Final at Lansdowne Road.

The week before the final, St Pat's were hit with a double blow when left-back Kharim El Kebir was ruled out through suspension, and Ugandan international left-winger Charles Mbabazi Livingstone was forced into retirement due to a medical condition. Both of them had played right through St Pat's Cup campaign, which culminated in a thrilling semi-final replay win over Bohemians. Suddenly the odds against Longford making history were not so great, and to reinforce the point, Mathews put a little 'h' in the back of each jersey. 'Making history for the club was our reference point,' he said, 'and the players bought into that. There was a great team ethic, with a lot of the players in their mid- or early-twenties. Two of them, Sean Dillon and Stephen Paisley, played in the U-20 World Cup in Saudi Arabia that season.'

A big help to Mathews's plans was a programme set up in Dublin City University by Darragh Sheridan and Dr Niall Moyna. 'It was to give players coming back from England an education and integrate them back into playing. We had signed Darragh and got Sean Dillon and Shane Barrett on to the programme. It was great while it lasted, but it only lasted a year.'

St Pat's manager Eamonn Collins, whose father Michael was an FAI Cup-winner with Transport in 1950, rearranged his team for the final, with centre-back Darragh Maguire switching to left-back and midfielder Keith Fahey moving to the left wing. It proved a fateful move for Fahey, who would later distinguish himself with Birmingham City and the Republic of Ireland. After Longford had made the early running, they were rewarded with a goal after thirty-three minutes from Sean Francis, and it could have been 2–0 four minutes later, only Ferguson repeated his penalty miss. Forced to chase the game, Pat's were fortunate not to concede another goal on the break, but in the seventy-seventh minute their world collapsed when Fahey was given a straight red card by referee Alan Kelly for a two-footed lunge at Prunty. The final minutes of the game were thrilling as St Pat's threw caution to the wind, with goalkeeper Chris Adamson joining in for set-pieces; but it was a pass by Man-of-the-Match Brian McGovern which set up Shane Barrett for Longford's second goal.

Longford Town had succeeded in winning the FAI Cup in their eighteenth season in senior football. Sean Dillon and substitute Graham Gartland subsequently moved to the Scottish Premier League with Dundee United and St

Johnstone respectively, while Stephen Ward, who scored twice for Bohemians in a second round win over Skerries Town, went on to play for Wolves and the Republic of Ireland. At twenty-eight, Alan Kelly followed in his father Pat's footsteps and became the youngest referee to take charge of an FAI Cup Final.

First Round

23 July	Everton	1	Waterford United	3
	R. O'Shea		Sullivan 3	
	(At Turner's Cross)			
24 July	Derry City	0	Cobh Ramblers	0
25 July	Bray Wanderers	6	Athlone Town	3
	Fox, K. O'Brien, C. Ryan,		Gavin 2, McCann	
	Zayed 2, Tresson			
	Cork City	0	Shelbourne	2
			J. Byrne 2	
	Finn Harps	1	Drogheda United	2
	McHugh pen.		O'Brien, Bradley o.g.	
	Kildare County	3	Crumlin United	1
	Nolan o.g., McNevin pen., Hughes		Murray	
	St Patrick's Athletic	3	Shamrock Rovers	2
	Maguire, Bird, D. Byrne		T. Grant, Molloy	
	UCD	2	Belgrove	0
	Griffin 2			
26 July	Cherry Orchard	3	St Mochta's	0
	Daly, Notaro, K. O'Brien			
	Limerick FC	2	Kilkenny City	1
	Sweeney, Purcell		Dunphy	
	Loughshinny United	0	Galway United	2
	(At Market Green, Balbriggan)		A. Murphy 2	
	Moyle Park	0	Sligo Rovers	2
	(At Baldonnel)		McTiernan, R. Gallagher o.g.	
27 July	Dundalk	0	Bohemians	2
			R. Doyle 2	
	Portmarnock	0	Dublin City	1
			A. O'Connor	
	Skerries Town	1	Monaghan United	0
	E. Doherty			
	Tolka Rovers	1	Longford Town	4
	Murphy		Kirby, B. Byrne, Barrett,	
			Whelan o.g.	

First Round Replay

30 July	Cobh Ramblers	0	Derry City	1
			E. Doherty	

Second Round

15 August	Bohemians	3	Skerries Town	0
	Morrison, Ward 2			
	Bray Wanderers	1	Waterford United	2
	McGuinness		Sullivan, O'Brien	
	Drogheda United	2	UCD	0
	Myler, O'Brien			
	St Patrick's Athletic	3	Dublin City	0
	Freeman, Osam, Mbabazi			
16 August	Kildare County	1	Cherry Orchard	0
	Hughes			
	Longford Town	2	Limerick FC	1
	Barrett 2		Finucane	
17 August	Galway United	2	Derry City	1
	Murphy 2 (1 pen.)		Holt pen.	
	Sligo Rovers	0	Shelbourne	0

Second Round Replay

21 August	Shelbourne	2	Sligo Rovers	3
	Cahill, J. Byrne		Keogh, Gaffney, Feeney	

(After extra time; 2–2 after 90m)

Quarter-Finals

12 September	St Patrick's Athletic	2	Kildare County	1
	Bird, K. Dunne		Whelehan	
13 September	Drogheda United	1	Bohemians	1
	Myler		Webb	
	Longford Town	3	Waterford United	1
	Francis 2, McGovern		Fenn	
	Sligo Rovers	1	Galway United	2
	Miller		Foley, A. Murphy	

Quarter-Final Replay

16 September	Bohemians Doyle, Morrison, Harkin	3	Drogheda United	0

Semi-Finals

3 October	Longford Town Francis	1	Galway United	0
5 October	Bohemians Crowe	1	St Patrick's Athletic K. Dunne	1

Semi-Final Replay

8 October	St Patrick's Athletic Oman o.g., Delaney, Hawkins o.g., Fahey	4	Bohemians T. Heary, R. Doyle, Lynch	3

(After extra time; 2–2 after 90m)

Final – Lansdowne Road

26 October	Longford Town Francis (33m), Barrett (90m)	2	St Patrick's Athletic	0

Longford Town: Stephen O'Brien; Alan Murphy, Barry Ferguson, Brian McGovern, Sean Dillon; Alan Kirby, Vinny Perth, Philip Keogh, Sean Prunty; Sean Francis, Shane Barrett. Sub: Eric Lavine for Kirby, 83m. Manager: Alan Mathews

St Patrick's Athletic: Chris Adamson; Barry Prenderville, Colm Foley, Clive Delaney, Darragh Maguire; Keith Dunne, David Byrne, Paul Osam, Keith Fahey; Gary McPhee, Tony Bird. Subs: Paul Donnelly for Byrne, 30m; Keith Foy for Delaney, 79m. Manager: Eamonn Collins

Referee: A. Kelly (Cork)   Attendance: 15,000

2004

Keegan Finally Delivers

There is nothing a striker fears more than a touch of the 'Gary Birtles'. Birtles was the England striker who cost Manchester United over £1 million in 1980 after he had won successive European Cups with Nottingham Forest, and who proceeded to endure a drought, which extended to thirty games before he scored a League goal for his new team. In 2004, the Gary Birtles of the League of Ireland was Longford Town's Paul Keegan. 'We jumped through hoops to get him,' recalled manager Alan Mathews, who saw the Bohemian striker as someone who could bring the 2003 Cup-winners to the next level. While Longford did improve to fourth in the Premier Division and won both the FAI and League Cups, Keegan endured the dreaded goal drought, failing to score in over thirty League and Cup appearances before the final. So poor was his form, in fact, that he only started one of Longford's eight FAI Cup ties.

'It was a difficult season for him, and he hadn't delivered,' said Mathews. 'He had also lost his father.' So en route to the final with Waterford United, Keegan slipped into the church at Saggart and said a prayer, asking for his father's help. When he came off the bench in the seventy-second minute, Longford were losing 1–0, and showed little sign of equalising. A quarter of an hour later, Keegan's prayer was answered: he had scored the winning goal – his first for Longford – in the Cup final, and the Town had joined the elite list of clubs who had retained the Cup. In those two years, they were unbeaten in twenty-three FAI and League Cup ties.

Mathews believes their trip to Vaduz to play a UEFA Cup tie in July helped their Cup campaign. 'I'm a good friend of Enda McNulty, the sports psychologist, and we're always sharing experiences. One he recommended was to have a common theme within the group, and we decided that it would be to read Lance Armstrong's book, *Every Second Counts*, in which he talks about going the extra mile to achieve his goal and how he would push his teammates outside their comfort zone. It's an inspiring story and all the players bought into it.'

Longford were the only team that didn't suffer because of their involvement in European competition. Cork City, tired by their Inter Toto exertions, lost to UCD; Bohemians sacked manager Stephen Kenny after losing to Levadia Tallinn and paid the price with a shock defeat at home to Kildare County, while Shelbourne, who had played their first round game against Finn Harps under duress before flying out to play Hajduk Split in the Champions League, were still involved in Europe when they lost to Derry City in the second round.

Players who subsequently made their mark in English and Scottish football were among the scorers in the first round, with Wes Hoolahan, Stephen Ward, Daryl Murphy and Sean Dillon all on target, while Roy Keane's brother, Pat, was on the mark in the quarter-final as gallant Rockmount took Waterford United to a replay before bowing out.

Centre-back Brian McGovern, who was Man of the Match in the 2003 final, watched this one from the terraces as he was on loan to Shamrock Rovers, while his partner at the back, Barry Ferguson, missed out because of suspension. Sean Dillon and Graham Gartland replaced them to good effect. Waterford native Alan Kirby, who scored Longford's equaliser in the final, declined to celebrate the goal in deference to his former teammates. Assistant referee Rhona Daly, from Roscommon, did have something to celebrate, though, as she was the first woman to run the line in an FAI Cup Final. Although he wasn't on the winning side on this occasion, Waterford midfielder Dave Mulcahy had the right pedigree, as both of his grandfathers, Jack Mulcahy and Paddy Grace, won All-Ireland hurling medals with Kilkenny in 1947.

First Round

22 July	Bohemians	8	Ringmahon Rangers	0
	T. Grant 2, Morrison,			
	O'Donovan o.g., Ward 3, Crowe			
	Dundalk	0	Drogheda United	0
23 July	Athlone Town	3	Tullamore	0
	Adrian Murphy 3			
	Bray Wanderers	0	Kilkenny City	2
			A. Mulcahy, Gorman	
	Cobh Ramblers	3	Limerick FC	3
	Brosnan, Wolfe, O'Shea		Hartnett, C.P. O'Brien 2	
	Galway United	0	Derry City	1
			McGlynn	
	Monaghan United	1	Dublin City	0
	Anto Murphy			
	St Patrick's Athletic	4	Wayside Celtic	1
	P. Sheppard 2, Foley, O'Keeffe		Callaghan	
	Waterford United	2	Sligo Rovers	1
	D. Murphy 2		S. O'Donnell pen.	
24 July	Kildare County	4	Glebe North	0
	B. O'Connor 3, McKenna			
	Shelbourne	4	Finn Harps	1
	Cahill, J. Byrne 2 (1 pen.),		Crossan	
	Hoolahan			
25 July	Leeds AFC	0	Longford Town	3
			D. Baker, Dillon, Kirby	
	Quay Celtic	3	Drumcondra	4
	Browne, Larkin, Dunne		M. Finn, Quinlan, Shanley, Doyle	
	Rockmount	3	Portmarnock	1
	M. Deasy 2, P. Oldham		Battigan	
	Shamrock Rovers	3	Carrick United	0
	Molloy, S. Grant, Deans			
29 July	UCD	1	Cork City	0
	S. Finn			

First Round Replay

27 July	Limerick FC	2	Cobh Ramblers	2
	C.P. O'Brien 2pens.		Yelverton pen., Brosnan	

(After extra time; 2–2 after 90m; Cobh won 3–2 on pens.)

Second Round

19 August	Shelbourne	1	Derry City	1
	D. Byrne o.g.		D. Byrne	
20 August	Athlone Town	1	Cobh Ramblers	0
	Silke			
	Bohemians	0	Kildare County	1
			Zellor	
	Drogheda United	2	St Patrick's Athletic	0
	Lester, O'Brien			
	UCD	5	Drumcondra	0
	Sullivan, McWalter, O'Donnell, McDonnell, R. Martin			
	Waterford United	7	Kilkenny City	2
	D. Murphy 4, Bruton 3		Maher, N. Andrews	
21 August	Longford Town	1	Shamrock Rovers	1
	D. Baker		K. Doyle	
22 August	Rockmount	2	Monaghan United	0
	M. Deasy 2 (1 pen.)			

Second Round Replays

24 August	Shamrock Rovers	0	Longford Town	1
			Barrett	

(After extra time.)

28 August	Derry City	0	Shelbourne	0

(After extra time; Derry won 5–3 on pens.)

Quarter-Finals

9 September	Derry City	1	Kildare County	0
	E. McCallion			
10 September	UCD	0	Drogheda United	0
	Waterford United	2	Rockmount	2
	P. O'Brien o.g., Bruton		S. Hurley, P. Keane	

| 11 September | Longford Town
Fitzgerald, Lavine | 2 | Athlone Town
Adrian Murphy, Hope | 2 |

Quarter-Final Replays

| 13 September | Athlone Town | 0 | Longford Town
Barrett, Alan Murphy, Keogh | 3 |
| | Drogheda United
O'Brien 2, Lester | 3 | UCD
R. Martin, McAuley | 2 |

(After extra time; 1–1 after 90m)

| 15 September | Rockmount
Busteed
(At Turner's Cross) | 1 | Waterford United
Bruton, Banville | 2 |

Semi-Finals

| 1 October | Derry City
D. Byrne | 1 | Waterford United
D. Murphy, Connor pen. | 2 |
| 3 October | Longford Town | 0 | Drogheda United | 0 |

Semi-Final Replay

| 5 October | Drogheda United
O'Brien | 1 | Longford Town
J. Martin, Dillon | 2 |

(After extra time; 1–1 after 90m)

Final – Lansdowne Road

| 24 October | Longford Town
Kirby (86m), Keegan (87m) | 2 | Waterford United
Bruton (62)m | 1 |

Longford Town: Stephen O'Brien; Alan Murphy, Sean Dillon, Graham Gartland, Sean Prunty; Alan Kirby, Dean Fitzgerald, John Martin, Shane Barrett; Eric Lavine, Dessie Baker. Subs: Paul Keegan for Martin, 72m; Vinny Perth for Barrett, 94m. Manager Alan Mathews

Waterford United: Dan Connor; Ben Whelehan, Pat Purcell, David Breen; Alan Carey, Alan Reynolds, Dave Mulcahy, John Frost; Willie Bruton, Daryl Murphy, Jose Quitongo. Subs: Vinny Sullivan for Carey, 61m; Kevin Waters for Quitongo, 61m. Manager: Alan Reynolds

Referee: J. Feighery (Dublin)   Attendance: 9,676

2005

Eight Out Of Nine For Hoey

When it comes to Drogheda, Vincent Hoey wears his heart on his sleeve. Whatever he can do to progress the cause of his native town, he will do to the best of his ability. At present he is working to get it city status. In 2004, with the appointment of Paul Doolin as manager, he was intent on making Drogheda United the kingpins of the League of Ireland. 'I'm Drogheda born and reared,' he says. 'I'm a community person and I'm associated with anything which can help the community. From a young age, the Drogheda team has been in my blood.'

A successful solicitor, Hoey joined forces with businessmen Chris Byrne and Eugene O'Connor to take over the club. 'We had nine objectives and we achieved eight of them,' he revealed. 'The ninth was the stadium, but it wasn't our fault that it didn't happen. We spent millions, but we were sabotaged.'

One of their main objectives was to bring a major trophy to the Boyneside town, and this was the year they achieved that goal. For manager Doolin, their defeat by Longford Town in the semi-final the previous year was the start of Drogheda's success. Attention to detail was the lesson learned, so for the first round tie at home to Limerick, Doolin hopped on a New York-bound plane and got off at Shannon to run his eye over the opposition. For the second round, away to Dundalk, in the first game played on Oriel Park's artificial surface, Doolin brought his team there to train on it. For the semi-final, he adopted a different tactic. 'I brought Vincent Hoey into the dressing room to read a letter that was in the local paper about how the club was always the bridesmaid. He was very passionate about the club, and sometimes things like that can work in your favour.'

The team that Drogheda met in the final, Cork City, had been crowned League champions two weeks previously. That made them favourites, but it didn't help their cause, according to manager Damien Richardson: 'We celebrated winning the League and got the trophy around the city. If the final had been a week rather than two weeks later, we would have waited until after the final.'

On a pitch that didn't do justice to the occasion, Drogheda proved the best team on the day. With goals from Gavin Whelan, grandson of Ronnie Whelan Sr, and captain Declan 'Fabio' O'Brien, the Cup travelled Boyneside for the first time. 'It was vindication of our decision to go full-time,' said Doolin. 'What we did at Drogheda was fantastic, and 25,000 turned up for the final. You can be lucky in the Cup, but it's what you do after winning – and we won the League.'

Drogheda had quite a cosmopolitan team, with Dutchman Jermaine Sandvliet and Finland international Sami Ristila lining out, and Scotland cap Paul Bernard a sub on the day. Centre-back Graham Gartland, at twenty-two, was winning his third FAI Cup medal in successive seasons, having signed from Cup specialists Longford.

Asked what it was it like to win the Cup, Hoey quoted Rudyard Kipling's 'if you can wait and be not tired of waiting,' declaring, 'we have waited and we weren't tired of waiting.' Then he visited a very despondent Cork dressing room and said: 'I hope you don't begrudge us this win, because I'm sure your time will come too.' His words were well received, helping to change the atmosphere in the dressing room, and proved prophetic as Cork won the Cup two years later.

Hoey, Byrne and O'Connor lost millions when their plans for a stadium complex designed to be self-financing were scuppered. Asked about his losses, he said, 'Not even winning the Lotto would repay me.'

However, he was repaid in other ways. 'In Drogheda there was one man, Tom Munster, who had been chairman and treasurer of the club for many years, and he was ninety. I brought the Cup to his house, knocked on the door, and it was one of the most emotional things I've ever done. If I'd given him a cheque for €5 million it wouldn't have meant as much to him.'

First Round

10 June	**Avondale United** (At Turner's Cross)	0	**Bray Wanderers** Charles	1
	Bohemians J. P. Kelly 2	2	**Athlone Town**	0
	Drogheda United Sandvliet, Rooney	2	**Limerick FC**	0
	Galway United	0	**Cork City**	0
	Shelbourne	0	**Derry City** Beckett, Delaney	2
	UCD McDonnell, Hurley	2	**Dublin City**	0
	Waterford United	0	**St Patrick's Athletic** Maguire	1
11 June	**Carew Park** Quinn	1	**Douglas Hall** Stanton, O'Connell, McSorley	3
	Cobh Ramblers	0	**Wayside Celtic** I. Callaghan	1
	Kildare County A. Byrne, McKenna 2, Cooney	4	**Galway Hibs** E. Ward	1
	Kilkenny City	0	**Finn Harps** McHugh	1
	Lissadell United	0	**Cherry Orchard** Thornton, Roache, Doyle 2	4
	Longford Town Keegan, Myler 3 (1 pen.), D. Baker	5	**Waterford Crystal**	0
	Sligo Rovers McTiernan	1	**Malahide United** K. Craven	1
12 June	**Monaghan United** Hughes	1	**Dundalk** A. Murphy, O'Kane, McCarthy 3, Hynes, C. Finnan	7
	Shamrock Rovers McDonagh, D. Mooney	2	**Fanad United**	0

First Round Replays

13 June	**Cork City** O'Flynn pen.	1	**Galway United**	0

408

| 14 June | Malahide United | 0 | Sligo Rovers | 2 |
| | | | McTiernan 2 | |

(After extra time.)

Second Round

26 August	Bohemians	2	Wayside Celtic	2
	Ward 2		W. Callaghan, O'Neill	
	Bray Wanderers	1	Cherry Orchard	0
	Fox			
	Dundalk	0	Drogheda United	2
			Leech, Lynch pen.	
27 August	Derry City	3	Kildare County	1
	Hutton, McGlynn, Farren		Zellor	
	Longford Town	1	UCD	1
	Keegan		R. Martin pen.	
	Sligo Rovers	2	St Patrick's Athletic	1
	Low, McTiernan		Armstrong	
28 August	Shamrock Rovers	2	Douglas Hall	0
	Roche, McGuinness			
29 August	Cork City	0	Finn Harps	0

Second Round Replays

30 August	UCD	2	Longford Town	1
	McDonnell, McWalter		Keegan	
	Wayside Celtic	1	Bohemians	2
	W. Callaghan pen.		T. Grant 2	
	(At Carlisle Grounds)			
3 September	Finn Harps	2	Cork City	3
	Asokuh, Breen		Kearney, O'Flynn, O'Donovan	

(After extra time; 2–2 after 90m)

Quarter-Finals

23 September	Bray Wanderers	3	UCD	2
	P. Murphy, D. Tyrrell,		R. Martin, McWalter	
	Kieran O'Brien			
	Cork City	3	Sligo Rovers	1
	Murray, O'Flynn, O'Callaghan pen.		Low	

	Drogheda United	2	**Bohemians**	1
	Keegan, Lynch		A. O'Keeffe	
24 September	**Derry City**	1	**Shamrock Rovers**	0
	Beckett			

Semi-Finals

21 October	**Cork City**	1	**Derry City**	0
	O'Callaghan pen.			
23 October	**Drogheda United**	2	**Bray Wanderers**	1
	O'Brien, Sandvliet		Tresson	

Final – Lansdowne Road

4 December	**Drogheda United**	2	**Cork City**	0
	Whelan (51m), O'Brien (83m)			

Drogheda United: Dan Connor; Damian Lynch, Graham Gartland, Stephen Gray, Simon Webb; Shane Robinson, Gavin Whelan, Stephen Bradley, Jermaine Sandvliet; Sami Ristila, Declan 'Fabio' O'Brien. Subs: Paul Keegan for Bradley, 72m; Mark Rooney for Ristila, 79m; Paul Bernard for O'Brien, 90m. Manager: Paul Doolin

Cork City: Michael Devine; Neal Horgan, Dan Murray, Alan Bennett, Billy Woods; Joe Gamble, Greg O'Halloran, George O'Callaghan, Liam Kearney; Neale Fenn, John O'Flynn. Subs: Denis Behan for O'Flynn, 63m; Colin O'Brien for O'Halloran, 83m. Manager: Damien Richardson

Referee: I. Stokes (Dublin)   Attendance: 24,521

2006

Kenny Exits in Glory

In 2006, Derry City enjoyed possibly its most exciting year in the history of the club. Three years previously, they had to battle through a relegation play-off to retain their Premier Division status, but now, with a young squad and a young, ambitious manager, they took not only the League of Ireland by storm, but Europe as well.

Featuring a five-man midfield with an average age of twenty-one, they bagged the scalps of Gothenburg and Gretna before going out of the UEFA Cup to Paris St Germain on a respectable 2–0 aggregate.

Their European exploits didn't distract them from their domestic campaign, and they came agonisingly close to emulating the treble-winning team of 1989. They duly won the League Cup, lost out on the League title by goal difference, and won the FAI Cup after an epic final played in near-impossible conditions of wind and rain at Lansdowne Road – the last football game before the ground was demolished to make way for the Aviva Stadium.

When Stephen Kenny took over as manager in 2004, the club was ninth in the Premier Division. The following year they lost the League in the last game in Cork, they won the League Cup and were beaten in the semi-final of the FAI Cup by Cork City. Kenny effected that transformation mainly through good management of the resources available. 'I didn't make many changes,' he recalled. 'I brought in goalkeeper David Forde and young midfielders Killian Brennan, who was released by Dublin City, and Ruaidhri Higgins, who was released by Coventry City.'

By the time the 2006 FAI Cup Final came around, Kenny had agreed to take over at Scottish Premier League side Dunfermline. 'They wanted me to take over a month earlier, but I had committed to Derry to the last game,' he said. 'Then, with Dunfermline in relegation trouble, they came over and said can you take over now, and I came to an agreement with Derry that I would stay on for the final, but Paul Hegarty and Declan Devine would prepare the team that week. I flew over on Wednesday, and Saturday after the game with Dunfermline.'

According to Kenny, the hallmark of his '06 team was its ability to come back. 'There was terrific spirit in the team. We won the League Cup with nine men after taking it to extra time and a penalty shoot-out. We went one down away to Gretna and won 5–1. We played nearly sixty games that year, and yet we won our last three games in the League 1–0, with Mark Farren scoring the winner each time, only for us to lose the League on goal difference. Then in the final, we were behind to St Patrick's Athletic three times, before Killian Brennan whipped-in a free kick and it went in off Stephen Brennan for the winner. That was the good thing about that team: it came back all the time.'

Derry weren't at full strength for the final, as midfielder Ciaran Martyn was suspended and centre-backs Ken Oman and Darren Kelly were injured. On the plus side, Clive Delaney, who had been injured most of the season, came back for the last few League matches, played in the final, and scored one of the goals.

'After the game,' Kenny recalled, 'I said to Declan Devine, "let's go to Hampden now" – and we were in Hampden Park for the Scottish Cup Final within six months, in front of a 50,000 full house. But winning the FAI Cup meant everything to me. It was a memorable game and helped me to finish on a high. It was also tremendous for the players because they had given so much that year.'

This was also the year of the walk-over and the takeover. The draw for the second round had already been made when Dublin City went out of football, conceding a walk-over to junior club Killester United into the quarter-final, where they took Sligo Rovers to a replay and extra time before going out 4–3. The weekend of the quarter-finals, the FAI completed its take-over of the League, with its search for a replacement for Dublin City at the top of its agenda.

First Round

26 May	**Athlone Town**	2	**Galway United**	1
	Moran, Sheridan		Murphy pen.	
	Bohemians	3	**Waterford Crystal**	1
	Arkins pen., Ward, Dunphy o.g.		Watson	
	Bray Wanderers	2	**Kildare County**	2
	Tresson, Fox		McKenna, Cooling	
	Limerick FC	0	**Drogheda United**	0
	Longford Town	2	**Cork City**	1
	D. Baker pen., D. O'Connor		J. O'Flynn	
	Waterford United	5	**Douglas Hall**	0
	D. Kavanagh, Doyle 3 (1 pen.),			
	S. Grant			
27 May	**Bangor Celtic**	1	**Shelbourne**	3
	Warren		Heary, J. Byrne, S. Byrne	
	(At Tolka Park)			
	Blarney United	1	**Derry City**	3
	Jennings pen.		Martyn, Farren 2 (1 pen.)	
	Carrigaline United	0	**Sligo Rovers**	4
	(At Turner's Cross)		Judge, Kuduzovic, McTiernan,	
			Foy pen.	
	Dublin City	0	**Monaghan United**	0
	Dundalk	1	**Cobh Ramblers**	0
	Hynes			
	Finn Harps	1	**Crumlin United**	0
	Gorman			
	Kilkenny City	0	**UCD**	2
			Cawley pen., McWalter	
28 May	**Castlebar Celtic**	0	**Shamrock Rovers**	2
			Doyle, Amond	
	Malahide United	0	**St Patrick's Athletic**	2
			M. Quigley, Molloy	
	Wayside Celtic	0	**Killester United**	1
			Keogh	

First Round Replays

29 May	**Drogheda United**	0	**Limerick FC**	1
			Guerin	

	Kildare County	0	Bray Wanderers	1
			P. Caffrey	
30 May	Monaghan United	2	Dublin City	4
	Harte, Lee		R. Collins, D. McGill, D. Brennan,	
			Freeman	

(After extra time; 2–2 after 90m)

Second Round

25 August	Shamrock Rovers	1	Bohemians	1
	Purcell pen.		Leech	
	Waterford United	1	Longford Town	1
	G. McCarthy pen.		J. Martin	
26 August	Finn Harps	0	Athlone Town	0
	St Patrick's Athletic	2	Dundalk	0
	Keegan, Murphy			
	Sligo Rovers	2	Bray Wanderers	1
	Mansaram, Singh		Georgescu	
	UCD	3	Limerick FC	1
	R. Finn 2, Hurley		Kelleher	
27 August	Killester United	W/O	Dublin City	SCR
	Shelbourne	0	Derry City	1
			Kelly	

Second Round Replays

28 August	Longford Town	1	Waterford United	0
	Paisley			
29 August	Athlone Town	3	Finn Harps	2
	N. McGee, Rushe, Gavin		Curran, Bradley	

(After extra time; 1–1 after 90m)

	Bohemians	0	Shamrock Rovers	2
			Cassidy 2	

Quarter-Finals

29 September	St Patrick's Athletic	4	Longford Town	1
	Molloy 3 (1 pen.), M. Foley pen.		R. Martin	
30 September	Athlone Town	1	Shamrock Rovers	2
	Sheridan		Rowe, Clarke	
	(At Dubarry Park)			

	Sligo Rovers	0	**Killester United**	0
1 October	**Derry City**	2	**UCD**	0
	Farren pen., McHugh			

Quarter-Final Replay

5 Octobe	**Killester United**	3	**Sligo Rovers**	4
	Keogh 2, Lacey		Bellew, Hughes, Peers,	
			McTiernan	

(After extra time; 3–3 after 90m)

Semi-Finals

27 October	**Shamrock Rovers**	0	**St Patrick's Athletic**	2
			Keegan, Molloy	
29 October	**Sligo Rovers**	0	**Derry City**	0

Semi-Final Replay

31 October	**Derry City**	5	**Sligo Rovers**	0
	McCourt, Farren 2 (1 pen.), Martyn 2			

Final – Lansdowne Road

3 December	**Derry City**	4	**St Patrick's Athletic**	3
	Farren (26m), Delaney (86m),		Mulcahy (20m),	
	Hutton (107m),		Molloy pen. (74m),	
	Brennan o.g. (110m)		O'Connor (104m)	

(After extra time; 2–2 after 90m)

Derry City: David Forde; Eddie McCallion, Clive Delaney, Peter Hutton, Killian Brennan; Kevin Deery, Barry Molloy, Ruaidhri Higgins, Paddy McCourt; Gary 'Bing'Beckett, Mark Farren. Subs: Gareth McGlynn for Deery, 72m; Kevin McHugh for Higgins, 78m; Sean Hargan for Beckett, 95m. Manager: Stephen Kenny

St Patrick's Athletic: Barry Ryan; Stephen Quigley, Colm Foley, Stephen Brennan, John Frost; Anto Murphy, Michael Foley, Dave Mulcahy, Mark Rutherford; Paul Keegan, Trevor Molloy. Subs: Sean O'Connor for Murphy, 45m; Mark Quigley for Keegan, 60m; Chris Armstrong for Foley, 110m. Manager: John McDonnell

Referee: D. Hancock (Dublin)   Attendance: 16,022

2007

Rico's Farewell

Before most FAI Cup Finals, the pressure is on the players, with the media building up the hype about who is likely to be the most influential player on the day. This year was different, as Cork City captain Dan Murray recalled: 'Most of the talk beforehand was about our manager, Damien Richardson, getting the sack. Everyone knew about it. It was the worst-kept secret in football.' Having lost two years earlier, Cork had unfinished business, according to Murray. 'Having lost in 2005 helped us,' he said. 'You have to lose one to win one.'

The early rounds featured goals from a number of players who were later to move to English clubs. Roy O'Donovan scored for Cork before moving to Sunderland for a big fee, while Keith Fahey, Paddy McCourt and Conor Sammon were on the mark for St Patrick's Athletic, Derry City and UCD respectively. Richardson replaced top scorer O'Donovan with Leon McSweeney, who was on the mark in the second round, along with John O'Flynn and Colin Healy, all of whom were transferred later to English clubs. In a second round replay, it took fourteen penalties to decide the shoot-out 4–3 in favour of Waterford United in Sligo. The next time Sligo were involved in an FAI Cup penalty shoot-out, the stakes were higher and the outcome was different.

Derry City, usually such doughty Cup fighters, lost their manager, Pat Fenlon, before the Cup began, and went out in the quarter-final to a Sammon goal for UCD. Manager Pete Mahon described this as the best result ever by the Students, but they couldn't repeat it when drawn at home to Longford Town in the semi-final. Former UCD striker Robbie Martin scored the winner as Gary Deegan, later to move to Coventry City, pulled the strings in midfield. Unfortunately, Deegan missed the final through suspension.

Longford were used to misfortune, as manager Alan Mathews recalled: 'At the start of the season things weren't right. There were financial issues, which resulted in the team being deducted ten points. This was reduced to six on appeal, but ultimately it resulted in our relegation. Apart from Sean Prunty and Dessie Baker, this was a brand-new team from the one that won in 2004. A lot of that team had been offered full-time terms by other clubs and had moved on. We did have the League's Player of the Year and top-scorer Dave Mooney. He was doing his finals as an electrician and was in the Irish U-23 team. The partnership between him and Dessie Baker was excellent. Dessie made sure Dave made the right runs.'

The season was defined for Mathews by a comment made to him after the team had qualified for the FAI Cup Final by beating UCD in Belfield: 'The Secretary said to me, "That's brilliant, now we'll be able to pay the taxman".'

For Richardson, it was also a difficult season: 'The club had been taken over by the Arkaga Group and all wasn't well. Still, the semi-final defeat of Bohemians in Dalymount was the best Cup performance I had during my time at Cork City. I knew the final was my last game with Cork, regardless of the result, but my only worry was when I saw how the strong wind at the RDS was making it most difficult for the players. Even though it was only 1–0, we won well in the end.'

The goalscorer was Denis Behan who, for Richardson, 'was the story of the Cup that season. He was from Abbeyfeale, and he won the quarter-final with four goals in two games against Waterford and then the one in the final. He was a big game player, but inconsistent.' Behan subsequently moved to Hartlepool, but returned to play for Limerick FC.

Rico's tenure at Turner's Cross ended in Cup glory, and the man selected to replace him was Alan Mathews. 'I had been in five finals with Longford in six seasons,' Mathews said, 'but I never had a chance at winning the League, so I took a career break from my job in Ulster Bank to go to Cork to win the League. Unfortunately, it didn't happen.' Moving back to Dublin, Mathews took over at Shelbourne.

First Round

15 June	**Derry City**	2	**Monaghan United**	0
	McCourt, Farren			
	Drogheda United	0	**Bohemians**	1
			Mansaram	
	Galway United	2	**Finn Harps**	2
	D. Glynn 2		Gethins pen., Parkhouse	
	Limerick 37	1	**Wexford Youths**	1
	Cosgrave		Keady o.g.	
	Malahide United	2	**Cherry Orchard**	1
	Doyle, Wright		Shields	
	Phoenix	0	**St Patrick's Athletic**	4
			Quigley, Maguire, Kirby, Cornwall	
	Shelbourne	0	**Cork City**	1
			O'Donovan pen.	
	Tolka Rovers	2	**Waterford United**	2
	R. Whelehan, Hayes o.g.		Sullivan, Warren	
16 June	**Douglas Hall**	4	**Cobh Ramblers**	1
	O'Donovan, O'Connell 2, Sweeney		Murray	
	Kildare County	0	**Kilkenny City**	1
			McDermott o.g.	
	Longford Town	1	**Celbridge Town**	0
	Mooney pen.			
	Salthill Devon	0	**UCD**	4
			Sammon, D. Doyle, C. Byrne 2	
	Shamrock Rovers	2	**Sligo Rovers**	3
	Purcell, Myler		Kudozovic 2, Judge	
17 June	**Bray Wanderers**	7	**St Mochta's**	0
	Buttner o.g., Dunphy 3, Tresson, Broderick, McCabe			
	Fanad United	1	**St John Bosco**	0
	P. McGrenaghan pen.			

First Round Replays

18 June	**Finn Harps**	0	**Galway United**	0

(After extra time; Finn Harps won 4–2 on pens.)

19 June	Waterford United	4	Tolka Rovers	1
	Harte, Brosnan 2, McCarthy		Doyle	
	Wexford Youths	0	Limerick 37	1
			Wall	

Second Round

16 August	Dundalk	1	UCD	2
	R. Doyle		D. Doyle, Sammon	
17 August	Bray Wanderers	1	St Patrick's Athletic	2
	Delaney		Quigley, Fahey	
	Cork City	5	Kilkenny City	1
	B. O'Callaghan, McSweeney, Healy, O'Flynn 2		McNicholas	
	Limerick 37	1	Douglas Hall	1
	Cosgrave		Moore	
	Waterford United	1	Sligo Rovers	1
	Bermingham		Hughes	
18 August	Finn Harps	0	Derry City	1
			Oman	
	Longford Town	2	Fanad United	0
	Doherty, Mooney			
19 August	Malahide United	0	Bohemians	1
			Crowe	

Second Round Replays

21 August	Sligo Rovers	2	Waterford United	2
	Kudozovic, Judge		McCarthy, Sullivan	
	(After extra time; 2–2 after 90m; Waterford won 4–3 on pens.)			
22 August	Douglas Hall	0	Limerick 37	1
			Tierney	

Quarter-Finals

21 September	Derry City	0	UCD	1
			Sammon	
22 September	Longford Town	3	Limerick 37	1
	D. Baker, Mooney, Duffy		Tierney pen.	

	Waterford United	1	Cork City	1
	Warren		Behan	
24 September	St Patrick's Athletic	1	Bohemians	2
	Fahey		Mansaram 2	

Quarter-Final Replay

25 September	Cork City	4	Waterford United	0
	Behan 3, Kearney			

Semi-Finals

26 October	Bohemians	0	Cork City	2
			Kearney 2	
28 October	UCD	0	Longford Town	1
			R. Martin	

Final – RDS

2 December	Cork City	1	Longford Town	0
	Behan 60m			

Cork City: Michael Devine; Cillian Lordan, Dan Murray, Brian O'Callaghan, Billy Woods; Leon McSweeney, Colin Healy, Joe Gamble, Liam Kearney; John O'Flynn, Denis Behan. Subs: Colin O'Brien for Woods, 67m; Gareth Farrelly for Kearney, 84m. Manager: Damien Richardson

Longford Town: Seamus Kelly; Pat Sullivan, Kevin Doherty, Damien Brennan, Sean Prunty; Jamie Duffy, Daire Doyle, Mark Rutherford, Robbie Martin; Dessie Baker, David Mooney. Subs: Ian Wexler for Baker, 55m; John Reilly for Duffy, 77m. Manager: Alan Mathews

Referee: D. McKeon (Dublin)　　　　　　　　　　　　Attendance: 10,000

2008

Kalonas Shows His Class

It was the final that had everything: the two best teams in the League, managed by the two most successful managers, a game that flowed from end to end, crowned by the drama and heartache of the first FAI Cup Final penalty shoot-out.

Even now, when Bohemians' manager Pat Fenlon talks about that game, he can't disguise his enthusiasm. 'It was a fabulous day, it had everything,' he said. 'It was a great game, and it was a privilege to be involved in a game so good it could have gone either way.' For Bohs, victory meant another League and Cup double; for Derry, there was the despair of losing out on the penalty 'lottery'.

Yes, lottery it is, as Fenlon explained the background to the selection of his penalty-takers: 'The night before all the players took a few, so we had seven or eight in mind, but Glenn Cronin wouldn't have been in that eight. Our first choice would have been Mark Rossiter, Jason Byrne, Killian Brennan, Gary Deegan and Neale Fenn, but towards the end of extra time I'm standing on the sideline with Liam O'Brien and it depended then on who was on the pitch.

'We had taken Jason off because he was playing wide right and ran out of legs. Deegan the same. He ran out of steam. I think he played the game in the hotel the night before, he was so excited at being in a final. And Fenn was also off. They were all taken off to freshen up the team. That's why Glenn and Mindaugas Kalonas took them. So, as the players were going up to take the penalties, the only one Liam fancied was Mark Rossiter – and he missed, smashing it over.' Rossiter's blushes were spared when goalkeeper Brian Murphy saved

421

from Kevin Deery and Ruaidhri Higgins, and Kalonas converted to take the Cup back to Dalymount after seven years.

The presence of Kalonas, so far the only Lithuanian to win an FAI Cup medal, was due to Fenlon's friendship with Englishman Paul Ashford, who had done his UEFA Pro Licence in Dublin alongside the Bohemian boss. 'Kalonas had played against us for FK Riga the year before in the Inter Toto Cup and Paul made enquiries for me and spoke to his agent, who said he'd come. He was a massive signing for us half-way through the season. He gave us a lift, offering something that was different to anything that was already in the team. I could play him in different positions and he was very difficult to mark. While at Bohs he went away to play for Lithuania against France and scored, so the fact that he was here proved that the standard was the highest it's ever been.'

Despite his huge impact in the League – he scored six goals in six starts and six substitute appearances – Fenlon didn't start him in either the semi-final or final, preferring Fenn on each occasion. 'With Kalonas on the bench I knew that if we had to chase the game he could come in and do that for us,' he explained. So it turned out: as Derry took the lead, two minutes later Kalonas was introduced, and within another two minutes he had laid-on the equaliser for Glenn Crowe.

In winning the penalty shoot-out, Bohs reversed a trend that had haunted Fenlon: 'Three times I lost to Derry in shoot-outs,' he recalled. 'As a player with St Pat's, I lost an FAI Cup Quarter-Final and with Bohs a League Cup Final, and as a manager, with Shels, I lost another League Cup Final, so this wasn't the way I wanted the game to go.'

On 26 September, the day St Patrick's Athletic qualified for the semi-final by beating Sporting Fingal 2–0 in a replay, the mood in Inchicore was sombre, for former club legend Noel O'Reilly had died earlier that day.

A sign of the times occurred a month before, when holders Cork City went into examinership. At least six clubs pleaded inability to pay their players, who were all forced to take cuts to keep the clubs afloat as the recession hit hard.

First Round

6 June	Athlone Town	2	Finn Harps	1
	Jinks, Hamm		Funston	
	Bohemians	3	Drogheda Town	0
	J.P. Kelly, J. Byrne 2			
	Derry City	2	Liffeys Pearse	0
	Deery, Farren			
	Douglas Hall	0	Drogheda United	3
			Hughes 2, Maher	
	Galway United	1	Waterford United	0
	O'Brien			
	Limerick 37	0	Cork City	2
			Mooney pen., Darren Murphy	
	Monaghan United	0	UCD	0
	St Patrick's Athletic	2	Longford Town	1
	O'Neill, Quigley		McKenna	
	Shelbourne	0	Dundalk	3
			Vaughan pen., Crowley 2	
	Sporting Fingal	2	Cobh Ramblers	0
	Hynes 2			
	Wexford Youths	0	Killester United	0
7 June	St Mary's	0	Wayside Celtic	1
			I. Callaghan	
	Shamrock Rovers	2	Sligo Rovers	1
	Amond, Price		Murphy	
8 June	Everton	0	Carrick United	2
			Cleary 2	
	Rockmount	0	Bray Wanderers	3
			Rowe, Whelan, Onwubiko	
24 June	Kildare County	3	Fanad United	0
	Kilduff 3			

First Round Replays

24 June	Killester United	1	Wexford Youths	2
	Lacey pen.		Sinnott, G. Doyle	
	UCD	0	Monaghan United	1
			Collins	

Second Round

15 August	**Bohemians**	1	**Drogheda United**	0
	Crowe			
	Bray Wanderers	0	**Dundalk**	0
	Galway United	4	**Athlone Town**	1
	Lester, Fitzgerald, Jorgensen, O'Shea		Hamm	
	Shamrock Rovers	0	**Cork City**	1
			Behan	
16 August	**Carrick United**	1	**Sporting Fingal**	3
	K. Walsh		Philip Byrne, McSherry o.g., Doyle	
	Kildare County	–	**Derry City**	–

(Postponed: waterlogged pitch)

17 August	**Wayside Celtic**	1	**Monaghan United**	0
	L. Flynn pen.			
	Wexford Youths	1	**St Patrick's Athletic**	3
	G. Doyle		Quigley, Murphy 2	

Second Round Re-Fixture

19 August	**Kildare County**	0	**Derry City**	6
	(At Brandywell)		Stewart 2, Delaney 2, Farren 2	

Second Round Replay

18 August	**Dundalk**	1	**Bray Wanderers**	3
	Crowley		Tresson, Kavanagh, J. Kelly	

Quarter-Finals

11 September	**Sporting Fingal**	3	**St Patrick's Athletic**	3
	Hynes, P. Byrne, James pen.		Quigley 2 (1 pen.), Dempsey	
12 September	**Galway United**	1	**Bray Wanderers**	1
	McCulloch		Myler	
13 September	**Cork City**	1	**Derry City**	1
	Darren Murphy		Morrow pen.	
14 September	**Wayside Celtic**	1	**Bohemians**	6
	I. Callaghan		Kelly, J. Byrne 2 (1 pen.),	
	(At Carlisle Grounds)		McGuinness, Fenn, Crowe	

Quarter-Final Replays

16 September	Bray Wanderers	0	Galway United Keane, O'Shea	2
26 September	St Patrick's Athletic Quigley, Fitzpatrick	2	Sporting Fingal	0
30 September	Derry City	0	Cork City	0

(After extra time; Derry won 5–3 on pens.)

Semi-Finals

24 October	St Patrick's Athletic Fahey	1	Bohemians Brennan, Deegan, O. Heary	3
26 October	Galway United	0	Derry City Farren	1

Final – RDS

23 November	Bohemians Crowe (64m), J Byrne pen. (70m)	2	Derry City Morrow (60m, 76m)	2

(After extra time; Bohemians won 4-2 on pens.)

Bohemians: Brian Murphy; Owen Heary, Ken Oman, Liam Burns, Mark Rossiter; Jason Byrne, Stephen O'Donnell, Gary Deegan, Killian Brennan; Neale Fenn, Glen Crowe. Subs: Mindaugas Kalonas for Fenn, 62m; Brendan McGill for Byrne, 76m; Glenn Cronin for Deegan, 106m. Manager: Pat Fenlon

Derry City: Ger Doherty; Eddie McCallion, Peter Hutton, Clive Delaney, Stephen Gray; Gareth McGlynn, Kevin Deery, Barry Molloy, Niall McGinn; Sammy Morrow, Mark Farren. Subs: Thomas Stewart for McGlynn, 91m; Ruaidhri Higgins for Molloy, 91m; Kevin McHugh for Morrow, 105m. Manager: Stephen Kenny

Referee: A. Buttimer (Cork)   Attendance: 10,281

2009

Fingal: Too Far, Too Fast

In 2007, Liam Buckley, the former manager of St Patrick's Athletic and Shamrock Rovers, made a presentation to Fingal County Council in its Swords headquarters that was so well received it was described by one councillor as 'a benchmark for other sports'.

At the time, Buckley, encouraged by John O'Brien, a senior Fingal County Council official, was making a play to enter a team in the League's A Championship, but Kilkenny City's sudden demise offered instant promotion to the First Division, which Fingal accepted in January 2008. Sporting Fingal, as it became known, was a prototype community-based club, representing an ideal for all League clubs, with its emphasis on establishing links with all levels of football in its area.

'We're delighted with the way things have gone,' O'Brien said at the time, 'but it all has to be viewed in relation to our overall plans for an academy and eventually our own stadium. The stadium is likely to be in Swords and there's a development plan for Swords, and the timeline for the stadium will be determined by that plan and by the Metro North's arrival.' Unfortunately, the recession caught up with Sporting Fingal, dashing its plans just as it delayed the arrival of Metro North.

However, Buckley and Co. left a remarkable legacy, not least for their FAI Cup triumph in only their second season, a feat unequalled in the competition's history. Sadly, their success on the pitch wasn't matched on the terraces, as they failed to build up a substantial support base. Despite eliminating Cup specialists Shamrock Rovers in the quarter-finals, they attracted an attendance of less than 900 when they hosted Bray Wanderers in the semi-final. For the final, their fans turned out in some numbers, but even then they were out-numbered three to one by the Sligo supporters in the 8,105-strong crowd.

Nothing, though, should take away from the achievement of Buckley and his players. He assembled a top-class squad who, in addition to winning the FAI Cup, also fought their way to promotion from the First Division via the play-off system. In fact, the extension of their season proved a blessing in more ways than one for Fingal, as it enabled striker Gary O'Neill, who had been out injured for almost three months and wasn't fit for the Cup semi-final, to regain his place for the promotion play-off – and retain it for the final, with dramatic consequences.

'Sligo took the lead,' O'Neill recalled, 'and being the Premier Division team people probably thought that was that, but we had a Premier squad and had a lot of confidence in our ability. We got a penalty and Colm James scored, then in the last minute the ball was played wide to Robert Bayly and I ran in to the box and met his cross with a diving header. I didn't know where it was going to go, but it ended up in the bottom corner. I was in the League ten years at that time, and you don't get many days like that.' O'Neill, who had played ten minutes as a sub for Bohemians when they lost the 2002 final to Dundalk, almost returned to Bohs for the 2009 season. 'I was with St Pat's and had a pre-contract agreement with Bohs, but that was pulled and then I couldn't go back to Pat's, so Liam Buckley rang and even though it was First Division football, I wanted to stay full-time, so I signed.'

Fast forward to 2011, and the Premier Division's list of casualties – Shelbourne, Drogheda United, Cork City, Bohemians and Sporting Fingal – had one common denominator: they were all funded by the property bubble. They all rode the crest of the wave with the country's developers, but when the bubble burst they were caught up in a rip tide, which brought them crashing onto the rocks. For Shels, Drogheda, Cork and Bohs, retrenchment secured their futures. Not so for Fingal, who were unable to find another backer to take over from NAMA-bound Gerry Gannon. They had, in effect, flown too far, too fast.

First Round

9 June	**Crumlin United**	1	**Shelbourne**	1
	D. Loughran pen.		McAllister	
	(At Tolka Park)			
12 June	**Blarney United**	0	**Sporting Fingal**	2
			Zayed, C. Byrne	
	Bohemians	8	**Mayfield United**	1
	Hurley o.g., A. Murphy, J. Byrne 2,		Wolfe pen.	
	Crowe 2, Fenn, Carey			
	Bray Wanderers	2	**Bluebell United**	1
	P. Byrne, McCabe pen.		A. Cleary	
	Cork City	2	**Sligo Rovers**	2
	Duggan, Behan		S. Feeney, Cretaro	
	Derry City	6	**Ballymun United**	0
	L. Byrne o.g., McChrystal,			
	Nash 3, Scullion			
	Limerick 37	0	**St Patrick's Athletic**	1
			Costigan	
	Mervue United	1	**Dundalk**	3
	Goldbey		Rowe, Shaun Kelly, O'Brien	
	(At Terryland Park)			
	UCD	3	**Arklow Town**	1
	Purcell, Reilly, Kilduff		D. Murray	
13 June	**Finn Harps**	0	**Galway United**	3
			Faherty 2, O'Shea	
	Kildare County	1	**Athlone Town**	2
	D. O'Riordan		S. Place, B. Cleary	
	Shamrock Rovers	1	**Drogheda United**	1
	S. O'Connor		Kenna	
	Tralee Dynamos	2	**Salthill Devon**	1
	B. Fitzgerald, M. O'Rahilly		M. Gilmore	
	Waterford United	6	**Carrigaline United**	0
	Kiely 2, J. Mulcahy,			
	Cummins 2 (1 pen.), Grincell			
14 June	**Cherry Orchard**	2	**Monaghan United**	2
	Leadbitter, G. Donohoe		Freeman, Clancy	

Wexford Youths	2	Longford Town	2
G. Doyle 2		G. Curran, Adrian Murphy	

First Round Replays

15 June	Shelbourne	0	Crumlin United	1
			M. Cramer	
16 June	Drogheda United	0	Shamrock Rovers	3
			D. Baker, Purcell 2	
	Monaghan United	4	Cherry Orchard	0
	S. Brennan, C. O'Connor,			
	Clancy 2			
	Sligo Rovers	2	Cork City	1
	Cretaro 2		Silagailis	

(After extra time; 1–1 after 90m)

17 June	Longford Town	3	Wexford Youths	2
	G. Curran, Glynn,		Malone, G. Doyle	
	Flynn O'Connor o.g.			

(After extra time; 1–1 after 90m)

Second Round

14 August	Bray Wanderers	2	Tralee Dynamos	0
	J. Flood, Webster			
	Crumlin United	0	Waterford United	0
	Dundalk	0	Bohemians	0
	Galway United	0	Longford Town	1
			L. Lynch	
	Sporting Fingal	4	Athlone Town	1
	O'Neill, C. Byrne 2, Bayly		N. McGee pen.	
	Monaghan United	0	St Patrick's Athletic	0
15 August	Shamrock Rovers	3	UCD	1
	D. Baker 2, P. Kavanagh		Kilduff	
	Sligo Rovers	1	Derry City	0
	Cretaro			

Second Round Replays

18 August	Bohemians	0	Dundalk	0

(After extra time; Bohemians won 4–2 on pens.)

	Waterford United	2	Crumlin United	0

Cummins, Waters

7 September	St Patrick's Athletic	1	Monaghan United	0

Ryan

(After extra time.)

Quarter-Finals

11 September	Bohemians	0	Sligo Rovers	0
12 September	Longford Town	0	Bray Wanderers	0
	Sporting Fingal	2	Shamrock Rovers	2

Williams, Maher   D. Baker, Chisholm

	Waterford United	1	St Patrick's Athletic	1

Kiely   Dempsey

Quarter-Final Replays

15 September	Bray Wanderers	2	Longford Town	1

J. Flood, Shields   Glynn

	St Patrick's Athletic	0	Waterford United	2

Carey, Kiely

	Shamrock Rovers	1	Sporting Fingal	2

Bradley pen.   Kirby 2 (1 pen.)

(After extra time; 1–1 after 90m)

	Sligo Rovers	2	Bohemians	1

O'Grady, Doyle   Cronin

Semi-Finals

23 October	Sligo Rovers	1	Waterford United	0

Blinkhorn

25 October	Sporting Fingal	4	Bray Wanderers	2

Zayed 2, Kirby, Bayly   McCabe, Mulroy

Final – Tallaght Stadium

22 November   **Sporting Fingal**   **2**   **Sligo Rovers**   **1**
James pen. (85m),   Doyle 57m
O'Neill (90m)

Sporting Fingal: Darren Quigley; Colm James, Shaun Maher, Stephen Paisley, Lorcan Fitzgerald; Robert Bayly, Shane McFaul, Shaun Williams; Conan Byrne, Gary O'Neill, Eamonn Zayed. Manager: Liam Buckley

Sligo Rovers: Ciaran Kelly; Romuald Boco, Gavin Peers, Alan Keane, Joe Kendrick; Brian Cash, Danny Ventre, Richie Ryan, Eoin Doyle; Raffaele Cretaro, Matt Blinkhorn. Subs: Owen Morrison for Cash, 55m; Darren Meenan for Cretaro, 69m. Manager: Paul Cook

Referee: A. Kelly (Cork)   Attendance: 8,105

It's a Record!

• The last soccer match at the old Lansdowne Road stadium was the 2006 FAI Cup Final, in which Derry City beat St Patrick's Athletic 4–3 after extra time.

• Martin Reilly was the first player to score a 'summer' goal in the FAI Cup, when he scored for Dundalk after twenty-eight minutes in their first round 2–2 draw with Shamrock Rovers in Oriel Park on 25 July 2002.

2010

Kelly's Penalty Show

There was a time when Shamrock Rovers and the FAI Cup were synonymous, while other clubs, such as Shelbourne, were convinced that there was a hex on them in the Cup. In the past twenty-five years, all that seems to have changed, as Shamrock Rovers have been on the receiving end of bad Cup luck, while Shelbourne, and clubs as diverse as Bray Wanderers, Galway United, Sligo Rovers, Drogheda United and Derry City, have enjoyed their day in the Cup sun.

The 2010 campaign was a good case in point, with Sligo Rovers denying Shamrock Rovers a League and FAI Cup double in a final, which was decided in sensational fashion after a penalty shoot-out. In winning, Sligo became only the fourth side to win the FAI Cup without conceding a goal, and their goal was still intact after the penalty shoot-out. All this, despite losing first-choice goalkeeper Richard Brush after the first round.

For Ciaran Kelly, Brush's replacement, the 2010 campaign helped erase the nightmare of the 2009 final, when he was controversially penalised, with Sligo winning 1–0 against Sporting Fingal. Colm James converted the spot-kick and Fingal went on to win. If Kelly was an unfortunate villain then, he more than made up for it with his heroics against Shamrock Rovers.

The final finished 0–0 after extra time and, before the shoot-out started, Kelly said 'a little prayer. If ever I was going to get a little help, it was then. I felt so confident going out for the penalties, as if I was in a different zone. I felt I was going to do well.' What happened subsequently saw him enter the record books, as he saved four successive penalties to help Sligo to a 2–0 win in the shoot-out. The only other occasion a goalkeeper has saved four in succession was in the 1986 European Cup Final, when Steaua Bucureşti's Helmuth Ducadam denied Barcelona for a 2–0 shoot-out win.

It was a memorable end of season for Kelly, who had spent most of the season as Sligo's reserve 'keeper, but took-over in time to win League Cup and FAI Cup medals, and also help Sligo secure third place in the League. Kelly was a late developer, only stumbling across his goalkeeping talents through playing Gaelic football. Yet, when Don O'Riordan signed him for Sligo Rovers from Ballinrobe Town, he recalled: 'I started off as number-one, to my surprise, and spent two seasons there. In eighteen months I had gone from starting to play in goal to being Sligo's number one.'

He subsequently played with Derry City, Galway United and Athlone Town before re-joining Sligo as number-two to Richard Brush. The unfortunate Brush missed out on three Cup finals through injury – two FAI Cup and one League that brought the FAI Cup back to Sligo. So what is his secret? After all, in twelve shoot-outs, he has only been on the losing side twice. 'It's something I study,' he explained, 'and it stood to me. I study on TV and, in general, it's all about body shapes and watching the players' run-up. That tells you where they are going to put the ball.'

Whatever about Kelly's confidence in facing penalties, manager Paul Cook, who has revolutionised the Sligo style of play, didn't share it. So nervous was he about the outcome that he hid in the Aviva Stadium car park during the shoot-out.

Moving the final to the Aviva Stadium proved a winner for the FAI, who reduced ticket prices and were rewarded with a 36,101 attendance, the largest since 1968. At the other end of the scale, it was a sign of things to come when holders Sporting Fingal could only attract 206 spectators when they began the defence of the Cup at home to Mervue United.

First Round

4 June	**Cork City Foras Co-Op**	1	**Bluebell United**	1
	Cummins		Meade	
	Derry City	1	**Bray Wanderers**	1
	Sweeney		O'Neill	
	Drogheda United	1	**UCD**	2
	Daly		Mulhall, D. McMillan	
	Dublin Bus	0	**Shelbourne**	2
	(At Tolka Park)		Gorman, Corcoran	
	Dundalk	0	**St Patrick's Athletic**	1
			Cash	
	Finn Harps	3	**Crumlin United**	0
	Mailey, McHugh 2			
	Galway United	5	**Malahide United**	0
	Meynell, Butler o.g., Flood, Sheppard, McBrien			
	Limerick FC	3	**Tolka Rovers**	1
	McGrath, Kelleher, Kelly		Hughes	
	Longford Town	1	**Waterford United**	0
	Lester pen.			
	Shamrock Rovers	5	**Wexford Youths**	1
	D. Baker, Twigg, Chambers 2, Turner		Sheehan	
	Sligo Rovers	1	**Athlone Town**	0
	Dillon			
	Sporting Fingal	1	**Mervue United**	1
	Zayed		Tierney	
5 June	**Belgrove**	2	**Avondale United**	1
	K. O'Brien pen., Dowler		Knowles	
	Tullamore	1	**Salthill Devon**	3
	Moylan pen.		Burke 2 (1 pen.), Kennedy	
6 June	**FC Carlow**	1	**Monaghan United**	1
	Quigley		K. Bermingham pen.	
	Glenville	1	**Bohemians**	7
	Hegarty		Madden 3, Oman, J. Byrne 2, Higgins	
	(At Richmond Park)			

First Round Replays

8 June	**Bluebell United**	0	**Cork City Foras Co-Op**	1
	(At Carlisle Grounds)		O'Neill	
28 June	**Bray Wanderers**	3	**Derry City**	2
	Kelly pen., O'Neill 2		Cassidy, P. McEleney	
29 June	**Monaghan United**	2	**FC Carlow**	1
	K. Bermingham pen., Hughes		A. Byrne pen.	
10 August	**Mervue United**	0	**Sporting Fingal**	4
	(At Terryland Park)		Williams, O'Neill, C. Byrne 2	

Second Round

27 August	**Bohemians**	1	**Shelbourne**	0
	Madden			
	Cork City Foras Co-Op	0	**Monaghan United**	1
			K. Bermingham	
	Finn Harps	0	**Sligo Rovers**	1
			Keane pen.	
	Galway United	1	**Salthill Devon**	1
	Molloy		Straut	
	Longford Town	1	**Shamrock Rovers**	2
	Lester		Deans o.g., Dennehy	
	Sporting Fingal	2	**Limerick FC**	2
	Finn, C. Byrne		Purcell, S. O'Flynn	
	St Patrick's Athletic	2	**Belgrove**	0
	Doyle, I. Bermingham			
	UCD	2	**Bray Wanderers**	3
	Kilduff 2		O'Neill, J. Kelly 2	

Second Round Replays

30 August	**Limerick FC**	0	**Sporting Fingal**	0
	(After extra time; Sporting Fingal won 4–3 on pens.)			
	Salthill Devon	1	**Galway United**	3
	Collins		Conneely, King 2	

Quarter-Finals

17 September	Bohemians	3	Bray Wanderers	0
	Quigley, Cretaro, Greene			
	Shamrock Rovers	6	Galway United	0
	Stewart, Meynell o.g., Chambers 2,			
	Twigg, D. Baker			
18 September	St Patrick's Athletic	3	Sporting Fingal	1
	Guy, Lynch, Faherty		Williams	
	Sligo Rovers	3	Monaghan United	0
	Keane pen., Boco, McGoldrick			

Semi-Finals

15 October	Bohemians	0	Sligo Rovers	1
			Peers	
17 October	Shamrock Rovers	2	St Patrick's Athletic	2
	Turner, Twigg		McAllister, Kavanagh o.g.	

Semi-Final Replay

19 October	St Patrick's Athletic	0	Shamrock Rovers	1
			Turner	

Final – Aviva Stadium

14 November	Sligo Rovers	0	Shamrock Rovers	0
	(After extra time; Sligo Rovers won 2–0 on pens.)			

Sligo Rovers: Ciaran Kelly; Alan Keane, Gavin Peers, Jim Lauchlan, Iarfhlaith Davoren; Romuald Boco, Danny Ventre, Joseph Ndo, John Russell, Gary McCabe; Eoin Doyle. Subs: Conor O'Grady for Ventre, 117m. Manager: Paul Cook

Shamrock Rovers: Alan Mannus; Stephen Rice, Pat Flynn, Craig Sives, Enda Stevens; James Chambers, Stephen Bradley, Chris Turner, Billy Dennehy; Gary Twigg, Thomas Stewart. Subs: Dessie Baker for Chambers, 69m; Pat Kavanagh for Stewart, 102m; Aidan Price for Baker, 112m. Manager: Michael O'Neill

Referee: T. Connolly (Dublin)   Attendance: 36,101

Roll of Honour

24

Shamrock Rovers: 1925, 1929, 1930, 1931, 1932, 1933, 1936, 1944, 1945, 1956, 1962, 1964, 1965, 1966, 1967, 1968, 1969, 1978, 1985, 1986, 1987

9

Dundalk: 1942, 1949, 1952, 1958, 1977, 1979, 1981, 1988, 2002

7

Bohemians: 1928, 1935, 1970, 1976, 1992, 2001, 2008.
Shelbourne: 1939, 1960, 1963, 1993, 1996, 1997, 2000

5

Drumcondra: 1927, 1943, 1946, 1954, 1957

4

Derry City: 1989, 1995, 2002, 2006

3

Sligo Rovers: 1983, 1994, 2010

2

Bray Wanderers: 1990, 1999
Cork Athletic: 1951, 1953
Cork City: 1998, 2007
Cork Hibernians: 1972, 1973
Cork United: 1941, 1947
Limerick: 1971, 1982
Longford Town: 2003, 2004
St James's Gate: 1922, 1938
St Patrick's Athletic: 1959, 1961
Waterford: 1937, 1980

1

Alton United: 1923
Athlone Town: 1924
Cork: 1934
Drogheda United: 2005
Finn Harps: 1974
Fordsons: 1926
Galway United: 1991
Home Farm: 1975
Sporting Fingal: 2009
Transport: 1950
University College Dublin: 1984